ENVIRONMENTAL LAW
FOR THE BUILT
ENVIRONMENT

Cavendish
Publishing
Limited

London • Sydney

ENVIRONMENTAL LAW FOR THE BUILT ENVIRONMENT

Editor
Jack Rostron, MA, DipLaw, ARICS, MRTPI

Contributors
RP Jackson
D Legge
EJ Longworth
J Parry
PJ Regan
FM Ruddock

Cavendish
Publishing
Limited

London • Sydney

First published in Great Britain 2001 by Cavendish Publishing Limited,
The Glass House, Wharton Street, London WC1X 9PX, United Kingdom
Telephone: + 44 (0)20 7278 8000   Facsimile: + 44 (0)20 7278 8080
Email: info@cavendishpublishing.com
Website: www.cavendishpublishing.com

Rostron, J
Environmental law and techniques for the built environment
1 Environmental law – Great Britain
I Jackson, RP
344.4'1'046

ISBN 1 85941 597 0

Printed and bound in Great Britain

FOREWORD

The growth in concern for the environment in recent decades has a dual focus, which is both internationalist and local. Internationalist in the sense that we can only address effectively global problems such as climate change through international co-operation. Internationalist also because such concern extends to the environment beyond our own borders. There is increasing recognition of the responsibility borne by developed countries to address the environmental impact of their own levels of consumption. There is also a growing awareness of the needs of those in the developing world whose dependence on natural resources makes them especially vulnerable to environmental changes such as desertification and the range of climatic effects likely to result from global warming.

The more 'local' aspect of concern about the environment relates to people's sense of how the environment impacts on their own and their family's standard of living in terms of their health and general well being. This includes the working environment, as highlighted in the book, for example, in the section on Sick Building Syndrome. To this human-centred concern for the environment is added a deep sense of the intrinsic value of the natural environment and its cultural importance and the book highlights the way in which the regulation of matters, such as environmental water quality, is critical for both human and intrinsically environmental protection. The local impact of global warming is also addressed, for example, in relation to the issue of flooding in Chapter 4. Different kinds of locality pose specific challenges as recognised in the final chapter which addresses the need to ensure both rural and urban regeneration.

Environmental concern has led to an enormous increase in legislation and to the development of new technologies aimed at reducing degradation of the environment. Information about these developments is increasingly accessible to those interested in the environment both through legislative provision for access to environmental information and through the use of information technology, in particular, the internet, by industry and civil society as well as by governments. Greater access to information facilitates informed scrutiny of the law and its operation but, in sifting through the vast amounts of information now available, it is important to have access to a comprehensive but readable guide to the laws which frame environmental decision making and which regulate activities that impact on the environment. This book makes a valuable contribution in that regard. More unusually perhaps, it also sets out the key technological developments which are likely to help to resolve the problem of environmental degradation and in this way provides the reader with a sense of some of the practical issues which underpin environmental law and policy.

The main focus of this book is on national law as derived from and influenced by European and international sources. Laws relating to the environment historically evolved and were administered by national jurisdictions but the global dimensions of atmospheric and oceanic pollution led to increased international regulation. Increased international co-operation has resulted in a large number of international instruments relating to the environment and the book refers to some of these, dealing with matters such as the protection of biodiversity, climate change, transboundary air pollution, biosafety (trade in genetically modified organisms) and trade in endangered species to name but a few.

It is not possible to cover in a book of this size all aspects of the environment and the book is necessarily selective in choosing those aspects of the pollution of land, water and air which are currently topical. The collection of writings include chapters on the development of environmental law, town and country planning (including environmental impact assessment), water pollution, air pollution (including climate change and energy efficiency), waste (including contaminated land), integrated prevention and pollution control and on the natural environment (including agricultural controls).

Concern for the environment can probably best be realised by making the goal of sustainable development a practical reality. The types of individual decisions which cumulatively determine how close we are to achieving sustainable development in practice are to a large extent subject to the laws described in this book. A number of the chapters examine the concept of sustainable development and the extent to which it is reflected in current law and policy. It emerges as the unifying theme underlying current thinking on the many different aspects of environmental protection. In this context, the twin approach of developing laws to regulate future activities which may lead to environmental degradation and developing technologies which help to remediate historical damage or which are cleaner and more energy-efficient is likely to be important. The format of the book reflects this, in that each chapter initially describes relevant policies and laws followed by the appropriate scientific and technological remedies. Thus, Chapter 5 considers developments in air pollution technology; Chapter 6, dealing with waste, discusses technical aspects of matters such as the reclamation of contaminated land and the design and construction of landfill facilities. Noise technology is considered in Chapter 7.

The precautionary principle has emerged as an important area of debate in relation to environmental decision making not least in relation to the release of genetically modified organisms, which is considered in Chapter 8 in the context of agricultural controls. Chapter 8 also looks more broadly at the way forward for agriculture including organic farming and the operation of agri-environment schemes.

Also of critical importance in delivering environmental protection and sustainable development are the mechanisms for ensuring that environmental standards are met: this book outlines the various enforcement mechanisms provided for as well as other ways in which the law facilitates the meeting of these standards such as the use of agri-environment schemes. In this regard, as Chapter 2 shows, mechanisms at the national level are complemented by those at the European level.

Another important development is the entry into force of the Human Rights Act 1998. As discussed in Chapter 2, where public authorities act in relation to the environment in ways that are incompatible with people's convention rights, the Act may provide a remedy. The full extent to which convention rights provide a basis for the protection of 'environmental rights' remains a matter for debate but the relevance of Art 8 (the right to respect for private and family life), in particular, is already clear from the case law of the European Court of Human Rights.

The book is written as a specialist text book for university students and introductory guide for practitioners. It is aimed at lawyers, civil engineers and the landed professions as well as those among the general public interested in environmental issues. It contains numerous footnotes and extensive bibliography for the reader to explore particular areas of interest in further detail.

I would have no hesitation in recommending this book as a clear and comprehensive guide to the environmental law that governs key sectors of policy. The great benefit of this book is the way in which it integrates reference to recent technological developments into an exposition of the law. As stated in Chapter 3: 'There needs to be an integration of sustainability into all levels of policy making.' This book will help equip the reader to assess how far environmental law has come and how far it still needs to go.

Cherie Booth
Matrix Chambers, London
February 2001

PREFACE

I have endeavoured in this book to describe the principles of environmental law and the germane scientific, technological and engineering remedies with as much precision, cohesiveness and system as the subject permits. I hope it is of sufficient detail and coverage to be of practical use to practitioners and students of law and the landed professions.

As editor, any shortcomings or criticisms are my responsibility, but any credit must rest with the co-authors; in particular, Debbie Legge for writing the law sections. I must also acknowledge the valuable contributions of Jim Parry (environmental impact assessment); Rob Jackson (water pollution); Jim Longworth (waste remediation); Pat Regan (buildings and the environment); and Fil Ruddock (air pollution and noise technology).

Jack Rostron
Liverpool
February 2001

ACKNOWLEDGMENTS

It is impossible to acknowledge all the people and agencies which have assisted with the writing of this book. However, my thanks are particularly extended to Anita Ellis, Fiona Fargher and Lynda Cunningham of the School of Law, Liverpool John Moores University, for help with developing the initial idea and commenting on drafts of the manuscript. Alan Pugh and Nerys Parry of Solicitors Hill Dickinson helped with style and content. Suzanne Fitzpatrick of JR Knowles, Liverpool, offered invaluable help regarding sick building syndrome. Paul Hodgkinson prepared the graphics.

The production of any law book requires the close assistance of the publishers, to whom I am especially grateful for their meticulous work on compiling the tables of cases and statutes.

LIST OF CONTRIBUTORS

RP Jackson, BSc, CEng, FICE, is Parkman Professor of Water and Environmental Engineering and Head of Civil Engineering Studies at Liverpool John Moores University. He has many years' experience in the water industry and consultancy.

D Legge, LLB, MA, PhD, is Lecturer in Environmental Law at Liverpool John Moores University. She is on the editorial board of several law journals, the author of numerous articles and co-author of *The Law Relating to Animals* (1997, Cavendish Publishing).

EJ Longworth, MSc, CEng, MIStructE, is a chartered structural engineer with many years' experience in consultancy and site supervision. He is currently Lecturer in Remediation Techniques concerning contaminated land at Liverpool John Moores University.

J Parry, BA, BEng, CEng, MICE, is Lecturer in Civil Engineering and Construction Management at Liverpool John Moores University. He has many years' prior experience in consultancy and site supervision.

PJ Regan, BSc, MEd, is Lecturer in Environmental Science at Liverpool John Moores University and a consultant chemist on waste management.

J Rostron, MA, DipLaw, ARICS, MRTPI, the editor of this collection, is a Lecturer at Liverpool John Moores University and sometime adviser to the World Health Organisation. He is the author of *Housing the Physically Disabled* (1995), co-author of *Adapting Housing for People with Disabilities* (1996), *Refurbishing Offices for People with Disabilities* (1996), *A Dictionary of Housing* (1997), and editor of *Sick Building Syndrome, An Anthology of Practice, Concepts and Issues* (1997) and *A Dictionary of Property and Construction Law* (2001).

CONTENTS

TABLE OF CASES

TABLE OF STATUTES

TABLE OF STATUTORY INSTRUMENTS

TABLE OF EUROPEAN LEGISLATION

Regulations

TABLE OF ABBREVIATIONS

AONB	Area of Outstanding Natural Beauty
APC	Air pollution control
ASSI	Area of Special Scientific Interest
BAP	Biodiversity Action Plan
BATNEEC	Best available technique not entailing excessive cost
BNFL	British Nuclear Fuels Ltd
BPEO	Best Practical Environmental Option
BRE	Building Research Establishment
BREEAM	Building Research Establishment Environmental Assessment Methods
BTCV	British Trust for Conservation Volunteers
CAA	Civil Aviation Authority
CAP	Common Agricultural Policy
CBI	Confederation of British Industries
CITES	Convention on International Trade in Endangered Species of Wild Flora and Fauna
COPA	Control of Pollution Act 1974
CPRE	Council for the Protection of Rural England
CSC	Customer service committee
DETR	Department of the Environment, Transport and the Regions
DG	Directorate General
DGWS	Director General of Water Services,
DOE	Department of the Environment
DPP	Director of Public Prosecutions
DWI	Drinking Water Inspector
EA	Environment Agency
EC	European Community
ECHR	European Court of Human Rights
ECJ	European Court of Justice
EEA	European Environmental Agency
EEC	European Economic Community
EELR	European Environmental Law Review
EIA	Environmental impact analysis
ELM	Environmental Law and Management
ELR	Environmental Law Review
EN	English Nature

EP	European Parliament
EPA	Environmental Protection Act 1990
ES	Environmental Statement
ESA	Environmentally Sensitive Area
EU	European Union
GDPO	General Development Procedure Order
GEMS	Global Environmental Monitoring Service
GMO	Genetically modified organisms
GNP	Gross national product
GPDO	General Permitted Development Order
GRID	Global Resonance Information Data Base
HMIP	Her Majesty's Inspectorate of Pollution
HNDA	High natural dispersal areas
HSE	Health and Safety Executive
HVAC	Heating Ventilating and Air Conditioning
ICRCL	Interdepartmental Committee on the Reclamation of Contaminated Land
IMPEL	Implementation & Enforcement of European Environmental Law
INECE	International Network for Enforcement and Compliance with International Law
IPC	Integrated pollution control
IPPC	Integrated Pollution Prevention and Control
IWL	International Wildlife Law
JEL	Journal of Environmental law
JPEL	Journal of Planning and Environmental law
LAPC	Local air pollution control
LAWDC	Local authority waste disposal committee
LMO	Living modified organisms
LPA	Local planning authority
MAFF	Ministry of Agriculture, Fisheries and Food
MOD	Ministry of Defence
NCC	National Customer Council
NCO	Nature Conservation Order
NDBG	Non-departmental government bodies

NII	Nuclear Installations Inspectorate
NTS	Non-technical summary
NWC	National Water Council
OEDC	Organisation for Economic Co-operation and Development
Ofwat	Office of Water Services
OPRA	Operator and pollution risk appraisal
PCB	Polychlorinated biphenyls
PPG	Planning policy guidance
RSPB	Royal Society for the Protection of Birds
RSPCA	Royal Society for the Prevention of Cruelty to Animals
SBS	Sick building syndrome
SOSETR	Secretary of State for the Environment, Transport and the Regions
SSSI	Site of Special Scientific Interest
TCPA	Town and Country Planning Act(s)
TPO	Tree Preservation Order
UKAEA	United Kingdom Atomic Energy Authority
UKELA	United Kingdom Environmental Law Association
UWWTD	Urban Wastewater Treatment Directive
VOC	Volatile organic compounds
WB	World Bank
WCA	Wildlife and Countryside Act 1981
WCED	World Commission on Environment and Development
WHO	World Health Organisation
WIA	Water Industry Act 1991
WQA	Water quality objectives
WRA	Water Resources Act 1991
WWF	World Wildlife Fund

CHAPTER 1

INTRODUCTION

> The environmental revolution amid which we live has a double face. It can be
> seen as a man made change, sudden and worldwide, in our natural
> environment. It can equally be regarded in the light of a transformation in our
> attitude to that environment. By going so far as he now has towards taking the
> earth from nature, man has made it inevitable, not only that he should manage
> nature, but also that he should henceforth learn to manage as a part of nature.

This declaration by Nicholson in his now, some may say, dated, but
nonetheless seminal, work, *The Environmental Revolution* (1968), indicates the
start of modern man's concern with the environment.

The creation of our current environmental awareness stems from man's
technical achievements in harnessing the power of nature for his own ends.
The Industrial Revolution of the Victorian period created the capability to
place Great Britain at the centre of a mighty empire. Then, and subsequently,
industrialisation was seen largely only in terms of its wealth producing
possibilities. Little, if any, thought was given to the longer term environmental
implications of these wealth creating activities.

At the dawn of the 21st century, man has to deal with his legacy. It is no
longer acceptable to create wealth without consideration of the immediate and
longer term effects that such activities have on the environment.

Man clearly has the ingenuity to develop technical solutions to both
remediate his past actions and, hopefully, prevent future environmental
degradation. In order to harness his technical capabilities appropriately, a
strong and evolving legal framework is necessary.

It is against this twofold approach – of first developing the technology to
remediate and prevent further environmental damage and, secondly, evolving
a legal framework to ensure that man's technical abilities are both restrained
and encouraged to create a better environment – that the idea for this book
was conceived. Perhaps it is an impossible task to produce in one text a
meaningful discourse on environmental law and technologies. Whilst it may
be impossible, it is certainly necessary to attempt to do so.

SCOPE AND PURPOSE

In order to meet some of these challenges, the authors of books on
environmental law and techniques have to make choices. On the one hand,
they can attempt to encompass everything, in which case the project becomes

unmanageable. On the other hand, they can attempt to limit their scope to that which they think is important, the consequence of which is the risk of omitting issues which are equally important to the reader.

In writing this book, the choice has been to lay emphasis on those areas which are topical and come within the purview of the built environment. Such terms can lay down artificial barriers, but limitations are necessary.

Those aspects of environmental law and technology which have been chosen are: the administration and sources of the law; town and country planning; water and air pollution; waste; integrated pollution control; and the 'natural' environment.

Chapter 2 describes the administration and sources of environmental law. It traces the evolution of 'modern' statutory controls from their historical routes in common law. It highlights the importance of cross-boundary control, describing in detail European and international law and enforcement regimes. A review of future developments is offered, particularly in terms of the impact of the new Human Rights Act 1998.

Chapter 3 discusses the town and country planning legal and administrative framework. In particular, it describes the agencies involved, the procedures at inquiries and enforcement measures and it looks at future developments. The important new protocol for assessing the environmental impact of new developments is explained in detail.

Chapter 4 describes the policy framework and legal processes involved in dealing with water pollution in terms of abstraction, supply, discharge and classification. It also explains the technical aspects of wastewater, water use, lead contaminants, flooding, groundwater and grey water.

Chapter 5 discusses the legal, regulatory and policy issues concerning air pollution. It does this in terms of energy efficiency, nuclear power, transport and future potential developments. Air pollution technology and the 'recent' phenomenon of sick building syndrome is explored in some detail.

Chapter 6 explains the law surrounding waste. It deals with the regulatory processes involved in dealing with contaminated land, recycling/re-use, incineration and import/export. The scientific and technological aspects of investigating and remediation of contaminated land are described in detail.

Chapter 7 deals with the law and policy of integrated pollution control. It specifically describes the background to the law, its application to certain processes, and offences and remedies. Noise technology and the environmental assessment of buildings is explained.

Chapter 8 describes the law regarding the use of land in rural areas and nature conservation. It offers a detailed exposition of the legal issues concerning protection of the countryside, birds and animals, the problem of genetically modified crops, forestry and mining.

CHAPTER 2

ADMINISTRATION AND SOURCES OF ENVIRONMENTAL LAW

BACKGROUND

The law sections of this book are there not to provide the last word on the law but to draw out the basics of the regulatory regime and to guide the user to where the details of the law can be found.[1] It is also the aim to show the general trends in environmental law, where it is going and what the issues may be in the future. It is based upon fundamental principles: that the highest level of environmental protection should be humanity's goal and that the precautionary principle should always apply. The issues raised in relation to the environment are fundamental to our survival and are relevant not just to legal practitioners, students or academics, but to us all, as humans; we are all part of the problem as well as the solution. This book is an attempt to put the problem of environmental degradation into perspective. It is a problem that often seems to be beyond our capacity or capability to do anything about or even to understand, but, as Albert Einstein said, 'The most incomprehensible thing about the world is that it is comprehensible'. If we can comprehend how the law has responded to this problem, then we are at least someway towards its solution. The key idea to remember is that law is a balance between utopian ideas and practical reality, so what has and will influence the development of environmental law depends upon the political/philosophical/social and economic debates taking place, as well as solving the practical legal problems.

The aim of this chapter is to put environmental law into its wider context and to explain some of the basic issues needed to understand how environmental law works.

---

1 There are a number of excellent environmental law books already published, including Bell and McGillvray, 2000, which provides not just a comprehensive look at the law but also puts it firmly into context. Hughes, 1996, is now rather out of date but provides a comprehensive coverage of the law. McEldowney and McEldowney, 1996, provides a straightforward look at the law but, again, is a little out of date. See, also, Harrison, 1997, pp 79–102, and Sunkin, 1998.

HISTORY[2]

Environmental law developed out of common law controls that were mainly based around the idea of property rights and nuisance.[3] This later took legislative form through the public health legislation that still concentrated on human needs, that is, health rather than the protection of the environment *per se*.[4] Since 1945, when a vast range of artificial, totally new substances were introduced into the environment, such as pesticides, there has been growing pressure and fear about whether we are upsetting the ecosystem to such a degree that we threaten the continuity of the system itself.

The UK was one of the first countries to industrialise and it has a long history of the problems that economic development can bring to the environment in terms of resource depletion, pollution, congestion and degradation of the rural and urban environment. The UK was also the first country to develop controls over pollution and it set up the first environmental agency – the Alkali Inspectorate, which later became Her Majesty's Inspectorate of Pollution (HMIP). The common law had responded to the problem of pollution through the development of nuisance and the law had been further developed through public health legislation. The development of town and country planning led to a more precautionary approach, but there was no real attempt to provide planning for long term problems such as pollution. This reflected the *ad hoc* nature of decision making in the UK and the pragmatic way in which governments often responded to the issues. This can be seen in relation to the statutes passed since 1945.

In 1945, a number of environmental statutes were passed which attempted to improve the life of ordinary people. In the environmental field, there had been calls for more access to the countryside and, in the National Parks and Access to the Countryside Act 1949, this aim was partially granted. The Town and Country Planning Act 1947 reflected the belief that society needed to be planned, but legislation was often passed on an *ad hoc* basis, such as the Clean Air Act 1956, which was passed to deal with the London smog problem.

The late 1960s and early 1970s saw a great upsurge in the public's interest in environmental policy through media coverage and pressure group campaigning, and popular interest increased dramatically in a short period of time. There were a number of reasons for this:[5]

- the growth of the media – media transmits ideas at great speed and can show specific pollution events;

---

2   For a more detailed look at the history of environmental law, see Clapp, 1994.
3   See McClaren, 1983.
4   See Routledge, 1981, pp 77–89; Osborn, 1997, pp 3–22.
5   See Brown-Weiss, 1992.

- rising educational standards;
- environmental disasters, such as the Torrey Canyon oil spill, where 120,000 tons of oil were spilt into the sea in 1967, and Chernobyl 1986;
- scientific advances;
- increased understanding about pollution and ecosystems;
- internationalisation of problems;
- economic consequences of growth became apparent;
- society's moral framework has changed;
- pressure from the European Community (EC).

However, the Control of Pollution Act (COPA) 1974 was the first attempt to legislate comprehensibly on environmental pollution. Nevertheless, there was still a tendency towards *ad hoc* law, as seen by the Deposit of Poisonous Waste Act 1972, enacted following the discovery by a local conservation group of cyanide dumping in the Midlands.

By the 1980s, it was clear that the shortcomings of the previous environmental pollution strategies left many problems unresolved and, in many cases, actually getting worse. This was often due to the rising standard of living in developed countries leading to more pollution. There was a realisation that long term planning was needed to deal with new problems and the concept of sustainability was developed. This led to a growing number of policy initiatives at an international, European and domestic level.

In the UK, the main Acts are:
- Water Industry Acts 1991 and 1999;
- Water Resources Act 1991;
- Wildlife and Countryside Act 1981 (as amended);
- Environmental Protection Act 1990 (as amended);
- Environment Act 1995;
- Pollution Prevention Control Act 1999;
- Town and Country Planning Act 1990;
- Planning (Listed Buildings and Conservation Areas) Act 1990.

The growth of regulation

So, since 1945, there have been two broad influences on the development of environmental law.[6] The first was the growth in the belief that economy/society needed to be planned, which has led to growing State

6   Pearce, 1990; Jacobs, 1991.

intervention in all facets of life, both economic and social. This was especially so after the Second World War, when people had become accustomed to the State regulating their lives in detail.

A recognition that the environment needs to be protected, not only due to the impact of pollution on human health, but also because the environment is seen as having intrinsic worth, led to the development of regulatory controls.[7] Regulation can be broken down into a number of steps:

- establishment of general policies, for example, clean rivers;
- setting of specific policies or standards, for example, water quality objectives for rivers;
- application of these standards to specific situations – licence conditions;
- enforcement of standards, permissions, licences, etc.

Administrative regulation is the application of rules and procedures by public bodies[8] so as to achieve a measure of control over activities carried out by individuals or firms. It is more coherent and less reactive than the common law and many market mechanisms need administrative/regulatory mechanisms to make them effective.[9] The UK regulatory structure used to be described as pragmatic and flexible, decentralised and discretionary.[10] This has changed to a certain extent, as decision making is now more centralised and there are more statutory standards set.[11]

EUROPE[12]

The EC

Although the UK has a long history of environmental protection and set up one of the first regulatory agencies – the Alkali Inspectorate, later to become HMIP and then amalgamated into the Environment Agency (EA) – most of

---

7   See Rugman and Soloway, 1999; Gunningham and Grabosky, 1998; Jewell and Steele, 1998.

8   See the *Better Regulation Taskforce Report*, 21 January 1998, which stated that the five principles of good regulation are: transparency – regulation that is clear, simple and easily understood; accountability – making the right people accountable, proper consultation, a fair and efficient appeals procedure; targeting – hitting the spot, no unintended side effects; consistency – national laws applied evenly and predictably; and proportionality – linking risks and protection to the cost and burden.

9   There are a number of economic instruments that can be used from emission trading to Eco taxes such as the landfill tax: see Bosselmann and Richardson, 1999.

10 Osborne, 1996.

11 *Setting Environmental Standards*, 21st Report of the Royal Commission on Environmental Pollution, Cm 4053, 1998.

12 Scott, 1998, is excellent, also Haigh and Usher, 1998.

the impetus for environmental change since 1945 has come from Europe and from international treaties.

The EC institutions

- The Commission proposes the bulk of legislation, employs the Community's civil service and has overall responsibility for the application and enforcement of EC law. The Commission members are nationals of the Member States but are there to represent the interests of the Community, rather than their Nation State.

- The Council of Ministers is where the interests of the Member States are represented. It consists of ministers from each Member State. There may be separate Council meetings for agriculture and environment. The presidency of the Council revolves.

- The European Council is where the heads of State meet.

- The Committee of Permanent Representatives is responsible for preparing the work of the Council and for carrying out tasks assigned by it. The Committee's members are senior diplomats.

- The European Parliament (EP) is directly elected. Legislation does not emanate from it but it has to be consulted before legislation is adopted under the Maastricht Treaty (Treaty on European Union 1992). Should the Council fail to take account of Parliament's opinion, Parliament can prevent adoption of the proposal. It also has power over the EC budget.

- The European Environment Agency (EEA)[13] is relevant only for advice and dissemination of information.[14]

- The EC departments relevant to this book are Directorate General (DG) VI (Agriculture); DG VII (Transport); DG XI (Environment, Nuclear and Civil Protection); and DG XVII (Energy).

- The European Court of Justice.

- The European Ombudsman.

---

13 The EEA published a Report on the environment in the EU in 1998. The Report looks at environmental trends in the Member States. It states that there has been an improvement in surface water quality but that more attention needs to be applied to climate change, ground water quality, habitat destruction and fragmentation: EEA, *Europe's Environment: The Second Assessment*, 1998.

14 European Environment Agency Regulations 1990 (SI 1210/1990).

EC legislation

- The treaties – for example, the EC Treaty and the Maastricht Treaty.
- Regulations – these are of general application and are directly applicable. This means that they can create legal relations between individuals.
- Directives – these are addressed to Member States but give them a discretion as to how they will be implemented, but this cannot be through administrative practice. Directives have to be implemented in the Member State by a competent authority.[15]
- Decisions – these relate to a specific addressee, such as a Member State or a commercial undertaking.
- Opinions and recommendations do not have binding legal effect, although a regulation may be used as an aid to interpreting national law.

Passing legislation

There are four procedures that can be used by the EC to pass legislation:

(a) Procedure without consultation – a Commission proposal is adopted by Council – consultation with the EP optional. Is it used very rarely, usually for emergency situations.

(b) Consultation procedure – proposal by the Council – Council consults the EP – EP adoption by Council. This is used for agriculture.

(c) Co-operation procedure – proposal by the Council in consultation with Parliament – 'adoption of common position' by Council – Council position communicated to EP with a full explanation of reasons and the Commission's position. The EP has three months to decide its position. Parliament can approve or reject it by an absolute majority – this means that the Council can only act at second reading with unanimity. Parliament can amend it again by an absolute majority – the Commission has one month to re-examine its proposal. The re-examined proposal can be adopted by the Council by qualified majority or the Council can amend it unanimously.

Since the Treaty of Amsterdam 1997, most areas are governed by the co-decision procedure, apart from economic and monetary union. All environmental legislation is to be adopted by the co-decision procedure.

(d) Co-decision procedure – here, Parliament has the power to reject a proposal for legislation. Parliament may indicate rejection or may propose amendments. If the Council agrees all amendments, the proposal can be adopted; otherwise, a Conciliation Committee must be convened. The

---

15 In the UK, this would be the EA. The body has to be independent from the bodies it regulates.

Committee operates as 'broker' between Parliament and Council and its task is to facilitate agreement on a joint text within a six week period. If no joint text is agreed, the Act is deemed not to be adopted. Although the Council does have the power to declare a common position during that six week period, and may incorporate some of the proposed amendments, adoption of the Act can still be prevented by an absolute majority decision of the EP. This procedure is used for matters including environmental programmes and policy, incentive measures on public health and areas such as consumer protection, education and freedom of movement of workers.

Thus, the Council and EP adopt the legislation jointly. Under the Amsterdam Treaty, the procedure can stop at the point at which there is agreement between the institutions or where there is outright rejection. If the EP rejects the common position by an absolute majority, there is no provision for conciliation, as the Act is deemed not to have been adopted.

The EC's environmental programme[16]

The Treaty of Rome 1957 did not contain any reference to the environment. The environmental programme arose out of the EC's economic policy – in particular, Arts 100 and 100A (now Arts 94 and 95 of the EC Treaty), which have as their aim the reduction in differences in Member States' laws which have an economic impact.

Through these general measures, the EC has laid down a plethora of secondary legislation of both directives and regulations covering the environment. This provides those wishing to improve the environment with standards by which to hold the Member States and other bodies to account, as well as a remedy in the case of any breaches of those standards.

However, it was not until the Single European Act 1986 and the Maastricht Treaty 1992 that the environment was protected as an end in itself. Europe developed its environmental policy through the Environmental Action Programmes, published in 1972, 1977, 1982, 1983, 1987 and 1992.[17]

Article 2 of the EC Treaty[18] sets out the EC's position:

---

16 Kraemer, 1999, pp 315–30; Doherty, 1999, pp 354–86; Gerard, 1998, pp 331–46. See, also, Gillies, 1999; Wyatt, 1998, pp 9–20.

17 The Fifth Environmental Action Programme (1993 EC Programme of Policy and Action in Relation to the Environment and Sustainable Development, *Towards Sustainability*, Com 138/5) covered: the integration of environmental considerations into the various target economic sectors; achieving policy objectives (including broadening the range of instruments and establishing shared responsibility); and at the same time programming new concepts such as sustainability.

18 See Van Calster, 1998, pp 12–25.

The Community shall have as its task, by establishing a common market and an economic and monetary union and by implementing common policies or activities referred to in Arts 3 and 4, to promote throughout the Community a harmonious, balanced and sustainable development of economic activities, a high level of employment and of social protection, equality between men and women, sustainable and non inflationary growth, a high degree of competitiveness and convergence of economic performance, a high level of protection and improvement of the quality of the environment, the raising of the standard of living and quality of life, and economic and social cohesion and solidarity among Member States.

Article 3 states that the Community shall develop a policy in the sphere of the environment and Art 6 (formerly Art 3c) that environmental protection requirements should be integrated into Community policies 'in particular with a view to promoting sustainable development'. Article 95 (formerly Art 100a) states that the Commission, when drawing up provisions, should have a high level of protection as its base, taking account of any new developments based on scientific facts (the EP and Council also have to seek to achieve this objective).

Article 174(1)[19] sets out the objectives of EC policy:

- preserving, protecting and improving the quality of the environment;
- protecting human health;
- prudent and rational utilisation of natural resources;
- promoting measures at international level to deal with regional or worldwide environmental problems.

The principles of EC environmental protection law are set down in Art 174(2). These are:

- the 'polluter pays' principle;
- a high level of protection, taking into account the diversity of situations of countries in the EC;
- the precautionary principle;[20]
- that preventive action is preferred to remedial measures;
- that environmental damage should be rectified at source.

Article 174(3) states that, when the EC is preparing its policy, it should take into account:

- available scientific and technical data;
- environmental conditions in the various regions of the EC;

---

19 Articles 130R, 130S and 130T are now Arts 174–76.
20 See *R v Secretary of Sate for Trade and Industry ex p Duddridge* [1995] 7 JEL 224: the precautionary principle in Art 174(2) was not formulated for specific action but instead governed future policy frameworks.

- potential benefits and costs of action or lack of action;
- the economic and social development of the EC as a whole and the balanced development of its regions.

Article 175 sets out the decision making procedure and states that all environmental legislation will be drafted using the co-decision procedure.

Article 176 states that:

... protective measures adopted pursuant to Art 175 shall not prevent any Member State from maintaining or introducing more stringent protective measures. Such measures must be compatible with this Treaty. They shall be notified to the Commission.

The Amsterdam Treaty has been important in including sustainability and the precautionary principles as part of the EC,[21] as well as the important principle of integration; and the principles of proportionality and subsidiarity will also have to take into account environmental policy.

International law[22]

International law was primarily concerned with establishing liability for trans-boundary damage and the allocation of resources. However, international law has now moved on to develop a more preventative, or precautionary, approach, mainly through the development of the concept of sustainability.[23]

The main international organisation is the United Nations (UN). It consists of:

- General Assembly – its role is to make recommendations on general principles of co-operation. It can discuss any matters within the scope of the UN Charter and can make recommendations to the Security Council or to the Member States;
- Security Council – only the Security Council can decide on matters of peace and security. It has 15 members, five of which are permanent;
- Secretariat – the UN Environment Programme is a subsidiary of the Secretariat. However, its members are elected by the General Assembly and it is responsible to that body;[24]
- International Court of Justice;
- International Law Commission.

---

21 See Bar Kraemer, 1998, pp 315–30.
22 Birnie and Boyle, 1994; Boyle, 1991, pp 229–45; Hurrel and Kinsbury, 1992.
23 Ailing, 1997, pp 243–70; Birnie and Boyle, 2000; Birnie 2000; Campbell, 1997; Gilespie, 1997; McIntyre Mosedale, 1997, pp 221–42; Sands, 1995.
24 There are other specialised bodies such as the World Health Organisation and the International Monetary Fund.

Its programmes include:

- Earth Watch;
- Global environmental assessment programme:
  - o environmental management;
  - o supporting measures;
- Global Environmental Monitoring System (GEMS);
- Global Resource Information Database (GRID);
- UN Environment Programme.

Since 1972, there have been hundreds of meetings and treaties. These will be looked at, where they are relevant, below. However, one of the fundamental principles that has emerged for the international arena is the issue of sustainability.[25] This was developed in the 1980 International Union for Conservation of Nature's World Conservation Strategy – which lays down that there should be a sustainable utilisation of species/ecosystems. In 1982 , the General Assembly of the UN adopted the World Charter for Nature – this states that there should be an optimal sustainable productivity of all resources, coupled with conservation/protection. In 1987, the World Commission on Environment and Development (WCED) reiterated the concept of sustainable development and stated that there should be co-operation on a worldwide basis to achieve these ends.

However, the most important recent conference was in Rio in 1992. The UN Conference on Environment and Development led to five important outcomes:

(a) Framework convention on Climate Change;

(b) Convention on Biological Diversity;

(c) Agenda 21;

(d) Rio Declaration on Environment and Development;

(e) Forest Principles.

This was followed by the Kyoto and Buenos Aires Conferences on measures to tackle global warming.[26]

International environmental crime is now a major problem. At an international meeting in April 1998, the 'Group of 8' major industrialised countries agreed the following measures:

- increased international efforts to train officials in environmental enforcement and raise the priority of environmental crimes for governments;

---

25 See below, Chapter 3.
26 See below, Chapter 5.

- continue to fight the illegal trade in ozone depleting substances, hazardous waste and protected species, through effective enforcement of the existing multilateral environmental agreements;
- aim to increase public awareness of environmental crime;
- share information internationally about environmental crime, and improve contacts and working relationships between police, customs officers and other enforcement agencies;
- help developing countries to comply with environmental agreements and tackle environmental crime.[27]

ENGLAND[28]

Agencies

There are a plethora of agencies involved in the protection of the environment. This is due to the *ad hoc* way in which environmental legislation has been passed – often reacting to problems with no overall, cogent view and no long term planning, unlike in the US, where one body, the Environmental Protection Agency, was set up.

Government departments[29]

- Department for the Environment, Transport and the Regions (DETR) – this has responsibility for environmental policy. Major operational requirements may be in the hands of executive agencies but the DETR holds the regulators to account. The DETR recommends changes to laws, allocates resources and exercises its powers under the legislation, but it has a wide remit, including transport and local government.
- Ministry of Agriculture, Fisheries and Food (MAFF) – this is responsible for agricultural matters, but it is also concerned with radioactive discharges, water pollution and flood defence.
- Home Office – this is responsible for wildlife crime enforcement, particularly in relation to the export and import of species and plants.

---

27 See DETR press release, 5 April 1999.
28 Since Devolution, Scotland and Wales are subject in many cases to a different legal regime. The London Mayor will also has some influence over environmental matters.
29 There are also hundreds of advisory bodies.

Local authorities

Local authorities have responsibility for town and country planning, waste disposal, nuisance and local air pollution control. Local authorities will also have a specific environmental remit under the Local Government Bill 2000.[30]

Statutory bodies

* Environment Agency (set up as the Alkali Inspectorate in the 19th century, becoming HMIP in 1987 as part of the then Department of the Environment). HMIP's Inspectors were civil servants and the Industrial Air Pollution Inspectorate of HSE and the Radiochemical, Hazardous Waste and Water Inspectorate of the then DOE were amalgamated into it. In 1996, the EA was set up under the Environment Act 1995, amalgamating HMIP and the National Rivers Authority, which had responsibility for pollution control in relation to water, water resources, flooding, land drainage and fisheries functions. This was a welcome step forward, but there was some concern that the body was still not responsible for countryside issues. Its general duties are:

  o s 4 – to protect and enhance the environment and to attain sustainable development;

  o s 5 – to prevent, minimise, remedy or mitigate the effects of pollution;

  o s 108 – sets up the unified system of enforcement powers for the agency, including inspection and entry powers.

  Section 39, however, was very controversial, in that it included cost benefit analysis for the EA in the enforcement of these duties, when choosing to exercise them. It applies to both strategy and individual cases.

* Countryside Agency.[31]
* English Nature.[32]
* Planning Inspectorate.[33]
* UK Round Table on Sustainable Development.

The Royal Commission on Environmental Pollution was established in 1970 and is an independent body. It is the only standing Royal Commission in existence and has been prolific in producing reports.[34]

There are also a number of parliamentary select committees in the House of Commons that examine government policy in relation to the environment.

---

30 See below, Chapter 3.
31 See below, Chapter 8.
32 See below, Chapter 8.
33 See below, Chapter 3.
34 See www.rcep.org.uk.

These include: the Agriculture Select Committee, the Trade and Industry Select Committee, the Environmental Audit Select Committee and the Select Committee on the Environment, Transport and the Regions. In the House of Lords, there is the European Select Committee.

The functional areas and implementing agencies are listed below.:

Town and country planning

The statutory agencies responsible for implementing the town and country planning system are:
- local authorities;
- Planning Inspectorate;
- DETR.

Water pollution

The bodies responsible for controlling water pollution are:
- EA;
- Ofwat;
- Drinking Water Inspectorate;
- local authorities for statutory nuisance.

Air

Air quality standards are monitored and and regulated by:
- EA;
- local authorities for statutory nuisance, Clean Air Act and smoke control, LAPC.

Waste

The organisations who statutorily deal with waste are:
- EA;
- local authorities for statutory nuisance.

Integrated pollution and prevention control

These measures are implemented by:
- EA;
- local authorities for statutory nuisance and noise pollution.

Countryside

- Local planning authorities;
- English Nature;
- Countryside Agency;
- Forestry Commission;
- National Parks boards.

Reforms

There are a number of changes being made to the regulators. The Royal Commission on Environmental Pollution has been reviewed.[35] The EA's[36] legislation is also to be reviewed in order to examine the mechanisms under which the Agency operates. The aim is to simplify the regulatory process and to 'identify any significant obstacles which hinder them from taking a holistic approach to safeguarding the environment'. The consultation process will take about a year and will not look at integration of the agencies or the philosophical approaches underlying the different regulatory regimes.[37] The Planning Inspectorate is also being reviewed.[38] A number of changes to the regulatory system have been outlined in the Green Paper on *Utility Regulation – A Fair Deal for Consumers*, March 1998, and the Government's *Response to Consultation*, May 1998.[39] Sustainability will also be part of the responsibility of the devolved Parliaments and the Regional Development Agencies.

The EA has published an *Environmental Strategy for the Millennium and Beyond*[40] and this has been followed by action plans on:

- water quality;
- process industries regulation;
- radioactive substances regulation;
- waste management and regulation;
- land quality;
- water resources;
- flood defence;

---

35 See DETR press release 035, 18 January 1999; Review of the Royal Commission on Environmental Pollution, *Financial Management and Policy*, 11 May 2000, available at www.rcep.org.uk.

36 House of Commons Select Committee on Environment, Transport and Regional Affairs, Session 99–2000, *The Environment Agency*, HC 34, 20 May 2000.

37 See DETR press release 292/ENV, 8 April 1998.

38 Quinennial Review of the Planning Inspector.

39 See Graham, 1998.

40 September 1997.

- fisheries;
- recreation;
- conservation;
- navigation.

Pressure groups

There are a number of pressure groups working within the environmental area. These include:

- Friends of the Earth;
- Greenpeace;
- Clean Air Society;
- Surfers against Sewage;
- Marine Conservation Society;
- National Trust;
- Open Spaces Society;
- Council for the Protection of Rural England;
- Environmental Law Foundation;
- Environment Council;
- UKELA;
- RSPB;
- RSPCA;
- Whale and Dolphin Conservation Society;
- Soil Association;
- Wildfowl and Wetland Trust;
- groups concerned with farming issues, including the National Farmers Union and the Countryside Alliance;
- direct action groups such as Earth First! and Genetix Snowball.

Enforcement

Enforcement action can take place on a number of levels, both European[41] and domestic. It can take the form of legal controls or through market mechanisms.[42]

---

41 See Hunter, Hendrickx and Muylle, 1998, pp 47–54.

42 This issue is not considered here, but includes taxes such as the landfill tax or the proposed pesticide tax, as well as subsidies and other payments, eg, self monitoring or clean up costs.

ENFORCEMENT[43] IN THE ECJ[44]

Actions against a Member State

The European Commission can bring Member States before the ECJ for failure to implement EC legislation. The Commission can impose penalties against a Member State (Art 226 of the EC Treaty).

Actions by another Member State

An action can also be brought by another Member State for failure to fulfil their obligations under the EC Treaty. The Commission has to be informed before the proceedings (Art 227).

Direct effect, indirect effect and *Francovich*

Under the doctrine of direct effect, provisions of Community law can create rights and obligations that can be enforced by individuals before their own national courts. There are certain requirements that need to be met:

• the provision must impose a clear and precise obligation;

• it must be unconditional;

• the Member State must not be left with any real discretion in relation to the application of the rule in question.[45]

Treaty provisions and regulations have direct effect, as well as decisions and some international agreements entered into by the Community, although this is not automatic. Directives are directly effective if they are sufficiently clear and precise. An individual cannot rely on a directive in relation to another individual – only a public body.[46]

Legislation may also be given effect indirectly – even if Community law does not have direct effect, it may still be applied indirectly in domestic law as a means of interpretation. There is no need for national legislation to have been enacted.[47]

---

43 Dollittle, 1999, pp 101–02; Paret De Prez, 1999, pp 224–28; Paret De Prez, 2000, pp 35–39.

44 See, also, Kunzlik, 1997, pp 46–52.

45 See Usher, 1998, p 147.

46 See Case C 188/89 *Foster v British Gas* [1990] ECR I-3133; Case 152/84 *Marshall v Southampton AHA* [1986] ECR 723; [1986] 1 CMLR 688.

47 Case 14/83 *Van Colsen and Kamann v Land Nordrhein-Westfalen* [1984] ECR 1891; [1986] 2 CMLR 430.

Legislation may also be given effect through the *Francovich*[48] principle. In this case, where a Member State had failed to implement a directive, under the principle of State liability, it would be obliged to compensate the individual for any damage suffered. That is, so long as the directive conferred rights on individuals, the content of the rights could be identified on the basis of the provisions in the directive, and there was a causal link between the State failure and the damage suffered by the person affected.[49]

The European Environment Agency

The agency for Implementation and Enforcement of European Environmental Law (IMPEL) was set up in 1992. It provides a framework of inspectors, licensing bodies and policy makers to exchange information ideas and develop enforcement structures. The European Commission has no environmental inspectorate and the EEA does not have an enforcement role. The responsibility for enforcement and inspection lies with the Member States. In 1996, the Commission issued a Communication on Implementation and Enforcement of European Environmental Law. It has four elements: the quality of the legislation; access to the courts; the minimum requirements for an inspection; and the introduction of IMPEL. This was adopted in June 1997. In May 1997, the EP stated that, in future, European environmental legislation should be accompanied by a minimum standard for inspection in relation to compliance.[50] There is also an International Network for Enforcement and Compliance with International Law (INECE).[51]

English environmental law enforcement[52]

This issue is looked at extensively elsewhere.[53] But the type of standards laid down are important in relation to how environmental law is enforced. In the past, enforcement was based on the 'British' style[54] of regulation.[55]

---

48 Cases C 6/90 and C 9/90 *Francovich and Others v Italian State* [1991] ECR I-5357.

49 There have been a number of UK cases that have looked at the operation of direct effect, including *Twyford PC v Secretary of State for Transport* [1990] JEL 273, *Wychavon DC v SOSE* [1994] JEL 351 and *R v North Yorkshire CC ex p Brown* [1997] Env LR 391 on the direct effect of the Environmental Impact Assessment Directive.

50 From Ministry of Housing, Spatial Planning and the Environment Factsheet, *Enforcement of Environmental Regulation at International Level*, October 1998, The Hague.

51 See www.inece.org.

52 There are a number of other mechanisms that can be used, including market mechanisms and environmental agreements. See Bailey, 1999, pp 170–79.

53 Birtles, 1993, p 615; Carson, 1970, p 396; Dickens, 1970, p 618; Hawkins Hutter, 1988; Jowell and Millichap, 1986, p 482.

54 Murdie, 1993, Rowan-Robinson, Ross and Walton, 1996, pp 19–42.

55 Vogel, 1986; Rowan-Robinson and Ross, 1994, p 200; Richardson *et al*, 1982; Hawkins, 1994; Jowell and Millichap, 1986.

Environmental offences were seen as 'morally neutral' offences or white collar crime. Whether a firm or individual was prosecuted depended upon the attitude of the enforcement agency, agency policy, intra-organisational pressure and the practical difficulties involved in a prosecution.

There has been a long history in the UK of a strategy of ensuring compliance through co-operation and consultation, and the number of prosecutions remain low. Friends of the Earth undertook a study which showed that companies had a one in 100 chance of being prosecuted by the EA. There were 2,152 breaches at 830 sites and 17 prosecutions.[56]

However, this has now changed. The EA recently issued an enforcement code. The EA has to specify in a letter the reasons for the action and representations can be made to the EA official concerned. The business has 10 weeks to object after being told of the enforcement notice, unless the EA believes that immediate action should be taken.

When enforcing environmental protection, the EA will follow the rules of:

* proportionality – enforcement action should be proportionate to the risks posed to the environment and seriousness of any breach of the law;
* consistency – a consistent approach is important but issues such as environmental impact, management actions and attitudes and offending history should be taken into account;
* transparency – it should be clear why enforcement action has been taken;
* targeting – the EA will target those activities that have the most serious environmental damage or where hazards are least well controlled.

The code states that, where there is sufficient evidence, the EA will normally prosecute for the following offences:[57]

* incidents or breaches which have significant consequences for the environment;
* carrying out operations without a relevant licence;
* excessive or persistent breaches of regulatory requirements;
* failure to comply, or to comply adequately, with formal remedial requirements;
* reckless disregard for management or quality standards;
* failure to supply information without reasonable excuse, or knowingly or recklessly supplying false or misleading information;
* obstruction of agency staff in carrying out their powers.

---

56 See *The Independent* (1997) 16 September, p 14.
57 The Common Incident Classification Scheme will record the gravity of incidents and how the agency has responded.

There is now greater incentive for the EA to take enforcement action (under ss 18 and 19 of the Water Industry Act 1991, as amended by ss 110–12 of the Environment Act 1995), because the penalties have increased. In the magistrates' court, a £20,000 maximum fine may be imposed, while in the Crown Court there is a provision for unlimited fines and two years' imprisonment. The bodies with the largest amounts imposed on them are Shell, which was fined over £1 million, and more in costs, and *The Sea Empress*,[58] fined £4 million and £825,000 in costs (See EA press release, 15 January 1999).[59]

There is also corporate liability under s 137 of the EPA 1990. This states that, where an offence committed by a body corporate is proved to have been committed with the consent or connivance of, or because of the neglect of, any director, manager or similar officer of the body, that officer is liable, as well as the body corporate itself. However, the cases indicate that the manager has to be part of the 'controlling mind' of the company. That person should have the power and responsibility to determine corporate policies and strategy. A company may also be vicariously liable for the action of its employees. In the case of waste, for example, if an employee knows of the illegal disposal of waste, the company may be vicariously liable and the employer may be fixed with knowledge of the deposit.

The EA has wider powers to help it in its enforcement functions – it can require information by notice and it is a criminal offence to fail to provide, without reasonable excuse, the information required, or knowingly to provide false information. Under s 108 of the EPA 1995, the EA has rights of entry to carry out investigations on premises, rights to take and remove samples, and, under s 109, an inspector may seize and render harmless any article or substance (that is, not just waste) which appears to be a cause of imminent danger of serious pollution or of serious harm to human health.

There are a number of provisions in the legislation for remediation and clean up powers, for example, under ss 92 and 161 of the Water Resources Act (WRA) 1991. The EA has widely drafted powers to prevent pollution incidents and, where they occur, recover the costs of cleaning up. It can also undertake remedial or restorative work. Under s 26 of the EPA 1990, clean up costs can be awarded and remedial work undertaken.

This change in enforcement strategy can be clearly seen, in that several water and sewage companies in England and Wales were found guilty of polluting rivers, streams and bathing waters on an average of once a week in 1998. The EA had successfully prosecuted eight out of the 10 companies for a total of 22 water pollution offences since 1 January 1998. All 10 companies had

---

58 *Environment Agency v Milford Haven Port Authority (The Sea Empress)* [1999] 1 Lloyd's Rep 673; [2000] W Law 331173 (CA (Crim Div)).

59 This was later reduced quite substantially.

been found guilty by the courts. The total sum in fines levied by the courts for offences was £95,300, which equates to an average fine per offence of £4,300. The largest fine levied during this period was £15,000 against Wessex Water. Since privatisation, the water companies have been found guilty of water pollution offences over 300 times. This works out to be, on average, around three prosecutions a month.[60]

England and Wales: court structure

- House of Lords – this is the final court of appeal in England and Wales in civil and criminal law. However, a case may go to the ECJ or the European Court of Human Rights (ECHR). They are two different courts, with separate jurisdictions.
- Court of Appeal – this has Civil and Criminal Divisions.
- High Court – this has three administrative divisions:
  - Court of Chancery (property and company law);
  - Queen's Bench Division (this deals mainly with contract and tort and some criminal cases);
  - Family Division.

  There is also the Queen's Bench Divisional Court, which hears appeals on points of law and judicial review.

  The High Court mainly sits in the Royal Courts of Justice in London, although it can sit anywhere in England and Wales.
- Crown Court – this hears criminal cases.
- County courts – these are composed of circuit and district judges.
- Magistrates' courts – these are composed of stipendary or lay magistrates.

Criminal law

Many criminal offences are of strict liability: this means that one does not have to prove fault or negligence; therefore, every breach should be an offence. This is the case in relation to water pollution offences under s 85 of the WRA 1991 and Pt I of the EPA 1990, as amended, and in relation to waste offences under s 33 of the EPA 1990.[61] There is a defence in s 33(7) that the defendant took all reasonable precautions and exercised all due diligence to avoid the commission of the offence.

---

60 See EA press release, 29 May 1998.
61 See *Shanks and McEwan (Teesside) Ltd v Environment Agency* [1997] Env LR 305.

Empress Car Co (Abertillery) Ltd v National Rivers Authority [1998] 1 All ER 481 looked at the offence of causing pollution. It concerned a diesel tank, parked in the yard of a business, whose contents drained into the local river. The tank was bunded to contain any spillages, but this was overridden by fixing an extension pipe to the outlet of the tank in order to connect to a smaller drum which stood outside the protective bund. This outlet had a tap but no lock. An unknown third party opened the tap and the entire contents of the drum polluted the river.

There is a difference between causing and knowingly permitting pollution. Causing involves some active operation or chain of operations. Lord Hoffman discussed the earlier cases on the issue, which required some positive act to be the immediate cause of the pollution. He stated that the Act does not require this; it requires only a finding that something the defendant did caused the pollution, and that maintaining a diesel tank was doing something. The question to ask is, did the defendants cause the pollution? He stated that, while forseeability is a relevant ingredient in the tort of negligence, it is not relevant when looking at the offence of causing pollution. In relation to the act of the third party, if a defendant has created a situation where the polluting matter could escape, and if the necessary condition of the escape is the act of a third party or natural event, the courts should look at whether the event should be regarded as a normal fact of life or something extraordinary, such as a terrorist attack.

Common law

This is a form of private law, regulating the relationship between individuals. It includes civil law, which provides a framework of legal rules through which individuals can assert their rights. The common law is 'case centred and hence judge centred, allowing scope for a discretionary, *ad hoc*, pragmatic approach to the particular problems that appear before the court'.[62] Briefly, it is law that has been made by the judiciary deciding cases.

---

62 See McClaren, 1983.

THE COMMON LAW AND THE ENVIRONMENT[63]

Nuisance

Private nuisance

Nuisance is the unlawful interference with a person's use or enjoyment of land, or of some right over it, or in connection with it. A person has to have a legal interest in land in order to bring an action.[64]

In the tort of private nuisance, the law's object is to provide guidelines to owners as to the extent to which their pursuit on their own land of continuing and intentional activities is protected from or inhibited by the interests of their neighbours. Nuisance cases can be about physical injury or sensibilities, that is, noise, dust and smell. If it is physical injury that is caused by a nuisance, then, as long as the damage is not trivial, liability will follow. However, in the case of the enjoyment of land, other factors come into play.

In relation to enjoyment of land, the test is one of reasonableness. A number of factors may be relevant, including locality, duration, hypersensitivity[65] and malice.[66] The court attempts to balance the conflicting interests of the parties, and, since the majority of nuisance cases involve noise and smells, the court will use external gauges of the reasonableness or otherwise of the defendant's conduct and the claimant's sensibility:

> ... the important point next for decision may properly, I conceive, be thus put: ought this inconvenience to be considered in fact as more than fanciful, more than one of mere delicacy, or fastidiousness, as an inconvenience materially interfering with the ordinary comfort physically of human existence, not merely according to plain and sober and simple notions among the English people [*Walter v Selfe* [1851] 20 LJ Ch 189]?

Whether this is so will often depend on the facts of each case. Nuisances have included noise and vibration, fumes, dust and smell; it is not necessary to prove an injury to health to succeed for an action in nuisance for smell.

The remedies for private nuisance are damages,[67] injunctions or abatement. Abatement means that, if a person is affected by a nuisance, the

---

63 See Pugh Day, 1992.
64 *Hunter v Canary Wharf* [1997] 2 WLR 684: in this case, the right to sue in nuisance was linked to ownership of land.
65 See *Robinson v Kilvert* (1884) 41 Ch D 88.
66 See *Hollywood Silver Fox Farms v Emmett* [1936] 2 KB 468.
67 *Savage v Fairclough* [2000] Env LR 183: in this case, it was established that forseeability of harm was required to establish a right to damages in private nuisance.

law allows them to abate the nuisance without going to court; however, there are restrictions on this – notice has to be given and unnecessary damage must not occur.

There are a number of defences, including prescription;[68] easement enjoyed for a number of years;[69] grant of right, that is, from one landowner to another to do something that would otherwise be unlawful; Act of God; act of a trespasser; and statutory authority. There is no defence of coming to a nuisance[70] or being one of many.

Public nuisance

An action can also be brought under public nuisance, which is a criminal offence at common law. On this basis, the Attorney General may bring a civil action for an injunction, or private nuisance, which is only a tort. Public nuisance is either a private nuisance which affects a larger number of people than is usual in a private nuisance situation or which involves the interference with the safety or convenience of the public generally but which does not satisfy the basic requirement for an action under private nuisance of interference with an individual's enjoyment of their own land. A private individual can bring an action for damages or an injunction for a public nuisance if it can be shown that they suffered special damage over and above that suffered by other members of the general public affected by the nuisance. In the absence of special damage, there can be no action, unless the Attorney General can be persuaded to bring one.

Statutory nuisance

The statutory control of nuisance is found in the EPA 1990. The main aim of the statutory nuisance provisions is to provide a quick and easy remedy to abate nuisances with which the common law is too slow or expensive to deal.

Local authorities are under a duty to inspect their areas for statutory nuisances (s 79 of the EPA 1990) and to act upon complaints. If an individual complains, the local council is under a duty to investigate. However, when investigating the complaint, the council only has to take such steps as are reasonably practicable.[71]

---

68 This is the defence that, if an activity causing the nuisance has been undertaken for 20 years, then it will not give rise to a legal action.

69 See *Sturges v Bridgeman* (1879) 11 Ch D 852.

70 See *Smeaton v Ilford Corpn* [1954] Ch 450.

71 *R v Carrick DC ex p Shelley* – duty to inspect and deal with nuisance. See Purdue, 1997, p 103.

The scope of nuisance was widened in the Noise and Statutory Nuisance Act 1993, which allows the council to take action against noise in the street, including vehicles, alarms, machinery and loudspeakers. There are increasing controls over noise at a national and European level, including proposed EC legislation on noise from outdoor equipment (COM (98)46).

Nuisance can be either prejudicial to health or a nuisance. This has the same meaning as under the common law. Under s 79(1) of the EPA 1990, the following may constitute such nuisances:

- physical state of the premises (79(1)(a));
- noise emitted from premises (s 79(1)(g));[72]
- smoke emitted from premises (s 79(1)(b));
- any accumulation or deposit (s 79(1)(e));
- any animal, in relation to the place or manner in which it is kept (s 79(1)(f)).

The general control of statutory nuisance is contained in s 80 of the EPA 1990. Where a local authority is satisfied that a statutory nuisance exists or is likely to recur it is under a mandatory duty to serve an abatement notice on the person responsible for the nuisance or, if they cannot be found, the owner or occupier of the premises.

The Act allows the authority to take action before the nuisance occurs. For example, if there is a party planned and there is more than a suggestion that powerful audio equipment may be used, if the local authority is satisfied that there is a nuisance, or that one is likely to occur, it is under a duty to serve an abatement notice. This must require the abatement of the nuisance, the prohibition/restriction of its occurrence/recurrence and the execution of works or other necessary steps to comply with the notice within the stipulated time limit. In *R v Falmouth and Truro Port HA ex p South West Water Ltd* [2000] 1 WLR 331, the Court of Appeal held that, whilst a local authority always has a discretion as to whether or not to specify the works required to abate a nuisance, if the authority does prescribe the manner in which the nuisance is to be abated, as opposed to leaving the choice to the perpetrator, the necessary works have to be specified in the notice. In a lower court ([1999] Env LR 833), it had been held that it was a matter of discretion as to whether an authority should consult prior to serving an abatement notice.

If the notice is contravened with no reasonable excuse – this does not include holding a birthday party or reducing noise levels on request, though this may be relevant as an issue in mitigation or in deciding whether there was

---

72 *Southwark LBC v Ince* (1989) 21 HLR 504, ie, lack of proper insulation of council owned flats against noise.

a noise nuisance in the first place (*Welling BC v Gordon* (1990) 155 JP 494) – then the defendant is guilty of an offence.

The person responsible can include the local authority or a landlord who has allowed a tenant to carry on offensive activities. If there is any difficulty in finding the person responsible, an action can be brought against the owner/occupier of the premises. The notice can be served either on the person or be left at their proper address or sent by post.

A right of appeal to a magistrates' court regarding the serving of an abatement notice lies within 21 days of serving the notice.

If an individual complains and the local authority takes no action, then the applicant may be able to take the council to court through a judicial review action. Therefore, any individual complaining to the council should ensure that proper evidence is gathered, that is, dates, times and the length of the nuisance. The SOSETR may also take action under its default powers if a local authority does not act.

Individuals can also bring an action themselves under s 82 of the EPA 1990 so long as the nuisance is in existence.

The penalties are set out in s 80(5) and (6) – the maximum level of fine in the magistrates' court is £5,000; if the offence continues after conviction, the defendant is liable under s 81(5) for a further fine not exceeding one-10th of that level for each day that the nuisance continues.

The local authority can also get an injunction to stop the nuisance if, for example, it feels that proceedings brought under an offence of contravening an abatement notice would not provide an adequate remedy. This is a discretionary remedy and the activity complained of must be of sufficient gravity/duration to justify stopping it.

There are certain defences available, such as reasonable excuse. Under statutory nuisance, this will be conclusive; however, in a private nuisance case, the fact that BPM has been followed is one of the factors to be weighed against the others.

Negligence

There have been environmental cases of negligence in relation to failure to warn. In *Scott Whitehead v NCB* [1987] P & CR 263, the water authority was held liable in negligence for failure to warn downstream riparian owners of known chloride pollution in the river which was so concentrated that it was clearly going to be damaging to crops. Negligence is:

> ... the omission to do something which a reasonable man guided upon those considerations which ordinarily regulate the conduct of human affairs, would do, or do something which a prudent and reasonable man would not do [*Blyth v Birmingham Water Works Co* [1856] 11 Exch 781].

The court takes into account the object to be obtained by the defendant's conduct and the practicability of precautions. Forseeability is an important part of the test for negligence.[73] Section 100 of the Water Resources Act expressly excludes civil liability for breach of statutory duty. Section 73(6) provides for liability for personal injury and property damage caused by an unlawful deposit of controlled waste and the contaminated land regime establishes liability for the clean up of contaminated land. Civil liability in relation to the nuclear industry is hard to establish. However, civil liability has for a long time been on the EC's agenda. On 9 February 2000, the European Commission adopted a White Paper on *Environmental Liability*. This would create an EU wide liability for harm to property, persons and protected natural resources and sites.[74]

Rylands v Fletcher (1865) 3 H & C 774 established a cause of action that is extremely limited, as it concerns the collection and storage of anything likely to do mischief if it escapes. If it does so, there is liability. However, it has to be a non-natural use.

Riparian rights

A riparian owner is a person whose land abuts a watercourse. He is entitled to water from the watercourse in its natural flow, without sensible diminution or increase and without sensible alteration to its character or quality. However, this is qualified, in that ordinary uses of water can be enjoyed notwithstanding their effects on a lower owner. An owner can also use the water for some extraordinary purpose but must do so in a way that does not cause any sensible damage to another riparian interest. An extraordinary use which damages another riparian owner will be actionable. The discharge of pollution would be considered to be an extraordinary use of the land and would only be acceptable if it did not cause any danger. To be a riparian owner, one must own or have an interest in land.[75]

---

73 See *Cambridge Water Co v Eastern Counties Leather plc* [1994] 2 AC 264; *Ryeford Homes Ltd and another v Fever Oaks DC and Others* (1990) JPL 36, where it was held that a planning authority did not owe a duty in negligence to any individual adversely affected by a planning decision.
74 See Poli, 1999, pp 299–309.
75 See *John Young & Co v Bakier Distillery Co* [1893] AC 691.

Public law[76]

Public law includes:

- administrative law, in relation to judicial review, the operation of local government, tribunals and inquiries;
- constitutional law, which is concerned with the operation of the uncodified constitution in the UK and the rule of law.

The following matters and bodies are covered by public law:

- civil liberties/human rights;
- Parliament, which passes legislation and scrutinises the executive through debates and questions;
- select committees, which are set up to look at various issues of government policy, such as the environment, transport and regions;[77]
- the Executive:
  - Prime Minister;
  - ministers who form the Cabinet;
  - civil service, which formulates and executes policy;
  - courts.

Public law is about the relationship between the individual and the State and includes statute law, that is, law which is created by Parliament in the form of legislation. There are a number of different types of statute:

- public Bills – these are Bills introduced by the Government;
- private Bills – these are Bills that alter the law in a particular locality, confer rights or relieve responsibility of a particular person or group;
- Private Members' Bills – these Bills are introduced by a backbencher MP, that is, an MP from either party who does not sit in the Cabinet as part of the Executive;
- delegated legislation – this is legislation made under a power conferred by Parliament. Acts such as the Pollution Prevention and Control Act 1999 are framework Acts, with much of the detail being left to the Secretary of State to pass on at a later date, in the form of regulations or directions. Delegated legislation includes bylaws made by local authorities.

---

76 There are a number of good books on public law, including Barnett, 2000, Bradley and Ewing, 1997, and Craig, 1994.

77 Reports can be found in *Hansard* or on the open government website, available at www.open.gov.uk.

STATUTORY OFFENCES

Judicial review

Increasingly, environmental control has been centred on statutory, rather than voluntary, controls, often as a result of pressure from the EC. This has meant that, under statutes such as the EPA 1990, the control of the environmental enforcement bodies often depends upon judicial review.[78]

The problem in general with judicial review is the restrictive nature of the grounds on which a court will intervene. However, judicial review is important both where a regulator has decided not to prosecute and in relation to a decision to permit a polluting activity by granting a licence.

How to apply for judicial review

An action has to be brought promptly and in any case within three months.

There are several limitations in relation to the availability of judicial review:

- The case can only be brought against a public body, for example, the Secretary of State for the Environment, Transport and the Regions, local authorities and the EA.

- The issue must be one of public law. However, there are exceptions to this; for example, a challenge to the validity of a bylaw was allowed as a defence to a criminal prosecution in *DPP v Hutchinson* [1990] 2 AC 783.

- There are no clear categorisations of the grounds of judicial review. However, three general categories have been set out:

    (a) illegality – a decision is illegal if it contravenes or exceeds the terms of the power which authorises the making of the decision, or if it pursues an objective other than that for which the power to make the decision was conferred;

    (b) irrationality – this is, the decision was made unreasonably;

    (c) procedural impropriety – this includes the duty to act fairly under natural justice. Natural justice embodies the right to be heard and the right to an unbiased trial.

- Other ideas are important, such as proportionality, legitimate expectations and human rights.

---

78 Hilson and Cram, 1997, pp 148–57. See, eg, *R v Secretary of State and Midland Expressway (MEL) ex p Alliance Against the Birmingham Relief Road* (1998) New Prop Cas 129.

An applicant has to establish *locus standi* (standing) – this means that he has to establish sufficient interest in the case. In civil actions, the claimant must show an identifiable and direct harm, and this test has been used as part of the basis for *locus standi*, although the courts are beginning to widen the notion. This is important, as public interest arguments are often at stake. There have been a few important recent cases in relation to this. In *R v HMIP ex p Greenpeace* [1994] 2 CMLR 548, although Greenpeace lost the case, it did establish standing and the judge widened the notion beyond that of a class action. This is important, as it explodes the myth of group actions in civil claims; that is, a group is seen as an amalgam of individuals where no individual is in a stronger a position than any others.[79]

There has been a large number of judicial review cases in relation to the environment and planning, and many pressure groups have been given *locus standi* to bring actions. Some examples include:

- *Twyford PC v Secretary of State for the Environment* [1991] 3 LMELR 89 (Tywford Down and the EIA);[80]

- *R v Secretary of State for the Environment ex p RSPB* [1997] Env LR 431 (Lappel Bank);[81]

- *R v Secretary of State for the Environment ex p Friends of the Earth and Another* [1996] Env LR 198 (Drinking Water Directive);[82]

- *Bushel v Secretary of State for the Environment* [1981] AC 75. Here, objectors in a motorway inquiry wished to cross-examine civil servants about the Government's methods of forecasting traffic growth. The House of Lords stated that the Government did not have to provide the materials, on the ground that these were matters of policy and confidential within the department.[83]

However, the problem with these developments is that they have been left to the discretion of individual judges, rather than being a statement of general principle. There is also a concern that there needs to be a specialist court to deal with environmental and planning matters.

---

79 See, also, *R v Secretary of State for the Environment ex p Rose Theatre Trust Co* [1990] 1 QB 504; and *R v North Somerset DC and Pioneer Aggregates (UK) Ltd ex p Garnett* [1998] Env LR 91; (1997) JPL 1015 for a limited view of standing. However, the test for standing has been widened by *R v Secretary of State for Employment ex p Equal Opportunities Commission* [1995] 1 AC 1; *R v Secretary of State for Foreign and Commonwealth Affairs ex p World Development Movement Ltd* [1995] 1 WLR 586; and *R v Somerset CC and ARC Southern Ltd ex p Dixon* (1998) 75 P & CR 175.

80 See below, Chapter 3.

81 See below, Chapter 8.

82 See below, Chapter 4.

83 See below, Chapter 5.

Information

Access to information and secrecy issues have been extremely important in relation to the development of environmental law. The first attempts to open up information to the public were made in the Control of Pollution Act 1974 and the Water Act 1973, which provided for public registers of consents. However, these were not enacted until 1985. It was the EC that again led the way on this issue, with Directive 90/313 on Access to Environmental Information. This led to the Environmental Information Regulations 1992/3240.[84]

The justifications for the policy of withholding information have centred around the ideas of the protection of trade secrets. In the past, it was argued that the public was incompetent at interpreting data, but this is less valid nowadays, with many of the pressure groups providing guidance and expertise. The other arguments are that the information will be abused and will lead to vexatious litigation.

All of these concerns are outweighed by the justification for allowing information into the pubic domain; these include encouraging public confidence, in that the public is able to assess an agency's work, and the degree of influence of industry can be revealed. It is also an important democratic principle, in that the Government should be held to account for its decisions. It also provides groups and individuals with the evidence to bring prosecutions themselves or put pressure on the regulators to bring an action.[85]

Access to information[86]

Legislation in relation to access to information at present consists of:[87]

- Water – the Public Register of Applications, Consents, Samples,etc, is kept under ss 189–90 of the WRA 1991; Control of Pollution (Registers) Regulations 1989 (SI 1989/1160); ss 195–96 of the Water Industry Act 1991. See, also, ss 202–03 of the WRA 1991. Restrictions on disclosure of information by the EA is contained in s 204 of the WRA 1991, as amended by the Environment Act 1995.

---

84 See Birtles, 1993, p 615.
85 See Hutter, 1988.
86 See Rowan-Robinson, Ross and Walton, 1996, pp 19–42.
87 Restriction on disclosures of information by the EA is contained in WRA 1991, s 204, as amended by the EA 1995, Sched 22, s 191(a), (b); EPA ss 20–22; Environmental Protection (Applications, Appeals and Registers) Regulations 1991 (SI 1991/507, 1996/667). See, also, the Environment Act 1995, ss 51–52, 113 on exclusion of information.

- Environmental Protection (Applications, Appeals and Registers) Regulations 1991 (SI 1991/507, 1996/667); see, also, ss 51–52 and 113 of the Environment Act 1995 on exclusion of information.

- Waste – s 64 of the EPA 1990; exceptions ss 65–66; Waste Management Licensing Regulations 1994 (SI 1994/1056). See, also, s 64(2)(a) on exclusions as inserted by the Environment Act 1995.

- Contaminated land – s 78 of the EPA 1990, as inserted by Environment Act 1995.

There is more information available now under the Freedom of Information (Environment) Regulations 1992,[88] as well as the Chemical Release Directory.[89]

The Government has drawn up a Freedom of Information Act.[90] It is also introducing legislation to ensure that the regulators will have to consult on and publish a Code of Practice about their consultation and decision making processes, and to publish reasons for key decisions.[91] The Government would expect regulators to include procedures in their Codes of Practice for consulting on and publishing their forward programmes.[92] The importance of consultation was stated in the Economic Regulation Report, which was published as part of the Round Table's Third Annual Report.[93] The EC has also been setting down new regulatory rules. The Aarhus Convention on access to information, public participation in decision making and access to justice in environmental matters took place in June 1998. It was the fourth ministerial conference on the theme of Environment for Europe.[94] This will ensure greater transparency in the European decision making process and covers EC institutions, as well as national authorities.

The importance of freedom of information is summed up by the following quote:

> There is no justification for keeping information about the state of the environment secret or, equally, for making access to such information difficult or prohibitively expensive. The general public should have a right to know the results of monitoring of the environment and to have it presented to them in an understandable manner. They should have the right to be informed in good

---

88 SI 1992/3240; EC Directive 90/313 on Access to Environmental Information.
89 *Maile v Wigan MBC* (1999) ENDS, in (2000) 12(1) Env Law and Mgmt 10.
90 See, generally, Bell and McKillvray, 2000, and *Your Right to Know: The Government's Proposals on the Freedom of Information Act*, Cmnd 3818, 1997. See, also, Twigg-Fleshner, 1999, pp 157–63.
91 See Graham, 1998, pp 149–56.
92 Government Green Paper on Utility Regulation and the Government's Response to Consultation, *A Fair Deal For Consumers*, 1998.
93 Round Table Third Annual Report. March 1998:10.
94 UN EC Commission for Europe, Aarhus Convention. See DETR press releases 514, 23 June 1998, and 524, 25 June 1998.

time, about the policies adopted to protect the environment and to have an informed input into the decision making process. This right of access applies equally to the industries concerned by regulation and to interested parties representing environmental or consumer interest ... a programme of measures implemented with the support of interested parties to tackle problems which they understand and appreciate has a greater chance of success than one which is imposed without explanation and justification.[95]

THE FUTURE

The Human Rights Act 1998,[96] which became operative on 2 October 2000, will have an impact on environmental issues, planning law[97] and regulatory control. Article 8 of the European Convention on Human Rights, which gives the right to respect for private and family life and home and correspondence, has been successfully used in relation to environmental pollution from a treatment plant which was releasing fumes and smells that were causing health problems and nuisance. The locals were evacuated and rehoused while part of the plant was closed down.[98] Article 8 may also be breached if quality of life has been affected[99] and where there has been a failure to provide information on the risks from pollution.[100] However, as Thornton and Tromans state, there are limits to Art 8 in relation to the fact that the State can interfere in family life and home under Art 8(2), that is, for reasons of national security, public safety and economic well being.[101] Thornton and Tromans note:

> It is not possible to conclude that any 'environment rights' have been established under the Convention. There is no express right to an environment of a minimum standard of quality. The Court and Commission have, however, accepted that the enjoyment of a certain quality of environment is part of enjoying the right to a family life and to peaceful enjoyment of possessions ... It may be that in this respect the procedural rights, such as a right to a tribunal and to access to information, offer a better opportunity to protect the environment.[102]

---

95 European Community Water Policy, Communication From the Commission to the Council and the European Parliament, Brussels, 21 February 1996. Com (96) 59 Final: 13.

96 See Thornton and Tromans, 1999, pp 35–57.

97 See Hart, 2000, pp 117–33.

98 See *Lopez Ostra v Spain* (1994) 20 ECHR 277.

99 See *Powell and Raynor v UK* [1990] 172 ECHR Ser A, para 41, in relation to aircraft noise from Heathrow.

100 See *Guerra and Others v Italy* (116/1996/735/932) 4 BHRC 63.

101 The article then goes onto to consider the possible issue of Art 2, the right to life; Art 6, the right to a fair trial; and Art 10, the right to freedom of expression.

102 Thornton and Tromans, 1999, p 45.

There is a problem with establishing a right to the environment or a biotic right. This is a belief that the integrity of natural ecosystems should be protected not simply for the pleasure of people, but as a biotic right. Nature has its own purpose, which should be respected as a matter of ethical principle.[103] Some 'dark greens', such as Arne Ness, want an environmental ethic where non-humans could be included in the moral community; that is, nature would have intrinsic value – value in itself – whatever its usefulness to people. The development of biotic rights is based on the abandonment of the Enlightenment project when intuition gave way to reason; in other words, reason is problematic, as it is based upon scientific, technological progress. Dark greens argue that science is at the root of the crises of the modern world and that, in order to develop an environmental ethic, we should go back to an intuitive way of life.

Thus, the argument is that, whilst it is difficult to ascribe environmental or biotic rights, it is easier to ensure that the way in which decisions are made about the environment are made in an accountable way.

Therefore, it is not good enough to have clean air/water in an economically stagnant or politically repressive and unjust State; environmentalism is allied to social justice, non-discrimination at all levels, including the international level, and political effectiveness.

The main problem in relation to an international solution is, how can a fragmented international system that is subject to many conflicts achieve the high levels of co-operation and policy co-ordination needed to remedy the global damage?[104]

In relation to Europe, there has been a strengthening of environmental protection in policy making after the Treaty of Amsterdam, but this Treaty does not fully establish rights for citizens to enforce environmental rights.[105] In an interesting article, Caliiess argues that we need a European environmental constitutional law:[106]

- there should be fundamental priority of environmental protection;
- nature should be respected in its own right – a recognition of the special rights of nature;
- environmental policy needs an ethical foundation: 'The law as a basic model of political development can, to a limited extent, impart a new ethical framework to society and to the relationship of humans and the environment, and thus, through steady interaction, influence the collective learning process ...;'[107]

---

103 Dobson, 1999, 1998.
104 Boyle, 1991, pp 229–45.
105 See Tromans, 1995, pp 779–96.
106 Caliiess, 1997, pp 113–20.
107 *Ibid*, p 114.

- access to justice by environmental associations should be introduced to take the roles of trustee and safeguard the special rights of the environment;
- the EEA should be reformed and a network of national environmental inspection agencies established;[108]
- the office of Environmental Ombudsman should be established;
- and Ecological Senate should be set up;
- the European Convention on Human Rights to include a fundamental right to a healthy environment.

In relation to the UK, there have also been calls for change,[109] particularly in relation to the idea of an environmental court.[110] Professor Malcolm Grant has undertaken a study for the DETR on the feasibility of establishing an environmental court for England and Wales.[111] The report looks at a number of different jurisdictions and the reasons for creating such a court.[112] The research identifies five alternative models :

(a) a planning appeal tribunal;

(b) an Environmental Division of the High Court;

(c) an Environmental Division of the High Court incorporating the Lands Tribunal;

(d) a separate environmental court;

(e) a two tier environmental court: the first tier would incorporate the regulatory appeals jurisdiction of the Planning Inspectorate, and the second would take over the jurisdiction of the Lands Tribunal.[113]

However, to have access to the court means that legal aid also needs to be reformed, as an action cannot be brought in the collective public interest. There should also be the development of more mediation and conciliation as an alternative to the courts in the environmental field.

---

108 See Macrory, 1992, p 347.

109 McAuslan, pp 195–208; Woolf, 1992, pp 1–14; Winter, 1989, pp 38–47.

110 Kramer, 1996, pp 1–18; Boyle Anderson Carnworth, 1999, pp 3–14; Miller, 1999, pp 157–76; Rugman Soloway, 1999; Stroup Meiners, 1999; Thornton and Tromans, 1999, pp 35–58; Wilson, 1999; Wolf, 1997.

111 See Grant, 2000.

112 Human Rights Act 1998, which may require a review of the Planning Inspectorate.

113 Review of tribunals and administrative justice by Sir Andrew Legget, available at www.tribunals-review.org.uk.

Some final thoughts[114]

The recent protests in relation to the World Trade Organisation[115] and the increasing concern over the global economy highlight the problems of the accountability of supranational organisations, and also multi-national corporations, which are increasingly seen as operating outside the traditional areas of accountability.[116] The conflict between trade and the environment has arisen in a number of cases.[117] It is clear that, whilst this book concentrates on the law in England, the issue of environmental improvement is a global issue.

114 Ekersley, 1992; Bookchin, 1991; Weale, 1992; Rowell, 1996; Wells, 1996; Lamb, 1996; Dobson, 1991, 1990; Norton 1991; Martell, 1994; Mccormick, 1995; Garner, 1996; Gunningham, 1974; Schumacher, 1974; Lovelock, 1995; Athanasiou, 1998.

115 See *The Journal of World Trade*, The Hague: Kluwer, in particular, Torres, 1999, and Cole, 1999.

116 See 'How to escape the global economy' (1998) 28(4) The Ecologist; 'Beyond the monoculture: shifting from global to local' (1999) 29(3).

117 See Cameron, Demaret and Geradin, 1997.

CHAPTER 3

TOWN AND COUNTRY PLANNING

LAW[1]

Planning controls[2]

Town planning was first introduced in the Housing and Town Planning etc Act 1909. This was strengthened in the Town and Country Planning Acts 1932 and 1943. However, the Town and Country Planning Act (TCPA) 1947 established the modern system of planning today. Current legislation is contained in the TCPA 1990 (as amended), the Planning and Compensation Act 1991, the Planning (Listed Buildings and Conservation Areas) Act 1990 and the Planning (Hazardous Substances) Act 1990.[3]

Agencies

- Local planning authorities (LPAs), including shire counties, metropolitan districts, shire districts and National Parks.

- The Planning Inspectorate Agency[4] was set up in 1992 and is in the process of being reviewed.[5] The Planning Inspectorate is an executive agency under the Department of the Environment, Transport and the Regions (DETR), which determines planning and enforcement appeals and the holding of inquiries into development plans. It also deals with planning-related casework, compulsory purchase orders, listed buildings and conservation areas and cases arising from environmental protection and water Acts. The Agency also manages the Lord Chancellor's panel of independent inspectors, which deals with trunk road and motorway cases.

Planning permission is required for individual developments and is granted by the LPA. It is based upon ideas of 'development'. The term 'development' is pivotal to the function of LPAs in controlling the development and use of

---

1   There are many detailed books on planning law, including Tromans, 1999; Greenwood, 1999; Telling and Duxbury, 1999; Weston, 1997; and Moore, 2000. For an interesting discussion of planning law and pollution control, see Purdue, 1999, pp 585–93.

2   French, 1999; Purdue, 1999, pp 585–94; Purdue, 1998, pp 837–48; Shelbourne, 1998, pp 1035–42.

3   Planning (Hazardous Substances) Regulations 1992 (SI 1992/596), as amended.

4   Shapley, 1999, pp 403–07.

5   See DETR press release 261, 21 March 2000.

land. It is defined in s 55(1) of the TCPA 1990 as 'the carrying out of building, engineering, mining or other operations in, on, over or under land, or the making of any material changes in the use of any building or other land'.

For the purposes of the TCPA 1990, 'building operations' includes demolition of buildings, rebuilding, structural alterations of or additions to buildings, and other operations normally undertaken by a person carrying on business as a builder.

The TCPA 1990 excludes the following from the definition of development, which therefore do not require planning permission: maintenance and improvement which affect the interior of a building and do not alter its external appearance; certain types of maintenance works undertaken by statutory authorities; uses within the boundary of a dwelling house for incidental purposes; and the use of land for agriculture or forestry.

The definition of 'development' includes certain specified exceptions concerning the division of a single dwelling house, waste disposal, fish farming and certain types of advertisements.[6]

The definition of 'development' and therefore the need for planning permission is refined in the Town and Country Planning (Use Classes) Order 1987[7] (see below, Appendix 1) and the Town and Country Planning (General Permitted Development) Order 1995[8] (see below, Appendix 2). These two Orders define in detail when planning permission is required for a change of use and for the physical development of land.

The LPA must have regard to the development plan and the determination should be made in accordance with the plan, unless other material considerations indicate otherwise.[9] The development plan sets out the planning policies of local authorities and forms the basis for decisions on planning applications. The plans can also be called in by the Secretary of State for the Environment, Transport and the Regions (SOSETR), who is a statutory consultee.[10] Development plans ensure that environmental protection is

---

6   Consent is required under the Town and Country Planning (Control of Advertisement) Regulations 1992, as amended; Town and Country Planning (Control of Advertisement) (Amendment) Regulations 1999. See Trimbos, 1999, pp 978–82.

7   Town and Country Planning (Use Classes) Order 1987 (SI 1987/764), as amended by SI 1995/297.

8   The Town and Country Planning (General Permitted Development) (Amendment) Order 1999 (SI 1999/1661) amends the 1995 Order in relation to permitted development rights for certain telecommunications developments, in relation particularly to masts. It also provides that SSSIs are to be treated in the same way as national parks, etc.

9   TCPA 1990, s 54A.

10   In *St Albans DC v Secretary of State for the Environment and Allied Breweries Ltd* (1993) JPEL 374, it was held that s 54A does set up a presumption in favour of the development plan but, for its rebuttal, it is sufficient that there are material considerations which indicate otherwise. See *Sainsbury (J) plc v Secretary of State for the Environment* (1993) JPEL 651, where an out of town supermarket was given planning permission even though it was not in accordance with the development plan.

considered at the level of policy making;[11] they set down the basic ground rules for development, but are increasingly being overtaken by central government circulars and policy guidance notes.

There are three types of plan:

(a) structure plans – these are a statement of general strategic policies, usually across a county, prepared by shire councils;

(b) local plans – these are more detailed and consist of written policies and specific land use allocations, prepared by district councils;

(c) unitary development plans, prepared by metropolitan districts. They are a hybrid of structure plans and local plans, containing the policy framework of the former and land use allocations of the latter.

The plans allocate land uses and can include environmental measures, for example, limiting traffic pollution by having a general commitment to developing green corridors, etc. Under the Planning and Compensation Act 1991, unless material considerations indicate otherwise, planning decisions should be made in accordance with the plans. The use of plans to ensure environmental protection has been given more prominence through recent legislation and guidance. The Planning and Compensation Act 1991 requires that development plans should include policies for the conservation of the natural beauty and amenity of the land and the improvement of the physical environment, whilst the Town and Land Planning (Development Plan) Regulations (SI 1999/3280) expressly require local authorities to take into account environmental considerations when preparing their development plans. Development plan and regional planning guidance (PPG 12) underlines the need for environmental concerns to be integrated into development plan preparation. The re-published PPG 12 on development plans promotes greater efficiency and effectiveness in the preparation of local and unitary development plans.[12]

The LPA also has to have regard to any other material considerations, for example, planning policy guidance notes, regional planning guidance notes and national and local policies.

---

11   Herbert, 1995, pp 121–29; Purdue, 1994, p 399; Wood, 1996, p 808.
12   See Nutley, 2000, pp 113–16.

Current planning policy guidance notes

PPG 1	General Policy and Principles
PPG 2	Greenbelts
PPG 3	Housing
PPG 4	Industrial and Commercial Development and Small Firms
PPG 5	Simplified Planning Zones
PPG 6	Town Centres and Retail Development
PPG 7	The Countryside: Environmental Quality and Economic and Social Development
PPG 8	Telecommunications
PPG 9	Nature conservation
PPG 10	Planning and Waste Management
PPG 11	Regional Planning
PPG 12	Development Plans
PPG 13	Transport
PPG 14	Development on Unstable Land
PPG 15	Planning and the Historic Environment
PPG 16	Archaeology and Planning
PPG 17	Sport and Recreation
PPG 18	Enforcing Planning Control
PPG 19	Outdoor Advertisement Control
PPG 20	Coastal Planning
PPG 21	Tourism
PPG 22	Renewable Energy
PPG 23	Planning and Pollution Control
PPG 24	Planning and Noise
PPG25	Development and Flood Risk

Regional policy notes are now more important, due to the setting up of the Regional Development Agencies.[13] The following points have to be taken into account when decisions on planning applications are made by the LPA:

- The LPA may have to consult statutory consultees, that is, the Environment Agency (EA) or English Nature if wildlife issues arise; for example, a survey may have to be undertaken for protected species such as bats.

- It may also have to take into account transport, number and size of buildings, its layout, design and its effect on neighbourhood.

- Permission can be granted with conditions – these are whatever the LPA thinks fit, but they have to be for a planning purpose, must fairly and reasonably relate to the development and must not be unreasonable.[14]

- May enter into a planning agreement for planning gain[15] under s 106 of the TCPA 1990 to carry out certain activities. The planning gain has to be capable of being a material consideration, and it must be necessary and relevant to the proposed development.[16]

- Planning permission can be granted unconditionally or refused.

- An applicant can appeal within six months if permission is refused, or if they object to a condition imposed.[17] If the LA does not make a decision within eight weeks, the applicant is entitled to appeal on the basis of a deemed refusal.

- The appeal is heard by a planning inspector, who may allow, dismiss or vary the decision. The appeal may be through a local inquiry, an oral hearing in front of the planning inspector or by written representations.

- The SOSETR can call in the application (s 77 of the TCPA 1990) where the issues are of more than local importance or where they conflict with national policy. This procedure is used very selectively. The guidelines published in *Planning Appeals, Call-In and Major Inquiries* (Cmd 43) include, *inter alia*, proposals for residential development of 150 or more houses, proposals for the development of green belts, and those which involve significant legal difficulties.

---

13 See DETR, *Guidance on Preparing Regional Sustainable Development Frameworks*, February 2000.

14 See *Newbury DC v SOSETR* [1981] AC 578.

15 Arnold, 1999, pp 869–77.

16 See Circulars 16/91, 11/97 on planning obligations. See, also, *Tesco Stores Ltd v Secretary of State for the Environment* [1995] 2 All ER 636, where the court stated that the test is: does the obligation give some connection with the development? The situations where planning gain is offered, and where it is required, should be distinguished.

17 *Newbury DC v Secretary of State* [1981] AC 578. It was held that a condition must be imposed for a planning purpose, must relate to the development and must not be manifestly unreasonable.

- A judicial review application may be brought against the LPA or the SOSETR if an applicant believes that the decision has been made unfairly. There is also recourse to the Local or Central Government Ombudsman in cases of maladministration.[18] Either party can use these forms of redress.[19]

Third party rights

Objections can be made to development plan proposals. The principal forum for making objections and representations is at a local public inquiry. Following an advertisement in the local press, members of the public and interested parties are notified of the timetable and venue. Representations and objections are made to the inspector, who takes these into account when preparing his recommendations. Regarding the examination in public for the approval of structure plans, interested parties may state their case, but may only appear to give evidence if invited to do so.

Concerning planning applications, these are held on a register which is open to public inspection. Applications which do not fit in with local policies and plans are advertised in the local press. Any objections or expressions of support are taken into account by the LPA in deciding whether to grant, refuse or attach conditions to any planning permissions. It is important to note that only the applicant can appeal against the refusal or attachment of conditions to a planning permission.

PLANNING INQUIRIES

A planning inquiry is a mechanism by which public views are heard and the Government is seen to be listening to those views. An inspector is appointed, who will hear evidence from supporters and objectors. Often, an inquiry leads only to a recommendation, which may or may not be accepted by the SOSETR.

Inquiries have very varied functions and aims – some may concern large projects which affect whole communities or large geographical areas; others may only affect one street, one housing estate, etc. The aim of inquiries is that the affected agency gets all the facts before making a properly informed decision. Traditionally, inquiries have been regarded as 'merely a stage in the process of arriving at an administrative decision' (*B Johnson & Co (Builders) Ltd v Minister of Health* [1947] 2 All ER 395, *per* Lord Greene). However, most decisions are now delegated to the inspector.

---

18   See above, Chapter 2.
19   See Scarse, 1999, pp 679–90.

The Franks Committee (Cmnd 2128)

The Franks Committee looked at inquiries. The Committee stressed the importance of ensuring openness, fairness and impartiality and emphasised the importance of the following matters to achieve the above aims:

- the individual should, in good time before the inquiry, be given full particulars of the case they have to meet;
- since the final decision will usually be made by a minister, it is not sufficient for the individual simply to be informed of a local authority's reasons and policies. Fair play requires that, whenever possible, some statement of the ministerial or department policy relevant to the particular case should also be made available to the inquiry;
- the inquiries should not be simply into objections to proposals. An objection cannot properly be considered or developed in isolation from the proposal or decision objected to. They should be conducted in accordance with published statutory codes of procedure, and the aim is that the inquiry should be simple and inexpensive, yet orderly.[20]

The Committee made the following points concerning inquiries:

- inquiries had a twofold purpose: to provide an opportunity for public participation in decision making; and to enable a minister to arrive at a better informed decision;
- the case against which objections are being raised at an inquiry should be clearly made out, and the objections themselves developed with sufficient detail in order to permit proper consideration.

As to the question of whether inquiries were administrative or judicial in nature, the Committee commented:

> Our general conclusion is that these procedures cannot be classified as purely administrative or purely judicial. They are not purely administrative because of the provision for a special procedure preliminary to the decision – a feature not to be found in the ordinary course of administration – and because this procedure, as we have shown, involves the testing of an issue, often partly in public. They are not, on the other hand, purely judicial, because the final decision cannot be reached by the application of rules and must allow the exercise of a wide discretion in the balancing of public and private interest. Neither view at its extreme is tenable, nor should either be emphasised at the expense of the other.[21]

The Committee recognised the need for some controls over ministers when considering inquiry inspectors' reports, without at the same time imposing

---

20 It should be noted that most of the evidence before the Franks Committee concerned the workings of inquiries dealing with land use.

21 Franks Committee (Cmnd 2128), para 272.

too much rigidity. It considered the position of inquiry inspectors and the arguments in favour of departmental inspectors as against independent ones. It recommended that inspectors be brought under the control of the Lord Chancellor's Department, thereby stressing their unquestioned independence and impartiality. It was nevertheless accepted that inspectors would have to be kept informed of central Government policy, where appropriate.

The principal findings and recommendations of the Franks Committee were:

- individuals should know, in good time before the inquiry, the case to be presented against them;
- the relevant lines of Government policy should be revealed at the inquiry;
- the inspector's report should be published confidentially, together with minister's decision;
- the decision letter should contain reasons for the decision;
- it should be possible to challenge the decision in the High Court on grounds of jurisdiction and procedure;
- inspectors should be under the control of the Lord Chancellor.

These recommendations were widely accepted, except that inspectors are not appointed by the Lord Chancellor. The Tribunals and Inquiries Act 1992 provides that the Lord Chancellor may make rules to regulate statutory inquiries, after consulting the Council of Tribunals. Certain codes are applied which are varied to suit particular inquiries.

Procedures

In many cases, the power to convene an inquiry is conferred by statute on the Secretary of State.[22] Following the Franks Report, inquiries are now bound by a statutory set of rules that set out their basic procedure. These are governed by s 78 of the TCPA 1990. There are two sets of rules:

(a) recovered cases – this is where the SOSETR makes a decision after the recommendation of the inspector;

(b) transferred cases – this is where the inspector makes the decision on behalf of the SOSETR.[23]

Under the old rules, once an appeal had been accepted by the SOSETR, the parties needed to take little formal action until 42 days before the opening of

---

22 Town and Country Planning (Inquiries Procedure) Rules 1992 (SI 1992/2038).

23 The Town and Country Planning (Determination of Appeals by Appointed Persons) (Prescribed Classes) Regulations 1999 (SI 1999/420) has extended the transferred cases procedure to a wider number of cases.

the inquiry, when the LPA's statement of case became due. Now, all the major stages in the appeal process take place from the relevant date, which is the date of the SOSETR's written notice to the applicant and the LPA that it intends to hold a public inquiry. This means that the period between the acceptance of the appeal and the inquiry itself can be used to greater advantage, and the new rules also provide for an early exchange of statements of case and the requirement of a pre-inquiry exchange of proofs of evidence and cross-examination.

The new rules have also made provisions for the early exchange of statements of case that set out the full particulars of the case at the inquiry. There is now a statutory requirement for pre-inquiry meetings, to ensure an orderly and efficient inquiry. In the case of a major inquiry, there is a special process which the SOSETR can follow if he feels that it is desirable, in that, under certain conditions, the inspector can proceed to make a decision without all of the evidence being available.

It is only the applicant who can appeal against a planning decision, but, once they have appealed, if a party has made representations within the time limits, they may have rights to be heard at an inquiry, but this may be at the discretion of the inspector.

Particular inquiries in relation to land use

There are many different areas of inquires:

- motorway development, for example, the Okehampton Bypass 1983;[24]
- airports, for example, the Roskill Inquiry 1967, Stanstead 1981–83;
- reservoirs;
- coalfields, for example, the Belvoir Inquiry 1979;
- nuclear, for example, Windscale, Thorpe 1977, Sellafield, Sizewell 1983–87.

These tend to be termed 'big' inquiries. Big inquiries:

- are controversial;
- are of national importance;
- have a high level of involvement of the sponsoring department;
- are technically complex;
- involve sensitive locations, both environmentally and politically;
- the proposal is regarded as the forerunner to further policy developments.

However, hundreds of smaller inquiries take place each year on smaller developments that have a large impact on peoples lives.

---

24   Brearley, 1999, pp 408–15.

Natural justice and fairness at inquiries[25]

The issue of representation arose in *Bushell v Secretary of State for the Environment* [1981] AC 75 regarding an inquiry into building an extension to the M40. The House of Lords emphasised that inquiries were to be regarded as quite different from courts of law – they were to be governed by a need to conduct themselves in such a way as to guarantee fairness to those who would be affected by any decision which followed from the proceedings.

How should a minster make up his mind as to what constitutes the public interest? In *B Johnson & Co (Builders) Ltd v Minister of Health* [1947] All ER 395, Lord Greene had indicated that the minster was entitled to be informed in a number of ways, but was also entitled to have his own policy and views as to what constituted the public interest. In *Franklin v Minister of Town and Country Planning* [1948] AC 47, it was held that it was inevitable that the minister would incline towards his own scheme. In *Save Britain's Heritage v Number 1 Poultry Limited* [1991] WLR 153, the minister's reasons were criticised as lacking clarity and precision, but it was held that reasons were to be read together with the inspector's report, which had been incorporated.

ENFORCEMENT

The types of enforcement that an LPA can take are:
- Planning contravention notices – these require information about the operations being carried out on the land; failure to provide information will result in a fine.
- Breach of condition notices – if there is any breach of the conditions, the notice will require compliance, including timescales after which it will become an offence.
- Enforcement notices – these state the breach of planning control and the steps needed to remedy the situation.
- Stop notices – these can be used to stop activity at any time if an LPA feels that there is a serious breach of planning control.
- Injunctions – these can restrain any actual or threatened breach under the Planning and Compensation Act 1991.

---

25 See the Tribunals and Inquiries Act 1992, s 1(1). See, also, above, Chapter 2.

Listed buildings

Listed buildings[26] are of special architectural or historic interest. Most buildings built before 1840 are listed; after 1840, a selection is made; and buildings less than 30 years old are listed if they are of outstanding quality and are under threat. Listed building consent may be required even if planning permission is not. It is an offence to carry out works requiring consent without obtaining consent first; or to fail to comply with a condition in a consent. The local authority also has the power to serve a Listed Building Enforcement Notice.[27]

Conservation areas

These are areas designated by an LPA on the basis of the quality and interest of the areas, rather than individual buildings within them.[28] Conservation areas were created under the Civic Amenities Act 1967. They are of special architectural or historic interest, the character or appearance of which it is desirable to preserve or enhance. Trees are protected in conservation areas (unless they are small, dead or dangerous).[29] The local council must be notified before any work is carried out on trees in a conservation area. If demolition work is to be carried out in a Conservation Area, consent is needed. An LPA has to consider whether any planning proposal, whether within or just outside a conservation area, would affect the setting or would preserve or enhance the character or appearance of the area.

Ancient monuments and archaeological areas

Under the Ancient Monuments and Archaeological Areas Act 1979, it is an offence to carry out works to an ancient monument without prior consent of the SOSETR or to fail to comply with any conditions attached to the consent.

Building Regulations

Failure to comply with the Building Regulations is an offence.[30] The Building Regulations are made under the Building Act 1984, which empowers the

---

26 Planning (Listed Buildings and Conservation Areas) Act 1990 and PPG 15 Planning and the Historic Environment.
27 Ynors, 1999; Scrase, 2000, pp 235–45.
28 Planning (Listed Buildings and Conservation Areas) Act 1990 and Regulations 1990 (SI 1990/1519), as amended.
29 See below, Chapter 8.
30 See below, Chapter 7.

SOSETR to make regulations. Under s 1 of the Act, the SOSETR may make regulations: first, to secure the health, welfare and convenience of persons in or about buildings and of others who may be affected by buildings; secondly, to further the conservation of fuel and power; and, thirdly, to prevent waste, undue consumption, misuse or contamination of water. New Building Regulations were made in 1985, replacing the 1976 set.

Outline procedures for environmental impact assessment (EIA) – developments[31]

The Town and Country Planning etc Regulations 1999 and EC Directive 85/337/EC on the assessment of the effects of certain public and private projects on the environment lay down the requirements for EIA.[32] Planning permission cannot be granted unless EIA has been carried out and taken into account, where required.

Schedule 1 to the Regulations lists those types of project for which an EIA is always required.[33] These are larger projects that include:

- crude oil refineries;
- thermal or nuclear power stations;
- radioactive waste storage facilities;
- integrated chemical installations;
- trading ports;
- waste disposal installations for the incineration or chemical treatment of special waste.[34]

Schedule 2 contains a list of projects that will require EIA if they will have a significant effect on the environment due to their size, location or nature; these are determined on a case by case basis by the LPA or the developer. They include:

- agriculture – poultry or pig rearing and salmon farming, etc;
- extractive industries – peat minerals, coal, natural gas, etc;
- the energy industry – power stations, etc;
- processing metals – ship yards, iron works and car plants;

---

31   See Jones *et al*, 1998; Alder, 1993, pp 203–20; Boch, 1997, pp 119–38; Carnworth, 1991, pp 57–67.

32   Town and Country Planning (Assessment of Environmental Effects) Regulations 1999 (SI 1999/293). Directive 97/11/EC amends 85/337/EEC and was implemented in March 1999.

33   These are required under EC Directive 85/337. See Directive 97/11/EC, amending 85/337/EEC.

34   For a full list, see Sched 11 to the Regulations (SI 1999/293).

- the chemical industry;
- the food industry;
- textile, leather, wood and paper industries;
- the rubber industry;
- infrastructure projects – industrial estate development, roads, harbours, dams, tramways, yacht marinas and motorway service areas;
- other projects, including holiday villages, hotel complexes, knacker's yards, waste water treatment plants, sites for depositing sludge, and installations for the disposal of controlled waste or water from mines and quarries which are not in Sched 1.

A developer can apply to the LPA as to whether, in its opinion, an EIA is needed.[35] The LPA has to respond within three weeks from date of receipt. If it is required and the developer disagrees, the developer can appeal to the SOSETR, who will try to issue a direction within three weeks; there is no appeal against the SOSETR's decision.

Procedure in outline

The developer should carry out a detailed survey of the site and project and design out any adverse environmental impacts. The developer must submit an Environmental Statement (ES) to the 'competent authority' – this will be the LPA if planning permission is also required; in other cases, it will be the public body with the responsibility for that particular area, for example, the Forestry Commission. It should record the developer's assessment of the project's likely effects on the environment and how those effects will be mitigated.

The statement should identify the potential environmental effects and the steps which it is envisaged will avoid, reduce or remedy the effects. The ES has to contain certain information, including:

- a description of the proposed development, site design and scale;
- the data needed to evaluate the environmental effects, both direct and indirect;
- a description of the measures proposed to mitigate significant adverse effects;
- a summary written in non-technical language.

The competent body then consults with others (for instance, English Nature) on the content of the ES and any other groups with specialist knowledge.

---

35 See *R v Rochdale Metropolitan BC ex p Tew* [1999] ELB (July) 12 in relation to the EIA and outline applications.

Members of the public can also comment on the Statement. The proposal must be publicly advertised and details given about where copies of the ES can be obtained or consulted. A minimum period, usually of 21 days, is allowed, and any representations made must be taken into account in the determination of the proposal. The competent authority should be fully informed about the environmental implications of the new development and must take these into account when making the decision.

The competent body must prepare an EA of the proposal before deciding whether it may go ahead. This should take into account the views of the public and consultees. If the EIA states that the development will have an adverse effect, this does not automatically mean that the development will not go ahead; the authority also has to look at other relevant factors, such as economic, social, public health and safety issues. Suitable mitigation measures may be imposed.[36]

If a third party feels that the proposal should undergo an EIA, they may contact the relevant LPA to set out their views. The SOSETR can issue a direction at any time as to whether an EIA is needed for a particular project.

The Town and Country Planning (Environmental Impact Assessment) (England and Wales) Regulations 1999 (SI 1999/293) replaced the 1988 Regulations.[37] The new Regulations extended the range of projects that were subject to EIA and made some procedural changes, including the following:

- reg 10 allows developers to obtain a formal Scoping Opinion from the relevant LPA on what should be included in the ES;

- for all Sched 2 developments (including that which would otherwise benefit from permitted development rights), the LPA must adopt its own formal determination of whether or not an EIA is required (a Screening Opinion), before (reg 5) or after (reg 7) a planning application has been submitted, and place it on the Planning Register;

- Pt II, para 2 of Sched 4 now requires a developer to include in the ES an outline of the main alternatives considered and the reasons for the choice;

- under reg 21, when determining an EIA application, the LPA or Secretary of State must inform the public of the decision and the main reasons for it, and whether it was granted or refused. The 1988 Regulations and Circular 15/88 apply to applications made before 14 March 1999.

The adequacy of the EIA procedure was looked at in *R v Poole BC ex p BeeBee and Others* (1991) JPL 643. In this case, the borough council gave itself planning permission to construct houses on Canford Heath, which was a rare Bronze Age heathland and had rare newts, toads, the 'Dartford Warbler' and the

---

36 See the DETR website for more information: www.planning.detr.gov.uk/eia/ assess/doc/01.htm.
37 Circular 2/99 gives guidance on the new Regulations.

Dorset Blue butterfly amongst its wildlife. The court held that the LPA did not have to undertake an EIA, as it already had all the relevant information before it. This decision was later reversed by the then SOSETR, Michael Heseltine. Similarly, in *Twyford PC and Others v SOSETR* (1992) JEL, the court refused to intervene in the decision, although it had been made illegally, the road had already been delayed for long enough and the applicants had not suffered any harm. In *R v Swale BC ex p RSPB* [1991] 1 PLR 6, it was held that LPAs have a broad discretion to decide whether work needs an EIA and a court should only exceptionally interfere in that discretion.[38] An EIA will often be needed in relation to Sites of Special Scientific Interest (SSSIs), as well as 'sensitive areas', or at least be screened for the requirement If a development is within 2 km of an SSSI, the developer should consult with the LPA.[39]

PLANNING IN THE FUTURE

The Government has set out its initiative for modernising planning in the Consultation Paper, *Modernising Planning* (January 1998). The Paper states that the Government 'does not propose to alter the basic principles'. However, it will look at:

- the European context for planning;[40]

- making clearer statements of national policy for the small number of projects where decentralisation is not possible;[41]

- effective arrangements for regional planning;[42]

- a continuous search for local efficiency;

- a willingness to consider economic instruments and other modern planning policy tools.

---

38 See *R v North Yorkshire CC ex p Brown* [1999] 2 WLR 452, which concerned whether an EIA was needed when an old mining consent was renewed with new conditions placed upon it. It was held that the imposition of conditions amounted to development consent. *R v Durham CC and Sherburn Stone Company Ltd ex p Huddleston* (1999) unreported, 13 December (CA) gave direct effect to the EIA Directive in relation to a mining permission. See above, Chapter 2, for a discussion of direct effect.

39 See below, Chapter 8.

40 In particular in relation to the European Spatial Development Perspective, an inter-governmental initiative for a framework for land use planning decision. It is not binding but is there as a blueprint. There is also another EC Spatial Planning Initiative.

41 This involves publishing more explicit national policy planning guidance, improving the public inquiry procedures and making more use of the parliamentary process to approve the broad principles and leave the detailed issues to be decided at a relatively short public inquiry.

42 This related to the changed regional policy guidance and the new regional development agencies. The paper also looked at the development plan process in relation to a draft PPG 12.

The Consultation Paper has already been implemented in a number of areas. These were outlined in *Modernising Planning: A Progress Report* (April 1999) and many of the changes have already taken place and have been included in the text above.[43]

The Government has published consultation papers on: development plan preparation;[44] regional planning guidance; planning appeal procedures; and development plans.[45] It has produced reviews of compulsory purchase procedure and new guidance on one-stop shops for development consents and the processing of major developments through the planning process.[46]

However, one of the major problems in relation to planning is the rights of third parties, who cannot appeal against the grant of planning permission – they can only make representations before the permission is granted. This means that the provision of notice is extremely important, in order that local residents can hear about proposals in good time. The provision of notice at present is inadequate and the planning system is heavily swayed towards the developers, rather than local communities. There has been an increase in judicial review of planning decisions. Some of the reasons for this are set out by Scrase;[47] these include the more liberal approach to *locus standi*.[48] However, there are problems in challenging decisions because of the lack of a statutory requirement to give reasons when refusing planning permission but not when giving it.[49] However, under the new EIA Directive, reasons have to be given, whether it is approved or refused.[50]

The Government has looked at the appeal process in *Modernising Planning: Consultation on Improving Enforcement Appeal Procedures* (December 1999). In this consultation document, the Government makes a number of proposals in relation to improving the enforcement appeal procedures. These are, in brief:

- to amend reg 3(a) of the Town and Country Planning (Enforcement Notices and Appeals) Regulations 1991 so as to require a list of all directly relevant development plan policies and the reasons why the LPA considers it expedient to issue the enforcement notice;

---

43 This includes measures to promote shorter, clearer plans and better targeted consultation for LPAs to announce timetables, and states that the plans should not be too complicated, that LPAs should make positive efforts to negotiate with objectors and that they must not make last minute changes to their plans.

44 PPG 12.

45 DETR, *Development Control and Development Plan Preparation: Local Authority Concerns and Current Government Action*, 17 June 1999.

46 Consultation Paper, *Modernising Planning: Streamlining the Processing of Major Projects through the Planning System*, May 1999.

47 Scrase, 1999, pp 679–90.

48 See above, Chapter 2.

49 See *R v West Dorset DC ex p Searle* (1999) JPL 331.

50 See, also, the Local Government Bill 2000.

- to amend reg 5 of the 1991 Regulations so as to state that appeals must be submitted to the SOSETR at the Planning Inspectorate and that a copy of the appeals document be sent to the LPA at the same time;
- to make changes to the deemed application;
- to amend reg 6 in relation to the questionnaire needed for an appeal;
- to amend reg 7 in relation to supporting evidence;
- to amend reg 8 in relation to third party representation.

There would also be changes made to the appeal process and the local inquiries procedure. These changes include, in brief, amending a number of regulations under the Town and Country Planning (Enforcement) (Inquiry Procedure) Rules 1992:

- amending reg 8 in relation to the timescale for submitting copies of statements;
- amending reg 14 in relation to proofs, summaries of evidence and statements on common ground;
- in relation to longer inquires (that is, those that last more than eight days), a pre-inquiry meeting should be held, unless this is considered unnecessary by the SOSETR, and a timetable for the inquiry should be established by the inspector at the pre-inquiry meeting;
- the discretion to allow cross-examination should remain unaltered;
- whether the main parties to an appeal are required to provide closing submissions in writing;
- the main parties to the appeal should state the number of witnesses and an estimate of the time needed to present their evidence, four weeks before the inquiry;
- interested persons who want to appear should normally inform the inquiry four weeks in advance;
- amend reg 14 in order to require proofs of evidence in advance for all grounds of appeal.

The Consultation Paper also looks at the suitability of the appeals procedure for the consideration of unilateral undertakings or agreements. However, the Paper does not consider whether third parties should be given the right of appeal to planning decisions.[51] The impact of planning permission can be enormous on a community or individual, whether in relation to the loss of green space or in relation to planning blight or the noise and pollution of a new road or airport.[52] It is important that the decisions are made in an accountable way:

51 Shepley, 1999, pp 2–6; Reid *et al*, 1998, pp 1028–34; Gillmore *et al*, 2000, pp 14–17.
52 Town and Country Planning (Blight Provisions) (England) Order 2000 (SI 2000/539), made under TCPA 1990, ss 149–71, in relation to people affected by planning and highway proposals to require the authority to acquire their interest in land.

In an increasingly articulate and informed society, decisions on projects having major environmental implications will not be left simply to ministers, civil servants and public authorities. Many people want to participate in decisions that will shape their lives, and are no longer prepared to leave matters to their parliamentary representatives. Will people remain governable if they are confronted by decisions to which they strongly and bitterly object, taken by procedures which seem to give them no effective means of debating the issues or influencing the final outcome?[53]

It seems clear that the planning system, if it is to be truly modernised, needs to take these issues into account, not just in theory, but also in practice.

Sustainable decision making

Planning is not just about the land use system – there is also the issue of policy planning. This is being driven at present by the idea of sustainability, which grew out of the 'no growth' debate. The prevailing assumption historically was that there were no limits to growth. This growth would lead to scarcity, pollution and famine on a catastrophic scale in the next 100 years unless something is done about it.

Criticism of the concept included the issue of how growth was measured. Economics is based around gross national product (GNP), while environmentalists tend to talk about growth in terms of the increasing consumption of natural resources. However, GNP does not distinguish between different types of economic activity; it records the overall total. At the moment, current patterns of economic growth cause major ecological problems, but this could change with the use of new technology, which could stimulate growth. The second form of growth is in relation to physical resource consumption, but, even for this definition, zero growth is not required; this is because, here, it is not the just growth which is the problem, but the rate of growth. The problem is not that production is worse this year than last year, because last year's was also too much.[54]

There is no generally accepted definition of sustainable development.[55] However, the most commonly used definition is that of the Brundtland Commission 1987:

[Sustainable development is] development that meets the needs of the present without compromising the ability of future generations to meet their own needs.

Sustainable development has three core beliefs:

---

53 Hughes, 1996, p 224.
54 See Jacobs, 1991.
55 Pearce, 1993.

(a) entrenchment of environmental considerations in economic policy making;

(b) commitment to equity, that is, fair distribution of resources, including intergenerational equity;

(c) a notion of economic welfare, that is, development (not growth) which acknowledges the non-financial components – health, education and the environment itself.

The issue of sustainability is being developed on an international,[56] European[57] and UK wide basis. The importance that the Government places on developing sustainable policies can be seen by the wide range of policy initiatives in this area and the range of organisations set up to look at the issues.

The Government has laid down four broad objectives for sustainable development:

> Social progress which recognises the needs of everyone; effective protection of the environment; prudent use of natural resources; maintenance of high and stable levels of economic growth and employment, so that everyone in Britain can share in high living standards and greater job opportunities.[58]

The UK Round Table on Sustainable Development was established in 1995. Its members are drawn from businesses, environmental organisations, local government and other sectors of the community. It aims to encourage discussion on major sustainable development issues. It provides an annual report and has published a number of reports on sustainable development. The Government Panel on Sustainable Development was established in 1994. The Convenor and members are appointed by the Prime Minister to provide independent advice to the Government on strategic issues arising from the sustainable development strategy. Its Fifth Report was published in February 1999. There is a proposal to merge the UK Round Table on Sustainable Development and the Government Panel into a Sustainable Development Commission.

Other Government initiatives include the 'Greening Government' initiative, which includes the identification of 'Green ministers', and the Parliamentary Environmental Audit Committee[59] has recently published a *Report on Greening Government*. The recommendations which have been

---

56 Boyle and Freestone,1999. See, eg, Sixth Session of the Commission on Sustainable Development (CSD-6), UN Headquarters, New York, 20 April–1 May 1998.

57 See above, Chapter 2.

58 The Government published its response to this consultation exercise in *A Better Quality of Life – A Strategy for Sustainable Development*, May 1999, Cmnd 4345.

59 House of Commons Select Committee on Environmental Audit, Eighth Report, *The Budget 1999 – Environmental Implications*, 27 July 1999, HC 326; Sixth Report, *The Greening Government Initiative*, 1 July 1999, HC 426; Fifth Report, *The Greening Government Initiative: First Annual Report from the Green Ministers Committee*, 28 March 2000, HC 341; Fourth Report, *The Pre-Budget Report 1999: Pesticide, Aggregates and the Climate Change Levy*, 29 Feb 2000, HC 76.

identified by the Government and on which action is promised include the following: the Cabinet Committee on the Environment's terms of reference have been amended so that its remit includes co-ordination of sustainable development issues; Green ministers will report regularly to the Committee (the first Annual Report was published in July 1999); the *Guide to Cabinet Committee Business* will be reissued, reminding Government departments that environmental costs and benefits of proposals should be included in papers for cabinet committees; and, where possible, departments will consult and make available their environmental appraisals. Whenever the Government creates a new body, the case for incorporating sustainable development into its remit will be considered and the Green ministers have been asked how far sustainable development can be incorporated into the remit of all existing departments and non-departmental government bodies.[60]

Other organisations include the Government's Sustainable Development Unit. Citizens' environmental initiatives to carry the message to individuals and communities include Agenda 21, the Sustainable Development Education Panel and the National Foresight Programme.

Sustainability is also being developed on a regional and local basis. Regional development agencies contribute to the achievement of sustainable development in the UK, where it is relevant in its area to do so.[61] Clause 2(1) of the Local Government Bill 2000 aims to promote and improve the economic, social and environmental well being of their areas and cl 2(3) states that a local authority must have regard to the effect which the proposed exercise of power would have on the achievement of sustainable development in the UK.

Sustainable development indicators

The European Environment Agency (EEA) has stated that it will publish regular indicator reports on the state of the European environment.[62] In the UK, the Royal Commission on Environmental Pollution's 21st Report, *Setting Environmental Standards* (Cmnd 4053/1997), was published in October 1998. The UK Round Table on Sustainable Development's *Report on Monitoring and Reporting on Sustainable Development* recommended that the features of reporting include the following: the fact that reporting should not be based upon one annual report but should include a number of reports; reports

---

60 DETR press release 966, 16 November 1998; Environmental Audit Committee Report, *Greening Government*, 2 July 1998, and Government's *Response*, December 1998.

61 DETR, *Guidance on Preparing Regional Sustainable Development Frameworks*, February 2000.

62 See DETR press release 514, 23 June 1998; EEA Report, *Europe's Environment: The Second Assessment*, 1998.

should be targeted at different audiences; a number of different formats should be used, including information technology; reporting should be open and transparent in order to create trust amongst the public; and reporting should be an interactive process, incorporating publication, feedback and re-examination, both of targets and of the reporting process.[63]

In *Quality of Life Counts,* the Government[64] published 15 headline indicators to give a broad overview of trends and 150 national indicators to look at specific issues and identify areas for action. In relation to the environment, the headline indicators include:

- climate change;
- air quality;
- road traffic;
- river water quality;
- wildlife;
- land use;
- waste – household;
- waste – other.

The future

The United Kingdom's Round Table has stated that:

> ... it is time to develop a new approach to planning, which would start from a process of rigorous consultation ... At regional and national levels, new ways of engaging the interest of the public will be needed. At a local government level, the planning process can use active community-led processes to identify the kind of community (and its physical manifestation) that people want to see evolve in the next 20 years. It would go on to guide and encourage communities and developers to work within the spirit of this plan, rather than seeking to drive ahead on their own lines against the spirit of sustainable development or the plan.[65]

The Report states that it would like to see tools developed to ensure that development addresses the social and environmental impacts and to ensure that development takes place on brownfield rather than greenfield sites; the development of more imaginative building regulations to provide sustainable buildings; PPGs need to be updated; vision and practice need to come together; decisions should be taken at the right level of competence; and there

---

63　See DETR press release 7, 2 November 1998.

64　See DETR, *Quality of Life Counts – Indicators for a Strategy for Sustainable Development for the UK – A Baseline Assessment,* 1999.

65　*Planning for Sustainable Development in the 21st century – A Contribution to a Study by the RCEP,* February 2000, p 3.

should be appropriate trade-offs between environmental assets and economic gains from development proposals. This is a particular problem in reaching decisions which result in the loss of habitats which, whilst those particular developments may be small scale, make a significant contribution to the overall habitat.

The lack of co-ordination between planning, the environment[66] and the aims of sustainability can be seen in a number of areas, but a few examples will be given in brief here.[67] It is projected that there will be 4.4 million more houses by the year 2016. The EA would like water resource issues to be considered during the planning process and the allocation of new housing. This should be the case in relation to the new EIA Directive and the inclusion of water resource projects into the area that will need an EIA, but it should be on issues that are considered in the planning process, through the development plan preparation process and in individual planning decisions.[68] Instead, planning and the environment are often only considered together on an *ad hoc* basis so as to comply with international or European considerations. For example, the Directive on Control of Major Accident Hazards now contains provisions for land use planning, which were implemented into the planning system in 1999.[69] There is also the issue of how well the planning system deals with environmental concerns in individual cases; this can be illustrated by *R v Exeter CC* [1991] QB 471, in which a housing development was given permission next to an animal waste processing plant, despite the owners arguing that it may be closed down in the future by the occupants exercising their rights in nuisance. The effect upon the environment is a material consideration but the final decision should balance all the factors in a case.

In general, there is a realisation that the concept of sustainability itself can mean all things to all people and that, at present, it is not sufficiently robust enough legally to lead to any real change. This will be the case in relation to the Local Government Bill 2000, and is also already clear in relation to the EA. Whilst the EA, for example, has to take into account sustainability, under s 4(1) of the Environment Act 1995:

> It shall be the principle aim of the agency (subject and in accordance with the provisions of this Act or any other enactment and taking into account any likely costs) in discharging its functions so as to protect or enhance the environment, taken as a whole, as to make the contribution towards attaining the objective of achieving sustainable development.

---

66 McAuslan, 1975.

67 For an interesting discussion of planning law and pollution control, see Purdue, 1999, pp 585–93.

68 See EA press release November 1998; EA, *The State of the Environment in England and Wales: Fresh Waters,* May 1998, para 3.2.

69 See Planning (Control of Major Accident Hazards) Regulations 1999 (SI 1999/981).

It is a vague power, with little real statutory force.

There needs to be an integration of sustainability into all levels of policy making[70] and a recognition that planning is not just about controlling development; it has a positive part to play in protecting the environment and building communities for the future, through inclusive and open decision making.

EIA: THE TECHNICAL PROCESS

There is a drive for mankind to develop. We talk of developed, developing and underdeveloped countries and continents. Indeed, even in those countries we regard as developed, there is a drive to develop further, and in underdeveloped countries there is a need to provide even basic necessities of life by development.

In the past, such 'progress' has almost always been at the expense of the deterioration, or even destruction, of the natural environment.

Within limits, the natural environment can always recover from such degredation. Recently, however, as mankind and his effect on the environment have grown, it has been realised that the scale of anthropomorphic changes is becoming such that some irreversible changes in the natural environment are in danger of occurring. Mankind has acquired the capacity to degrade the environment on an industrial scale. Such degradation, if allowed to continue and grow, will have very serious consequences for the future of the environment upon which man, in his place, depends.

Over the very recent past, a movement has grown which advances the regard for preservation of the environment even while we continue to develop. We now realise that any development must be sustainable (defined in the Bruntland Report for the UN in 1987) or we will be in danger of causing irreversible damage to the systems which are necessary to sustain life. Accepting the fact that all development should be sustainable, there is, then, an identified need to manage development into the existing environment without degrading it. Such development should be based on a balanced strategy that will combine the need to protect the existing environment with the benefits of economic growth accruing from that development.

EIA is an important technique, or process, for ensuring that the likely environmental effects of new development are fully understood and taken into account before the development is allowed to happen. It is, therefore, an environmental management tool, which, if carried out properly, should become a key element in an environmental management programme. It is not

---

70   See DETR press release 898; MAFF press release 449/98.

a procedure intended to stop development; rather, it is aimed at ensuring that they are authorised and executed in the full knowledge of the environmental consequences. Properly used EIA should enable mankind to make better informal decisions about development. It should lead to the abandonment of environmentally unacceptable developments and enable us to alter or mitigate other proposals to the point that they are environmentally positive, or at least neutral.

The following discussion aims to explain the process of EIA in the framework of the UK legislation. It will consider the steps in the process, the participants in the process and some of the science involved. Any environmental system will have many aspects and, within each of those aspects, there are whole areas of science, law, expertise and experience. It is not within the scope of a simple discourse to explain all of these but the following discussion will endeavour to give an idea of the complications that EIA might have to deal with in certain circumstances.

As one final word of introduction, a caveat: EIA takes place within a real world context. There is the environment to take account of but there are also politics, economics and social/societal factors which the decision makers have to consider as well. EIA is an aid to making the correct decision in terms of the environment, but sometimes the decision makers will let the other factors override the environmental factors. We often see that in practice where, for example, the availability of new jobs can sway the decision to allow a development that might not be allowed on environmental grounds. The EIA process, then, is not a waste of time because it can still be used to ensure the best possible mitigation measures and the best practicable environmental option to be achieved. This should ensure that damage to the environment is at least minimised. After all, the definition of 'practicable' is left to the courts and the decision makers.

Definition

At its simplest, EIA is a systematic procedure for considering the possible effects of any proposed development on the environment before a decision is made about whether the project should be given approval to proceed.

More fully, EIA refers to the entire process and all the techniques by which the impact of a proposed development on the environment can be assessed. Information about environmental effects is collected by the developer and from other available sources. This information is taken into account by the LPA when it is deciding whether or not to allow the proposal to proceed. EIA is a systematic and comprehensive assessment of significant impacts. It involves the participation of the developer, the LPA, relevant information sources and the public. Any information gained from the assessment is passed to the LPA in the ES and presented to the public in a non-technical summary. This statement allows the importance of the significant effects and the scope for modifying or mitigating them to be evaluated by the LPA in the environmental appraisal, before a decision is made.

The environment concerned is both the natural and social environment and includes all aspects of the surroundings of humanity, individually and in social grouping.

The environment can perhaps best be defined as:

- human beings;
- flora;
- fauna;
- soil;
- water;
- air;
- climate;
- the landscape (the interaction between any of the above);
- material assets;
- the cultural heritage.

History

The history of EIA begins in the US. The first piece of legislation in this area was the National Environmental Policy Act 1969. The next development was the United Nations Conference on the Environment 1972 in Stockholm. This conference really started the ball rolling around the world, with increasing environmental awareness being promulgated among the populations and among governments.

The problem is a whole world problem, and eventually it must have a whole world solution. Organisations such as the UN, World Health Organisation (WHO), World Wildlife Fund (WWF), the World Bank, etc, are all involved and there have been conferences and world level meetings about the environment; EIA is universally accepted as desirable, if not mandatory, in most countries in the world.

In Europe, the EC has developed its environmental policy as the EC has developed itself, beginning with the Paris Declaration of 1972. In 1973, the EC started its series of Action Programmes on the environment (we are now in the fifth Action Programme). In 1975, the EC initiated research on EIA. Realising from this research the role of EIA in the 'level playing field' scenario, the EC published a draft Directive in 1980 and followed this up in 1985 with the actual Directive (85/337/EEC). As with all directives, Member countries are treaty bound to transmute them into local law. It is worth noting that, at this stage, in 1985, there was no basis in European law for environmental measures and the Directive was issued under Art 100 (now Art 94) of the EC Treaty , which basically deals with harmonisation measures.

The EC, however, passed the Single European Act in 1987 and introduced a new environmental basis for legislation. This was reinforced in the Treaty on European Union 1992 (Maastricht Treaty) under Art 2. The EC continues to legislate on environmental matters, and in EIA the most recent piece of EC legislation was the update of the 1985 Directive (97/11/EEC).

In the UK, we have had a land use planning system in place since 1947. As an integral part of that process, there has always been a requirement to take environmental factors into account in the planning process. In some ways, the UK led Europe on environmental matters, having its own legislation in place, for example, the Control of Pollution Act 1974, and having a department dedicated to the environment – the Department of the Environment, established in 1970.

After some resistance to the Directive, however, because it was felt to be unnecessary, the British Government passed the 1998 Regulations requiring EIA as part of the planning process.

EIA is now almost universally seen as a good environmental management tool and is a requirement in most developments throughout the world.

The EIA process

The EIA process in the UK consists of several stages where the developer considers the potential effects of his proposal and submits an ES, containing details of the significant effects, to the planning authority, with his application for approval. This is the simplest explanation and the full process is as detailed below. The process is a series of iterative steps and each stage can feed back into any previous stage or stages.

Alternatives

In EIA, alternatives, location, process, configuration, etc, including the no action alternative of not proceeding, need to be considered. Under the new Regulations, this consideration also has to be documented

Designing the selected alternative

The best practice in EIA is where it is done in parallel with the design process. The EIA can always indicate ways in which the design can be modified or even changed completely to give 'the best practicable environmental option'. For instance, consultation, mitigation measures or some particular impact might sometimes, in iteration, cause design changes. If the EIA moves with the design as intended, this can provide efficiencies for the developer, avoiding costly changes to a rigid design or lengthy delays in the planning process.

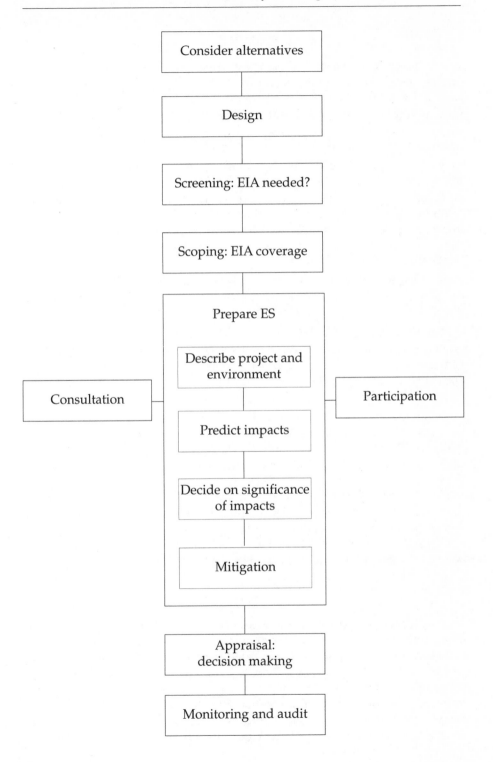

Screening

This is basically the process of deciding whether an EIA is necessary for the project concerned. This screening narrows EIA to those projects likely to have significant environmental impacts. Screening is largely determined by the laws governing EIA in the country involved. Whether or not a particular project requires EIA is subject to screening criteria and thresholds. It is worth mentioning that it also depends on whether LPAs apply the criteria.

The significance of effects is likely to hinge on the nature, size and location of the project. 'Nature' means projects that are likely to give rise to complex or particularly adverse impacts, for example, in terms of polluting discharges. In terms of size, this depends on whether the project is of more than local importance. Any projects intended for sensitive locations will require EIA. Sensitive locations would include SSSIs, Areas of Outstanding Natural Beauty, local nature reserves and National Parks.

The screening process is now formalised under the new Regulations. The developer can obtain a screening opinion from the LPA or a screening directive from the Secretary of State.

Nearly all types of public and private projects are subject to EIA. The original regulations excluded some projects, such as private motorways, wind generators, coastal protection, etc. These gained coverage under the Planning and Compensation Act 1991, whereby the Secretary of State is allowed to require EIA for them.

Some major civil engineering schemes seek permission for development by means of a private Bill in Parliament. Thus, they fall outside the terms of the Directive. The House of Commons, on 20 May 1991, approved Standing Order No 27, which requires private and hybrid Bill schemes involving development activity to conform to the EIA requirements of the Regulations. Schemes that come under this provision include the Jubilee Line Extension to the London Underground and the Channel Tunnel Rail Link. As well as this, there is nothing to stop a developer doing an EIA voluntarily, even though it is not a legal requirement. Many developers these days believe that it is a beneficial business enhancer to be seen as 'green' in the eyes of the public.

Scoping

This is the process of deciding on the aspects to be considered in the EIA. This narrows the EIA to the likely most significant impacts and defines those areas of the environment to be studied. Each project and the environment into which it will be placed will be different. It is therefore a necessary antecedent to each EIA to decide what to cover in the exercise. This enables proper focus in the EIA. Scoping involves discussion with the environmental authorities, the public and other interested groups. This is part of the process of consultation within EIA and it can be used to help the developer formulating the EIA. Under the new Regulations, the LPA can be asked for a scoping opinion and the Secretary of State for a Direction.

Carrying out scoping in the early stages can help the developer and can focus the EIA so as to make it much more effective in the decision making process.

The ES

This is the statement of environmental information which the developer must submit with his planning application. It will be discussed below.

Appraisal and decision making

Based on the ES, opinions expressed on it by interested parties and, of course, on policies, the LPA will make a decision on whether or not to allow the project to proceed.

Monitoring and audit

If the development proceeds in order to ensure that the environmental impact is minimised, and to learn for future projects, it is essential that it is audited in operation and the mitigation measures are monitored to ensure they are effective. The overall EIA process can be audited to compare predicted and actual impacts. Since the process is relatively new, this is a very necessary part of the learning curve in environmental management. Being the final iteration, it should also feed into future EIAs.

The team

The developer is responsible for the execution of the EIA and the submission of the ES. The task, however, is so complex, requiring many different specialist skills and knowledge, and the timescale limited, that the actual assessment is usually done by a developer lead team. For a smaller EIA, most of the work would probably be done by one firm of consultants together with the appropriate specialists, as required by the nature of the project. For larger, higher profile projects, such as the Channel Tunnel, the Channel Tunnel Rail Link or, for example, a new airport development, a consortium of consultant firms might be required. Again, these would consult with the relevant specialist professions. An example of the scale of this consultation can be gauged from the fact that one of the consultants engaged for the Channel Tunnel EIA consulted 48 organisations.

Among the specialisms involved are town planners, civil engineers, architects, landscape architects, agricultural scientists, economists, geologists, hydrologists, archaeologists, sociologists, chemists, ecologists and meteorologists. The list of possible involvement is almost endless but it does illustrate the vast numbers of facets of the environment that might be involved in any EIA. It is the developer's responsibility to decide, within the confines of the law, what is required in his particular EIA and to build his team accordingly.

The ES

This is a document setting out the developer's own assessment of the project's likely significant environmental impacts and other relevant information, including mitigation measures. It is prepared by the developer, who is required by the Regulations to submit it with his application to the LPA for planning consent.

The ES can be thought of as the report of the EIA process. The aim of the report is to give interested parties an accessible document which details the assessment and gives due weight to the significant effects or impacts.

The public's interest in a proposed project is often expressed as fear of the unknown and how it will affect them. If the ES provides a full analysis, it informs the public and should allay their fears. A good ES should enable readers to understand the conclusions and to form their own judgment on the environmental issues.

The LPA may express opinions about the content of the ES and has the power to call for further information. Any disagreement is addressed through the planning appeals procedure.

The developer will usually engage consultants for the EIA, in whole or in part and for the preparation of sections of the ES. The preparation of the statement, if it is to be effective, should be a collaboration, involving the LPA, the statutory authority, other consultees and the developer. There is no prescribed form for the statement, except that it must satisfy the Regulations. The best form is probably a systematic and objective account of the significant environmental impacts which will result from the project. It is important that the statement gives sufficient detail to enable interested parties to confirm the conclusions. Note that EIA often includes very detailed scientific work, too exhaustive to be included wholesale in the statement, and, if summarised, it must be done in sufficient detail.

The ES must also contain a non-technical summary (NTS), which is intended to allow non-experts to understand the conclusions of the EIA.

This NTS highlights the findings in brief in non-technical language and it must be free standing. It should include a description of the project, a map or diagram showing the location, and a simple explanation of the significant impacts and proposed mitigations. The document should be widely available for the public and must explain how they can make their views known.

Schedule 4 to the Regulations sets out the information which should be included in the statement. The Regulations also indicate additional information which may be provided. There is a distinction between what is specified information, which must be included, and additional information, which may be included by way of explanation or amplification.

There is considerable guidance available on the writing of ESs. There are also several sources dealing with the analysis of statements that have been submitted and, of course, their effectiveness. For live projects, the ES, and especially the NTS, is widely available for study; for schemes that have proceeded, the ES is often kept in the local public library and is available to anyone wanting to study it. Some ESs are available for sale. For example, the ES for Manchester Airport's second runway is available for purchase and, as a state of the art EIA, is a very valuable resource for anyone studying EIA.

Impacts

These are basically adverse effects causing deterioration in or destruction of the existing environment.

Impacts can be direct, that is, primary, or indirect, that is, secondary. They can be short, medium or long term, and temporary or permanent. They can also be positive or negative, although, obviously, in the usual sense the main interest must be in negative effects. Impacts can also be cumulative in effect and this cumulation can be simply additive or it can be synergistic, where the result of combinations of, for example, pollutants causes multiplier effects. Sometimes, of course, the cumulative effects will be antagonistic where one pollutant affects another. This does need attention and assessment in order to ensure that the expected result is achieved.

Major projects can give rise to a wide range of impacts and, as environmental systems do not exist in isolation, it is essential that all impact possibilities are assessed.

For each effect, or likely impact, there are certain areas that need to be looked at in the context of the EIA. A checklist for each of the significant impacts is given below:

- Definitions and concepts

  For each impact, it is necessary to understand the basic science and technology of the problem. For instance, in the area of noise impacts, it is essential to know how noise is generated, how it is attenuated and the effects of noise on the environment.

- Legislative background

  All of the aspects of EIA have their own specialist areas of legislation. The field of environmental law is burgeoning all the time, especially with the interest of the EC and the UK's legislation in this area of law. An example would be the 'water quality field'. These are a multitude of statutory instruments and other standards governing water quality from both the fresh and waste water points of view. Obviously, in EIA, there would be a need to satisfy all of these requirements.

• Interest groups

For each of the aspects of the environment studied, there is likely to be a number of interest groups who will have a view on the impact of the development. These will vary from international groups, through national ones, down to very local groups.

They will also vary from general interest groups to special interest groups. Examples would include the WWF, the RSPB, local fishing clubs, Friends of the Earth and local residents' committees.

It is essential that the views of all these special interest groups are known and accounted for. The alternative is a real risk of disruption to the project's passage through the planning process.

• Baseline studies

Appraisal of each potential impact should begin with this. It is essential that the developer carries out an environmental audit or inventory – a complete description of the environment as it exists and into which the project will be placed.

To help him do this, there is an enormous amount of information about the environment in the UK and in Europe. It is in the possession of governmental and quasi-governmental organisations, the LPAs, the water companies, heritage organisations, interest organisations and local organisations.

In Europe, a useful source of information is *Europe's Environment* (the 'Dubris Assessment'). This is a comprehensive report, published in 1995 by the EEA, and is a useful source on the state of the environment and the stresses being placed on it in Europe.

Before it is possible to do anything else, it is essential that the existing environment is understood.

• Impact prediction

Once the existing environment is understood, and given the fact that the developer knows the likely effects of his project, the next step is to predict the likely impacts, both in a qualitative and quantitative sense. The developer must also then assess the significance of these impacts.

• Mitigation

Once the significant impacts are identified and quantified for each aspect of the environment, it is then necessary to consider the mitigation of the impacts.

- Monitoring

  In order to ensure that the mitigation measures and the management of the project into the environment has been successful, and in order to ensure the success of the idea of EIA, it is essential that monitoring is included.

  The process of EIA is a very new process and some of the theories and practices behind it are relatively innovative. If it is to be used well, and it is essential that it is, a commitment to monitoring by both developers and LPAs is fundamental.

Mitigation

This refers to measures which the developer proposes to take in order to prevent, avoid or ameliorate the actual or potential impacts of the project. The mitigation measures relate to the significant impacts detailed in the ES. They might include substitution of techniques, clearer methods, pollution control measures, compensations or attenuations.

Decisions on mitigation measures are an integral part of the design and planning of the project. This is an interactive process and, as the design develops and information becomes available, feedback loops will be needed to modify various facets of the design. Mitigation measures are classified as:

- avoidance;
- reduction;
- remedy.[71]

It must be borne in mind when deciding on mitigations that there are two principles central to EC policy on the environment:

(a) preventative action is better than remedial measures;

(b) where possible, environmental damage should be rectified at source.

On this basis, the best mitigation is modification to the project, rather than containment or repair. It must also be remembered that some mitigation measures are required by law for new plants, for example, flue gas desulphurisation systems for power plants.

The question for the developer is how far the mitigation measures should go. Should the mitigation be total, or complete, with no regard to cost? The alternative is to settle for what is reasonably practicable, although to some extent this has been overtaken by the best practicable environmental option (BPEO). For the developer, the ultimate aim must be to mitigate far enough to ensure success within the planning application. The overall objective of EIA is

71   DOE, 1994.

not to prevent schemes from going ahead, but to mitigate them in order to be environmentally acceptable. For the developer, however, the question of cost must be a big one; expensive mitigations might financially obviate the project. Some mitigations might require long term management to ensure effectiveness, and this must be ensured in the proposal.

Because the process of EIA and the science of mitigation is relatively new, it is also essential that the success of measures is monitored and audited. This should ensure feedback for practitioners and the build-up of a database for successful mitigation.

Consultation and participation

It is a statutory requirement that various bodies which have statutory responsibilities related to aspects of the environment and the general public must be consulted when EIA has to be undertaken. The statutory consultees are English Nature, the Countryside Commission, HM Inspectorate of Pollution and certain other bodies. The list of such other bodies will depend on the nature of the development and of the environment. On complex EIAs, the number of consultees is likely to be large. The legal requirement is for the LPA to consult the parties involved and each must be provided with a copy of the ES. It is better, however, if the consultees are involved as early as possible by the developer, after discussions on scoping with the LPA. This should make for a more efficient process and a more effective statement. The developer has to assess the environment involved and the consultees hold a list of the data about this environment. They are obliged to provide this information for the EIA. Note that they are only required to provide information already in their possession and not to undertake original research. The statutory consultees can make a charge for this information and they are not obliged to give an opinion on the development to the developer – they have an opportunity to do this at a later stage in the EIA. As well as the statutory consultees, the developer should consult the general public and local amenity groups during the preparation of the ES. This will give the developer an indication of what are likely to be key issues in the appraisal, especially if the application is likely to go to public inquiry.

There are many methods of consultation, some formal and some informal. They include:

- questionnaires and surveys;
- advertisements to the media;
- displays and developments;
- community outreach;
- workshops;
- public meetings.

All can be used to elicit response and might be useful at different times in the process.

Overall consultation, as well as being an obligation, can be a very useful source of information and, if used properly, can help the EIA.

Methods

EIA is not a single specific analytical method or technique; it is more of a combination of methods, techniques and sciences which are available for identifying, predicting and evaluating the environmental impacts imposed by a particular development.

As with the rest of the EIA process, the developer is responsible for the assessment methods used. There is nothing in the Regulations which specifies EIA methods or techniques to be used. The *Guide to Procedures* advocates a flexible approach designed for the individual set of circumstances:

> Assessment techniques used and degree of detail on which the subject is treated depends on the character of the proposal, the environment likely to be affected, and the information available.

> A careful study of the baseline conditions will be needed but original scientific research is not needed.

The trend is towards an increasing focus on indirect, cumulative and transboundary impacts (pollution from one country to another, for example acid rain from UK to Norway or from Czechoslovakia into the rivers of Germany).

There is considerable research into these topics, much larger databases being built, and geographical information (GI) system computer models are being developed.

Measurement of the existing environment and prediction of the impacts of specific processes on aspects of that environment are well established in their own particular scenario, with appropriate techniques and much expert opinion being available, for example, traffic surveys and computer models for impact prediction; noise surveys and the body of knowledge of noise sources and attenuation; a surveyor can value land or buildings; and a botanist can quantify the rarity of a plant species.

Many of the aspects and impacts also have accepted standards in existing legislation, for instance, statutory controls on noise, EC directive standards on waste water quality and discharges, WHO standards on drinking water quality, etc. There is a great deal of science involved in many of the aspects and impacts. Some, however, are not so objective and can involve opinion and public feeling.

This is certainly true of visual impacts, such as large road schemes through country areas. It is also true of some social impacts and in amenity perceptions. There are no generally accepted standards to apply to these impacts, so the developer must be prepared to explore them with appropriate consultees.

There are many good books on the subject of EIA methodologies and they deal with the science of EIA in breadth and depth. There are, however, techniques which are evolving for use in EIA in general.

One of the simplest is a checklist of impacts. These must, however, be detailed and no impact can be overlooked. Checklists can also lead to lack of careful thought, but they are very suitable for projects where there is a lot of experience available.

Matrices are another way of approaching assessment. Simple ones with project components along one axis and environmental aspects along the other can be useful. These are in the process of being developed. They can be time consuming to construct and can, if really effective, be too detailed, revealing some impacts which are not the responsibility of the developer. Matrices can also be used as a check on the assessment. The Leopold Matrix, one of the most sophisticated matrices, has 8,800 cells, 88 environmental parameters and 100 development characteristics. Obviously, this is complicated to use, although for most projects many of the cells will not be filled.

Network analysis can also be used. Environmental systems are complex and there are generally chains of effects leading to harmful impacts. Networks can be used to show this and may prove very useful. Flow diagrams can be used in a similar fashion. Maps can be used in EIA, and one of the most common uses is the sieve map. In this technique, a series of maps is prepared, each showing one aspect of the environment, for example, social areas, noise impacts, habitats, SSSIs, water features, etc. These are then overlaid manually or by using a computer and thus show areas susceptible to the impacts of development, and vice versa.

Much use of statistical data analysis is also used in EIA. This can be used for individual impacts or in assessing cumulative or interacting impacts.

Computer simulations based on aerial photographs or field data are often used. GI systems are being used to a greater extent as the systems build up. They are essentially computer based databases. They include maps, aerial photos, field data, etc – basically cartographical systems and a database management system. They can be used to show spatial relationships for different variables. Information can be stored, displayed, combined or analysed with relative ease on a machine and at considerable speed. With the advent of the internet, there is considerable scope for making these systems very powerful indeed.

The merits of available alternatives can be analysed using decision analysis or cost benefit analysis. One of the problems associated with these techniques is the subjective nature of some areas of EIA, for example, cost benefit analysis. Decision analysis can take account of subjectivity, and so it is possibly a more useful technique in EIA.

There is no limit to the techniques which can be used. Many are still under development and there is considerable research being carried out in relation to appropriate, cost and time efficient methods. It is certain that EIA is a complex phenomenon and this can lead to complex assessment. The methods for this are not yet agreed upon completely.

There is certainly work to be done on project interaction, transboundary effects and growth effects arising indirectly from projects.

CHAPTER 4

WATER POLLUTION[1]

HISTORY

The modern system of regulation[2] of the water cycle was implemented after the process of industrialisation had begun to put a strain on the river system, especially in the largest manufacturing areas. In 1847, Edwin Chadwick facilitated legislation[3] which allowed for municipalities to include standard waterwork clauses which would speed up the passage of private Bills; these included requirements to supply water constantly and at a reasonable pressure. The legislation also made it an offence to foul drinking water supplies.[4]

The early regulation of water was placed firmly in the hands of local government and their role was increased with the passing of the Public Health Act 1875 and the Rivers (Prevention of Pollution) Act 1876. The new legislation made the municipal councils the enforcement agencies for the new offence of discharging or dumping sewage, industrial or mining wastes into the rivers. However, the new legislation was largely ineffective, due to the defence of 'best practicable and available means' of rendering any waste harmless. This often led to inertia, as industries often argued that there were no means by which to clean up the pollution, and the municipalities had a problematic role, having the function both of promoting manufacturing industries in their regions and ensuring that the same industries were not polluting.[5]

Water resources during this time were not addressed but boards were created in the Thames and River Lee catchments and for land drainage and fisheries.[6] However, it was recognised by later governments that these areas needed to be integrated into a more specialised agency, but that such an agency would need to maintain its local character. Therefore, until the water industry was reorganised in 1973, water and sewage supply was essentially seen as part of municipal local government, as water could then be co-

---

1   For a general discussion of water law, see Howarth, 1998, and Garner, 1995.
2   For an interesting discussion of the law on water before this time, see Sharman, 1982, pp 222–45. For the common law controls and their adequacy, see Maclaren, 1983, p 155.
3   Waterworks Clauses Act 1847.
4   See Kinnersley, 1988, p 47.
5   *Ibid*, p 51.
6   *Ibid*, p 50.

ordinated with land use planning and the water industry could respond to public opinion through the local authorities' political mandate.[7]

Three Royal Commissions sat in the early part of the last century, reporting on sewage disposal, salmon fisheries, canals and waterways. They advocated that a central agency should be created for water conservancy. However, no action was taken until the Central Water Advisory Committee was set up in 1934.[8]

In 1945, the law was significantly changed by the Water Act 1945. This gave central government stronger powers over most water supply functions. This was followed in 1948 by the River Boards Act, which created 32 river boards in addition to the two boards already in existence. The large number of bodies involved in the water cycle made administration of the system complicated and it was felt necessary to rationalise the bodies into multi-functional agencies. This was achieved by the Water Act 1973, which created the 10 regional water authorities. The Water Act 1983 finally removed the local authority representation that had characterised the regulation of the water industry since the 19th century. The National Water Council (NWC) was abolished, removing the little national planning for water that there had been. Privatisation was first suggested to the Government in 1985. In February 1986, the DOE published a White Paper on privatising the water industry.[9]

The most recent Water Act was passed in July 1989. Since privatisation, additional changes have been made in environmental regulation by the Environmental Protection Act 1990, whilst the Director General of Water Services (DGWS) has additional statutory powers under the Competition and Utilities Service Act 1991[10] and the Competition Act 1998. The Water Act 1989 has since been consolidated into six Acts: the Water Industry Act (WIA) 1991; the Water Resources Act 1991; the Land Drainage Act 1991; the Statutory Water Companies Act 1991; the Water Consolidation (Consequential Provisions) Act 1991; and the WIA 1999 .

---

7   See Purdue, 1979, pp 122–24.

8   See Hall, 1989, pp 18–19.

9   *Privatisation of the Water Authorities in England and Wales*, London: HMSO 1986 Cmnd 9734.

10 The Competition and Utilities Service Act 1991 strengthened the powers of the various Directors General of the utilities to improve the standards of service provided, especially in relation to customer complaints, and gave them scope to enhance competition in the industries.

THE POLICY FRAMEWORK

Many of the institutional and substantive changes in the regulation of water have arisen due to pressure from the European Community (EC). Measures to combat water pollution were among the first to be taken by the EC, mainly because this problem seemed to be the most urgent at the time. More than 25 directives or decisions have been adopted since the mid 1970s, adding up to one of the more complete and comprehensive bodies of Community legislation and initiatives in relation to the environment.

The EC water directives tend to follow two basic models:[11]

(a) those which adopt emission standards, which are mainly used for reducing dangerous substances, that is, regulating quality of emission;

(b) those which impose quality objectives on waters, which are mainly set according to the use that is to be made of that water.

For the quality approach, there are a number of stages:

- water with particular uses must first be identified (this is usually left to the discretion of the Member States);

- the EC must establish a number of parameters – these are normally expressed either as imperative (I) values, which must be kept to, or guide (G) values, which Member States must try to achieve;

- environmental quality objectives must be set for the waters, having regard to the parameters;

- a competent national authority must be established for monitoring purposes and uniform sampling techniques are set by EC directives (for example, Directive 79/869 on Sampling Surface Water for Drinking).[12]

Procedures are established for updating I and G values in the light of new knowledge.

Several directives have been adopted which set objectives for various types of water. These include:

- Quality of Surface Water Intended for Abstraction – 75/440/EEC;
- Drinking Water – 98/83/EC;[13]
- Bathing Water – 76/160/EEC;[14]
- Water for Shellfish – 79/923/EEC;
- Detergents – 73/404/EEC;
- Nitrates – 91/676/EEC.

---

11   Somsen, 1990.
12   As amended by 90/2/EEC.
13   98/83/EC.
14   As amended by 91/692/EEC.

There are also a number of directives covering specific substances, such as the Dangerous Substances Directive (76/464 EEC).[15] This Directive has as its object the prevention or limitation of groups of substances, either directly or indirectly, into groundwaters,[16] for example, lead, cadmium and asbestos. For pesticides, the Directive additionally requires Member States to draw up programmes for the progressive reduction and eventual elimination of pollution caused by waste from existing establishments. Further substances were added to the list with Council Directives 88/347/EEC and 90/415/EEC. Other areas include Titanium Dioxide Wastes (78/176/EEC); 87/217/EEC Asbestos; and 83/513/EEC Cadmium. Directive 84/491/EEC lays down limit values and quality objectives in relation to discharges of hexachlorocyclohexane (HCH). Directive 82/176/EEC covers mercury; this lays down limit values for emissions of mercury discharged from industrial plants which produce chlorine by electrolysing alkali chlorides. It also sets quality objectives for mercury in the aquatic environment, reference methods for measurement and monitoring procedures. Council Directive 84/156/EEC governed emissions of mercury from industrial processes other than the chlor-alkali process.

The Commission is currently drawing up a Water Quality Framework Directive[17] that will provide the basis of all future Community water legislation. This Directive would contain both environmental quality standards and emission limit values from point sources. It will address both quality and quantity issues. The aim of the Directive will be to ensure the quality of EU waters (both surface and groundwater) by 2010; an Annex to the Directive will contain quality standards and limits for substances that must not be exceeded. It will also require that the price of water reflect its true cost by 2010, with no cross-subsidies between industry, agriculture and households. The Framework Directive would repeal a number of other directives by 2007.[18]

---

15 As amended by 90/415/EEC.

16 For the meaning of discharge in the Dangerous Substances Directive, see *Nederhoff and Zonen v Dijkgraaf en Hougheemraden van het Hoog-heem-raadscap Rijnland* (C 232/97) (2000) 2 ELM 2000 12, pp 50–51.

17 COM (97) 49, House of Lords Select Committee on the European Union, Eighth Report, *Community Water Policy*, 1 Dec 1997, HL 36.

18 See EC Water Policy (COM (96) 59 Final 21 February 1996. Proposal for a Council Directive for Community Action in the Field of Water Policy (COM 97) 49 Final 26 February 1997 OJ 1997 C184/20). The Framework Directive would repeal by 2007 Directives 75/440/EEC; 77/795/EEC; 78/659/EEC; 79/869/EEC; 79/923 and 80/68/EEC. The proposed directive COM (93) 0680 covers the ecological quality of water.

DIRECT ABSTRACTION

Water resources are increasingly becoming an issue both globally[19] and in the UK.[20] To abstract water, a licence is required from the Environment Agency (EA).[21] The EA is under a duty to conserve, redistribute or otherwise augment water resources and secure their proper use – subject to the qualification that it is not to be construed as relieving a water undertaker of the obligation to develop water resources for the purposes of performing a duty of the undertaker with respect to the water supply.[22] Minimal acceptable flows for inland waters may be set.

Water resources can be conserved through drought orders, which were previously provided for under the Drought Act 1976.[23] Now, the Secretary of State for the Environment, Transport and the Regions (SOSETR) can make whatever provisions are expedient with a view to meeting the deficiency under a drought order. The application is usually made by the EA/water undertakers, and these can be either general or, where the situation is more serious, they can issue emergency drought orders.[24]

The Government is concerned about over-abstraction on sites covered by the Habitats Directive (92/43/EEC) and the Birds Directive (79/409/EEC) and Sites of Special Scientific Interest (SSSIs). It would like improvement work to be undertaken on other rivers where low river flows are affecting the environmental amenity of the rivers.

The Government called a Water Summit on 19 May 1997 as part of its plans for a better water industry[25] and has announced as part of its review of the abstraction system that nearly all types of water abstraction and water transfer will be controlled.[26] It will also withdraw, in due course, requirements to provide adequate notice and compensation for the variation or revocation of licences that are causing environmental damage,[27] and plans to place a time limit of 15 years on new and existing licences, to secure the efficient use of

---

19 See Salman and Boisson de Chazournes, 1998.

20 See Legge, 2000.

21 DETR, *Trading in Water Abstraction Licences – A Consultation Paper*, 9 May 2000.

22 WRA 1963, as amended by WRA 91, s 16 and Environment Act 1995, s 6.

23 Legge and Jackson, 1998, pp 490–91.

24 See Environment Act 1995, Sched 22, p 139 amending the WRA and inserting a new s 79(a) to provide for drought permits.

25 DETR news release 180, 1997.

26 See DETR, *Taking Water Responsibly – Government Decisions following Consultation on Changes to Water Abstraction Licensing System in England and Wales*, 21 April 1999.

27 The Government is concerned about over-abstraction on sites covered by the Habitats Directive (92/43/EEC) and the Birds Directive (79/409/EEC). It would like improvement work to be undertaken on other rivers where low river flows are affecting the environmental amenity of the rivers. See DETR, *Raising The Quality – Guidance to the Director General of Water Services on the Environment and Quality Objectives to be Achieved by the Water Industry in England and Wales 2000–2005*, 1998.

abstracted water, remove abstractors' future protection from liability, where the abstractions are causing financial loss to others, and streamline the administration of abstraction authorities.[28] Ofwat wants to see more trade in abstraction licences by revocation and compensation and wishes to make revocation simpler. But Ofwat is concerned that the time limits on new and existing licences may make the future too uncertain for the water companies and that this may have an impact on consumers' bills.[29]

In *Taking Water Responsibly: Government Decisions Following Consultation on Changes to the Water Abstraction System in England and Wales*, April 1999, the Government set out its plans to establish abstraction amendment strategies, extend licensing to all forms of abstraction and reduce compensation for the removal of abstraction rights. It will also simplify procedures, particularly in relation to abstraction authorisation appeals. Voluntary action by abstractors who are damaging special areas of conservation, special protection areas or SSSIs will have their licences withdrawn if no agreement is reached.

Legislation will be enacted to undertake the following changes:

- alteration to the application and succession requirements so that the only requirement is the right of access to the point of abstraction;
- two new forms of abstraction licences will be created – permits and consents;
- removal of most of the authorisation exemptions – these are currently on the grounds of use;
- develop a register of exempt abstractions and abolish exempt area status, instead establishing volume exemption thresholds on a catchment basis;
- provide the power to revoke an authorisation after four years without beneficial use, with no compensation payable;
- removal of the defence against civil action in relation to future financial losses incurred as a result of continuing water abstraction;
- more enforcement power for the EA in relation to the breaching of conditions;
- removal from 1 July 2012 of the right to compensation if a licence without time limit is withdrawn on the direction of the SOSETR on the grounds that an abstraction is causing significant environmental damage;
- EA powers to require abstractors to enter into enforceable water management agreements and to recover the reasonable costs from the abstractors;

---

28 DETR Press Release 503/98; DETR, *Review of Water Abstraction Licensing System in England and Wales*, 19 June 1998; *op cit*, DETR, fn 26.

29 Ofwat press release 28/98.

- provision of EA powers to allow water companies to seek bulk supply from others and to transfer abstraction licences from one water company to another;

- powers to gather and provide information and to agree public drought plans;

- creation of enforceable duties on the water companies to conserve water in carrying out their functions and other abstractors to use water abstracted under authorisations in an efficient and effective manner.

There are a number of other measures being taken to improve the longer term planning for water resources.[30] There are also provisions in relation to the water companies to encourage customers to save water.[31] Under the legislation, the water companies have to supply water in an efficient and economic way. There has been a concern that water supplies are lost due to leakage. However, work has been undertaken in this area and leakage levels are improving. Leakage levels in England and Wales fell from 3,981 megalitres a day in 1997–98 to 3,537 megalitres a day in 1998–99 – a reduction of 11%.[32] This is due, in part, to mandatory leakage targets that have now been set. The DGWS has set new targets for 1999–2000.[33] The Government has reiterated its commitment to provide a sustainable water resource system.[34] It has also introduced a number of measures to improve the efficiency of water use. Metering and tariffs to reflect water use are an important mechanism, the Ofwat Report states, in relation to the sustainable and efficient use of water. However, it also states that other areas that need to be addressed are leakage and water efficiency. Regulatory action will be taken where companies fail to meet targets. Companies will also be expected to provide water saving devices, as well as water efficiency advice through water audits, efficient domestic appliances and advice on garden watering. All water companies agreed to changes in their licences suggested by the regulator, to ensure that customers would receive compensation if domestic supplies were interrupted during a drought.[35]

---

30 See the Water Conservation Research Database; DETR Consultation Paper, *Economic Instruments in Relation to Water Abstraction*, 25 May 2000. There are also proposed amendments to the Reservoirs Act 1975. Water Regulations Advisory Committee Guidance on Water Recycling Systems (Reclaimed Water Systems IGN/1) www.wras.co.uk.

31 See EA, *Managing Water Abstraction: Towards a Shared Strategy*, April 2000.

32 Ofwat press release 36/99.

33 See Ofwat press release 16/97; DETR press release 844, 14 October 1998, which states that water companies will be required to cut leakage by over 25% in the three years to the year 2000.

34 Sustainable development: Government Consultation Paper, *Opportunities for Change*, 4 February 1998, p 14.

35 See Ofwat *Annual Report* 1997; Annual Report of Ofwat National Customer Council (ONCC) and the 10 regional Ofwat Customer Service Committees (CSCs), *Representing Water Customers 1997–98*, 1998.

REGULATION

Flooding

Flood defence[36] is regulated under the Water Resources Act 1991.[37] The Environment Act 1995 contains powers for the creation of flood defence committees.

Groundwater (Directive 80/68)

This Directive complements Directive 76/464 by controlling the discharge of dangerous substances into underground water sources. It aims to prevent pollution by List I (black list) substances and reduce pollution by those in List II (grey list). To this end, direct discharges of List I and all discharges of List II substances are to be made subject to prior investigation and, where appropriate, consent. Sewerage and radioactive discharges are excluded from the ambit of the legislation.[38]

The Groundwater Regulations 1998 (SI 1998/ 2746)

The Groundwater Regulations[39] implement the Groundwater Directive (Protection of Ground Water Against Pollution as Used by Certain Dangerous Substances) (80/68/EEC). The Regulations cover the discharge or disposal of certain dangerous substances, where they are not already covered by existing legislation. An authorisation is needed for disposal onto or into land; this may be accepted with conditions or refused. The substances that fall into List 1 are the most toxic and include pesticides, solvents, sheep dips, hydrocarbons, mercury, cadmium and cyanide. List 2 substances are less harmful but, if disposed in large amounts, could be harmful to groundwater; they include some heavy metals, ammonia and phosphorous. Entry must be restricted for these substances, whereas List 1 substances must be prevented from entering groundwater. Groundwater is water that is contained in the ground, below the water table. The EA can stipulate areas of unsuitability, where there must be no entry of List 1 substances unless it is permanently unusable. Statutory

---

36 See, also, the Land Drainage Act 1991.
37 See the proposed new PPG 25 – development and flood risk: consultation draft, 15 April 2000, to replace the existing guidance contained in 30/92.
38 Commission Proposal Com ((1996) 315 final) Proposal for a European Council and Parliament decision on an action programme for integrated ground water protection and management.
39 Groundwater Regulations 1998 (SI 1998/2746): Draft Guidance November 1999.

Codes of Practice will be drawn up and, where there is a risk of groundwater pollution, notices can be served, prohibiting the activity or allowing it, subject to conditions. An authorisation is not required for certain circumstances, including: spreading onto land certain substances for nutrient benefit; if there is an IOC authorisation or waste management licence or a discharge consent; or if it is covered by the Radioactive Substances Act 1993. Authorisation will only be granted if adequate groundwater surveillance is carried out, and the cost is to be borne by the applicant. There is a right of appeal to the SOSETR within three months of the authorisation being issued and, if the allocation is refused, it will be an offence to dispose of listed substances onto land without an authorisation.

Water supply

The protection of drinking water is important not just for the protection of human health; it is also important in relation to the additional controls it places on water quality, which have an environmental impact. The main controls are set out in the EC Drinking Water Directive.

EEC Drinking Water Directive

This Directive (EEC Drinking Water Directive 98/83)[40] sets standards or parameters for drinking water quality.[41] It specifies the bacteriological, chemical and aesthetic requirements that all drinking water supplies should satisfy, and there are 62 different parameters. Compliance with these standards was required by 18 July 1985, unless derogations had been made or delays granted. These would only be allowed in certain circumstances, for example, in relation to situations arising from the nature and structure of the ground in the area in which the supply in question emanates; situations arising from exceptional meteorological conditions or following emergencies; or when a poor quality water supply, for which adequate treatment is not possible, must be used consistently.

The Directive makes it clear that these derogations do not apply to toxic or microbiological parameters, and that derogations must not constitute a public health hazard.[42]

---

40 Council Directive 98/83 on the Quality of Water Intended for Human Consumption replaces 80/778.

41 Legge and Jackson, 1998.

42 See Case C 337/89 *Commission v UK* [1992] ECR 6103, where the Commission brought an action against the UK due to high nitrate levels. The court held that, except within the derogations provided by the Directive, the UK could not rely on special circumstances to justify the failure to comply (the UK had tried to argue that its failure to comply was due to agricultural techniques). The Court stated that the UK could not say that it had taken all practicable steps to achieve the standards, as the standard had not been achieved.

There is an obligation on the water undertaker to supply domestic water.[43] The SOSETR designates a company as a water company under s 11 of the WIA 1991.[44] This lays down the duties of the water companies. If the company breaches these duties, then the DGWS can issue a s 20 enforcement order; however, this is unlikely to be used because it is a serious sanction. The water supplied must be wholesome, constant and sufficient.[45]

The standards have been laid down in the Water Supply (Water Quality) Regulations 2000. Wholesomeness was not officially defined until these Regulations were passed. The Regulations are monitored by the local authorities, which have a duty to keep themselves informed of the wholesomeness and sufficiency of supplies. They only have the power to monitor private supplies, as the water companies undertake[46] their own monitoring.[47] The Drinking Water Inspectorate (DWI),[48] part of the DETR,[49] was set up to ensure that there was a competent body to enforce EC directives.[50]

In *McColl v Strathclyde RC* (1984) JPL 351, the court held that the duty on local authorities was to provide wholesome water – this did not empower them to improve dental health by the addition of fluoride.[51] This led to the Water Fluoridation Act 1985, which does allow fluoride to be put into water. It is an offence to supply water unfit for human consumption (s 70 of the WIA 1991). Prosecutions can only be brought by the SOSETR/DPP. There is a defence that there were no reasonable grounds to believe the water would be used for human consumption and all reasonable steps were taken/all due diligence was exercised to ensure the above.

The Surface Water for Drinking Directive (75/440/EEC) has imposed significant controls on the quality of inland water. It ensures that water abstracted is fit for drinking.

---

43 Obligation to supply to non-domestic users – WIA 1991, s 55.

44 The SOSETR can issue directions to Water Undertakers – WIA 1991, s 208.

45 WIA 1991, Pt II, s 67.

46 The Drinking Water (Undertakings) (England and Wales) Regulations 2000 (SI 2000/1297) were made to comply with the ECJ's judgment in Case C 340/96 *Commission v UK*, in relation to water undertakers' undertakings.

47 Local Authority monitoring role – WIA 1991, ss 77–85.

48 Report by the Chief Inspector of the Drinking Water Inspectorate, *Drinking Water 1998*, July 1999.

49 Director General of Water Services: see WIA, s 1; Drinking Water Inspectorate: see WIA, s 86.

50 Council Directive 98/83/EC on the Quality of Water Intended for Human Consumption. See C 340/96 *Commission v UK* Case (1999) 22 April. It was held that the system of undertakings used by the UK from water companies was not enough to ensure compliance with the Directive. See W Law June 1999, vol 10, issue 3, pp 93–94.

51 *R v Northumbrian Water ex p Newcastle and North Tyneside HA* (1998) QBD, 15 December in W Law June 1999, vol 10, issue 3, pp 96–105.

Discharges into sewers

Before 1989, the water authorities carried out all the functions in relation to water and sewerage on an integrated basis. After the Water Act 1989 (as consolidated), there is now a split in functions: the private water and sewerage undertakers provide the public water supply and own and operate the sewerage network and the sewage works, as well as regulating any discharges to the sewers; whereas the EA regulates abstractions from and discharges to the natural environment and has responsibility for surface water pollution.

Trade effluent from trade premises is subject to a consent system.[52] It is a criminal offence to discharge any trade effluent from trade premises into sewers unless a trade effluent consent is obtained from the sewage undertakers – this is the only example of a private body exercising functions in relation to environmental protection. Trade effluent is effluent discharged from premises used for carrying out of trade or industry other than surface water and domestic sewage, including agriculture, fish farming and scientific research and development institutions.

In relation to the procedure, a Trade Effluent Notice is served on a sewerage undertaker; this must be done at least two months prior to the commencement of the discharge. The sewerage undertaker may grant or refuse consent, or attach conditions.[53] The conditions can include: the nature, temperature and composition of the discharge; the place of the discharge; the rate and timing of the discharge; and conditions on payments for effluent charges. The conditions do not specify specific treatment plant of the effluent standard that should be met – this is left to the individual dischargee. Appeal lies to the DGWS but not in relation to the charges.[54] Variation is possible after two years[55] and, exceptionally, variation is allowed within two years. There is a public register of consents only (s 196 of the WIA). There is no public right to information on any samples taken and there is no right to bring a private prosecution, unless the person is aggrieved or has the consent of the Attorney General.[56]

Drains and private sewers are built to comply with the Town and Country Planning Act 1990 and the Building Act 1984.[57] They need planning permission, as they are engineering operations,[58] whilst public sewers are built to comply with the WIA 1991.[59]

---

52 WIA 1991, s 141.
53 *Ibid*, s 121.
54 *Ibid*, s 124.
55 *Ibid*, s 119.
56 Offences and enforcements: see the Environment Act 1995, s 130(7).
57 Schedule 1, Pt H.
58 See PPG 23 – planning and pollution control, and Circular 3/99.
59 Sections 94, 98, 101A, 104, 112.

Pollution of inland waters

A person is guilty of an offence if they 'cause or knowingly permit any poisonous, noxious or polluting[60] matter or any solid waste matter to enter any controlled waters'.[61] Controlled water is defined in s 104 as:

(a) relevant territorial waters;

(b) coastal waters;

(c) inland waters;

(d) groundwaters.

Cause is seen as a strict liability offence because there is no need for knowledge.[62] Knowingly permitting is more limited because of the knowledge requirement. In *Empress Car Co (Abertillery) Ltd v National Rivers Authority* [1998] 1 All ER 481,[63] the court stated that the question to ask in relation to the strict liability offence of causing pollution was, 'Did the defendants cause the pollution?'. Lord Hoffman stated that, whilst forseeability was a requirement for the tort of negligence, it was not relevant to this offence. The court went on to state that, in relation to the act of a third party, if the defendants had created a situation where the polluting matter could escape and the necessary condition of the escape is the act of a third party or a natural event, the courts should look at whether that event is a normal facet of life or something extraordinary, such as a terrorist attack. Whether this is relevant to other offences of causing pollution is unclear.

There is also a specific offence of discharging trade or sewage effluent without a consent and a further offence of substantially aggravating pollution by impeding the proper flow of inland non-tidal waters.

The defences[64] include: a consent under the Water Resources Act 1991 (or Authorisation under the Environmental Protection Act 1990); deposit in accordance with a Waste Disposal Licence under Pt II of the Food Environmental Protection Act 1985, a local Act or statutory Order; water from abandoned mines can be prosecuted under s 58 or 69 of the Environment Act; if it is an emergency ('to avoid danger to life or health'); refuse from mines, if the EA grants permission for the deposit; trade or sewage effluent from a waterborne vessel; Crown property.

In relation to trade effluent and discharges to sewers, there is no right to bring a private prosecution unless the person is a person aggrieved or has the

---

60 See *R v Dovermoss Ltd* [1995] Env LR 258.

61 See WRA 1991, s 85.

62 See *Alphacell Ltd v Woodward* [1972] AC 824; *NRA v Yorkshire Water Services Ltd* [1995] 1 AC 444.

63 See Stanley, 1999; Parpworth, 1998, pp 752–61; Ryan, 1998, pp 347–62.

64 See WRA 1991, ss 87, 88, 89.

consent of the Attorney General.[65] Under s 87(2) of the Water Resources Act 1991, there is a defence that contravention of the discharge consent was due to an unconsented discharge made into the sewer which could not have been reasonably prevented.[66]

The EA has widely drafted powers to prevent pollution incidents and, where they occur, recover the costs of cleaning them up. It can also undertake remedial or restorative work.[67] The penalties are those for integrated pollution control, as is the provision of enforcement notices.[68]

The procedure[69]

Consents are granted under Sched 10 and the EA can attach 'such conditions as it may think fit' (para 2). The EA will set the consent by reference to a water quality objective (WQO). The Water Resources Act 1991 has altered the law so that conditions requiring a specified treatment plant or process are legal; before this, it was left to the individual owner's discretion. Conditions can also be staggered so that they become progressively stricter.[70]

Applications for discharge consents are made to the relevant authority and have to contain all the relevant information; these are then published in the *London Gazette* and in a local newspaper. A copy is also sent to the water undertakers and local authorities. The authority then considers any written representations made within six weeks.[71]

Consent is deemed to have been refused if consent is not given within four months or any longer time agreed between the authority and the applicant. Publicity and notification requirements can be withdrawn if it would prejudice, to an unreasonable degree, a trade secret or would harm the public interest. The existence of a certificate must appear on the register. The publicity requirements can be waived if the discharge has 'no appreciable

---

65 See the Environment Act 1995, s 130(7).

66 See WRA 1991, ss 92, 161.

67 Anti-Pollution Works Regulations 1999 (SI 1999/1006). See, also, below, Chapter 5.

68 Environmental Protection Act 1990, s 145; WRA 1991, s 90B. See *EA v Shell (UK)* [1990] W Law 40; *Wychevan DC v NRA* [1993] 2 All ER 440.

69 Control of Pollution (Application, Appeals and Registers) Regulations 1996 (SI 1996/2971).

70 Effluent charges: WRA 1991, s 131; Environment Act 1995, ss 41, 42.

71 WRA 1991, Sched 10.

effect' on controlled water.[72] Variation and revocation of consents may take place after two years, or, exceptionally, within that period. The SOSETR can call in applications and acts as an appeal body, the authority has to abide by the SOSETR's decision. Local inquiries can be held, and this power can be exercised by the SOSETR where a request is made by the authority or the applicant. An opportunity to be heard is given to anyone who has made representations or objections to the SOSETR in relation to the application.

The classification of water

WQOs are an important innovation, brought about by the Water Act 1989, as consolidated (see the Water Resources Act 1991).[73] Previously, water quality objectives were set by administrative practice; this meant that water was often classified as 'to use'. This has now been put on a statutory footing, in order, ostensibly, to comply with various EC directives and also in response to a House of Commons Environment Committee Report published in May 1987. This made the case for water authorities needing clearer water quality objectives related to timetables for achieving them and stated that improved sewage works performance should be achieved. Also, it stated that pollution control and a more active prosecution policy should be pursued in the hands of an independent body not involved with sewage works operations and more prosecution of water authorities which caused pollution.

The general effect of the new provisions under the Act are that the obligations to implement Community directives on water quality, such as directives relating to dangerous substances, bathing waters and the quality of fresh water to support fish life, can be realised by legal means, rather than as a matter for administrative discretion, as was the case previously. The Water Resources Act 1991 allows the SOSETR to set up a classification scheme for controlled waters and to set WQOs. The system of classification has to be prescribed by regulation, but the classifications themselves have no legal effect

---

72 This was defined in an Annex to Circular 17/84. This laid out three criteria when the pollution would have no appreciable effect on the environment: the discharge should not effect an area of amenity or environmental significance, ie, beaches, SSSIs, marine nature reserves; the discharge should not result in a major change of flow to the receiving waters; and, taken together with previously consented discharges, the discharge should not lead to a change in water quality so as to damage existing/future uses of the water, or alter by more than 10% the concentration of a substance which is important for the quality of the water and the well being of its flora and fauna, eg, nitrates, phosphates and dissolved metals.

73 Classification of quality of waters – WRA 1991, s 81; Surface Water (Classification) Regulations 1989 (SI 1989/1148); Surface Waters (Dangerous Substances) (Classification) Regulations 1992 (SI 1992/337); Bathing Water (Classification) Regulations 1991 (SI 1991/1597); Surface Waters (River Ecosystem) Classification Regulations 1994 (SI 1994/1057).

until incorporated into WQOs.[74] This is important, as it is the duty of the SOSETR and the EA to exercise their water pollution powers so that, 'as far as practicable', the WQOs are achieved at all times.

The Bathing Water Directive (76/160) and the Urban Waste Water Directive (91/271)[75]

These are important directives in relation to coastal discharges. The Urban Waste Water Directive lays down minimum standards for waste water treatment at sewerage treatment works.[76] The Bathing Water Directive was adopted in 1976.[77] A new Bathing Water Directive is in the process of being agreed.[78] The two objectives of the Directive are to improve or maintain the quality of bathing waters and to protect health.[79]

Under the Water Act 1989, the EA is the 'competent authority to implement the EC Bathing Water Directive in England and Wales'. The EA wishes to improve the level of compliance with the Directive by ensuring that discharges near bathing water comply with the relevant water quality criteria, and this will be an integral part of the statutory WQOs. The quality of sea water has been raised by the ban on dumping sewerage sludge which will help to lead to the development of secondary and primary treatment at STWs, rather than relying on the methods of diffusion and dispersion.

There are a number of controversial issues in relation to bathing water.[80] These include the fact that the Government had failed to designate beaches. The UK was taken to the ECJ, as Britain defined its bathing beaches so narrowly that it did not even include Blackpool, which North West Water had

---

74 Between 1990 and 1998, the following improvements took place in water quality: 25% in rivers and canals and the length of good quality rivers rose from 44% to 55%. In 1997, 82% of rivers complied with their river quality objectives. See DETR, *Water Quality – A Guide to Water Protection in England and Wales*, 24 March 2000.

75 OJL 135 30.5.91, as amended by Directive 98/15/EC.

76 EA press release 30/7/98: Agency announces higher level of sewage treatment for coastal discharges under the Urban Waste Water Directive (91/271).

77 See Bathing Water (Classification) Regulations 1991 (SI 1991/1597).

78 The new Bathing Water Directive is still in the process of being negotiated.

79 The Bathing Water Directive (76/160/EEC) presently uses total coliforms, faecal coliforms, faecal streptococci, salmonella and enteroviruses as indicator organisms to set standards of cleanliness for water in which people are likely to bathe. The Directive sets both a minimum (mandatory value) and an optimum (guideline) standard, and lays down how frequently the water should be tested for each of the indicators. For bathing water to comply with the Directive, 95% of all samples must meet the mandatory standards. Bathing water which does better than this and achieves the guideline standard is eligible for consideration for blue flag status. It is deemed to have achieved guideline standards if 80% of tests for total and faecal coliforms and 90% of tests for all other organisms meet the relevant guideline standards.

80 See Legge, 2000.

estimated would need £30 million to bring it up to standard.[81] Of 600 beaches in England and Wales, the Government designated 27 at 18 resorts and none at all in Scotland, which was considered to be too cold and so people would not stay in for long enough for any damage to be done. France and Italy designated 3,000 beaches. Now, 496 beaches have been designated.

A number of controversial issues were looked at by the Environment, Transport and Regions Select Committee, including the definition of 'bathing waters' and the need for full tertiary treatment.[82] In the Government's Response to the Select Committee Report (July 1998), it did not state that full treatment would be required, but that there should be increased treatment, that companies would have funding for secondary treatment and that high natural dispersal areas should be removed in many cases. The Government also stated that there should be a significant increase in bathing water standards, particularly in the level of compliance with guideline standards under the Bathing Water Directive, with the aim of enabling more resorts to gain blue flag status. The programme to improve unsatisfactory sewer outflows, which deposit unhygienic and distasteful solids on riverbanks and beaches during rainstorms, should also be accelerated.[83]

Many of these concerns will, in part, be remedied under the new EC Directive on bathing waters.[84] New standards have been set out and recreational users have been added to the Directive.[85] In areas where the pathogenic loading exceeds the new standards, the Directive states that disinfection should be applied. Some water companies have adopted ultraviolet (UV) treatment or microfiltration techniques, including Wessex Water, Yorkshire Water and Welsh Water. South West Water is in the process of upgrading its treatment plants. Jersey has been held up as the way forward, with its water meeting the target for faecal strepococcoli in 99.99% cases, after installing a £2 million UV treatment plant rather than a long sea outfall. However, North West Water has consistently failed to meet the standards. As the Directive is 24 years old, it would seem that it is time for better

81 See Case C 56/90 *Commission v UK* [1993] ECR 4109, where the UK stated that it had taken all practicable steps to comply with the Directive by undertaking studies at Blackpool and Southport and had the works ready to proceed. The Court stated that the Directive had not been complied with.

82 See *op cit*, DETR, fn 74, paras 175–82.

83 DETR press release 778/23, September 1998.

84 Commission Proposal (Com 1994 036), Final Proposal for a Council Directive Concerning the Quality of Bathing Water, OJL 112, 22.4.94, as amended by (1997) 585 final.

85 Draft WHO bathing water guidelines cover recreational waters, including coastal and inland waters.

compliance, a view reiterated by the Government in relation to the 1998 bathing water results.[86]

The quality of bathing waters should be improved with the Urban Waste Water Directive.[87] This lays down minimum standards for waste water treatment at sewerage treatment works. Council Directive 91/271/EEC, as amended by 98/15/EEC,[88] aims to protect the environment from the effects of collection, treatment and discharge of urban waste waters, discharges from certain industrial sectors and the disposal of sludge. It sets requirements regulating effluent discharges at a common fixed standard, allowing exceptions under specified conditions. It has set deadlines (ranging from 1995 to 2005) for urban areas of different population levels to provide for collection and at least secondary treatment of urban waste waters. It establishes requirements for urban waste water treatment plants and controls on discharges of industrial waste water into urban waste water treatment plants. It also required that Member States identify sensitive areas by the end of 1993; sensitive areas[89] are classified as those subject to eutrophication and those waters used for drinking water which might not meet the requirements of other Council directives.

The Environment Agency has detailed further coastal sewage outfalls which will require secondary level treatment under the Urban Waste Water Treatment Directive.[90] It means that to date the Agency has required discharges from 12 outfalls on the south and east coasts of England to be subject to the higher level of treatment. The Government has also accepted Agency recommendations to remove high natural dispersion area status

---

86 Of the 496 identified UK coastal bathing waters sampled in 1998, 89% passed the EC mandatory coliform bacteria standards, compared with 88% in 1997 and 90% in 1996. In England, 90% passed, compared with 88% last year. Results from samples taken by the EA for bathing waters in England showed the following: a record number of coastal bathing waters (349 out of 389) met the Directive's coliform standards; of the 40 which failed, half of them missed compliance by only one of the 20 samples; more coastal bathing waters (146) met the higher 'guideline' standard needed for a European blue flag than in 1997 (136); all nine inland bathing waters included in the survey for the first time in 1998 passed the mandatory coliform standards; and, despite an improvement, the North West still remains (at 62%) very poor: DETR press release 982, 19 November 1998.

87 See Roger, 1999, pp 24–27.

88 See Commission Report on implementation of Directive 91/271/EEC, 21 May 1991, concerning waste water treatment, as amended by Directive 98/15/EEC, 27 Feb 1998 – survey of the measures implemented by the Member States and assessment of the information received pursuant to Arts 17 and 13 of the Directive (Com (98) 75).

89 See *R v SOSETR ex p Kingston-upon-Hull CC* [1996] Env LR 248.

90 Urban Waste Water Directive (91/271); see Urban Waste Water Treatment (England and Wales) Regulations 1994 (SI 1994/2841).

(HNDA)[91] from a number of locations. This decision means three further coastal discharges, serving population equivalents in excess of 15,000, will also require secondary treatment.

The Government has set down its proposals for improving bathing water quality, stating that, for secondary treatment, or treatment laid down by the EA, it has to comply with the Urban Waste Water Directive (91/271/EEC). Investment will be needed to meet the requirements for nutrient striping of discharges in new and extended eutrophic sensitive areas. The Government has also decided that secondary treatment will be the minimum requirement for all coastal discharges. It wants to bring forward work on intermittent discharges: this was to be completed by 2015, but the Government wishes to see at least two-thirds of the discharges completed by 2005. In relation to bathing water, improvements will be needed to meet the failure at identified beaches to reach the mandatory targets set down in the Directive and to achieve compliance with the guideline standards targeted at particular holiday resorts to achieve blue flag status. The use of untreated sewage sludge on agricultural land will be phased out by 2001. Further restrictions were placed on the use of untreated sludge by the beginning of 1999.[92]

At the 1987 North Sea Conference, the Government accepted an undertaking in principle not to dump sewage at sea unless there were no practical land based alternatives. In 1990, it decided to ban all sewage sludge dumping at sea from the end of 1998, and this later became one of the requirement of the Urban Wastewater Treatment Directive (UWWTD) (91/272), adopted in 1991. Alternative methods for disposal include[93] recycling onto agricultural land, incineration or gasification with energy recovery and use for land reclamation schemes, while organisations such as Surfers against Sewage[94] point to the benefits of recycling waste water.[95]

---

91 Under the Urban Waste Water Treatment Directive, where it can be shown that estuarine or coastal waters do not exhibit eutrophication, have good levels of dissolved oxygen and exhibit good dispersion, then these waters can be designated as less sensitive areas (HNDAs in the UK). The effect of this is that relevant sewage discharges into these areas can be subject to reduced treatment requirements – provided that comprehensive studies show that the discharge will have no adverse environmental impact. See EA Press Release 30/7/98.

92 Op cit, DETR, fn 26.

93 See DETR press release 1120, 30 December 1998.

94 See the Surfers against Sewage website at www.sas.org.uk.

95 See House of Commons Select Committee on the Environment, Transport and Regions, 20th Report, Sewage Treatment and Disposal, February 1998.

ion and short sighted regulation has left us with a legacy of
he past few years, in varying degrees and to varying speeds, the
oastal environment is being cleaned up.[116] There have been a
dies on the water environment[117] and, although there have been
s,[118] only 15% of lowland rivers and streams are in their natural
mber of issues have arisen in relation to who should pay for the
ater pollution and other resource measures, which have caused
during the periodic review when the prices are set for the water
he EA has set out its proposals for water in *Water Resources*
ne and *An Environmental Strategy for the Millennium and Beyond*.
n a number of changes to the regulatory structure for water[121]
nat there will be a new Water Act when the current draft Water
The challenges for water in the future are essentially the same
leal with the legacy of pollution, but some may be new
sing out of climate change, where drought or flooding may
ended with.

WATER POLLUTION TECHNOLOGY

logy has great potential for waste purification and disposal,
rtain dilemmas facing the UK. Take, for example, the case of
dustrial wastewaters. Even well designed treatment works
rloaded will produce residual sludges in addition to treated
estion is, how should this sludge, or the waste from waste, be
d, sea or air? For the UK, in 1997, the percentage breakdown
rage sludge were:

)%;

24%;

36–37; Legge, 1999, p 250.

tate of the Environment in England and Wales: Fresh Waters, May 1998;
rvey.

cussion of water quality, see, DETR, op cit, fn 74.

rvey: see EA press release 11/6/98.

0, 85–89; Legge, 1998, pp 147–48; Legge, 1999, pp 113–19.

in England and Wales a new approach Response to consultation Water
9: Consultation on Regulations Water Industry Act 1999 Delivering the
ctives: see www.environment.detr. Gov.uk/wia99/index.htm.

Titanium Dioxide Wastes Directive (78/176)

Titanium Dioxide (TiO_2) is a white pigment, the manufacture of which produces large amounts of polluted water. The directive lays down specific guidelines controlling manufacture and discharge.

Dangerous Substances Directive (76/464 EEC)

The Directive has as its object the prevention or limitation of groups of substances either directly or indirectly into groundwaters,[96] for example, lead, cadmium, asbestos and pesticides. In addition, the Directive requires Member States to draw up programmes for the progressive reduction and eventual elimination of pollution caused by waste from existing establishments. These programmes are to form the basis of a further directive, co-ordinating action at Community level.

Detergent Directive (73/404)

The Council had adopted a series of directives on detergents, partly to protect the natural environment and partly to remove obstacles to intra-Community trade by the adoption of common standards. Directive 73/404 lays down the basic principle that no detergent marketed within the EEC (now EC) should contain a surfactant (active constituent) which is less than 90% biodegradable. 'Hard', or less biodegradable detergents, cause foaming in rivers.

Preventive powers

The EA has widely drafted powers to prevent pollution incidents[97] and, where they occur, to recover the costs of cleaning them up. It can also undertake remedial[98] or restorative work. The SOSETR can designate water protection zones.[99] These establish a system of local law within the zone in relation to water pollution and are useful for protecting sensitive areas. However, to date, only one has been designated.[100]

96 In C 231/97 *Van Rooij v Dagelijks Bestuur van het Waterschap de Dommel* [2000] Env LR D16, the meaning of 'discharge' was considered in relation to the Dangerous Substances Directive (76/464). It was held that discharge included the release of a contaminated stream falling initially onto land or buildings or coming into contact with surface water.

97 WRA 1991, ss 92, 161.

98 WRA 1991, s 161A, inserted by Environment Act 1995, s 22. See, also, the Water (Prevention of Pollution) (Code of Practice) Order (SI 1998/3084).

99 WRA 1991, Sched 11, s 93.

100 Water Protection Zone (River Dee Catchment) Designation Order 1999 (SI 1999/915).

Nitrates Directive (91/676)

Nitrate pollution was controlled through the use of nitrate sensitive areas. These were areas designated by the DETR and farmers received compensation for not using nitrates. They were initially criticised by groups such as Friends of the Earth because of the voluntary nature of the scheme. Mandatory designations[101] are now made under nitrate vulnerable zones.[102] Nitrate vulnerable zones designation is a mandatory action programme to protect ground and surface waters against nitrate pollution by protecting the quality and timing of nitrogen[103] fertiliser and livestock manure applications; these are uncompensated, as they equate to good agricultural practice.[104]

In the case of *R v SESTR ex p Standley* (268 ENDS Report 47), it was held that, where agriculture was a significant contributor to nitrate pollution, all known areas of land that drained into waters containing more than 50 mg per litre of nitrates must be designated a vulnerable zone and it was unnecessary to determine that nitrate pollution above the specified limit was caused solely by agriculture; and that, in any case, a Member State had power to designate their entire territory a vulnerable zone, even if nitrate pollution due to agricultural causes did not exceed 50 mg per litre. The right to property was not an absolute right in isolation and had to be reconciled with measures to protect public health and promote the general interest.

Codes of good agricultural practice[105]

The Code sets down good practices for farmers to follow in relation to water pollution.[106] They were set up under s 93 of the Water Resources Act 1991, as amended by the Environment Act 1995. The farmers will not be prosecuted if they breach these codes but they can be used as evidence of bad practice if they are being prosecuted for another offence.[107]

Sewage sludge

The Sewage Sludge Directive[108] regulate farmland and puts controls on the stora sludge on agriculture is to be stopped a Disposal Directive. The Control of Pollu Fuel Oil) Regulations 1991 set minimum or improved waste stores. They can app serious pollution. Smells may be a statut

Environment Agency figures show incidents of water pollution by agricu incidents, and agriculture was responsib pollution incidents in that year. Betwee of separate incidents of water pollution

Animal slurry, which contains man more polluting than raw untreated d the liquid produced when preservin green so that they can be kept for fodd polluting.[111] For necessary remedial w notice requiring action to be taken as pollution, if someone has knowingly p

Nuisance

See the cases of *R v Falmouth and Tru* and, in relation to sewage on a beach *Shelley*.[114]

The future[115]

In the UK, water protection has bee public health and increasingly fro

industrialisa
pollution. In
aquatic and
number of stu
improvement
state.[119] A nu
clean-up of w
some conflict
industry.[120]
Planning Outli
There have be
and it seems t
Bill is enacted.
as now – to
challenges, ari
need to be con

Waste water

Modern techno
but there are ce
domestic and i
that are not ove
effluent. The qu
disposed? To la
of outlets for sev

- farmland – 5
- landfill – 9%;
- sea disposal –

---

101 See Protection of Water Against Nitrate Pollution (England and Wales) Regulations 1996 (SI 1996/888); Action Programme for Nitrate Vulnerable Zones (England and Wales) Regulations 1998 (SI 1998/1202). Under these Regulations, farmers have to implement programmes to reduce nitrate pollution, such as keeping records of crops grown and the addition of fertiliser.

102 See Case 337/89 *Commission v UK* [1992] ECR I-6013.

103 The EA is also drawing up a strategy: *The Aquatic Eutrophication in England and Wales: A Proposed Management Strategy*, December 1998.

104 See Case C 293/97 *R v SOSETR and Another ex p Standley and Others* ECJ (Fifth Chamber) 22 April 1999 on the designation of nitrate vulnerable zones.

105 The Crop Residue Burning Regulations 1993 (SI 1993/1366) prohibit the burning of crop residues as waste.

106 Codes of good agricultural practice: WRA 1991, s 92.

107 See the Environment Act 1995, s 60; new code of good agricultural practice under the Water (Prevention of Pollution) (Code of Practice) Ord 1998 (SI 1998/ 3804).

108 86/278/ EEC, as amended by Directi

109 See the Control of Pollution (Silage, (SI 1991/324). See, also, Agriculture 1990/ 880; Code of Practice for Agric

110 MAFF website.

111 *Ibid*.

112 Water (Compulsory Works Powers)

113 See above, Chapter 2.

114 Purdue, 1997, pp 103–18 on *R v Cari*

115 Legge, 2000, pp 3–19.

116 Legge, 1999, pp

117 From EA, *The* River Habitat Su

118 For a general di

119 River Habitat Su

120 Legge, 1994, pp

121 *Water Charging* *Industry Act 19* *Government's obj*

- incineration – 8%;
- other – 9%.

However, changes in legislation will mean that these percentages are set to change quite dramatically over the next few years, with significant implications for the relative waste exposures to air, land or water as the primary disposal medium.

Sludge comprises solid matter that has settled out of suspension during sedimentation and is the mixture of wastes which remain after treatment processes. The quality of sludge is as important as the quantity which is to be disposed of: the more hazardous the substances discharged from industrial processes, the more likely they are to appear in the resulting sludge. This will, in turn, make the disposal of sludge to agricultural land more problematic. Hence, the utilisation of sludge (biosolids) from treatment works is strictly controlled.

Alternative methods for sludge disposal have historically comprised: disposal to agricultural land, landfill, dumping at sea and incineration with some sludge dried and sold as fertiliser. It may be applied to agricultural land in its raw form but, in order to reduce odour and bulk, it may be treated by a variety of different methods, including dewatering; thickening; digestion; composting; thermal drying; and incineration/combustion. When digested in purpose built tanks by micro-organisms to reduce the organic content, the volume of sludge decreases and the residue achieves relative inoffensiveness, having attained the character of humus. The treatment of sewage sludge by thermal combustion is controlled by licences issued by the EA and incineration requires appropriate technology and controls to limit the degree of air pollution. Domestic sewage sludge is viewed as a valuable resource, due to its soil conditioning properties and fertiliser value, and its utilisation on agricultural land if undertaken in accordance with the detailed requirements.

Water use

The crucial issues of water asset ownership and responsibility are increasingly becoming potential areas of conflict. Consequently, the increasing use of water metering to preserve water means that leakage control, the attendant problems of liability for any leaks and difficulties with water meters themselves are proving to be expanding areas of importance.

The increasing demand for water, coupled with prolonged periods of drought, have put existing resources under great pressure and led to concerns that over-abstraction of water may result in ecological damage. Climatic variation is very complex and our climatic system, like most other natural systems, is dynamic and behaves in a non-linear fashion. Severe droughts are probably expressions of our climate's natural internal variability, rather than of externally forced changes such as the greenhouse effect, and meteorologists and geologists recognise that major gaps still exist in the explanation of climatic change.

Water undertakers find it increasingly necessary to provide affordable engineering solutions which strike an informed balance between cost, benefit, sustainability and acceptability. Whilst a supply of water sufficient for the basic public health needs of every user is essential, and should be available at all times, supplies over and above this requirement necessitate the use of demand management measures to reduce the consumption of water and delay or remove the need for new water resources. Effective demand management will involve a combination of efficient water use, equitable charging arrangements and reduced leakage.

The considerable hydrologic imbalance caused by droughts leads to water shortages, crop damage, streamflow reduction and depletion of groundwater and soil moisture; it occurs when evaporation and transpiration exceed precipitation for an extended period. Unpredictable drought involves an abnormal rainfall failure, whilst invisible drought can be recognised in summer when high temperatures induce high rates of evaporation and transpiration. In such cases, even frequent showers may not supply sufficient water to restore the amount lost, resulting in a borderline water deficiency that diminishes crop yields.

Water saving devices often alleviate difficulties, and the re-use of 'grey' water and collection of rainwater for garden watering are ways in which existing resources can be used efficiently. However, there is a growing need for water companies to be empowered to carry out water supply audits leading to mandatory recommendations.

Water companies are able to maintain high standards of environmental awareness, and improve their environmental performance, by fostering the concepts of sustainable development and environmental protection and achieving an appropriate balance between environmental and economic factors. However, one recent area of concern has been in relation to water companies imposing minimum payments for metered water. Portsmouth Water has imposed a minimum payment on customers apparently causing problems for homes which use very little water, such as residences that are only used at weekends. Ofwat is concerned about this issue but urges customers to complain to the water company if and when this occurs. It would appear that there does not seem to be an effective mechanism by which Ofwat can ensure that a water company does not impose this type of charge. This is clearly an area which may need to be reformed if water meters are to play an effective part in preserving water.

Flooding

Because of global warming, the danger of urban flooding becomes more real each year, with wetter winters and more frequent storms. Added to this, an increase in air temperature over the next 50 years of between 1–3°C will raise sea levels through thermal expansion by between 100–500 mm.

Sea levels have risen by 100–250 mm over the past 100 years and, currently, there are 46 million people around the world at risk of flooding from storm surges; a predicted maximum 500 mm rise would increase this number to 92 million people. There are already signs of more variable and extreme weather patterns, with floods occurring in 1997 in eastern Germany, Poland, China, USA and Canada of a severity which should only occur once in 100 years. The recent acute flooding problems in England have lead to major concerns regarding the adequacy of flood defence and drainage systems. In response to this, the SOSETR has allocated a further £51 million for emergency alleviation measures.

Business and domestic premises are at risk and, in England and Wales alone, there are over 1.3 million premises and four million people at increased risk of severe flooding; in April 1998, flooding caused £400 million worth of damage and 21 deaths.

The EA has recently launched a three year flood awareness campaign and, since taking over the task of alerting the public to flood threats from the Police in 1996, the Agency's main target is for zero lives to be lost in floods. Furthermore, water treatment systems will have to be upgraded because of higher rainfall, with winter rainfall rising by between 8 and 14%.

The dynamics of rainfall are such that weather radar, computerised river flow and flood modelling cannot always exactly predict the pattern of rainfall events, thereby limiting the overall effectiveness of any flood prediction and warning system.

Flooding of an urban property from external sources can become an increasingly complex issue, specifically in relation to both the cause of the flooding and the 'ownership' of the relevant drainage systems. The true cause of urban flooding is often difficult to isolate, due to the interdependence of and interaction between separate and distinct drainage facilities. Flooding may be the result of inefficiency/insufficiency of the individual drainage systems in whole, in part or in combination.

Flooding may also occur in an urban area due to a number of reasons, such as deficiencies within the land drainage or highway drainage system, which usually falls within the remit of the local authority; deficiencies within the sewerage system; or excessive storm flows which exceed the design capacities of the existing systems, resulting in hydraulic inadequacy. A sewer may be considered hydraulically inadequate when the flow from a storm with a known return period cannot flow down it due to a permanent problem.

Often, however, the statistical frequency of storm will not be known until sufficient years have elapsed to enable statistical analyses to be used. It may also be the case that, once the statistical data has been collected, the flooding can be shown to be caused by a storm of a longer return period than that corresponding to the reference level of service.

In order that a full appreciation of flooding problems in urban areas is demonstrated, it is necessary that potential mechanisms of flooding are described. Flooding can occur in an urban area for a number of reasons, as listed below.

Land drainage

- Inadequate capacity – cross-section of hydraulic flow too small.
- Inadequate maintenance – blockages, etc.
- Actual storm intensity exceeds design storm intensity.
- System has not been upgraded to deal with increased urbanisation and development.
- Rainfall run-off cannot enter the land drainage system.

Sewerage: surface water or combined systems

- Inadequate capacity – cross-section of hydraulic flow too small
- Inadequate maintenance – blockages, etc.
- Actual storm intensity exceeds design storm intensity.
- System has not been upgraded to deal with increased urbanisation and development.
- Rainfall run-off cannot enter sewerage system.

Highway drainage

- Inadequate cross falls or road gully provision.
- Inadequate maintenance – blockages, etc.
- Actual storm intensity exceeds design storm intensity.
- Rainfall run-off cannot enter the highway drainage system.

Lead contamination of drinking water

The principal concern in relation to drinking water is centred around the fact that water can dissolve lead from the supply pipes between the mains supply and the tap. Lead can be a health risk if consistently consumed over a number of years. Chemical injury through poisoning is characterised by a poison's ability to cause damage at particular sites within the body. Lead is probably the most ubiquitous metal poison and, like mercury, it is toxic to the nervous system and kidney, with the extent of damage depending upon the amount of exposure. As a cumulative toxin, it can induce adverse effects on mental development and behaviour and, as the body's ability to eliminate lead is poor, chronic ingestion of non-toxic amounts can result in a build up that may eventually reach toxic levels.

Lead was formerly used as plumbing pipe material and, until the 1930s, was the only material available for small diameter underground pipes. It was used until 1974 in some areas, and some older houses will today have pipes and cisterns made of lead. Like other inorganic chemicals, lead can often appear in chemical forms that are quite harmless, but it is the soluble salts of inorganic lead that are strong systemic poisons, with poisoning able to occur through the ingestion of water from lead pipes. To combat this problem, treatment methods are often revised to include the addition of phosphate, which reduces the ability of water to dissolve lead and soldered joints; water companies are replacing lead supply pipes; and ongoing customer replacement of private pipework is supported by efforts to reline small bore pipes *in situ*.

Many of the lead pipes are found in customers' properties. By way of example, one water company states that their mains network contains no lead and that any dissolved lead is picked up in the service pipe or from internal plumbing. The pipes on an owner's property are their responsibility. The water undertakers will test for lead, for no charge. If the concentration of lead exceeds the limit, the undertaker will replace any pipes owned by them, but the householder is responsible for removing his own pipes. The new pipe is connected to the main, at a place agreed with the water undertaker, and this would not entail a charge. The water undertaker will also ensure that the old pipe is properly disconnected. If an owner cannot afford to undertake domestic pipework replacement, typical advice from the water company is to flush the toilet or to take a shower in order to remove the five litres or so that stands overnight in the pipes, which can have a lead concentration of approximately double the normal amount.

The Drinking Water Directive is at present in the process of being revised and the proposals are being considered by the European Parliament; thus, the extent of any revisions and the possible timescale for the changes are presently uncertain. There is a proposal to provide for a stricter lead standard: an interim standard of 25 mg/l must be achieved five years after adoption and a final standard of 10 mg/l after 15 years. The sampling regime has not yet been proposed by the European Commission; however, it seems clear that there will be new regulations and procedures for enforcement in the near future.

Groundwater pollution

The change from an essentially rural agricultural society and economy to an industrial society with worldwide connections began in the UK in the 18th century and two-thirds of the then six million population worked on land. Industrialisation increased substantially after 1750, with metallurgical industries becoming widespread and newer industries developing. Even so, industry was small-scale and domestic in character, water was the main source of power, and manufacturing industries were mainly geared to satisfying the needs of the home market.

In time, waterpower was applied to larger textile machines, larger factories became a feature of the landscape and the modern industrial landscape began to take shape. However, it was only in the 19th century, with the coming of the steam age, that environmental injury to the landscape began, with industrial towns, atmospheric pollution, the pollution of streams and rivers and physical damage as a byproduct of industrial activity. Waste products from industrial processes were usually tipped on or adjacent to factory sites and contaminants allowed to leach into the ground. Liquid waste was often discharged directly into rivers or onto the ground surface, from where it found its way into watercourses and streams. Pollution and contamination were accepted as part of the price of progress and the benefits of income outweighed health risks.

There is growing evidence that many chemicals in the environment, whether from industrial pollution or in end products, are having a huge impact on human health and the health of the environment. It is often extremely difficult to prove what impact any chemical may have, since some chemicals may be toxic for a short time, while others may be damaging for hundreds of years. The rate of exposure is also extremely important, with a single dose in a short space of time being potentially more serious than the same total dose spread over a long period of time. Some organic pollutants will degrade rapidly once they enter the environment; others require more time or will hardly degrade at all. For instance, silage liquor will degrade provided there is enough oxygen, whereas polychlrorinated biphenyls (PCBs) will hardly degrade.

Furthermore, how a chemical is dispersed will have a significant impact on toxic levels in the environment, with weather conditions making a significant difference. For example, pollution released into a river will usually be transported downstream, though some pollutants may bind to the sediment near to where they are released. Wet weather and high flows will flush more of the pollution away, though high flows through treatment facilities, such as sewage works, may reduce the efficiency of the treatment. Moreover, the exposure to chemicals may be indirect, with a chemical released into the air but deposited on the ground or to surface waters.

Today, there are upto 100,000 hectares of contaminated land in the UK, with costs of treatment of ground and polluted groundwater estimated at £30–£35 billion. Any material or chemicals that find their way into the water resource may need to be removed before supply, and their removal is generally technically difficult and expensive. However, instead of applying universal controls over land or soil use and effluent discharge to the ground, it is often more cost effective, and less prejudicial to economic development, to utilise the natural contaminant attenuation capacity of the strata overlying the saturated aquifer.

Derelict land, which has been so damaged by industrial exploitation as to be incapable of beneficial use without treatment, is becoming increasingly available for reclamation as wastefill areas reach their capacity. Wastefills present many hazards, including poor engineering properties, contamination, biodegradation effects, gas and leachate production and, perhaps most importantly, groundwater pollution. Constraints on development arise from the interaction between the hazards on a derelict site and the end use proposed for that site. Furthermore, contamination on a derelict site may pose a threat to piped drinking water supplies and to ground and surface water resources. Drinking water piped through contaminated ground may be at risk from defects in the pipes or joints arising from aggressive attack or mechanical failure. Moreover, certain organic compounds, such as phenols or solvents, can diffuse through plastic pipes and taint the water without pipe damage.

Local contaminated perched water tables may be severely affected even though the main aquifer may be unharmed, while site works may aggravate water contamination problems and, even at contaminant concentrations well below toxic levels, the aesthetic quality of water may be affected. Hence, the rehabilitation of polluted groundwater is expensive and often may not be technically feasible. It is important that a robust policy of groundwater protection is available to protect the resource from pollution. It is, therefore, interesting to review definitions of pollution and contamination, particularly with respect to contaminated land and groundwater.

The problem is clearly complex. Even if all chemical emissions could be accurately measured, it would still be difficult to gauge their precise effect. Pollution that is not degraded and is not transported away from its source may accumulate in the soil of the local area, as is particularly the case with pollutants such as lead and dioxins. Some pollutants concentrate in the bodies of plants, animals and humans, often resulting in those at the top of the food chain having higher levels of contamination than those at the bottom. Equally, with dwindling water resources and ever increasing demands, it is inevitable that water will have to be re-used over and over again, with pressure to exploit water from resources of poor quality. Furthermore, as groundwater is easily contaminated, it is subsequently very difficult to treat or control, and contaminants can be transferred over large distances within regional groundwater systems.

Greywater

Within the UK, 40% of total water use is within the domestic sector; hence, urban water re-use through water recycling is a particularly attractive option for helping to meet future predicted increases in population and per capita demand. However, to date, houses have not generally been designed with water conservation in mind, even though there is sufficient greywater produced in the majority of UK households for toilets to be flushed using recycled greywater alone.

Consequently, in previous years, the housing sector has made little progress in reducing its water consumption, with water seen as a cheap, readily available commodity in inexhaustible supply. It is significant, therefore, that domestic users increasingly recognise that the reduction of water consumption is a necessary component of good environmental practice. Hence, it is now acknowledged that new construction should no longer consider water simply as a utility but should embrace the use of water as part of the process of environmental assessment.

The relatively low levels of microbiological contamination within greywater make it suitable through re-use as a source of non-potable water such as toilet flushing, but there are significant technical challenges. The practicality of operating a greywater recycling system depends on the nature of the contamination, the operability of the recycling unit, the integration of water streams and an understanding of water chemistry.

Greywater recycling processes are required to protect public health and must function properly if re-use water quality is to meet acceptable standards. Equally, within an urban housing development, greywater re-use is best achieved where it affords advantages in cost, design and operation via communal recycling systems. That said, communal systems do pose particular concerns regarding their social acceptance and the reliability of treatment for unsteady State operation. Threats to process reliability are borne from occasional substance spiking, where problem substances including bleaching and cleaning agents enter the greywater stream. In their favour, the capacity of larger communal greywater recycling systems to buffer occasional substance spiking makes their processes less sensitive to greywater changes and increases their inherent attractiveness as the preferred option.

CHAPTER 5

AIR POLLUTION CONTROL

HISTORY

There has been a long history of air pollution control (APC) in the UK. However, the starting point for any discussion of the law on air pollution really has to start with the alkali industry, which began in the late 19th century. In *St Helens Co v Tipping* (1865) 11 HL Cas 642, the limitations of the common law as a remedy for industrial pollution were highlighted and, instead, statutory controls were placed on the alkali industry through the Alkali Act 1874, which introduced the concept of best practical means (BPM).[1] The legislation was consolidated in the 1906 Alkali Works Regulation Act. The Alkali Act 1863 set up the Alkali Inspectorate, later to become Her Majesty's Inspectorate of Pollution and now amalgamated into the Environment Agency (EA).[2] In 1926, the Public Health (Smoke Abatement) Act was passed, but this did not cover domestic smoke. In December 1952, London suffered from the 'London Smog', which led to 12,000 deaths and Clean Air Act 1956, which controlled domestic smoke for the first time. However, it was not until the Health and Safety at Work Act 1974 and the Control of Pollution Act 1974 that any coherent regulatory structure was set up. In 1993, the Clean Air Act consolidated the previous legislation in relation to clean air. But, whilst many of the air pollution problems of the past, such as dark smoke, have been controlled, new problems have emerged such as the destruction of the ozone layer, acid rain and global warming.

THE POLICY ISSUES

Climate change[3]

In 1990, the Intergovernmental Panel on Climate Change (IPCC) was set up. In 1992, the Rio Earth Summit agreed on a Framework Convention on Climate Change. This Convention was the first to recognise the problem of the greenhouse effect. Articles 2 and 3 set out the objective of the Convention:

---

1   See above, Chapter 2.
2   See above, Chapter 2 .
3   French, 1997, pp 227–40.

... to achieve ... stabilisation of greenhouse gas concentrations in the atmosphere at a level that would prevent dangerous anthropocentric interference with the climate system. Such a level would be achieved within a timeframe sufficient to allow ecosystems to adapt naturally to climate change, to ensure that food production is not threatened and to enable economic development to proceed in a sustainable manner.

The panel concluded that there was a need to cut greenhouse gases by 60%. This limit was not agreed on; instead, countries agreed different targets, with the US following a 'business as usual' scenario.[4] This was followed by the Kyoto and Buenos Aires Conferences.[5] Under the Kyoto protocol, the targets set were legally binding. The European Community (EC) and its Members agreed to an 8% cut, while the US agreed to a 7% cut. The UK has agreed to reduce emissions from a basket of six greenhouse gases by 12% below 1990 levels by 2008–12. The UK's strategy is to stabilise emission levels by the year 2000 to 1990 levels but wishes to go beyond the targets set down for it at Kyoto of 12% to a target of 20% below 1990 levels by the year 2010.[6] One of the controversial issues was in relation to carbon trading. This allows countries that have reached emission targets over and above those required by the Kyoto target to sell them to other countries which are finding it too difficult or expensive to meet their targets. The Kyoto protocol also allowed targets to be offset by carbon sinks or the absorption of carbon dioxide by forests. In Buenos Aires, a timetable was set down for completion of any outstanding issues, such as how the Kyoto mechanisms will operate, from November 2000.

This has been implemented in the EC[7] through Council Decision 93/389/EEC for a monitoring mechanism of carbon dioxide and other greenhouse gas emissions in the EC.[8] In June 1998, the Environment Ministers of the EC agreed a list of priorities:

- taxation of aviation fuel;[9]

- an action plan for improving the energy efficiency of appliances and equipment;

---

4   If there is a 'business as usual' scenario, then it may be 1.6% warmer, the seas may rise by 20 cm and carbon dioxide levels may increase.

5   The Fifth Conference to the Parties in Bonn in October/November 1999 reviewed the progress since Buenos Aires.

6   See the UK Consultation Documents, *UK Climate Change Programme*, DETR, October 1998; *Climate Change Consultation Report*, August 1999, DETR.

7   Council Resolution on the Greenhouse Effect and the Community OJC 183 20.7.89.93/389; EC Council Decision for a Monitoring Mechanism of Community Carbon Dioxide and other Greenhouse Gas Emissions OJL 167, 9.7.93.

8   See the European Commission Communication, *Preparing for Implementation of the Kyoto Protocol*, June 1999.

9   In the UK, the Government is drawing up a Consultation Paper on civil aviation, which will lead to a new air transport White Paper.

- a programme to promote the take-up of energy efficiency best practice;[10]
- an action plan for reducing methane emissions;
- a policy framework for tackling emissions of hydroflurocarbons, perflurocarbons and sulphur hexafluoride;
- mandatory energy labelling;
- minimum energy efficiency standards;
- future directive on access for electricity from renewable sources to the internal electricity market;
- further work on energy labelling;
- SAVE programme;
- the Euro best practice programme: revised monitoring arrangements that require annual monitoring by the Member States and the Commission.

In the UK, the Government's policy has been set out in the *Climate Change Draft UK Programme*.[11] The consultation document outlines the problems that the UK may face in the future and some strategies for dealing with climate change. This will have wide ranging implications on all aspects of life in the UK.[12] The Report sets out some of these:

- changing patterns of water quality and availability and changes in water demand;[13]
- increased risk of river flooding and foul flooding;[14]
- sea level rise, increased risk of storm surges on the coast and impacts on built assets in coastal and river flood plain areas;
- increased storminess and winds;[15]
- deterioration of the built environment;
- impacts on tourism and agriculture;
- impact on biodiversity and habitats;[16]

---

10 See Reg 93/389 and the energy efficiency Directives 93/76 and 93/500.
11 *Op cit*, DETR, 1998, fn 6.
12 See Climate Research Centre and Hadley Centre, *Climate Change Scenarios for the United Kingdom: UK Climate Impact Programme, Technical Report No 1*, September 1998. See, also, the Climate Impacts LINK project and the Hadley Centre at www.met.office.gov.uk; the Climate Impacts programme at www.ecu.ox.ac.uk/ukcip.htm.; the British Atmospheric Data Centre at tornado.badc.rl.ac.uk.
13 See above, Chapter 4.
14 See above, Chapter 4.
15 See Met Office, 'Climate change and its impacts: stabilisation of carbon dioxide in the atmosphere', in Bunyard, 2000.
16 See below, Chapter 8.

The Report sets out the strategies that the Government is introducing in order to meet its Kyoto targets. These include:

- the climate change levy:[17] agreements with the energy sector to set challenging targets and to improve energy efficiency;[18]

- integrated pollution control;[19]

- a new obligation on the electricity suppliers to help to increase the proportion of electricity provided by renewable sources by 10% by 2010;

- a new target to double the capacity of combined heat and power by 2010;

- a new energy efficiency standard of performance, placing an obligation on electricity and gas suppliers to help domestic customers, particularly those on low incomes and the elderly, to save energy and cut their fuel bills;

- EC level agreements with the car manufacturers to improve the average fuel efficiency of new cars by at least 25% by 2008–09;

- implementation of policies to cut congestion and pollution;[20]

- changes to transport taxation;

- a new drive to improve energy efficiency in the public sector;[21]

- a new home energy efficiency scheme, improvements to community heating and more efficient appliances;

- integration with other policies, for example, waste,[22] construction,[23] planning,[24] housing, building,[25] agriculture.[26]

---

17 House of Commons Select Committee on Trade and Industry 1998–99, 11th Special Report, 26 October 1999, HC 834, *Government observations on the Ninth Report for the Trade and Industry Select Committee* (session 98–99) *on the Impact on industry of the proposed climate change levy,* 19 July 1999.

18 The climate change levy will come into effect in April 2001.The levy is expected to save 1.5 million tonnes of carbon by 2010. Firms can, however, trade carbon as a way of meeting targets.

19 See below, Chapter 7.

20 Cleaner Vehicles Taskforce Report, *Driving the Agenda,* July 1999; the Powershift programme encourages a market for cleaner fuel vehicles in the UK. See, also, the fuel duty escalator reforms to the vehicle excise duty, which encourage the use of more environmentally friendly vehicles and reforms of company car taxation based on carbon dioxide emissions.

21 See Pt II, Chapter 8 of the Report: this includes new targets for improving the energy management of public buildings; energy efficiency targets for local authorities, schools and hospitals; and the development of transport plans in the public sector.

22 See *Implications of the EC Landfill Directive and the Draft Waste Strategy on the UK Greenhouse Gas Emissions: a Preliminary Study,* February 2000, AEA Technology.

23 See *Building a Better Quality of Life – a Strategy for Sustainable Construction,* DETR, April 2000.

24 See the Urban White Paper, *Planning for the Communities of the Future,* DETR, February 1998. See, also, PPGN 13 on transport.

25 Review of Pt L of the building regulations on energy efficiency.

26 See below, Chapter 8.

- sustainable development when planning permission is sought.
- energy efficiency best practice programme.

Thus, the Government has set out how it will meet the challenges faced by climate change,[27] but are the policies already in place adequate to ensure that, in the long term, the climate change programme is sustainable?[28] The two main areas of concern are in relation to the production of energy[29] and transport.

Energy efficiency

The abolition of the Department of Energy in 1992, with its supply functions going to the Department of Trade and Industry and the Department of the Environment, Transport and the Regions (DETR) having responsibility for the efficient use of energy, means that in the past there has been no co-ordinated national plan for energy.

However, a number of pieces of legislation[30] have been passed that set down measures that can be taken to improve energy efficiency. This includes the Home Energy Conservation Act 1995. This Act requires local authorities with housing responsibilities to prepare and publish an Energy Conservation Report, which is submitted to the Secretary of State. The Report sets out the local authorities' energy conservation measures. The Secretary of State has to make a report to Parliament. The first report was made in 1998.[31] Guidance for energy conservation authorities was published as DOE Circular 2/96 and set down the 30% base line for improvements. Further guidance notes were issued (155) on energy efficient refurbishment of existing housing. Section 15 of the Energy Conservation Act 1996[32] allows advice to be given on energy conservation measures.[33] There are a number of bodies that can provide information on energy efficiency, including:

---

27 House of Commons Select Committee on Environmental Audit, Second Report, *Climate Change: Government Response and Follow Up*, 12 February 1999, HC 88.

28 See *Climate Crises Special Issue* (1999) 29(2) The Ecologist; 'Power to save the planet – is it possible to have an eco-friendly energy industry?' (1998) New Statesmen special supplement, 25 September.

29 House of Commons Trade and Industry Select Committee, *Report on Energy*, June 1998.

30 IPPC now includes energy efficiency in the Pollution Prevention and Control Act 1999; see below, Chapter 7.

31 For a review of how energy conservation authorities have implemented the Home Energy Conservation Act, see *Implementation of the Home Energy Conservation Act*, September 1999. See, also, the Home Energy Conservation Act Report to Parliament April 1999.

32 Energy Conservation Act 1996; DOE Circular 5/97.

33 Guidance was set out in Circulars 2/96, covering the Home Energy Conservation Act 1995; 5/97, on the Energy Conservation Act 1996.

- Energy Efficiency Advisory Service for local authorities;[34]
- Energy Saving Trust;
- Energy Efficiency Best Practice Programme;
- Home Energy Efficiency Scheme.[35]
- Energy Efficiency Standards of Performance.

Energy conservation[36] is also central to the Government meeting the targets for climate change and energy efficiency. It has been considered in the Climate Change consultation paper (1998) and the Response to Consultations and Technical Support paper (1998) on energy efficiency in the domestic sector.[37]

Renewable energy[38]

Whilst energy efficiency is the most important target in relation to preventing pollution, it of course does not wholly solve the problem. Some energy has to be produced. That energy should be produced in the least polluting way.

Thus, there is a need to develop renewable energy supplies. The Government has committed itself to renewable energy and wishes to achieve 10% of electricity generation from renewable energy by 2010.[39] At present, only 2% of the UK's energy comes from renewables.[40]

There are a number of technologies that can be used to provide renewable energy. These include:[41]

- tidal barrages;
- wind power;
- wave and tidal power;
- coal fired combined heat and power stations;
- geothermal power.

---

34 Discussion document, *Energy Efficiency and Local Wellbeing – a Corporate Priority for Local Authorities*, DETR, 1998.

35 See the Home Energy Efficiency Scheme Regulations 2000 (SI 2000/1280).

36 House of Commons Select Committee on Environmental Audit, *Energy Efficiency*, Seventh Report, 22 July 1999, HC 159; House of Commons Environmental Audit Committee 1998–99, *Energy Efficiency*, 30 March 1999, HC 159.

37 See, eg, the Energy Information (Lamps) Regulations 1999 (SI 1999/1517); Energy Information (Dishwashers) Regulations 1999 (SI 1999/1676).

38 See the Budget 1999 and the proposed energy tax and EC energy tax.

39 See DETR press release 509/ENV 1999.

40 See *New and Renewable Energy: Prospects for the 21st Century*, DETR, March 1999.

41 See Flood, 1983.

The review of new and renewable sources of energy and the non fossil fuel obligation began in 1997.[42] However, the Government published its consultation paper, *New and Renewable Energy – Prospects for the 21st Century* in March 1999 and the *Conclusions to the Report* were published in February 2000.[43]

Planning

The Government published guidance on preparing regional sustainable development frameworks[44] to supplement the guidance in PPG 22.[45] It has stated that planning was important in relation to renewable energy. The Government's regional offices are preparing regional assessments and targets for renewable energy provisions. The frameworks will work alongside regional planning guidance and regional development agencies' economic strategies; these will be set out in the revised Planning Policy Guidance Note (PPG) 11 on regional planning. In relation to buildings, there has been a review of Pt L of the Building Regulations.[46]

However, all forms of energy production have some impact on the environment. In relation to barrages, these will need planning permission and will probably be subject to an inquiry. This is because there are concerns about the environmental impacts on wildlife and countryside by interrupting the natural tidal cycle of the estuaries.

Wind farms need planning permission. There has been much concern over the Government's plans for more wind farms. Wind power at present only makes up 1% of current energy from 700 turbines;[47] this is because wind power developers need to seek the windiest sites, which are also likely to be the most environmentally sensitive.[48] There is a concern that development will impair the countryside in sensitive locations.[49] Local authorities, when deciding whether to grant planning permission, have to take account of both the immediate impacts of renewable energy projects on the local environment and their wider contribution to reducing emissions of greenhouse gases.

---

42   See, also, Council Decision 93/500 on renewable energy.

43   House of Lords Select Committee on the European Union, First Report, *Electricity from Renewables*,17 December 1999, HC 18; House of Lords Select Committee on the European Union, 12th Report, *Electricity from Renewables*, 7 July 1999, HL 78.

44   The DETR published *Guidance on Preparing Regional Sustainable Development Frameworks* on 2 February 2000.

45   See DETR press release 161, 6 March 2000.

46   See below, Chapter 7.

47   *Op cit*, fn 43.

48   Cooper, 1998, pp 432–37; *Hove BC and Adur DC v Appis* (1995) JPL 868.

49   Eg, the Marine Conservation Society: while it supported renewables, it wished that the marine environment be protected; see (2000) 4(8) Marine Conservation.

In 1998, the Government launched a drive to encourage more communities to change to combined heat and power.[50] It encouraged combined heat and power through the publication of a *Good Practice Guide to Community Heating* in May 1998 (Guide 234). This was published under the DETR's Energy Efficiency Best Practice Programme, which requires that the technology is up to date and that plants are operated at maximum temperatures to ensure that there is no air pollution.[51]

Conventional sources

Traditional energy sources have had a major impact on air quality. Smoke dust and fumes are covered under the air quality regime. However, energy production is important in ensuring that the UK meets its greenhouse gas and acid rain targets. Energy efficiency is obviously central to this strategy.[52]

The main way in which proposed coal, gas and oil burning power stations are controlled is through the planning process, that is, through environmental impact assessments, as well as public inquiries.[53] There are some specific controls, such as under Sched 7 to the Electricity Act 1989: when building power stations, regard must be had to the desirability of preserving flora and fauna, etc. Most of the UK's electricity is still produced through conventional power stations.[54] The Secretary of State for Trade and Industry is responsible for the general supervision of electricity supply under s 3 of the Electricity Act 1989. Under s 1 of the same Act, a Director General of Electricity has been established to regulate the industry and issue licences for the generation of electricity. Section 32 lays down the provision for companies to take some energy from non fossil fuels;[55] this is the non-fossil fuel obligation.[56] It is now possible to buy energy from renewable sources. The Utility Bill,[57] if passed,

---

50 See DETR press release 1998 356/ENV.

51 See below, Chapter 6.

52 See below, Chapter 7.

53 See above, Chapter 3.

54 Cooling waters are subject to water pollution controls. See above, Chapter 4.

55 The Fossil Fuel Levy Act 1998 amends the Electricity Act 1989, s 33.

56 The non-fossil fuel obligation. The Electricity Act 1989 empowers the Secretary of State to require by Order that public electricity suppliers in England and Wales secure a specified amount of generating capacity from non-fossil fuel and for a levy to be raised on electricity customers to meet additional costs involved. Contracts are placed by the Non-Fossil Purchasing Agency on behalf of the Regional Electricity Companies for up to 15 years.

57 The Utilities Bill was introduced on 20 January 2000 a number of policy documents were passed, including *A Fair Deal for Consumers: Modernising the Framework for Utility Regulation*, March 1998; the *Response to Consultation*, July 1998; *Consumer Councils*, September 1998; the *Response*, April 1999; *The Future of Gas and Electricity Regulation*, October 1998; the *Response*, October 1999; the Draft Regulatory and Environmental and Equal Treatment appraisals, October 1999.

will set energy efficiency targets and energy efficiency standards of performance.[58]

Nuclear power[59]

It has often been suggested that the development of nuclear power is a means by which energy can be produced cleanly.[60] However, the use of nuclear power is controversial, as the nuclear fuel cycle raises pollution risks at each level from radioactivity.[61] The history of the nuclear power programme is inextricably linked to nuclear weapons in the UK; this has influenced much of its control and is one of the reasons for the high level of secrecy that permeates this industry.[62]

Only 20% of world power comes from nuclear power stations, Europe has 221 reactors, although no country is planning any new reactors. 30% of the UK's electricity is from nuclear power.[63]

At Windscale, now Sellafield, reprocessing first began in 1952 to extract plutonium from spent fuel to enable the development of a British atomic weapon. A second plant, known as B205, began operations in the early 1960s to reprocess fuel from the first generation of civil nuclear reactors, the magnox reactors. Thorp (Thermal Oxide Reprocessing Plant) is the third reprocessing plant to have been built on the Sellafield site.

There are a number of bodies involved in the control and running of the nuclear industry. The two main Government departments concerned are:

- the DETR – planning permission, transportation, registration of users and waste disposal licences under Radioactive Substances Act, 1960;

- the Ministry for Agriculture, Fisheries and Food (MAFF) – waste disposal licences.

There are also controls over nuclear weapons by the MOD. There are a number of regulatory bodies, including UKAEA.[64] This is concerned primarily with research into the nuclear power programme, especially in

---

58 See *Energy Efficiency Standard of Performance 2000–01*, DETR, 9 March 2000.

59 Tromans and Fitzgerald, 1997; Purdue, 1994, pp 297–349; Millar, 1990 p 65; Guruswamy, 1991, p 209; De La Fayette, 1993, p 31.

60 See Ragner Gerholm, 1998.

61 The international policy in relation to plutonium is increasingly being seen as a liability, as there are increasing and growing international stockpiles due to decommissioning of nuclear weapons and reprocessing capability.

62 See 'The madness of nuclear energy' (1999) 29(7) The Ecologist Special Issue; and Kronick, 1999, pp 135–37. For an alternative view, see the BNFL website at www.bnfl.com/index/htm.

63 Brown, 1999a.

64 See the Atomic Energy Act 1954.

relation to fast breeder reactors. Private bodies include the electricity companies, which have to take a percentage of their energy from British Nuclear Fuels Limited (BNFL), and Amersham International, which carries out radiochemical work in connection with radioactive substances and stable isotopes.

The EU has an unambiguous role in relation to nuclear power: it is committed to develop nuclear power through Euratom. The main controls are in relation to health and safety of workers and prior authorisation is required for producing processing transportation and disposing of nuclear materials.

The Nuclear Installations Inspectorate (NII) was established under s 24 of the Nuclear Installations Act (NIA) 1965, but has the same powers as other Health and Safety Executive (HSE) inspectorates under s 20(2) of the Health and Safety at Work Act 1974. The NII has wide discretion on granting, varying and revoking licences and in relation to the operation of reactors, and does not use formal controls such as Repairs and Prohibition Notices under the HSWA. The NII has 4 branches:

(a) design and construction of reactors;

(b) licensing and regulation of operational reactors;

(c) assessment of future systems;

(d) processing, reprocessing and waste management.

International bodies and action[65]

The main agencies responsible for nuclear energy at the international level are:

• International Commission for Radiological Protection;

• International Atomic Energy Agency;[66]

• EURATOM;

• World Energy Council.

Nuclear installations – licensing[67]

A licensing system was set up in 1959 and is covered by the NIA 1965:

---

65 Nuclear Safeguards, etc, Act 1978, Nuclear Material (Offences) Act 1983; Atomic Energy Act 1989.

66 See Nuclear Safeguards Act 2000 on information and access needed for the Secretary of State to comply with the Additional Protocol on information to be given to the Intentional Atomic Energy Agency. See Cmnd 4282.

67 Nuclear Explosions (Prohibition and Inspection) Act 1998; Radioactive Substances Act 1993, implementing the revised Basic Safety Standards Directive (Euratom 96/29); Transfer of Functions (Nuclear Installation) Order 1999 (SI 1999/2786).

- s 1: site licensing by HSE (N11) for nuclear reactors and plants (there is an exception for the United Kingdom Atomic Energy Authority (UKAEA) and Government departments);

- s 2: UKAEA permit (or MOD permit) for enrichment or extraction plants;

- s 4: allows 'such conditions as may appear to the HSE to be necessary or desirable in the interests of safety';

- s 6: register of sites licensed.

Prior registration to keep and use radioactive material or mobile radioactive apparatus, and prior authorisation to accumulate radioactive waste and to dispose of it at or from premises, is required under the Radioactive Substances Act 1993. Some premises and activities do not need to be registered or authorised, as they are covered by exemptions made under the Act.[68]

Use and transportation of radioactive materials

This is covered by the Radioactive Substances Act 1948, which empowers ministers to make regulations on import, sale and use. The transportation of radioactive materials is also regulated. The Radioactive Substances Act 1960 set up a system of registration of premises with the DETR. Prior approval is required for the import of radioactive materials from EC Member States. Prior approval is required before the trans-frontier shipment of radioactive waste.[69]

Disposal of radioactive waste

The disposal of nuclear waste is one of the most controversial environmental issues generated through the production of nuclear power.[70] The problem of waste and its disposal is that it will not reduce its radioactivity for many half-years.[71]

To discharge waste into the sea, BNFL must apply to the EA and MAFF, which are the joint authorising departments for a licence to discharge liquid wastes.[72] To be granted a discharge authorisation, BNFL has to show that it

---

68 Consultation Paper, *Control and Remediation of Radioactively Contaminated Land*, DETR, February 1998.

69 Radioactive Substances Act 1993 (as amended). Council Directive 92/3/Euratom on the Supervision and Control of Shipments of Radioactive Waste between Member States and Into and Out of the Community; Transfrontier Shipment of Radioactive Waste Regulations 1993 (SI 1993/3031).

70 Royal Commission on Environmental Pollution, Sixth Report, Cmnd 6618, Chapter 8.

71 House of Lords Select Committee on Science and Technology 1998–99, Third Report, *Management of Nuclear Waste*, HL 41, 24 March 1999.

72 *R v HMIP ex p Greenpeace* [1994] 4 All ER 329.

has complied with Government policy on radioactive waste management,[73] which states that any production of radioactive waste has to be justified.[74]

The issue of the possibility of putting nuclear waste into landfill sites has been very controversial.[75] At the moment, it is stored and vitrified at Sellafield. However, it is not feasible to store all the waste indefinitely, due to the half-life of much of the waste, especially high level waste. BNFL stores waste,[76] NIREX was set up by BNFL and UKAEA as a managerial body. It is charged with the responsibility for disposing of low and intermediate level waste. This is a commercial body.[77] However, in the past, public pressure has led to the cancellation of underground storage of nuclear waste outside of Sellafield.[78]

Any authorisation for disposal will be granted by the DETR. The EA grants licences where nuclear material is accumulated for disposal but not at those sites that are licensed. There are provisions for consultation of local authorities, water companies and the EA, unless to do so would be against the interests of national security. There must also be a hearing before any decision is made. However, the adequacy of the public inquiry as a way of determining these issues is questionable. There are also provisions for disposal records to be kept. The main offences relate to unauthorised disposal of radioactive waste or accumulation of such waste with a view to its subsequent disposal; to breaches in the limits or conditions attached to such authorisations; and to failure to comply with the terms of enforcement or prohibition notices.

The Government is in the process of establishing a control regime for radioactively contaminated land under Pt IIA of the Environmental Protection Act 1990. The Act gives the Secretary of State powers to make regulations applying Pt IIA with any modifications to radioactively contaminated land.[79]

---

73 See *Magnox Power Stations: Explanatory Documents and Draft Authorisations*, EA, May 2000. This is part of the public consultation exercise as to whether BNFL should be allowed to dispose of waste.

74 DETR press release 1115, 19 November 1999 announced new limits to certain radioactive discharges at BNFL's Sellafield Site.

75 In 1997, Nirex was refused planning permission for a rock characterisation facility near Sellafield. The Radioactive Waste Management Advisory Committee was set up in 1978 to advise the Government on these issues. The House of Lords Select Committee on Science and Technology looked at the management of radioactive waste between November 1997 and March 1999. The Government response was published in November 1999.

76 Consultation Paper on the *Control and Remediation of Radioactively Contaminated Land*, DETR, February 1998. Criteria for the designation of radioactively contaminated land have been developed for the EA.

77 Nirex, 1982; CPA, 1990; HASWA, 1974.

78 See DETR website on radioactive waste management.

79 See DETR website and the Consultation Paper on the *Control and Remediation of Radioactively Contaminated Land*, DETR, February 1998; see, also, Nuclear Reactors (Environmental Impact Assessment for Decommissioning) Regulations 1999 (SI 1999/2892).

In general, the clean-up costs for nuclear power are enormous. The estimated bill for cleaning up the four main UKAEA sites in Harwell, Dounreay,[80] Winfrith and Sellafield is £7.1 billion, It will take 50 years to dismantle and 250,000 years for the radioactivity to decay.[81]

Enforcement[82]

There have been a number of long standing concerns in relation to the way that the nuclear industry is, and has been, regulated. These include:

- problems in staffing in relation to the NII and the EA;
- zero discharges are an impossibility – therefore, the legislation is not to be interpreted and applied so as to impose such an absolute requirement on licences;
- concern has been expressed about the management of the site at Sellafield. The NII stated that management at Sellafield were responsible for the failures in safety that have occurred at the site. It produced three reports,[83] the first of which looked at safety, and the second at the falsification of data about mixed fuel manufactured at Sellafield for sale to Japan – the Report stated that this had begun as long ago as 1996 and was the result of worker boredom from the tedium of checks. The third report was into the backlog of high level liquid nuclear waste kept in tanks; the NII was concerned that this was not being dealt with properly.[84]

Damage arising from nuclear installations[85]

There are a number of strict liability offences in relation to licenced users of nuclear power sites.[86] However, while the offence is strict liability, if there is

---

80 House of Commons Select Committee on Trade and Industry HC 678, 1998–99, 7 March 2000. *Advice to Ministers on radioactive waste management issues at UKAEA Dounreay.*

81 Brown 1999b, p 6.

82 Radioactive Substances Act 1993; Consultation Paper, *Implementing the revised Basic Safety Standards Directive (Euratom 9629)*, DETR, March 1999. House of Lords Select Committee, *Report on the Management of Nuclear Waste: a New Move to revise the Radioactive Substances Act PR*, 26 March 1999.

83 Nuclear Safety Directorate HSE, HSE Team inspection of the control and supervision of operations at BNFL's Sellafield site An investigation into the falsification of pellet diameter data in the MOX demonstration facility and the effect of this on the Safety of MOX fuel in use.

84 Brown, 2000b.

85 Tromans 1999, pp 59–65 – on *Blue Circle Industries PLC v MOD* [1998] 3 All ER 385.

86 See the Paris Conventions on Third Party Liability in the field of Nuclear Energy, 1960 and 1963; Vienna Convention on Civil Liability for Nuclear Damage 1963. These were applied in UK law by NIA 1965, ss 7–21. Section 7 establishes absolute liability for licensed sites (and s 8 for UKAEA and Government Department sites), subject to limited defences in s 13. See, also, *Merlin v BNFL* [1990] 2 QB 557; 3 All ER 711.

damage to person or property, this must be physical, and not merely economic loss; however, there is no need to prove an escape from the site. Compensation can be reduced through contributory actions. The time limit is 30 years from the occurrence, or 30 years from the last relevant date, if it was a continuing occurrence.

However, there are problems due to the need to prove causation and the time limits, that is, intergenerational problems. Under the Congenital Disabilities Act 1976, if a child is born disabled, due to an injury in breach of the NIA 1965, then the injuries are to be regarded as injuries caused on the same occasion and under the same breach, unless it preceded the child's conception and the parents knew that there was a risk that their child may be born disabled. If there was a large scale release, the funds are also limited. The Government published a National Response Plan to deal with the consequences of overseas nuclear accidents in January 1998 after the Chernobyl accident.[87] European Directive 96/29 lays down safety standards for workers and the public against the dangers of ionising radiation. This is implemented in England by the Radioactive Substances Act 1993, which is in the process of being revised.[88]

ENERGY: THE FUTURE

The Government's White Paper, *Energy Sources for Power Generation,* published in October 1998, set out the broad objective of energy. This includes the following policy developments:

- opportunities for change – prudent use of natural resources, including renewable resources, is one of the key objectives;

- industrial energy efficiency – the use of economic instruments to improve business uses of energy and helps reduce greenhouse gas emissions.

- the climate change levy on business from April 2001, which was announced in March 1999.

- the Government's Foresight Programme identified alternative sustainable energy technologies amongst its key priorities 'where further work was absolutely vital and demanding top priority';

- the Energy Saving Trust (EST) Renewable Energy Accreditation Scheme (REAS), which will ensure that suppliers' green claims are supported by independent auditing and that consumers know the mix of generation used to meet the tariffs they are choosing;

---

87 See DETR website response to radiological emergencies.
88 See Radioactive Substances Act 1993, implementing the revised Basic Safety Standards Directive (Euratom 96/29).

- the Wind Fund was launched in 1995 by Triodos Bank, investing in small hydro and wind generation;
- the Government's White Paper, *Our Competitive Future – Building the Knowledge Driven Economy*, states that the development of sustainable technologies for the future, such as renewables, will be a key feature of a forward looking economy;
- crops grown for MAFF and the Forestry Commission are to be used for energy;
- international policies – the World Bank, Global Environmental Facility and International Finance Corporation has launched a series of aid schemes. These include the Solar Initiative, the Solar Development Corporation and the Market Technology Initiative.

There are a number of proposals for directives and communications from the Commission, as well as a variety of actions that Member States are expected to implement.

Topics covered include:

- fair access for renewables to the electricity market;
- taxation of energy products;
- start-up subsidies for production plants, small and medium sized enterprises, and job creation;
- development/harmonisation of 'green' funds;
- increasing market share of liquid biofuels in transport;
- renewables to be among the main priorities in allocating regional development funds;
- promotion of biomass in the Common Agricultural Policy and rural development policy;
- renewables to feature in work with third countries under the Lomé Convention, and EC support schemes such as PHARE, TACIS and SYNERGY;
- support through the Fifth Framework Research and Technology Development Programme;
- relaxation of competition and State aid rules to favour renewables.[89]

---

89 Council Directive 93/76/EEC to limit carbon dioxide emissions by improving energy efficiency (SAVE) (OJL 237 22.9.93); Council Decision 96/737/EC concerning a programme for the promotion of energy efficiency in the Community (SAVE II) (OJL 335 24.12.96); Council Directive 96/62/EC on ambient air quality assessment and management (OJL 296 21.11.96); Council Decision 98/352/EC concerning a multi-annual programme for the promotion of renewable energy sources in the Community (OJL 159 3.6.98, as amended by OJL 079 30.3.00); Council Resolution on a Community strategy to promote combined heat and power (OJC 004 8.1.98); Council Resolution on energy efficiency in the EC (OJC 394 17.12.98).

The UK will be one of the few countries that will meet its Rio targets.[90] The Government has highlighted energy efficiency measures, including turning off unnecessary lights; only boiling the required amount of water when making drinks; switching off televisions, computers and hi-fis when not using them; and using public transport or walking.[91] However, there is a need for a world solution.[92] It is important to implement the Rio summit's proposals in relation to climate change to which the UK Government has committed itself to reduce carbon dioxide emissions to 1990 levels by the year 2000. In the UK, the aim of the Government is to achieve this target on the switch to gas in electricity production. However, this is unlikely to be enough; there needs to be a large improvement in energy efficiency and a switch to non fossil fuels.

The UK's energy intensity fell by 2.2% between 1973 and 1988; however, much of this was due to the loss of energy intensive industries such as iron and steel. However, further reduction cannot be achieved through market mechanisms alone. Most households' and businesses' energy costs are a relatively small percentage of total costs; the lack of capital in industry and the public sector, as well as in many households, makes it easier to pay fuel bills than to invest in energy saving measures. Responsibility for paying the bills and investment to conserve energy is often separated, as in the landlord/tenant relationship.

There also needs to be a change in the law to ensure that tighter regulations are imposed, with higher fines and better enforcement in relation to private businesses, government owned buildings and local authority property.

Much of the law protecting the environment in relation to energy production is found in planning legislation, for example, the planning inquiries for Sizewell and the Vale of Belvior coalfield, etc.[93] The law needs to ensure that there is an adequate regulatory framework so that the energy sector can be held to account.[94] It is also important that finance is put into renewables; as *The Economist* has put it:

> It is hard to believe that if the cash thrown at nuclear power had been put into almost any other technology – even hamster-powered fly wheels – it would have produced something commercially viable.[95]

---

90 See Spencer, Fossil, Cruch, 1999, pp 125–28; Boyle, 1999, pp 129–32.
91 See 'Are you doing your bit?' campaign.
92 Wysham, 1999, p 108; Kronick, 1999.
93 See above, Chapter 3.
94 A 1991 Report from the European Commission has concluded that energy efficiency is not only the most effective way of reducing carbon dioxide emissions but would serve many national or Community objectives in addition to minimising the risk of global warming (*Cost Effectiveness Analysis of Carbon Dioxide Education Options – Synthesis Report*).
95 (1991) *The Economist*, 31 August.

There is no doubt that current patterns of energy production are unsustainable. *The Economist* summarised the situation thus:

> Using energy in today's ways leads to more environmental damage than any other peaceful human activity (except perhaps for reproduction). From deforestation to urban smog, from acid rain to airborne lead, from valleys flooded for hydroelectric schemes to rivers polluted with coal mining waste, from Chernobyl to the Exxon Valdez: all are consequences of the production or consumption of energy.[96]

Transport[97]

Transport[98] and energy production is central to developing an effective air pollution strategy.[99] The Government's transport strategy is set down in *A New Deal for Transport*[100] – *Better for Everyone*[101, 102] which highlights the importance, particularly of road transport, to climate change, in that 'emissions of carbon dioxide from road transport are the fastest growing contributor to climate change'.[103] Car use is expected to rise by one-third, and van and lorry traffic will increase more quickly.[104]

The Report sets out the following aims:

- new local transport plans, which will provide integrated strategies;
- local targets will be set for improving air quality,[105] road safety, public transport and road traffic reduction;

---

96 (1991) *The Economist*, 31 August.

97 See 'Can Prescott steer us through a transport revolution?' (1998) New Statesmen Special Supplement, 22 May.

98 Each year, the Government publishes the Bulletin of Transport Statistics at a national and regional level. The 1999 report stated that the number of passenger journeys by rail increased by 5% in the UK during 1998–99 to 1.9 billion. Local bus passenger journeys decreased by 1% in England as a whole, although in some regions, such as the South East (excluding London), they increased by 6%. Domestic air travel increased by 45%. The 2000 edition, published on 30 March 2000 looked at transport in an ageing society and in relation to school journeys.

99 The Government's strategy for an integrated transport policy was set out in the White Paper, *A New Deal for Transport: Better for Everyone*, Cm 3950 in July 1998.

100 House of Commons Select Committee on Environment Transport and Regional Affairs 1997–98, *Integrated Transport White Paper*, HC 1141, 18 November 1998.

101 House of Commons Select Committee on Environment, Transport and Regional Affairs Session 1998–99, Third Special Report, 13 July 1999.

102 See, *A New Deal for Trunk Roads*, July 1998; *Breaking the Log Jam: the Government's consultation paper on fighting congestion and pollution through road user and work place parking charges*.

103 *Ibid*, p 11, para 1.8.

104 See the National Travel Survey, July 1999, Focus on Public Transport: Great Britain, 1999 edn.

105 *Driving the Agenda: the First Report of the Cleaner Vehicles Taskforce*, DETR, July 1999; Motor Vehicles (Type Approval of Reduced Pollution Adaptations) Regulations 1998 (SI 1998/3093).

- more certainty of funding;
- greater use of traffic management;[106]
- new powers for road user charging and levies on parking;
- new sources of funding for local transport;
- tackling pinch points in transport networks that lead to congestion;
- a new airports policy and a stronger role for regional airports;
- a new deal for the motorist, which includes better management of the road network, better information and more efficient cars;
- to encourage cycling[107] and walking;[108]
- better and cleaner buses, with quicker, more reliable services, special funding for buses on the countryside, concessionary fares for elderly people and better bus contracts;
- better trains through the proposed strategic rail authority,[109] and new passenger dividends from passenger railway companies;[110]
- tougher regulation;
- better interchanges and networks;
- a cleaner vehicles taskforce;[111]
- better safety and personal security, including a review of speed policy and traffic management, calming and reduction;
- strengthening the interrelationship between planning and transport.

The report also looks at freight and shipping.[112]

Agencies

There are a number of agencies concerned with transport, including the following:

106 See Highways (Assessment of Environmental Effects) Regulations 1999 (SI 1999/369); Highways (Road Bumps) Regulations 1999 (SI 1999/1025); Highways (Traffic Calming) Regulations 1999 (SI 1999/1026).
107 See *National Cycling Strategy: Second Report*, DETR, May 1999; *Promoting Cycling: Improving Health*, DETR, April 1999; *Safety Framework for Cycling*, DETR, April 1999. The Traffic Advisory Unit also produces traffic advisory leaflets.
108 *Walking in Great Britain*, DETR, 1999.
109 House of Commons Select Committee on Environment, Transport and Regional Affairs 1998–99, 21st Report, *Railways Bill*, 10 Nov 1999, HC 837.
110 *A New Deal for the Railways*, July 1998, Cm 4024.
111 Motor Vehicles (Type Approval of Reduced Pollution Adaptation) Regulations 1998 (SI 1998/3093); Vehicle Excise Duty (Reduced Pollution) Regulations 1998 (SI 1998/3094); Vehicle Excise and Regulation Act 1994, as amended by the Finance Act 1998.
112 *Sustainable Distribution – a Strategy*, DETR, March 1999.

- the Highways Authority is responsible for roads;
- Traffic Commissioners,[113] who are responsible for the licensing of operators, goods and public service vehicles and the registration of local bus services. They also have a disciplinary role in relation to holders of entitlements to drive goods or passenger carrying vehicles, such as buses and coaches;[114]
- the Commission for Integrated Transport;
- the Strategic Rail Authority.[115]
- local authorities, which deal with traffic reduction, road charging and planning.

Emissions

In the UK, emissions from motor vehicles are regulated under the Environment Act 1995. Vehicles must be properly maintained so that they do not discharge noxious fumes or particles into the atmosphere and must meet statutory emission standards. It is an offence to use a vehicle that emits such substances as oil, which are likely to cause damage to any property or injury or danger to other road users. It is also an offence to cause unnecessary emissions by leaving a vehicle's engine running unnecessarily whilst stationary. It is an offence to operate a vehicle that emits avoidable smoke or other visible vapour.

The EC[116] is also negotiating agreements with the car manufacturers on improving fuel efficiency and the fuel economy labelling scheme. Other areas which the EC is drawing up legislation on include the sulphur content of liquid fuels and other measures relating to car use, including a Council Agreement Position on auto oil vehicle emissions and fuel quality directives. This sets stringent emission standards for cars and light vans, to apply to all new cars sold from 1 January 2001 (known as Euro III standards) and 1 January 2006 (Euro IV standards). There are also tighter fuel specifications that have applied to all petrol and diesel powered vehicles since 1 January 2000 and further ones that will apply from 1 January 2005. There has also been a general ban on the marketing of lead petrol from 1 January 2000. New emission standards for heavy duty diesel engines have also been set out in a

---

113 The Commission for Integrated Transport has published *Work Programme National Road Traffic Targets: Guidance on Provisional Local Transport Plans*.

114 Traffic Commissioners Annual Reports October 1999.

115 Bulletin of Rail Statistics, February 1999; see, generally, the Railways Act 1993.

116 See Council Directive 77/306/EEC on the measures to be taken to avoid the emission of pollutants from diesel engines for use in vehicles.

Directive.[117] There are proposals to look at methane emissions, the ambient air quality standards and incineration of non-hazardous waste and minimum energy efficiency requirements for industrial equipment.

Aircraft emissions are regulated by the Civil Aviation Authority under the Civil Aviation Act 1982 and are increasingly seen as a problem in relation to climate change gases.[118] Between 1986 and 1996, the number of aircraft using Britain's airports increased by 55%.[119] In *A New Deal For Transport – Better for Everyone*, the Government will publish an airports policy which will cover the next 30 years and encourage the growth in regional airports to meet local demand, where it is consistent with sustainable development principles.[120]

Traffic reduction

The Road Traffic Reduction (National Targets) Act 1998 sets out the requirements for a national road traffic reduction target. Under s 2 of the Act, the Government has to provide a report.[121] The 2000 Report states that 'we should focus our targets on the outcomes we want to achieve, rather than crude national traffic volume figures. It analyses the effect of *A New Deal for Transport* and concludes that:

> ... even if the measures in *A New Deal for Transport* are applied very intensively, national forward traffic levels would still be well above 1996 levels in 10 years' time. Our present judgment is that reducing national road traffic to below 1996 levels is unlikely to be achievable.

The Government is concentrating on outcomes such as reducing congestion and pollution, including air quality and greenhouse gas emission,[122] health and road safety, and the effects on land and biodiversity.[123]

---

117 Commission proposal – COM (1998) 348 Final proposal for a Council Decision establishing scheme to monitor the average specific emissions of carbon dioxide from new passenger cars as amended by Com (2000) 044.

118 See Friends of the Earth, *Report on Pollution from Air Transport*, 2000; *Aviation and Global Climate Change*, published by Friends of the Earth, the Aviation Environment Federation, the National Society for Clean Air and Environmental Protection and HACAN/Clear Skies. This Report states that the world's 16,000 commercial jet aircraft produce more than 600 million tonnes of carbon dioxide every year. Friends of the Earth want people to take more holidays near home.

119 DETR Transport Statistics Great Britain 1997, Table 7.1a.

120 Commission proposal – Proposal for a Council Directive on the Limitation of the Emission of Oxides of Nitrogen from Civil Subsonic Jet Aeroplanes COM (1997) 629 Final.

121 See DETR, *Tackling Congestion and Pollution – The Government's First Report under the Road Traffic Reduction (National Targets) Act* 1998, January 2000.

122 The Report states that 23% of carbon dioxide emissions are from transport, in particular road traffic. It outlines some of the measures taken, including the graduation of fuel excise duty for cars and the reform of company car taxation.

123 See Snape, 1999, pp 95–124.

The Road Traffic Reduction Act 1997 requires local authorities to provide reports relating to the levels of road traffic in their area, forecasts of growth, and targets for the reduction. Local transport plans have to be drawn up every five years by local authorities.[124] Road traffic reduction targets should be set, unless the local authority can explain why such targets are not appropriate. The Transport Bill 2000[125] gives local authorities new powers to improve local bus services. It also requires local authorities to prepare five year plans to improve local transport, putting the plans on a statutory basis. Local authorities will also be able to introduce road charges or levies on parking at the workplace to tackle congestion and pollution. There must be local consultation first and the revenue must be used to improve local transport. The Bill will also require local authorities to offer half price concessionary fares or better for pensioners.

However, for there to be any real improvement, there needs to be a fundamental shift in attitude towards car use and road building.[126] Under the Highways Act 1980,[127] the creation, improvement and maintenance of roads is required by the SOSETR, the Highway Agency or the county council.[128] Under s 10(2) of the Act, the minister is under a duty to review the national road scheme.[129]

The issues of congestion[130] and driving into city centres has been examined in *Breaking the Logjam: Charging Policy – A Consultation Paper on Implementing Road User Charging and Workplace Parking Charges* (DETR, December 1998) and *Breaking the Logjam: The Government's Response to Consultation* (22 February 2000). These looked at how workplace parking levies and road user charging could be developed. Local authorities will implement the proposals as part of the Local Transport Plan and the money will be ring-fenced for improving local transport. However, before the

---

124 Guidance for local authorities on local plans was given by the Government in *Guidance on Producing Local Plans*, April 1999. This included a specific requirement that the local authorities should address the problem of climate change.

125 This contains measures to set up a strategic rail authority to ensure better regulation and some co-ordination to provide a national rail service between the fragmented rail companies.

126 See Tyme, 1978.

127 New Roads and Street Works Act 1991.

128 *What Role for Trunk Roads in England?* Consultation Paper, RTRDA, 1997.

129 See, generally, the Highways Act 1980, which covers the main provisions on road building. See, also, the Road Traffic Act 1991 and the Road Traffic (Regulation) Act 1984, which allows for the development of priority routes; National Audit Office Report, *Department of Transport: Environmental Factors in Road Planning and Design*, HMSO, 1994. See Highways (Inquires Procedure) Rules 1994 (SI 1994/3263); Transport and Works Act 1992 for improved procedures in relation to major projects. On environmental impact assessments, See PPG13; s 54A of the Town and Country Planning Act 1990 on traffic reduction policies. See, also, *A New Deal for Trunk Roads*, DETR, August 1998.

130 See *Tackling Congestion and Pollution The Government's First Report under the Road Traffic Reduction (National Targets) Act 1998*, January 2000.

schemes are approved, the local authorities will have to provide well thought out plans for spending the proceeds. Public transport must be improved to offer motorists a choice, the technology must be in place to make sure that the schemes work and there must be consultation; local authorities may also be able to charge on trunk roads.

Planning[131]

Many of the decisions in relation to roads and development are governed by the planning process.[132] PPG 13 (Transport) was published in March 1994. The aim of the guidance note was to integrate land use planning and transport policies. A number of studies have looked at the effectiveness of the guidance note, the first in 1994–96, and the most recent one was commissioned in 1997 and published in January 1999. PPG 13 is at present being revised. It provides guidance to ensure that local authorities carry out land use polices and transport programmes in a way that will reduce the time and length of motorised journeys and encourage alternative means of travel. The revised PPG 13 will strengthen policy integration at a local, national and regional level. Regional planning guidance will also consider public transport issues. Under s 331 of the Highways Act 1980, roads need planning permission for their construction/modification.[133] For many public transport proposals, planning inquiries are held into road projects, such as at Twyford Down and Newbury, or for the expansion of airports, such as at Manchester,[134] all of which were very controversial.[135] Environmental impact assessments are often needed; indeed, they are compulsory for airports and major road projects. There are also provisions for the compulsory purchase of land.[136] Roads can be made subject to traffic regulation orders in areas of sensitivity, for example, national parks, under s 22 of the Public Transport Regulation Act 1984.

The future

Car use has grown enormously: 'Between 1952–86, car use, in terms of distance travelled, has risen over 10 times; and whereas in 1952 cars accounted for 27% of distance travelled, this had risen to 86% in 1996'.

---

131 See Brearley, 1999, pp 408–15.

132 See PPG13.

133 See Town and Country Planning Act 1990, ss 294, 55(2)(b) for the exceptions to this.

134 See Airports Act 1986, s 57.

135 Public inquiries can be held under the Highways (Inquiries) Procedures Rules 1994 (SI 1994/3263).

136 There are also powers of compulsory purchase under ss 41 and 44 of the Civil Aviation Act 1982.

Therefore, in relation to long term planning, the Government is also drawing up a 10 year transport plan which is being led by the Integrated Transport Taskforce and the Minister for Transport. The plan will look at roads, local transport and what investment is needed for transport of both passenger and freight[137] and access to ports and airports.[138] The plan will endeavour to deliver broad outcomes, rather than listing projects.[139] It is central to the strategy to develop proper public transport and the Government has issued a number of consultation documents.[140]

The EU Action Plans on Transport suggest that the following measures should be taken:[141]

- new national and local strategies for reducing levels of road transport growth;
- prompting more use of public transport;
- promoting better environmental performance of vehicles by reducing fuel consumption, emissions and noise;
- developing a comprehensive set of indicators of the sustainability of transport;
- promoting awareness campaigns of the environmental impact of transport and assessing the potential for greener vehicles;
- receiving reports from the Commission and further meetings of the Joint Council.

Alternative Traffic in Towns (ALTER) is a Europe-wide initiative to give greener vehicles special exclusive rights to city centres. Athens, Stockholm, Oxford, Barcelona, Florence and Lisbon are implementing the scheme.[142] Under it, any participating city will:

- renew their own public transport and services on a low or zero emission basis;
- only allow vehicles that meet stringent emission standards into sensitive parts of towns and cities.

The need for all of these policy documents to come together is shown by the surveys[143] undertaken to monitor transport trends.[144] They state that:

137 *Sustainable Distribution: a Strategy* Fright policy, March 1999.
138 Air transport will be looked at in a White Paper and shipping was covered *in British Shipping – Charting a New Course*, DETR, December 1998.
139 See DETR Ten Year Transport Plan (Explanatory Note), 8 March 2000.
140 In a *New Deal for Railways*, Policy: a Response to the Third Report of the Environment, Transport and Regional Affairs Committee.
141 See DETR press release 484/ENV, 18 June 1998.
142 See DETR press release 320, 26 April 1998.
143 Focus on Personal Travel is the successor to the National Transport Survey.
144 Focus on Public Transport Great Britain 1998 and Encouraging Walking – Advice to Local Authorities, 28 March 2000. DETR press release 349, 11 May 2000.

- only 9% of journeys are made by public transport;
- one-quarter of all car journeys made are of less than two miles;
- we each travel on average 6,666 miles a year;
- whilst car use is increasing, walking and bus use is decreasing;
- rail use is constant;[145]
- taxi and minicab use has increased;
- for long journeys in the UK the domestic air service is increasing;
- the proportion of people travelling to work by car increased from 68–71% from 1993–97 and 87% of households in Great Britain live within six minutes of a bus stop.[146]

It is hoped that the Roads Review will not lead to a large scale road building programme. In the end, it seems that the UK still has some way to got before it can be said to have developed a truly effective and sustainable transport system.

The ozone layer[147]

It was not until 1974 that scientists put forward the theory that CFCs may damage the ozone layer.[148] In 1985, the British Antarctic Survey reported a hole in the ozone layer over Antarctica and, in 1985, the Vienna Convention was signed. This Convention incorporated Principle 21 of the Stockholm Declaration 1972 and provided a framework for international co-operation in the research of and agreement on measures for the protection of the ozone layer. The Convention was a framework document, requiring action by the member parties, but 1985 had achieved little in relation to the problem of the ozone layer. In 1987, the Montreal Convention was signed. This led to the Montreal Protocol in 1989, which required the development of alternatives to CFCs, technology transfers and international funding for technology development by 2000.

The 1987 Montreal Convention imposed a series of controls on the production and consumption of ozone depleting substances which should lead to a 50% reduction in the production and consumption of CFCs by the year 2000 and a cap on the production and consumption of halons. These were implemented into European legislation through Decision 88/540/EEC and Regulation 3093/94. In June 1990, the second meeting of the parties agreed to

---

145 Bulletin of Rail Statistics – DOE press release 455/98.

146 Se DETR press release 962, 12 November 1998.

147 See Bunyard, 1999, p 85.

148 See Lean, G, 'Where did all the fresh air go?' (1995) *The Independent on Sunday*, 5 March, p 5.

phase out CFCs, halons and carbon tetrachloride by 2000 and 1,1,1 trichloroethane by 2005. A financial mechanism was also set up to help developing countries. In March 1991, EC Regulation 594/91 came into force, which phases out the use of CFCs within the EC by 1997. In June 1991, the second meeting of the parties to the Vienna Convention and the third meeting of the parties to the Montreal Protocol met. The Montreal Protocol was implemented through EC Regulation 3093/94.[149] The European Commission adopted, on 1 July 1998, proposals for a new Regulation that will tighten the existing controls on ozone depleting substances.[150] The new Regulation will, if agreed, prohibit the use of CFCs from the date that the Regulation comes into force, except for use in air conditioning and refrigeration equipment, which will be allowed until 31 December 2000; the use of halons in non critical fire protection systems after 31 December 2002; and the use of 1,1,1 trichloroethane and carbon tetrachloride from the date that the Regulation comes into force.[151]

In the UK, the Government has been implementing policies though Regulations 1994/1997 and 1996/506, Ozone Monitoring and Information Regulations. The Environmental Protection (Controls on Substances that Deplete the Ozone Layer) Regulations 1996 (SI 1996/506) impose restrictions on the supply of other ozone depleting substances and controls the use of HCFCs. It also requires that all precautionary measures be taken to prevent leakage of ozone depleting substances, such as aerosols, refrigeration[152] and air conditioning systems. These Regulations provide powers to enforce provisions of EC Regulation 3093/94, as they relate to HCFCs and leakage of controlled substances, and are enforced by the HSE and local authorities.[153]

Acid rain

Acid rain is controlled at an EC level through Directive 80/779/EEC, which established annual and winter limit values and guide values for sulphur

149 Council Regulation 3093/94/EC on substances that deplete the ozone layer (OJL 333 22.12.94).

150 A proposal on substances that deplete the ozone layer currently before the Commission will amend Regulation 3093/94 to bring EU legislation into line with the latest changes to the provisions of the Montreal Protocol which took place in 1995 and 1997. The changes include the following: phasing-out of methyl bromide by the year 2010; phasing out HCFCs by 2020 with derogations for old equipment (these were previously to be phased out by 2030); phasing out CFCs in developing countries by 2010.

151 COM (1985) 106 final recommendation for a council decision concerning the signature of a global framework convention on the protection of the ozone layer and COM (1998) 398 final proposal for a council regulation on substances that deplete the ozone layer as amended by Com (1999) 067.

152 Environmental Protection (Non-Refillable Refrigerant Containers) Regulations 1994 (SI 1994/1999); Environmental Protection Act 1990, ss 33, 34.

153 DETR's *Towards More Sustainable Construction*, s 31 gives details of alternatives to halons. See DETR website on greening Government.

dioxide and suspended particulates in the atmosphere. In 1997, an acidification strategy was proposed. This would reduce emissions of sulphur dioxide, nitrogen oxides and ammonia and thus reduce the area in Europe at risk from acid rain from 6.5% on the basis of existing commitments to 3.3% by 2010. This was agreed in 1997 and has been implemented through the Directive on the Sulphur Content of Certain Liquid Fuels, which sets limits on the sulphur content of heavy fuel oil of 1% from 2003 and gas oil 0.1% from 2008. An amendment was made to the EC Large Combustion Plant Directive, which will further reduce emissions of SOx and NOx and particulates. In the UK, this was implemented through the Sulphur Dioxide National Plan. The National Emissions Ceiling Directive and Daughter Directive (Ozone) is in the process of being agreed in the EC. The EC Solvents Directive aims to reduce VOCs from certain industrial installations by around 57% by 2007, compared with a 1990 baseline.

Transboundary air pollution

In 1958, the Geneva Agreement was signed. This was updated by the 1979 Geneva Convention on Long Range Transboundary Pollution. The aim of the Convention is to protect human health and the environment by monitoring, and gradually reducing, air pollution, with particular reference to transboundary air pollution by sulphur dioxide. Information goes to the UNEP Global Environmental Monitoring Service (GEMS). This has been implemented in the EC through EC Regulation 94/63.In relation to monitoring information, Council Decision 97/101/EC established a reciprocal exchange of information and data from networks and individual stations measuring ambient air pollution within the Member States.[154]

Other controls

These include Directive 85/203/EEC on nitrogen dioxide and Directive 87/217/EEC on asbestos. COM (96) 538 (amended in June 1998) aims to reduce by 53% VOC emissions from 1990 levels by 2001.[155] Sectors affected would include the printing, textile, pharmaceutical, vegetable oil, wood impregnating and coating industries. In relation to indoor air, most people spend 90% of their time indoors and 60% of their time at home. In the light of

---

154 Council Directive 85/203 EEC (OJL 087 27.3.85) amended OJL 163 29.6.99 on air quality standards for nitrogen dioxide; Council Decision 86/277/EEC on the conclusion of the Protocol to the 1979 Convention on long range transboundary air pollution on the long term financing of the co-operative programme for monitoring and evaluating the long range transmission of air pollutants in Europe (OJL 181 4.7.86).

155 See the Solvents Directive, which aims to reduce emissions of VOCs by 57% as compared to a 1990 baseline by 2007.

this, the Government has developed an indoor pollution strategy to reduce levels by 2003, through guidance provided in leaflets. The HSE sets limit for occupational exposure.[156]

GENERAL AIR QUALITY[157]

Air Quality Directive[158]

Council Directive 96/62/EC on ambient air quality assessment and management is a framework Directive which has as its main aim the establishment of air quality limits to avoid, prevent or reduce harmful effects on human health and the environment. The Directive sets objectives for ambient air quality and a timetable within which the Commission must present proposals on limit values and alarm thresholds for each pollution list. European limit values aimed at the protection of vegetation and ecosystems have been agreed for oxides of nitrogen and sulphur dioxide. The UK Government proposes to introduce these limit values as additional obligations in the National Air Quality Strategy. This will also include particulates and lead. Forthcoming air quality directives include one on ozone, which again may cover the protection of vegetation and ecosystems, as well as directives on poly-aromatic hydrocarbons, cadmium, arsenic, nickel and mercury.[159]

In June 1998, at Aarhus in Denmark, two new protocols were signed. The first, aimed at preventing persistent organic pollutants, set up procedures for tightening the existing controls and for identifying and controlling other pollutants with similar properties.[160] The second, on heavy metals, provides emissions limits for cadmium, lead and mercury and allows for other metals to be added later, if international action is needed.

---

156 There are also proposals for a National Emissions Ceiling Directive, which would set limits for sulphur dioxide, nitrogen oxides, VOCs and ammonia.

157 Commission Proposal (COM 1998 591 final) proposal for a Council Directive relating to limit values for benzene and carbon monoxide in ambient air; Commission Proposal (COM 1999 125 final) proposal for a Directive of the EP and Council on national emission ceiling for certain atmospheric pollutants and ozone in ambient air; Council Decision 97/101/EC establishing exchange of information and data measuring ambient air pollution within the Member States (OJL 035 5.2.97). See Miller, 1997, pp 303–20.

158 See Lefevre, 1997, pp 10–14.

159 The Aarhus Convention's Protocol on POPs, signed in 1998, aims to control, reduce or eliminate discharges, emissions and looses of 16 POPs to the environment. The Heavy Metals Protocol, also signed in 1998, covers emissions to the air of cadmium lead and mercury. The protocols will come into force once all the Member States have ratified them. The Aarhus Convention has two new protocols on persistent organic pollutants and heavy metals in the atmosphere.

160 See DETR press release 521, 24 June 1998.

The Clean Air Act 1993

This Act covers dark smoke controls to all trade and industrial premises, and not just chimneys. It includes: chimneys (s 14);[161] furnaces (s 1); railway locomotives (s 43); vessels in harbour (s 44); and smoke from trade premises (s 2). There are certain exemptions under the Act, as well as time limits. There are also defences of lighting of a coal furnace; mechanical failure; unavoidable use of unsuitable fuel; and any combination of the above. There is also a defence if there is an inadvertent release and the operator took all practicable steps to avert it. The Act also introduced smoke control areas and standards for chimney heights under s 18.

In smoke control areas, it is an offence to emit smoke from the chimney of premises or to burn an unauthorised fuel. If smoke is emitted which is judged to be a statutory nuisance, a local authority must serve an abatement notice. An individual may also apply to the magistrates' court for an abatement order. Failure to comply with a notice or order is an offence. There is a right of appeal against both. It is enforced by the local council and EA. There may also be issues of air pollution from the burning of illegal deposits of waste.[162]

The Air Quality (England) Regulations 2000 (SI 2000/928)

These were made in 1989 and updated in 1997 under Pt IV of the Environment Act 95 and were recently updated in 2000. They impose mandatory air quality standards to ensure that levels of sulphur dioxide, lead and smoke do not rise above EC limits and set up a system of sampling stations to measure air quality.

The UK signed a new agreement to combat air pollution across Europe in December 1999. This Protocol aims to reduce levels of ground level ozone, acidification and other Ecosystem damage through proposed emission level reductions, namely, a reduction of sulphur dioxide, VOCs, ammonia and nitrogen oxides, with a ceiling for reducing national emissions by 2010. The Protocol was signed under the UN Economic Commission for Europe's Convention on Long Range Transboundary Air Pollution, which is designed to reduce the four atmospheric pollutants stated above by the year 2010.

National air strategy

The UK National Air Quality Strategy was published in March 1997 under s 82 of the Environment Act 1995. The strategy set out policies for the

---

161 The Smoke Control Areas (Exempted Fireplaces) Order 1999 (SI 1999/1515).

162 See, also, below, Chapter 6, in relation to the burning of material and the waste provisions.

management of ambient air quality, with a target date of 2005. Objectives have been set for eight major pollutants: lead; benzene; particles; nitrogen dioxide; sulphur dioxide; 1,3 butadiene; carbon monoxide; and ground level ozone. There are two main levels for the pollutants: an alert threshold, which is reached when air quality is so poor that an immediate response would be justified to prevent serious damage to health or the environment; and the guideline level, which is seen as a long term goal. There are a number of other bodies with advisory functions, including the Expert Panel on Air Quality Standards, which consists of independent experts who make recommendations on air quality standards to the Government; the Quality of Urban Air Review Group; and the National Environmental Technology Centre. At present, the National Air Strategy is being revised. This will take into account proposals by the Expert Panel on Air Quality,[163] including a recommendation for lower levels of lead in air. The Strategy was amended in January 2000.[164]

The Advisory Expert Panel on Air Quality Standards is a scientific body, set up to advise the Government to recommend air quality standards for the UK for the purposes of developing air pollution strategy and increasing public knowledge and understanding of air quality, taking into account the best available evidence of air pollution on human health and the wider environment, and of the progressive development of the air quality monitoring network. Its recommendations have been incorporated into standards in the UK National Air Quality Strategy, which was set out in 1997 on objectives to be achieved by 2005. Under Pt IV of the Environment Act 1995, the objectives for each pollutant (except ozone) have been given statutory status in the Air Quality (England) Regulations 2000 (SI 2000/928).[165] Under the local air quality management legislation in the Act local authorities are under a duty to review air quality periodically. Within this area, action plans have to be drawn up and a more detailed assessment of air quality undertaken within 12 months. This covers the eight pollutants in the national air strategy, except ozone, because it was felt that concentrations of ozone are heavily influenced by transboundary pollutants and, therefore, it was inappropriate to require local authorities to take steps locally.[166]

---

163 This body was reviewed in 1998: see DETR press release 96/ENV, 12 February 1998.

164 See *Air Quality Strategy for England, Scotland, Wales and Northern Ireland*, DETR, January 2000, Cmnd 4548.

165 The Air Quality (England) Regulations 2000 (SI 2000/928) under Pt IV of the Environment Act 1995 review the quality of air within their area during the relevant period laid down by regulation; an assessment has to be undertaken as to whether any prescribed air quality standards or objectives are being, or are likely to be, achieved within the relevant period.

166 See *Report on the Review of the National Air Quality Strategy Proposals to Amend the Strategy*, DETR, 11 January 1999, para 11.

Part I of the EPA 1990[167]

This provides for area pollution control (APC) that broadly follows the regulations. Best Practicable Environmental Option (BPEO) does not apply to APC and the HSE has only to be notified under APC. APC guidance notes are drawn up centrally by the DETR. Registers are provided for under ss 20–22. If there is an overlap between the two systems, the EA is the regulator. Local authorities are the regulators for smaller polluting processes emitting to air only.[168] The Environment Agency is responsible for regulating the potentially most polluting processes and processes emitting to more than one medium. Local authorities are under a duty to regulate air pollution from approximately 13,000 factories under Pt I of the EPA 1990; these factories are regulated through authorisation, which must contain conditions aimed at minimising pollution using the best available technique not entailing excessive cost. This is known as the local APC regime. In 1998, the Government published an action plan to improve the inspection and enforcement of industrial air pollution legislation. The plan aims to ensure a more consistent approach to the inspection of air pollution across the country; to encourage local authorities to sign up to the Cabinet Office's Enforcement Concordat; to monitor centrally local authority action; to undertake four year reviews of authorisations; to provide a local management guide for local authorities; to help compliance by metal and plastic coating enterprises; and to consolidate local authority networking on local air pollution control issues.[169]

Emissions from industrial plants

These are subject to integrated pollution control under the EPA 1990; Pt A by local authorities and Pt B by the EA.[170] If there is an overlap, the EA can take control. There are also directives aimed specifically at large combustion plants, including the Large Combustion Plant Directive (88/609/EEC). This Directive was reviewed in 1998[171] and is implemented through Pt 1, s 3(5) of the EPA 1990.

---

167 As amended by the Pollution Prevention and Control Act 1999.

168 There are a number of air quality guidance notes: Local Air Quality Measurement (LAQM) G1 G2 G3 and G4, all issued in 1997 on the framework for review and assessment of air quality, developing local air quality strategies and action plans.

169 See DETR press release 836, 13 October 1998 on an action plan that was developed to improve the inspection and enforcement of air pollution legislation.

170 For the new IPPC regime, see below, Chapter 7.

171 Commission Proposal (COM 1998 415 final) for a Council Directive amending Directive 88/609/EEC on the limitation of certain pollutants into the air from large combustion plants, as amended by Com 1999 611 final). Council Directive 88/609/EEC on the limitation of emissions of certain pollutants into the air from large combustion plants (OJL 336 7.12.88, as amended by OJL 337 24.12.94).

Incineration[172]

Council Directives 89/369/EEC and 89/429/EEC regulate air emissions from new and existing municipal waste incineration plants. These two Directives came into force in December 1990. Directive 94/67 on the Incineration of Hazardous Waste was passed into law in December 1994. This Directive has as its goal the minimisation of emissions resulting from the incineration of hazardous waste that might be detrimental to human health and the environment. The Directive sets stringent licensing, technical, design and operational criteria for all hazardous waste plants and facilities. Existing facilities will be required to upgrade to meet the new standards.

Land use planning

In December 1997, guidance was issued to local authorities on air quality and land use planning.[173] This stated that air quality considerations on the use and development of land are capable of being a material planning condition and that local authorities are expected to have regard to the national air quality objectives when preparing development plans. Local authorities should also consider the impact of development in relation to both its operational characteristics and its transport implications.

Common law controls

Traditionally, air pollution problems have been controlled under the common law through nuisance actions. Whilst nuisance has been considered above, Chapter 2, it is particularly relevant in the control of air pollution problems. The statutory control of nuisance is found in the EPA 1990. The local authority is under a duty to inspect their areas for statutory nuisances (s 79) and to act upon complaints. If an individual complains, the council is under a duty to investigate; however, the council only has to take such steps as are reasonably practicable when investigating the complaint. In particular, the following provisions are relevant to APC: smoke emitted from premises has to be prejudicial to health or a nuisance (s 79(1)(b)) – this can include dust, steam and odours. Machinery must be operated such that noxious fumes and particulates are not released to the atmosphere (Pt III of the EPA 1990, as amended). Failure to comply with the special control is an offence. If smoke fumes, grit or dust are emitted, a local authority may serve an abatement notice. A person aggrieved by the fumes may apply to the magistrates' court for such a notice. Failure to comply with the notice is an offence.

---

172 See, also, below, Chapter 6 on the regulation of waste.
173 See LAQM G4(97).

The general control of statutory nuisance is contained in s 80. Where a local authority is satisfied that a statutory nuisance exists, or is likely to recur, it is under a mandatory duty to serve an abatement notice on the person responsible for the nuisance, or, if they cannot be found, on the owner or occupier of the premises. If the notice is contravened with no reasonable cause, then the person is guilty of an offence. The notice can be served either on the person, or it can be left at their proper address or sent by post. There is the right of appeal from the serving of an abatement notice to a magistrates' court, which lies within 21 days of serving the notice.

Individuals can also bring an action themselves under s 82 of the Act so long as the nuisance is in existence. The local authority can also get an injunction to stop the nuisance, for instance, if they feel that proceedings brought under an offence of contravening an abatement notice would not provide an adequate remedy. This is a discretionary remedy and the activity complained of must be of sufficient gravity/duration to justify stopping it. There are certain defences, including reasonable excuse/BPM. Under statutory nuisance, this will be conclusive; however, in a private nuisance case, the fact that BPM has been followed is one of the factors to be weighed against the others. If air pollution is properly controlled under APC, the Secretary of State's consent is needed before an action can be brought under statutory nuisance. However, it is not a prohibition.

The future

In the Royal Commission on Environmental Pollution's 20th Report, *Transport and the Environment – Developments Since 1994* (Cmnd 3752, 1997), the Commission raised concern that action on transport had been 'too little and too slow'. *A New Deal for Transport* laid out a number of initiatives to deal with the problem. However, if the new forms of pollution are to be dealt with effectively, there must be more investment in public transport, less use of aircraft, more energy efficiency statutory targets and tough statutory targets for renewable energy. The EC has committed itself to a target of reducing carbon dioxide by 8% and the UK will meet its target. But, internationally,[174] the will is not there, particularly from the large emitters such as the US. The UK Round Table on Sustainable Development stated that setting targets for reducing the pace of climate change and cutting traffic pollution should be the priority of the UK. The Chair of the Royal Commission on Environmental Pollution argues that the 20% goal is not enough: the UK should aim for a 60% target and energy prices should be raised to encourage energy efficiency.[175]

---

174 See Brown, 2000c, p 7.
175 *Ibid*, p 10.

Climate change and air pollution problems need international solutions if we are really to have the power to save the planet.

AIR POLLUTION TECHNOLOGY

Incineration

Incineration is a process used in several industries, and it inevitably produces a certain amount of pollution. Incineration of coal and other fossil fuels provides the basis for the electricity generation industry: many industrial processes require burning, and it is a method of disposal of waste. The incineration of certain types of waste (for example, hospital waste) has been practised for many years, while the incineration of municipal solid waste, and wastewater sludge, have developed more recently.

The level of pollution will depend on what is being burned, the incineration process itself, the cleaning processes and the chimney height.

Chimneys

Raising the level of emissions to allow for greater dispersion has been used for some centuries as a method of controlling the impact of the pollution. It does not reduce the amount of pollution emitted. However, it does disperse this over a greater distance, and the idea is that this should reduce the pollutant concentrations to a level at which they do not cause significant problems. In many ways, this approach is successful, although problems with long range transport of pollutants, particularly acid pollutants such as sulphur oxides (SOx) and oxides of nitrogen (NOx), which combine with water to form sulphuric and nitric acid respectively, have been created.

Raising the level of pollutants above ground level allows for both dispersion and reduction, as reactions occur in the atmosphere before the pollutants reach the ground. The question that then occurs is one of chimney design.

A fundamental question is that of height. The method for calculating the required chimney height depends on the fuel. For 'conventional' fuels such as coal and oil, the height is calculated using methods specified in HMSO's Memorandum on Chimney Heights (3rd edn, 1981). It is based on the requirement to keep sulphur dioxide concentration at ground level to an acceptable limit, because, historically, sulphur dioxide has been regarded as one of the worst pollutants. For other fuels, or other unusual conditions, an alternative guidance note, Technical Guidance Note (Dispersion) D1,

Guidelines on Discharge Stack Heights for Polluting Emissions (HMSO, 1993) has been produced. Both publications specify methods of calculating the required height based on emissions and local buildings.

There is also a requirement to ensure that the emissions from a chimney rise above the chimney. If the efflux velocity is too low, then the emissions can cling to the chimney and fall down to the ground. Wind passing the chimney will leave an area of low pressure in its wake, and the efflux velocity must be sufficient to overcome the tendency to move towards this region of low pressure. This principle is similar to that of a milk bottle: if one does not tip the bottle far enough, the milk will cling to the bottle and drip off its base. Additionally, if the efflux velocity is too low, then the surrounding (cold) air may enter the chimney. This would mix with the hot air and cool it, thereby reducing its efflux velocity further. Historically, this was not a great problem, as the heat of the air was usually enough to send the emissions upwards. However, this is less true in modern chimneys, which often contain several devices for cleaning the emissions, each of which removes heat from the air flow. This problem can be overcome by the use of forced draught systems, which may be in the form of a fan or post-heating the air after it has been through the cleaning systems.

Tall buildings near to a chimney can also cause a downdraught, and chimney height is adjusted to take account of the surrounding buildings.

Many chimneys serve several boilers. If a chimney is designed for, say, four boilers, and only three are in use (due to maintenance, lack of demand, failure or some other reason), then the efflux velocity will reduce. To overcome this problem, most chimneys contain one flue for each boiler, so that the efflux velocity remains the same in each operating flue.

The design of a chimney itself is subject to both physical and planning constraints. Physically, the chimney must withstand high temperatures, internal loading, corrosion and the wind. For a tall chimney, the wind loading can be considerable. In earthquake regions, earthquake forces must also be accounted for. The traditional material for chimneys is brick, but many chimneys are now built of steel, which is generally the most economic material for higher chimneys. The outer shell of the multiple flue chimney will withstand the loading. Many chimneys can be observed to have a spiral band up their length, which helps to maintain their structural integrity. Additionally, it will be beneficial in maintaining an immediate upward flow of air around the chimney.

Planning considerations may be problematic, as air emissions have a bad press and can be an emotive subject with the public. Recent planning applications for incinerators have had considerable opposition from local residents. There is no way of making a chimney unobtrusive. One solution is to 'cover up' the chimney with an architecturally more pleasant surround. However, this can add to the problems of low pressure around the chimney, and is thought to contribute to plume grounding (the emissions falling to the ground) in some cases. Post-heating of the emissions immediately before release can be useful here; if the gases are not cool enough to condense, then they will be less visible. There is also a problem with too high an efflux velocity; although useful in other respects, too high a velocity can lead to noise. The noise of air whistling out of a chimney can be annoying.

Incinerator design and operation

Careful design and operation of an incinerator can reduce emissions significantly. Choice of fuel is one consideration and much has been done over the past 20 or so years to reduce pollution from chimneys simply by using less coal and more gas and oil. This approach, however, has its problems; there is a limited supply of any fossil fuel.

There are four vital components to the burner itself. These are as follows:

(a) adequate oxygen;

(b) temperature control;

(c) turbulence;

(d) time of residence.

Combustion requires oxygen, so it will not take place completely without adequate oxygen. This will mean that the burner is not operating at its maximum efficiency (thus increasing emissions) and unburnt hydrocarbons will escape into the exhaust stream. Additionally, combustion in conditions of low oxygen means that carbon monoxide is produced, rather than carbon dioxide.

Temperature control is necessary in order to destroy pollutants. In particular, dioxins (which are known to be carcinogens in rats, and thought to be carcinogens in humans) are destroyed above 850°C. They are formed at temperatures of 250–400°C, if there is chlorine present. This means that they are most likely to be formed in waste incinerators. They can also be reformed in the same temperature range, after combustion. Hence, the incinerator gases need to be rapidly cooled, to minimise dioxin reformation.

Formation of NOx occurs at high temperatures, either from the nitrogen and oxygen in the atmosphere, or from atmospheric oxygen combining with nitrogen in the fuel. Low oxygen in the burning process would limit NOx emissions, but, as seen earlier, low oxygen causes other problems. One solution to this is to use a two stage burner. The first, high temperature burner has a low oxygen concentration, while a second burner, operated at a lower temperature to minimise NOx formation, has a higher level of oxygen to ensure complete combustion and to convert carbon monoxide to carbon dioxide.

Further control of emissions takes place through the use of 'end of pipe' solutions, cleaning the air flow on its way from the boiler to the chimney. The exhaust air will contain both gases and particulates. Particulates are generally measured in terms of PM 10, which are those particles which would pass through a sieve with holes of diameter 10 microns. Other PMs are also in use: PM 20 includes larger particles, of up to 20 microns in diameter, while PM 2.5 (up to 2.5 microns in diameter) is thought to be the size of particles which cause the greatest health problems.

Particulates are generally collected in cyclones, filters or electrostatic precipitators (ESPs). Cyclones consist of a cylinder, into which the air enters tangentially. Particles go to the side of the cylinder under centrifugal force and collect together to form larger particles, which slide down the cylinder wall into a collecting bucket. These are relatively cheap to install and run, and work well on large particles. They are less effective on smaller, less heavy particles.

The ESP consists of a series of metal plates and wires. The wires are charged with a high voltage, while the plates are earthed. The air flows past the wires, which give the particles a charge which then attracts them to the earthed ESP plate. The plate is rapped at regular intervals to remove caked particles, which then fall into hoppers below. An ESP can collect particles which are rather smaller than those collected by a cyclone, and is reasonably efficient at dealing with particles as small as 5 microns in diameter.

Filters act by preventing particles from going through them. They may either have very small holes in the filter, or work by filtering through the caked material. It is expensive to make filters with very small holes, and so most filters work by allowing a certain build up of particles, which themselves reduce the size of hole (or tunnel) for particulates to travel. Filters are generally long and thin and are grouped together in a formation known as a baghouse. Usually, the flow is inwards, through the individual filters, so that the particles remain on the outside of the bags. They clean by blowing jets of air back out through the filter.

Gases can be removed in a rather similar way, by adsorption. This is a mass transfer process in which the gas is bonded to a solid. It is a surface phenomenon. The gas (adsorbate) penetrates into the pores of the solid (adsorbent) but not into the lattice itself. The bond may be either physical or chemical. Physical bonding is by electrostatic forces, whereas chemical bonding is by reaction with the surface. Pressure vessels, having a fixed bed, are used to hold the adsorbent.

Common adsorbents are activated carbon, molecular sieves, silica gel and activated aluminium. The common property of these adsorbents is a large active surface area per unit volume after treatment. They are very effective for hydrocarbon pollutants. In addition, they capture hydrogen sulphide (H_2S) and sulphur dioxide (SO_2). With the exception of the activated carbons, adsorbents have the drawback that they preferentially select water before any of the pollutants. Thus, water must be removed from the gas before it is treated. All adsorbents are subject to destruction at moderately high temperatures (150°C for activated carbon, 600°C for molecular sieves, 400°C for silica gel and 500°C for activated aluminium).

Scrubbers are use for the removal of acid gases. The principle is that an alkaline material (usually limestone, as it is relatively cheap and available) comes into contact with the acid gases in the exhaust. There are three basic ways in which this can be achieved: dry scrubbing is one option, which basically consists of adding limestone to the boiler. This is the least efficient of the options. The other two options are wet and semi-dry scrubbing. A wet scrubber is a tower packed with limestone, through which water flows. Air flows in the opposite direction. The air, therefore, comes into contact with the alkaline water, and sulphur dioxide in the exhaust gas will combine with the limestone in the water (and atmospheric oxygen) to form calcium sulphate and carbon dioxide. Thus, the sulphur dioxide (and other acid gases) are removed from the airstream. One problem with this method is the resultant waste water, which needs to be treated. The alternative is to use the semi-dry method, which is basically similar but involves less water. The quantity of water used is such that the water will evaporate when it comes into contact with the hot gases. Of the three methods, the dry is the least efficient, while the wet process is the most efficient.

Other methods are available for treatment of waste gases, but they are more specialised. It is worth noting that methods for treating waste gases will also remove some particulates, while gases may be trapped with particulates in cyclones, filters and ESPs.

Air pollution monitors

Legal controls on emissions are of no use unless they can be policed. This requires methods for testing the pollutants. Monitors within flues need to ensure isokinetic sampling. The monitor itself is liable to distort the air flow, leading to the air flow being either too fast or too slow, which would give an untrue reading of the concentration of particulates.

Particulate sampling can be done by any of the collection methods. A measured volume of air passes through either a filter or a cyclone, and the amount of particulates is measured. Continuous monitoring of particulates is possible by using either a tape with small filters, which passes over the air flow like an old fashioned film reel, or by a device known as a TEOM (tapered element oscillating microbalance). This is a tapered cylinder with a filter mounted on its top. It is vibrated at its natural frequency, and this frequency is continuously recorded. The air passes through the device, leaving particulates on the filter at the top. This alters the mass of the top, which then alters the natural frequency of vibration. Thus, the particulate concentration is related to the rate of change of the natural frequency of vibration.

Gas sampling methods depend on the gas. There are a variety of methods, related to the characteristics of the particular gas in question.

One method which can detect a variety of gases is differential optical absorption spectroscopy. This is a 'long path' instrument which measures the amount of various substances along a path between a light source and a receiver. This makes it more representative than a standard 'point' sample. Being a spectroscopic method, it also allows for simultaneous measurement of several pollutants such as sulphur dioxide, nitrogen dioxide, ozone, toluene, benzene and formaldehyde. A typical system is as follows:

light source   ⟶   receiver   ⟶   spectrometer

The light source is a high pressure xenon lamp, which generates light of wavelengths 200–2000 nm.

The path for the light is typically 300–800 m long. The receiver collects the light, sending it via a fibreoptic cable to the analyser. The analyser uses a grating to defract the light into its different wavelengths. The detector measures the amount of light received in a chosen part of the spectrum, relevant to the particular substance.

Nitrogen dioxide can be measured by use of diffusion tubes. Molecules of a gas diffuse from high to low concentrations. Stainless steel discs coated with triethanolamine (a good absorber of nitrogen dioxide) are held in the closed end of a diffusion tube. A tube is placed in the sample area for two to four weeks, then sealed and sent to the laboratory for analysis. The discs are reacted with sulphanilamide and N-(1-naphthyl)-ethylenediamine dihydrochloride. Together, these form a dye with the nitrogen dioxide, and the colouration can be measured either visually or in a spectrophotometer to determine the nitrogen dioxide concentration in the air. The tubes are small (less than 10 cm long) and require no source of power.

Sulphur dioxide is measured using the principle of ultraviolet (UV) fluorescence. A narrow beam of UV light is shone onto the sample. The sulphur dioxide absorbs the UV light, some of which is then emitted as fluorescence. A photomultiplier tube is placed at right angles to the UV light source, so that it gets no direct light, but only light from the fluorescence. This is then related to the sulphur dioxide concentration. A drechsel bottle can be used to measure sulphur dioxide. This bottle will contain a specified concentration of hydrogen peroxide, which rapidly reacts with sulphur dioxide to form sulphuric acid. The resulting amount of sulphuric acid can be measured by titration – titrating with an alkaline solution of sodium tetraborate to a given pH value.

Monitors for carbon monoxide measure the absorption of electromagnetic radiation in the infra-red band of the spectrum. Infra-red radiation is passed through two tubes, one containing the air for analysis. Carbon monoxide will absorb the energy from this radiation and, hence, the amount remaining for heating a sample beyond the tube will be reduced. A diaphragm separates the receiving samples, and this will be distended by the difference in heat in each receiving sample. The amount by which this diaphragm is distended is proportional to the carbon monoxide concentration.

Hydrogen chloride and hydrogen fluoride can be measured by adding the sample to a liquid in which the gas dissolves, and measuring the resulting ion concentration in the solution.

Stratospheric ozone is measured in Dobson units. The instruments (spectrometers) measure the ratio of radiation intensities at two wavelengths, one in the UV-A range (little absorption by ozone), and one in the UV-B range (partly absorbed by ozone). Ozone levels at the South Pole have been monitored since 1961. Despite its importance in shielding us from UV-B radiation, the amount of ozone in the stratosphere is very small. It if were collected into one layer around the world, that layer would have a thickness of only 3 mm. Three is a small number to deal with, so it has been multiplied by 100 to give sensible units for measuring ozone loss. These are known as Dobson units.

Ozone soundings are also taken regularly over the Antarctic by using electrochemical concentration cell (ECC) ozonesondes. The ozonesonde consists of a small piston pump which bubbles ambient air into a cell containing a 2% iodide solution. The current generated by the cell reaction is proportional to the incoming ozone. These are sent up in balloons and take readings until they get to the height at which the balloon bursts. They also record temperature, pressure and humidity, and transmit the data to the receiving station.

Lichens are extremely sensitive to air pollution, and so provide useful biotic indicators of pollution. It is noted that some lichens are almost totally absent from large industrial urban areas.

Control of greenhouse gases

One of the major debates of the times is that of global warming. There is evidence to suggest that temperatures are increasing globally due to the 'enhanced greenhouse effect' caused by humankind. However, the evidence is not conclusive, and it may be that the activities of humans since the Industrial Revolution are not leading to a significant raising of the global temperature. The question remains as to whether action should be taken to reduce greenhouse gas emissions on limited evidence. However the consequences of failing to take action, if the greenhouse effect is causing significant warming, may be catastrophic.

The major greenhouse gases are:

- carbon dioxide (CO_2);
- methane (CH_4);
- nitrous oxide (N_2O);
- ozone (O_3);
- CFCs;
- water vapour

If there was no atmosphere (and, hence, no greenhouse effect), the earth would be at a temperature of about $-18°C$.

Solar energy is mainly in the visible part of the spectrum, which is logical, as our eyes have evolved to make use of the available energy. These visible wavelengths (0.4–0.7 mm) pass through the earth's atmosphere virtually unchanged. Common molecules do not trap energy at these wavelengths. Some are reflected back into space.

The wavelength of this radiation (known as black body radiation) is determined by the temperature of the body giving it off. The sun's temperature is about 6,000 K. As the warmth from the sun heats the earth's surface, the earth also gives off radiation. But the earth is at a lower temperature (about $15°C = 288$ K). At this temperature, the radiation peaks at higher wavelengths (4–100 mm). At these wavelengths, the greenhouse gases can trap some of the outgoing energy. Water vapour absorbs in the range 4–7 mm. Carbon dioxide absorbs in the range 13–19 mm. The window between 7 and 13 mm allows about 70% of the radiation from the earth's surface to escape into space. However, this 'window' is being lost, as other absorbing gases have an effect.

The trapped radiation warms the troposphere. In turn, this warmed air radiates (mainly in the infra-red) in all directions. Some goes up and out, while some goes back into heating the surface again.

This has been known about for a long time. Fourier suggested the existence of a greenhouse effect in 1827, and in 1863 Tyndall published a paper on water as a greenhouse gas. In the 1890s, Arrhenius and Chamberlain both considered the problems which may be caused by a build up of carbon dioxide from coal burning.

In the early 20th century, temperatures rose slightly ($0.25°C$ between 1880 and 1940). However, between 1940 and 1970, there was a worldwide cooling of $0.2°C$. Researchers began to take measurements of carbon dioxide at Mauna Loa (Hawaii) and at the South Pole during International Geophysical Year 1957. Those sites were chosen because they are far from sources of pollution and hence represent 'well mixed' atmosphere. They show seasonal changes, in line with the activity of vegetation in the Northern Hemisphere (there is more land there than in the Southern Hemisphere). However, superimposed on these seasonal changes is a clear upward trend. Studies of bubbles of air trapped in the Antarctic ice show a similar trend. An ice core at Siple (Antarctica) shows carbon dioxide levels rising steadily from about 280 ppm in 1800 to above 350 ppm in recent years. Other cores show that the concentration had remained fairly constant, at about 280 ppm for the past 10,000 years or so. The 'background' level is generally taken to be 270 ppm.

Between 1850 and 1950, about 60 Gt of carbon were burnt, mainly as coal. The same amount is now being burnt every decade. The observed increase in carbon dioxide in the atmosphere corresponds to about half of the amount we know to be produced. The rest must therefore go to carbon sinks, such as vegetation (which will use excess carbon dioxide to grow more vigorously), land and the ocean. Water contains dissolved carbon dioxide and, as concentrations increase in the atmosphere, more will move across the air/water boundary.

Carbon dioxide dominates the debate because there is more of it in the atmosphere. However, on a molecule for molecule basis, it is not the 'worst' greenhouse gas. The effect of the various gases has been analysed, and the concept of *global warming potential* (GWP) has been developed. The GWP of a greenhouse gas is the ratio of global warming from one kilogram of a greenhouse gas to one kilogram of carbon dioxide over a period of time. The IPCC-recommended time is 100 years. On this basis, the following GWPs are found:

Gas	GWP
carbon dioxide	1
methane	32
nitrous oxide	150
ozone	2,000
HFCs	140–11,700
CFCs	15,500
carbon tetrafluoride	6,500
sulphur hexafluoride	23,000

Photochemical contributors, which include NOx and VOCs, are not included in this, because it is difficult to know how to measure them – they contribute only indirectly by the creation of ozone under sunlight.

This needs to be put into context of the relative amounts emitted. The relative effects of the various greenhouse gases, taking into account the GWP and actual emissions, is calculated to be approximately:

Gas	Relative contribution (%)
carbon dioxide	50
methane	20
nitrous oxide	5
ozone	10
CFCs	15

This does not include some of the minor contributors. Note that HFCs will take over the position of CFCs as the manufacture of CFCs reduces dramatically according to the Montreal Protocol to protect the stratospheric ozone layer. However, CFCs have a long lifetime in the atmosphere, and their concentration is reducing only slowly.

There is considerable dispute over whether the world is indeed warming, and whether any warming is due to the greenhouse effect. Global mean temperatures can be measured at ground level or in the atmosphere. Surface average temperatures do, indeed, seem to be rising, by about 0.5°C since the early part of the 20th century. This could in part be due to urban heating influences, as more people either heat or cool their homes and places of work and travel by vehicles, which give off heat. Atmospheric temperature measurements do not show the same overall mean rise.

The 1980s was the warmest decade on record, containing seven of the eight warmest years up to 1990. The coldest year of the 1980s was warmer then the warmest year of the 1880s. However, the trend reversed in the early 1990s. Mount Pinatubo in the Philippines erupted in June 1991, throwing an enormous amount of debris into the atmosphere. This shielded the earth from part of the sun's radiation, thus causing cooling for a couple of years. However, 1995 nearly equalled the 'warmth' record set by 1990. There is speculation that global warming is contributing to volcanic activity.

The 'aerosol effect' of volcanic activity is similar to that of coal burning, and it is thought that this effect has dampened the degree of global warming. Thus, global warming has increased as clean air legislation has increased, reducing the number of particulates in the atmosphere.

The IPCC projects that global temperatures will rise by between 1°C and 3.5°C, with 2°C being the 'best estimate'. The 'best' warming rate is predicted at 0.2°C per decade. This is about 50 times faster than the warming which brought an end to the most recent Ice Age.

One effect of global warming is likely to be a rise in sea level. This is caused by both the thermal expansion of the warmer water and the inflow of melted glaciers and/or ice caps which are currently over land. Sea level rose by about 15 cm during the 20th century. A global temperature increase of 2°C would increase the sea level by a further 30 cm. This may not seem to be a large amount, but it could cause devastation to low-lying areas such as Bangladesh.

Other effects include changes in habitats for various species of flora and fauna. Within the UK, this could lead to possible agriculture changes, including vine growing in the North, but it is also likely to bring with it pests such as the anopheles mosquito, which can carry malaria.

On a global scale, widespread desertification is likely, together with an increase in severe weather, such as droughts, floods and hurricanes. Longer dry periods, coupled with heavy storms, are likely to make water supply more difficult.

Some calculations suggest that the Antarctic ice sheet might collapse (probably over several hundred years) if the temperature increases by 4°C. There is evidence (in the form of large cracks in outlying parts of the ice sheet) that this could be beginning. If the entire ice sheet melted, the sea level could rise by about 70 m.

Although various ingenious technological fixes to global warming (such as pumping carbon dioxide to the ocean depths) have been suggested, none have so far been even approaching workability. Control of global warming is therefore a matter of controlling emissions.

Carbon dioxide is an inevitable consequence of both combustion and respiration. Without anthropogenic influence, the carbon dioxide emitted in respiration is balanced by that used by plants in photosynthesis. Ways of controlling carbon dioxide emissions include the following:

- increase efficiency of combustion (thus causing fewer wasted emissions);
- use of catalysts, which allow the combustion process to occur at lower temperature and hence less energy is required for input;
- use of renewable energy sources;
- use of new technology such as computer and video conferencing, which reduce the need for travel;
- good building design, making use of shade in hot weather to reduce the need for air conditioning, and insulation to reduce the need for heating in cold weather.

The other method suggested for controlling carbon dioxide levels in the atmosphere is that of forestation. In the short term, growing new forests will use excess carbon dioxide. However, in the long term, the forests will reach a state of equilibrium. There is scope for good forestry here, as certain trees use more carbon dioxide than others, and young trees use more than old trees.

Methane is produced by decomposition under anaerobic conditions. Hence, any anaerobic situation is liable to produce methane. The major sources of methane are animals, such as cows, which chew cud; insects, such as termites, which eat wood; landfill sites; rice paddy fields; and marshland. It is difficult to control animals, termites and mice, although a change in eating habits could control emissions of the latter.

Methane from landfill sites can be captured and used, and this is being done increasingly. A network of pipes links the site to an electricity generator, or boiler, to make use of the methane. If this is not possible, particularly during the early years of a site, when the gas contains a high proportion of acidic gases, or during its final year when the concentration reduces, then the methane can be flared. The combustion of methane produces one molecule of carbon dioxide for one molecule of methane. Consideration of the GWPs of each, means flaring reduces the greenhouse effect by a factor of 21.

Reservoirs that flood land that was previously under cultivation can produce methane. This is evidenced by Furnas Dam in Brazil, which suffered from an explosion in its intake tunnel. It is thought that methane production will continue for up to 100 years after the dam was built. Removing vegetation before flooding a reservoir could reduce this source of methane.

CFC concentrations are reducing (albeit slowly) because of the Montreal Protocol's aim of protecting the stratospheric ozone layer. However, in terms of the greenhouse effect, the problem is getting worse, because CFCs are generally being replaced by HFCs. These are less harmful to the ozone layer but have a greater GWP. Alternative substances are needed to reduce this problem.

Tropospheric ozone concentrations depend to a large extent on VOCs, NOx and other photochemical precursors. Traffic control is largely the answer to this.

VOCs and the control of photochemical smog

VOCs (volatile organic compounds) are generally subdivided into methane (CH_4) and others, known as non-methane VOCs (NMVOCs). Methane is associated with global effects such as global warming and background ozone production, while NMVOCs are associated with more local effects. Most VOCs are non toxic, but some, such as benzene and 1,3-butadienne are carcinogens. The major environmental impact is the formation of tropospheric ozone through the action of sunlight (photochemical oxidation). All VOCs contribute to ozone formation, but in differing amounts. This is quantified by their photochemical ozone creation potential (POCP). For example:

VOC	POCP
methane	0.7
ethane	4.0
ethylene	100.0
benzene	18.9

High ozone concentrations can lead to chest constriction and irritation of the mucous membrane. Eye, nose and throat irritation can occur, as well as headaches. Children and young adults can suffer pulmonary deficiency at concentrations in the range 80–150 ppb. Ozone also damages rubber products (such as tyres), and causes damage to vegetation.

In addition, VOCs contribute to the formation of other compounds such as peroxyacetyl nitrate (PAN), which is an eye irritant.

The major source of emissions is transport, leading to high urban concentrations. However, the photochemical process is slow, so that ozone can be generated some distance from the VOC emission source. The situation can be worse in rural areas because nitrogen oxide levels, which are generally higher in urban areas, 'mop up' ozone.

Control of photochemical smog is difficult, as it is dependent on weather conditions and is caused by emissions from dispersed sources. Catalytic converters do reduce the emissions, but the major control is the reduction of vehicles when weather conditions are favourable to smog formation. Thus, control depends mostly on transport policy.

Use of catalysts

Catalytic converters are best known in cars, although the same principles can be applied to a variety of emissions. Catalytic converters in petrol engined cars reduce emissions of NOx, carbon monoxide and hydrocarbons. The converter itself consists of a box containing a honeycomb structure, plated with metals such as platinum, palladium (which assist in the removal of carbon monoxideand hydrocarbons by oxidation) and rhodium (which assists in the reduction of NOx). The honeycomb structure of the converter allows the air to come into contact with a large surface area, which increases the probability of any particular molecule of gas coming into contact with the catalyst and, hence, converting. The surface area of the honeycomb is approximately the same as that of a football pitch.

The efficiency of the catalytic converter in removing the pollutant depends critically upon the air:fuel ratio. Efficient removal of all three pollutants requires an air:fuel ratio close to 15:1. A sensor (known as a lambda probe) is generally used in the exhaust stream to provide a feedback mechanism to the engine to ensure that this air:fuel ratio is maintained.

The use of catalytic converters has also led to the removal of lead from petrol, as lead in the petrol will poison the catalyst. Thus, as a by-product of the advent of catalytic converters, lead emissions have been reduced.

Unfortunately, the same is not true of other emissions. In particular, the use of catalytic converters increases carbon dioxide emissions, for two reasons. First, its use reduces slightly the overall efficiency of the engine; and, secondly, the carbon monoxide is converted to carbon dioxide. It is also worth noting that the converter does not work while cold, so emissions are high when a car starts.

SICK BUILDING SYNDROME

Can buildings actually make people ill? This is a question posed by many people, yet no definitive answer can as yet be given. Some experts believe that this so called 'illness' is all psychological and can be caused by dissatisfaction amongst employees (Barnett, 1995). Curell (1993) argues that there is no such thing as a sick building, just sick people. For every one argument against the case of sick building syndrome (SBS), numerous counter-arguments can be found.

SBS is recognised by the World Health Organisation (WHO) as 'a syndrome of complaints covering non-specific feelings of malaise, the onset of which is associated with occupancy of certain modern buildings' (Wilson *et al*, 1987). A syndrome is defined as 'a collection of signs and symptoms fitting a recognisable pattern' (WHO, 1983). Symptoms characterising SBS are commonplace in the general population, but it is the pattern of their expression that points to the diagnosis of SBS.

Here, it is important to note that some authors (and studies) speak of building related illnesses (BRI). BRI is distinctly separate from SBS. SBS is when occupants display symptoms that disappear shortly after they leave the building. Conversely, Singh believes, BRI includes sicknesses such as Legionnaire's Disease, which may be contracted as a direct result of entering a building, but may continue to have an effect after the sufferer has vacated the building. Goldman (1996) also differentiates between SBS and BRI. For him, SBS is where the occupants of a building are affected over an indefinite period, and is directly connected with the building itself. BRI, however, refers to a pathological condition, harmful not only to the regular, everyday occupants, but also to visitors and passers by. Goldman also believes that the symptoms characterising SBS, first noted in the 1950s, appeared to be correlated with the development of post-War, energy efficient, airtight buildings, at a time where the architects main brief was to keep costs low.

Although variations of the words used to characterise the phenomenon do exist, there is a clear consistency in the way in which the syndrome is being described. We will hereon accept SBS to be a phenomenon whereby people experience a range of symptoms for a few hours after leaving the building, yet are relieved of these symptoms after then (Raw, 1992). The terms 'SBS' should be restricted to multi-factorial problems, where no single cause factor exceeds the level of generally accepted recommendations (Potter, 1988).

In more recent years, SBS has emerged as a significant problem in the workplace, with it not only being restricted to the UK, but present in most European countries, North America, Australia and Japan.

Within and between nations, there is a recognisable variation in the phrase used to describe the phenomenon, for example, building sickness, sick office syndrome, tight building syndrome, office eye syndrome, etc, with non truly and accurately fitting the condition. But SBS has been accorded recognition by the WHO (1982) and is therefore the most widely used and accepted definition (Raw, 1992).

It should be noted that SBS is most often, but not exclusively, spoken of as being present in places of work, for example, office buildings, and occupants of naturally ventilated buildings, in general, appear to experience a lower prevalence of the symptoms (again with exceptions) (Raw, 1992). It should also be noted that, for SBS to be suspected within a building, it is not necessarily the case that all occupants will display symptoms.

National and international sources indicate that up to 80% of buildings in which the occupants display the symptoms have present within them some 'service faults' of 'contaminants' which can be relatively easily identified as being the source of the problem. It is therefore more appropriate to term these buildings 'problem buildings', and not 'sick buildings'. As 'sick buildings' are those in which the problem(s) is/are caused by a cocktail of different factors, not readily identifiable, and therefore makes diagnosis very difficult (Potter, 1988).

Problems in the operation of buildings may originate from any of the disciplines involved, from architectural design to maintenance to facilities management. Possible sources of symptoms include interior furnishings and fabrics and design of workshops, and some researchers suggest psychological factors, such as occupational stress. Potter (1988) suggests that the issue of problem buildings should not be viewed as a psychological myth, but it should be acknowledged that designers, architects, building operatives, consultants, maintenance engineers and managers have an 'intertwined role'.

The range of symptoms displayed by occupants depends on various factors. Sykes (1988) identifies a number of 'common factors':

- symptoms are most prevalent in air conditioned buildings, but symptoms can also be displayed in naturally ventilated buildings;
- complaints are higher in the public sector than in private sector, with more 'sufferers' being clerical staff;
- the people who display higher levels of symptoms have the least perceived control over their environment;
- symptoms present themselves more in the afternoons than in the mornings.

Rostron, in his research into SBS (1997), obtained what WHO believe to be common to SBS buildings:

- they often have forced ventilation – WHO does not specifically refer to air conditioning systems, although it falls into this category;
- they are often of light construction;
- often, internal fittings and finishes are covered in textiles;
- usually, they are energy efficient buildings – having a homogenous thermal environment;
- often, they are 'closed buildings', for example, no windows that open.

Symptoms

The symptoms of SBS have been fairly well established over the years. A study by Molhave (1987) (cited in Potter, 1988) concluded with a refined list of five 'symptoms criteria', namely:

- Sensoric irritation in eyes, nose or throat:
    - dryness;
    - stinging, smarting, irritating sensation;
    - hoarseness, changed voice.
- Skin irritation:
    - reddening of skin;
    - stinging, smarting, itching sensation;
    - dry skin.
- Neurotoxic symptoms:
    - mental fatigue;
    - reduced memory;
    - lethargy, drowsiness;
    - reduced power of concentration;
    - headache;
    - dizziness, intoxication;
    - nausea;
    - tiredness.
- Unspecified hyperactions:
    - runny nose and eyes;
    - asthma-like symptoms in non-asthmatic persons;
    - respiratory sounds.

- Odour and taste complaints:
  o changed sensitivity;
  o unpleasant odour or taste.

Mulhave (1987) stipulates that sensoric irritation must be one of the dominating complaints, and also stresses that systemic symptoms, for example, complaints arising from problems in lower airways or stomach, should not be a dominant complaint, and there should be no identifiable single cause in relation to the problem.

Raw (1992) suggests that taste and odour anomalies are not necessarily symptoms; it is most probable that they are environmental perceptions unique to individuals and, therefore, are best excluded from the list of symptoms. Likewise, breathing difficulties should be treated with the same caution (the criteria could possibly be identifying people with asthma rather than SBS).

Some investigators have produced more extensive lists of symptoms, including (amongst others) airway infection; coughs; wheezing; nausea; dizziness; and high blood pressure. Even the possibility of miscarriage has been suggested by Ferahrian (1984). Also of note is the fact that the range and prevalence of the symptoms reported may be directly related to the number and the nature of the questions used in the research process. Also, the use of different frequency scales to report the frequency of symptoms and discomfort may distort and/or manipulate the findings (Raw, 1994).

The general nature of the symptoms means that they will be reported to some degree in all buildings. It has been found, however, that the level of symptoms varies between buildings, and buildings where symptom rates are high do tend to have a number of common features – as mentioned previously (Goldman, 1996).

The more generalised condition of tiredness, aches, and pains can at times be so severe that they result in loss of appetite and loss of weight (Walker, 1991). The symptoms occur whilst the person is at work, but disappear shortly after the person leaves the building. The condition has been described by some authors as 'Monday complaints'. However, their frequent recurrence while at work indicates that the symptoms are not due to infections, but are more likely to be as a result of an irritant or some form of allergic reaction.

Research indicates that there is unlikely to be one isolated cause for the symptoms displayed, with the level of reporting varying significantly between different offices, with the so called ' healthy' offices averaging one or two symptoms per worker, compared against the four or five symptoms per worker in relatively 'unhealthy' offices (Jones, 1995). Nearly always the most frequent reported symptoms are headaches and lethargy, whilst at the other end of the scale (being reported least often) are tightness of the chest and breathing difficulties. Unlike cigarettes, buildings do not come with warning labels – maybe they should!

It is important to acknowledge a clear distinction between SBS and complaints about comfort, for example, thermal control; perceived air quality; lighting; noise and intrusion; and privacy in open planned offices. It is highly debatable whether SBS should be diagnosed only if there appears to be no apparent obvious cause for the problem of a given building. The logic to this theory would be that there is no point expending time and money into uncertain solutions to SBS if there is a clear, identifiable fault which may be readily put right.

SBS at present, like many of the health problems of the past, is defined in terms of symptoms and occurrence, rather than cause. A possible and plausible reason for this being so is due to the fact that there is no single and proven cause, and any attempt to introduce cause into the definition is likely to be misleading.

The implications of SBS

Some may argue that the symptoms of SBS could easily be regarded as minor, as there have been no reports of any lasting physical damage – symptoms normally disappear rapidly after leaving the affected building. However, these symptoms are not minor to those affected in their place of work.

SBS can have serious wider implications, including reduced productivity – many sufferers have reported that their productivity levels have been reduced by up to 20% (Tong, 1991); reduced overtime; increased staff turnover – the population of office workers is a volatile one, with workers regularly changing jobs, as opposed to dedicating their career to one company. It is likely that office conditions are slowly beginning to influence the decisions of workers when considering a change, another implication is increased sickness, leading to increased absenteeism. Private litigations against employers by workers who have become ill as a consequence of foul air have resulted in substantial financial settlements.

Some buildings affected may require costly and dramatic remedial works, for example, replacement of air conditioning systems, windows and furnishings. For some buildings, however, demolition may prove to be the only, or the most economic, action. The Inland Revenue gave up on its 19 Storey building in Bootle, Merseyside, in 1995, after intolerable levels of staff absenteeism, with a reported half of the 2,000 strong staff over the previous five years suffering from SBS symptoms (Goldman, 1996).

Therefore, it can clearly be seen that the cost of reduced productivity, replacement staff and litigation make prevention unarguably better than cure.

Why now?

So, why has SBS emerged now? There are several reasons for this.

It has been estimated that, through our changing habits, the average person spends between 80–90% of their time indoors, with the majority of time being spent in the workplace (Holdsworth *et al*, 1992; Jones, 1995; Parker, 1993). Therefore, for most of our time we are subjecting ourselves to an artificial internal environment. And, with the population of the world increasing, a higher majority of people will begin to find themselves imprisoned in building erected with little courtliness and with minimum planning for health.

Even those earning their living in the best of the world's modern architecture suffer a range of medical problems throughout their working days. Buildings all over major cities and towns are havens of bacteria and other health threats. Could this be the result of misuse of the buildings? But, then, doesn't everyone misuse their buildings to some extent in ways that the designers never intended?

It is true to say that, in today's world, organisations are placing greater demands on their buildings. They are being used far more intensively and for longer periods of time. Technically, buildings are now much more complex than ever before.

To complicate matters even further, there has been a substantial increase in the average concentration of various pollutants in the internal environment, being introduced into buildings in the form of partitions, carpets, paints, cleaning compounds, equipment, ventilation systems, etc. Actual building services themselves are rarely sources of pollution, but they can act as carriers of internal pollutants.

Sealey and Holdsworth (1991) put forward that, in 1987, 5,000 different chemicals and synthetic substances were being used within building materials. With this cocktail of substances, each emitting different pollutants and chemicals, the problem is becoming increasingly difficult to control.

Concerns about the quality of internal air are becoming a major consideration for designers, constructors and operatives of buildings. A report published by Robertson (1989) – a US Government study – found that many of the chemicals detected indoors were 100 times greater in concentration than that found outdoors, with many of the chemicals believed to be animal and human carcinogens. Slowly, we are beginning to learn that the human body, along with the world's natural ecosystem, appears to be weakening in its immune defence systems. When undesirable levels of substances build up in our enclosed environments, the result is that the quality of air inside is often worse than the air outside (McHarry, 1994). Ultimately, the result is human health deterioration.

Research indicates that there is no single identifiable cause for SBS and, fairly or unfairly, fully sealed buildings with air conditioning systems are regarded as the worst possible scenario. One thing that we can say for sure with regard to artificial environments is that they are becoming better insulated and sealed and, therefore, dramatically reduce the levels of heat loss from buildings.

Air conditioning is largely to blame, due to its inherent nature of spreading airborne toxins from outside, or circulating those released from within the building itself. It could be said that a building's air conditioning system acts in the same way as a human lung. Any microorganisms that exist within the structure can pass through the entire system.

To support this reasoning, Rowe (1994) observes that the reporting of symptoms were significantly more widespread in buildings with reduced air ventilation. At around the same time, it was noted that trace quantities of a large number of VOCs were being released from man made materials that were previously not found indoors (Rowe, 1994).

This lead to the conclusion by investigators that theses VOCs were being able to accumulate to excessive levels, due to the reduced level of ventilation, and therefore contributing to, if not causing, the conditions of illness being displayed amongst occupants.

It is logical to suggest that the frequent connection between air conditioned building and SBS is due to the fact that air conditioned buildings are more likely to be deep-plan, having low levels of natural daylight and therefore higher levels of artificial light, with a higher level of noise.

However, it is not clear whether air conditioning is so strongly related to the health (or ill health) of the occupant. Although there is a familiar association with the 'lack of fresh air', actual measurements show that air conditioned buildings have better ventilation rates than naturally ventilated buildings (Robertson, 1991).

Numerous studies (see, for example, Purcell and Thorne, 1976; Husband, 1991; Bordass and Leaman, 1993; Rylander, 1993, all cited in Rowe, 1994) have proposed that there may be other plausible contributing factors – poor lighting, noise, stress, lack of local control or personal environment, lack of privacy and dull and boring work, amongst other factors:

> Put 100 employers in a modern multi-storey office block, stir in emissions from computer equipment, add a touch of bad light and poor ventilation, and what do you get? SBS (according to some health experts and employers) [Barnett, 1995].

The 1980s witnessed the transformation of the office environment. It was during this period that the microcomputer took the forefront of information technology (IT). IT created its own problems, due to unpredictable heat gains from machinery causing discomfort amongst staff.

The 1980s saw the rise of so called 'tight buildings'. With the onset of the energy crisis in the 1970s, energy efficiency was a major concern. Buildings in advanced countries were constructed to be energy efficient, with less air exchange between them and their surroundings. Among the problems that arose in such buildings as a result of this energy efficient drive were the following:

- retention of higher temperatures;
- higher humidity levels;
- decreased ventilation;
- increased odour retention.

The advent of higher temperature and increased humidity levels in buildings gave birth to the proliferation of microorganisms in indoor environments.

Traditionally, ventilation rates have been set in response to 'human body odour'. However, the 1980s began to see a significant increase in the use of photocopiers and laser printers, each generating chemicals, and yet there has been no recommended change in the ventilation rates (Tong, 1991).

Finally, on the subject of why SBS has emerged now, could it be that many sick buildings are simply getting old, and so too are their air conditioning systems? Air conditioning systems do not have a long history in the UK, so is it possible that SBS has emerged at a time when these systems have degraded to the extent where they are no longer satisfactory in their performance?

However SBS is viewed, it appears that we are doomed to be victims of our own technological advances; clearly, man made contaminants are tipping the natural balance, and once again nature wins hands down!

Building for health

The phrase 'sick building syndrome' was originally used by the medical profession to categorise symptoms displayed by patients who appear to be caused by various physical factors in the design and operation of state-of-the-art office buildings.

Until recently, attention was focused on the physical elements of the problem, for example, respiratory problems, eyestrain, etc. However, attention has begun to shift towards psychological factors, that is, what it actually 'feels like'. It is now widely accepted that SBS must be considered a serious issue by all involved, from design stage, to construction, to management. It is becoming more common to involve psychologists and sociologists in advising on the psychosocial aspects of building design.

The concept of a healthy building is one that is well balanced in all aspects:

- functional yet aesthetically pleasing;

- man made balancing with the natural;
- well managed, not over managed.

Curwell (1996) initially thought that the technical performance and the aesthetic merit of materials would need to be considered as separate entities. However, in reality, the aesthetic considerations given to building materials are not as great a priority as originally surmised, so combining the two factors has proved to be appropriate.

When designing a building, architects must take into consideration not only the cost aspect, but also the impact on the environment – both internal and external. The question which could logically be put forward is, do designers consider cost, aesthetics, technical performance and internal/external environment during the designing process?

Possible causes of SBS

Much research has been carried out in an attempt to establish conclusively the cause(s) of SBS. Unfortunately, this has not yet been achieved (White, 1993). The pattern of occurrence of the symptoms – for example, during the working day and week – rules out the possibility of the problem being that of an infection. It is important to understand that a consideration of the physical environment should also be given attention. In all probability, there are different combinations of causes in different buildings (Morris *et al*, 1995).

Many possible causes of SBS have been suggested, with the majority of explanations focusing on air quality within the building and the systems that are used to ventilate the building. Other factors which have been implicated are noise, artificial lighting, control by occupants, cleaning of the workplace, stress and psychological effects (amongst others).

Heating, and ventilation systems and thermal comfort

Mechanical ventilation of buildings differs from natural ventilation in a number of ways:

- with natural ventilation, occupiers have a choice of opening/closing windows. This is not the case in mechanically sealed buildings;
- any mechanical system is subject to design fault, and poor installation, components may fail and have a devastating impact on the system's performance;
- ventilation systems can harbour organic growth and may distribute contaminants from one area throughout the building.

Evidence for a correlation between ventilation rate and SBS symptoms is at best patchy. Generally, air conditioned buildings have higher rates of symptoms than naturally ventilated buildings.

There are many reasons why ventilation may be inadequate in buildings: malfunctioning ventilation systems; badly maintained systems; badly designed or ill-controlled systems; or distribution of air within the space may be inadequate.

Even if appropriate volumes of fresh air are delivered to a space, it may not reach the occupants in the way intended. Distribution is susceptible to problems caused by changes in layout of office spaces and to unregulated covering of air inlets by building occupants.

Probably the most crucial aspect of ventilation is the practice of maintenance of ventilation systems. Fresh air is required in air conditioning systems to supply air for respiration and to dilute carbon dioxide and other contaminants. Ventilation is required to maintain personal comfort. Standards have been set for ventilation and fresh air rates, usually based on the air required to dilute body odours.

With the increase in building plan size, there has been an increase in the need to ventilate mechanically. Within small plan areas, it is easy to naturally ventilate by opening windows, and the occupants can control their own environment. However, with larger, open plan office arrangements, the opening of windows is not always possible or effective.

Evidence indicates that an inadequate volume of fresh air is unlikely to be a sufficient explanation for SBS, although it is likely to be a contributory factor.

Temperature

There is fairly strong evidence that there is a correlation between temperatures at and above 23°C and the prevalence of symptoms. Therefore, temperature should be limited to 22°C during winter heating.

Indoor air pollutants

The subject of indoor air quality (IAQ) is far too in-depth to be covered in detail here; therefore, a brief discussion of indoor air pollutants (IAPs) will be given.

Within buildings, there are many sources of pollution, including the occupants, the buildings and furnishings, office materials and equipment, building services and the environment outside the building. Consequently, there is a wide range of pollutants in the indoor environment. Due to the low levels of each pollutant found, it has proved very difficult to show clear differences between 'sick' and so called 'healthy' buildings with respect to levels of pollutants.

Inorganic gases such as carbon dioxide and ozone may occasionally create problems, but they are not thought to be widespread causes of SBS. One's sense of smell is an unreliable indicator of some of the most dangerous contaminants (Rowe, 1994).

VOCs, for example, formaldehyde, are released by a large number of materials and processes in buildings and by the occupants, often reaching moderately high levels.

Few studies have analysed the role of VOCs in SBS in a controlled way; therefore, the measurement and effects of a mixture of VOCs are not sufficiently and clearly understood. However, it is thought that the levels of VOCs will be significantly higher in new buildings than in older buildings.

SBS has been shown to be related to the size of areas in which dust and air can collect in the building, which provide breeding sites for microorganisms and the like. Microorganisms are more likely to be present in older buildings than in newer buildings.

Studies have shown that airborne dust levels are a significant factor. Dust cannot be regarded as simply an air pollutant, effective only when inhaled, since it can be transferred direct to the skin or ingested with food/drink.

It is clear that there are many combinations of sources of pollutants, and, in addition, the sources may not be independent. The potential range of pollutants in the office environment is therefore enormous.

Pollutants may be introduced into a building via a large and diverse range of sources, which can be summarised as:

- building users and their activities;
- building and furnishing materials;
- office materials and equipment;
- heating, ventillating and air conditioning (HVAC) systems;
- outdoor air and soil;
- environmental tobacco smoke (ETS).

ETS is a vastly complex area in its own right, with evidence often being contradictory. Again, it is outside the scope of this study to speak in detail about ETS. It deserves special attention.

The long term impact of the increasing proportion of synthetic building materials and furnishings is unknown (McHarry, 1994).

Noise and speech privacy

Noise transmission and speech privacy are complex topics. Noise can contribute to SBS, but in differing ways. Whether or not the noise level is disturbing or annoying to an occupant depends on numerous factors, psychological and physiological, varying from person to person (Potter, 1988).

Traffic or external noise is not usually considered to be a problem in air conditioned building with sealed windows. But, in older buildings that rely on open windows for ventilation, external noise can be a cause of serious inference. If this is the case, it can only be prevented by careful location of openings, to try to prevent direct transmission pathways.

Sometimes, low noise-emission is acceptable and may even be useful to help dampen the general noise level in open planned offices. Nevertheless, there are occasions when unacceptable levels of intrusive noise appears in occupied spaces. If necessary, a suitable contaminant or hearing protection partition should be provided. If the problem is that of low frequency noise from office equipment, this could be 'deadened' by introducing a level of background noise into the office (Rostron, 1997; Rowe, 1994). However, by careful design, for example, the re-routing of services and treatment, forms of intrusive noise can be avoided.

Noise can cause headaches and affect concentration by a combination of its intensity, frequency, location and its acceptability. People also vary widely in their subjective response to a given noise situation.

There is no direct evidence on the role of noise in SBS, for many workplaces are as noisy as 'sick' buildings, without any reports of SBS symptoms. Noise can, however, contribute to stress levels and therefore exacerbate complaints.

There are potential problems with certain proposed remedial measures. Removing possible sources of indoor pollution, for example, carpets, soft furnishings and false ceilings, could create new problems, due to the effects on absorption and reflection of sound.

Lighting and tinted glazing

The subject of lighting is an extremely detailed topic, and ideally should be spoken about in depth. However, the aim of this chapter is simply to make the reader aware of the potential problem, and nothing more.

Lighting has the potential to affect health and comfort. Visual environments which fall outside the generally accepted design recommendations (for example, those given in the Chartered Institute of Building Services Engineers (CIBSE), [1994] Code for Interior Lighting) are those most likely to lead to unsatisfactory conditions.

Lighting is related to both general satisfactions in the indoor environment and the comfort of visual performance. Eye-work under inappropriate lighting can be a very obvious cause of SBS, producing eye discomfort, eyestrain and fatigue.

The interior lighting of a building has three main purposes:

(a) to enable occupants to work and move about safely;

(b) to enable tasks to be performed properly;

(c) to enhance appearance.

The main aspects of lighting which have been attributed to SBS are the provision of daylight and the quality of artificial lighting provided in the workplace. Many existing buildings have been designed with a simple approach based on illumination levels.

The basic quantity of illumination required for performing tasks depends largely on the age and eyesight of workers, as well as on the task being carried out.

Lighting has to be designed for most office situations reasonably early in the overall process, to fulfil contractual and installation obligations. The values of reflectances are agreed with the architect at this early stage. However, the final decision on finishes very often takes place much nearer the completion of the project and, therefore, there is a higher probability that reflectances will differ greatly from those used in the lighting calculations. It is not clear as to whether or not colour finishes contribute directly to SBS.

Repeated dilation and contraction of the pupils of the eyes can bring about eye irritation. This can result from repeated adaptation to variations in brightness of adjacent parts of the field of view. A change of the tone or colour of wall surfaces to reduce the variation is the simplest remedy.

There appears to be a correlation between tinted windows and a higher incidence of symptoms. It is possible that this is because of a direct link between tinted windows and a particular generation of buildings.

People seated near windows tend to have fewer symptoms although no reason for this has yet been established; possibly it is psychological.

There is little evidence to suggest that glare increases all symptoms of SBS, especially eye related symptoms. Yet the visually imperceptible flicker of some tubular florescent lamps has been reported as a possible cause of illness among some office workers. Excessive luminance from glazing is most readily controlled by internal blinds or louvres, but consideration should also be given to external shading devices.

The use of visual display units (VDUs) coupled with less than ideal lighting solutions in the past may be a contributing factor to SBS. The provision of matt screens on VDUs may reduce the effects.

So, to conclude, one could argue that there is some evidence that lighting can contribute to the eyestrain and headaches of SBS; however, it is unlikely to explain the whole magnitude of symptoms of SBS. For example, it is difficult to see how lighting could influence the occurrence of a dry throat or a runny nose, and yet headaches and eye irritations are more easily associated with the lighting conditions.

Hygrothermal factors

Hygrothermal factors include temperature, humidity and air movement, all of which have an effect on the comfort of building occupants. The complex way in which these factors interact to produce feelings of thermal comfort and dryness may be responsible for some of the complaints of SBS.

Temperature, humidity and air movement must be considered as determinants of indoor air quality. They affect not only comfort, but also the rate of emissions and depositions of pollutants from materials in buildings and from people.

Various standards have been set for optimum comfort. However, in reality, no single thermal environment is ideal for everyone; even if conditions are 'ideal', there will still be a percentage of occupants who will be dissatisfied.

Dissatisfaction with the thermal environment is often greater in larger air conditioned buildings than in smaller, naturally ventilated buildings. In naturally ventilated buildings, the occupants are able to open windows and control radiators and, therefore, are able to vary, to some extent, the thermal environment, whereas air conditioned buildings are generally 'tight' and there is little that the occupant can do to improve conditions.

To conclude on hygrothermal factors, it is clear that little is known about the effects of fluctuations in the thermal environment. Large and slow fluctuations reduce thermal comfort, whilst small rapid fluctuations decrease worker productivity and cause sleepiness and fatigue. A constant thermal environment seems to be preferable to either type of fluctuation.

Although SBS does appear to be strongly associated with complaints of physical discomfort and lack of local control over the indoor environment, it is ambiguous to suggest that SBS could result solely from either thermal discomfort or a lack of control. It is probable that, if there is any relation between SBS and comfort complaints, it is due partly to ill health of the complainant exacerbating discomfort. Two important studies (Hedge *et al*, 1986 and Robertson *et al*, 1985, cited in Raw, 1992) conclude that there were no differences in air temperature or air velocity between 'sick' and 'healthy' buildings.

Design of building services

The traditional route to the design of building services is as follows:
- client informs architect of requirements;
- architect produces outline sketches;
- outline sketches passed to structural engineer, who carries out structural design;
- architect passes both sets of drawings to the service engineer.

Some would argue that a more appropriate route would be to gather all designers together at the earliest possible opportunity, to discuss all aspects of the building. Therefore, the service engineer can design the services parallel to the design of the building shell. If services are designed in isolation, there is no knowing how they will behave within the building as a whole unit.

Elements such as heating, ventilation and lighting should be designed so as not to impair one another's effective operation.

Construction practice

The installation of systems (especially air conditioning systems) must be carried out in such a manner as to ensure that the system is not susceptible to breakdown, that it is clean to begin with and that it is easy to maintain. A paper produced by the Heating and Ventillating Contractors Association in 1991 sets out a guide to good practice with regard to internal cleanliness of new ductwork installations.

Specialist cleaning

High levels of cleanliness should be specified to prevent SBS. With regard to air conditioning, ductwork shall be cleaned after installation by a specialist cleaning contractor. There should be adequate access to allow cleaning of the installation to be undertaken thoroughly.

Industrial cleaning of the workplace

Cleaning and maintenance are two of the most important factors influencing SBS (Rideout, 1995). Regular cleaning and maintenance of items from air conditioning, building fabrics, lighting, etc, creates a sense of wellbeing amongst employees, indicating to them that they are appreciated by company's management, in that it is concerned to create a pleasant working environment.

An untidy workplace is hazardous and looks unprofessional. It has been estimated that, if workplaces were kept as clean as domestic dwellings, the number of accidents that occur could be halved.

It is often the case that janitorial services for office buildings are often near the bottom of the list of priorities. A survey carried out by Dyna-Rod (cited in Rostron, 1997) concluded that the majority of building owners carry out crisis maintenance – that is, they wait for the system to fail before carrying out repairs.

Industrial cleaning is a specialised industry, involving trained staff with specialist equipment and detergents. By using such specialists, there may be a reduction in the symptoms of SBS if pollutants are believed to be the main cause, or even a contributory cause, of SBS.

Personal environments systems

A personal environment system (PES) is a system of individual environmental control for open plan offices. Each workstation within the office has access to facilities – electricity, telecommunications, data communications and conditioned air. The individuals are able to adjust the system to meet their own needs.

The personal environment module (PEM), which acts as the control centre, is mounted beneath the work surface of open plan office furniture. It enables the occupant to have control over:

- air flow/speed;
- heat/temperature;
- the generation of background noise;
- light.

An infra-red sensor in the control panel automatically turns the PEM off or on when the station is unoccupied or occupied, respectively.

If we assume that everyone's personal preferences in respect of temperature, lighting, noise, etc, differs, then it would be impossible to design a HVAC system to suit all needs. Therefore, the possible use of PEMs may be one way in which to eradicate SBS from the workplace.

If the occupant is more content with their working environment, then they are more likely to stay at their desks for longer periods of time; this will therefore increase productivity levels.

Type of job

Job stress and dissatisfaction are probably more important causes of symptoms than physical and chemical factors in the indoor environment.

The prevalence of symptoms appears to be highest among clerical staff than among professional staff, possibly due to their more routine work. Where concentration may stray, it is likely that a greater examination of the environment may take place, and, therefore, they will be far more aware of minor changes in the working environment, especially if inactive for long periods of time. Those with more interesting, involving jobs and more control over their environment report significantly fewer symptoms (HSE, 1995; Building Use Studies, 1988) .

The proportion of work time spent in front of computers is very important when considering eye symptoms and satisfaction with lighting conditions. Very often, computers are thought to be the cause of problems, but it is not the actual computer itself that is the problem; rather, it is the work carried out on them.

Recent studies indicate that the degree to which workers feel integrated into their organisation also affects the occurrence of symptoms (Jones, 1995).

Management

Having looked at non-human factors in relative detail, we are led to the last issue of management as a possible contributing factor to the problem of SBS.

It is important for management both to show that they recognise environmental problems, where they do exist, and to react in an appropriate manner. Staff with no environmental control will be more frustrated and feel more helpless if they are confronted by a manager who refuses to acknowledge the importance of their complaint (Rowe, 1994).

Psychologically, it is far better to have investigated the complaints and communicated the reasons why action cannot be carried out, than to have ignored the complaint altogether. Management attitudes are a prime influencing factor. According to Besch and Besch (1989, cited in Raw, 1992), if problems are not dealt with rapidly and effectively, staff can lose confidence in management and become frustrated and despondent about their environment.

The subject of management factors contributing to SBS has two lines of thought:

(a) poor quality management can lead to inadequate environmental conditions, which are a direct cause of SBS symptoms;

(b) poor quality management affects the sensitivity of staff, so that they suffer or report symptoms even in environmental conditions which would otherwise be considered adequate.

People seem to be more sensitive to their environment and report higher levels of symptoms at times when there are management or organisational changes, so communication between all levels is of vital importance.

To claim that bad management causes SBS can be seen either as claiming an obvious truth or an unfair nonsense (Raw, 1992). The true balance between these two views can only be reached by establishing specifically what management could have done to avoid the problem.

Taking a wider view, management could be seen as contributing to SBS if it does not do everything possible to create a good indoor environment so as to avoid symptoms and stress. One symptom which could be avoided by improved management is the perception of lack of control over personal environment.

To conclude, management does have the potential to influence the occurrence of SBS, in both a direct and indirect way. However, it is difficult to scientifically prove an association between the two (management and SBS).

Psychological issues

One reason for the lack of an accurate cause or 'cure' for SBS is that the majority of investigations into SBS only look at part of the problem. If the problem were purely physical, then a solution would have been found to eradicate the problem, so it is logical to reason that SBS is not purely a physical problem. Therefore, is there an element of psychology, such as job satisfaction, lack of local control, work related stress, attributing to the problem of SBS, and is the problem far more complex than originally postulated?

However, it has proved difficult to demonstrate objectively any pathophysiological changes in the subjects affected or associated with the problem of SBS (Ohm, 1997).

For an accurate diagnosis of work related illnesses, the investigation must include: a thorough industrial hygiene examination which documents levels of pollutants in the air; building characteristics; the working environment; job demands and work related stress; social support; perceived environmental control; and management issues.

Other important factors include the attitudes and belief systems of the individuals concerned, certain personality and behaviour patterns and the presence of current stress or pre-existing psychological distress. Workers' perceptions of the competence and credibility of managers and professionals, and the influence and involvement of the media, pressure groups and the legal system, will all have an impact (Spurgeon, 1997).

One major need of individual workers is that of control of their personal working environment. This need is closely associated with the need to be independent of the controls and restrictions of others, and to be able to manage one's own actions. When this freedom of control is lost, people react by reasserting their freedom and display symptoms of SBS – 'psychological reactance'.

Continued loss of control is likely to result in 'learned helplessness', for example, continuous expression of SBS symptoms. The effects of 'learned helplessness' are not easily changed, but, with persistent positive reinforcement, the association can be changed to a positive behaviour or reaction.

Occupants of buildings generally accept that they have no control over their working environment. Working environments are usually set at appropriate levels (temperature, lighting, desk height, etc) prior to the users' arrival into the building. If the occupant suffering from SBS related symptoms does make some attempt to question the working environment, and this request is ignored, then it is likely that the symptoms will become exaggerated – resulting in increased levels of absenteeism, which, in turn, results in a reduction in the organisation's productivity level.

Dr Wyon (cited in Rostron, 1997) identified that the use of individual environmental control systems can increase productivity by up to 7% and, therefore, also reduce absenteeism. Building occupants will feel in control of their working environment and will thus become less susceptible to displaying SBS symptoms.

Over the past eight to 10 years, there has been a change in the current business environment. Where organisational changes create uncertainty, resistance to change is likely to be evident. Seemingly, this resistance is not so much a resistance to change, but a resistance to the personal loss which is believed to accompany the change. This resistance will probably manifest itself, in some cases, as psychological reactance.

Possible sources of resistance to change include:

- habit – a change to a well established routine of procedures and practice could result in discomfort on the part of the person who is familiar with the current system;
- security – familiarity is security; therefore, loss of familiarity is loss of security;
- economic considerations – change may threaten their jobs, or lead to loss of wages/salary;
- fear of the unknown – any disruption of familiar patterns may create fear;
- lack of awareness.

When looking to assess the nature of SBS, there are three factors within the organisation that must be examined.

(a) environmental factors – comfort, layout of workspaces, temperature, lighting, air flow, air quality, and HVAC systems;

(b) psychosocial factors – work/organisation, nature of work, stress factors, management styles and cultures;

(c) physiological factors – the impact of the above on individual physical and behavioural attitudes.

SBS depends on a number of individual characteristics, and it should not be attributed to hysteria or stress. Symptoms are generally more likely to be reported by women, and by staff employed in clerical, low paid jobs. These factors should not be considered as causes, but as factors which contribute to making the individual more sensitive to environmental pollutants.

A popular view is that the causes of SBS are of a psychological nature. Two commonly named possible psychological causes are hysteria and stress. It is unfitting to characterise hysteria as attributable to SBS. Hysteria is an identified psychological illness; stress is a psychological phenomenon which can cause or contribute to a wide range of symptoms, and should be seen as generally having an environmental cause. Stress is more appropriately dealt with under the issue of management.

Yet, a study carried out by the Ministry of the Environment for Singapore confirmed stress to be a significant and an independent determinant of health complaints, and symptoms compatible with SBS, in many cases, were stress related (Ooi, 1997).

Where there is an effect, there must be a cause. The cause could be the office environment itself, the job or the individual.

Hedge *et al* (cited in Raw, 1992) emphasised the importance of individual factors. When a comparison between air conditioned and naturally ventilated buildings was carried out, it was found (as expected) that the air conditioned building displayed the highest levels of symptoms. Yet, within the air conditioned building, different departments displayed different levels.

It was found that a department comprised mainly of female workers reporting low job satisfaction displayed higher symptom rates than a department composed mainly of male professionals reporting high job satisfaction. It should be noted that both departments were served by the same air conditioning plant but were located on different floors.

It can be said that there is a higher rate of symptom reporting by females than males, and this is generally not solely specific to SBS (Wilson and Hedge 1987, Skov *et al*, 1987; both cited in Raw, 1992). Wilson and Hedge also highlighted a few factors which may explain the effect of job type in relation to symptom reporting.

- increased sensitivity to environmental conditions, due to routine work;
- inability to leave office during the day;
- physical stress due to work demands (for example, typing);
- general quality of working conditions;
- power to change working conditions.

It is correct to say that there are similarities between symptoms of SBS and symptoms of psychological origin, but there is little solid evidence to link SBS with outbreaks of psychological illness. Finnegan and Pickering (1986, cited in Raw, 1992) concluded that symptoms of SBS are unlikely to be of psychological origin, except in a minority of cases.

To conclude, if SBS is not primarily psychological in origin, then it possibly does have psychological consequences, and it may be amplified by psychological effects due to the way in which the individual perceives the environment and the responses of other building occupants. Psychological factors will not so much affect the symptoms themselves, but (more likely) the reporting of the symptoms.

There is a clear need for further research into the area of stress, personality and physical factors associated with SBS. There is also a need to assess the validity of the historical and self-reported methods used to assess SBS, concerning the possibility that the environment causes the problems and psychological factors determine the reporting of the symptoms.

POSSIBLE CONSEQUENCES OF SBS

There is evidence that, although SBS does not cause serious damage to health, it does result in potentially problematic consequences. Apart from being distressing to the people experiencing the symptoms, SBS does cause widespread loss of productivity and increases sickness absence, and takes up valuable time in the making of complaints and dealing with those complaints. If a building acquires a reputation for being 'sick', it can prove to be difficult to rehabilitate its reputation, even if it is clear that the building itself is improved (Raw and Goldman, 1996; Tong, 1991). Extreme cases may lead to building closure or even demolition.

The direct economic cost of SBS would comprise reduced staff efficiency while the staff are actually working; increased probability of unofficial extended breaks and reduced overtime; increased sickness absence; and increased staff turnover.

Productivity

Employees, who drag themselves into an unpleasant and disliked workplace every day will not do much for productivity. If workers believe that the office environment affects their productivity, that belief is important, whether it is correct or not. The belief itself may affect productivity, or the worker may leave for a job which offers a better perceived environment. Dressel and Francis (1987, cited in Raw, 1992) found that improvements to the office environment have resulted in higher productivity.

Commitment to the organisation is of vital importance. Failure on the part of management to do anything about a disliked and unhealthy working environment is clearly counter-productive.

Absenteeism

Data on the relationship between SBS cases and absence from work has proved to be difficult to collect, due to the fact that investigators in the past have found it difficult to obtain reliable data.

Staff turnover

If unhealthy environmental conditions persist, or remain unsolved, then, often, employees want to leave and go to a healthier working environment. Because different organisations and industrial sectors may have differing turnover rates, the question of whether this has reached the level of a serious problem depends upon how the suspected 'sick' building compares with the average turnover rates for that particular industry.

The national population of office workers is becoming increasingly mobile. Professional office workers do expect, in this day and age, to change from job to job, rather than spend their career in one company. As workers move from job to job, and office to office, it is possible that office conditions are beginning to influence this move. The increasingly attractive trend of working from home means that organisations will have to improve standards in office accommodation in order to reach a similar standard to that which can be achieved at home.

Along with the three major potential problems – reduced productivity, increased absenteeism and increased turnover – there are other potential spin-offs.

- private litigation against employees by unhealthy working environments has resulted in punitive financial settlements;
- Government legislation – both UK and European Union legislation clearly lay down the necessity to monitor the working environment, especially with respect to air conditioning systems, with potentially serious consequences for non-conformists;
- serious health risks – the toxic effects of poor indoor air quality can cause a myriad of allergies and infections.

Legal ramifications of SBS

Sick buildings have become a cause for concern in many quarters, including the legal world. At present, there is huge legal controversy surrounding whose liability it is to put sick buildings right and eventually compensate the victims.

Employers may not be solely responsible, as it is possible for the original designers, architects or builders to be held accountable where negligence can be proved. In 1990, a computer programmer in the US received a $600,000 settlement from a claim that he suffered head injuries by falling during a dizzy spell caused by exposure to (alleged) toxic substances re-circulated in the (allegedly) inadequately ventilated airtight building where he worked. He sued the architect, building contractors, engineers, manufacturers and installers of the air conditioning system, and the manufacturers and distributors of the floor covering and furnishings (Goldman, 1996).

If an employer has done all that is reasonably practicable but fails to achieve a totally satisfactory solution, this would probably constitute a safe defence in law. However, the extent of an employer's responsibility in this connection is still the subject of debate.

Rooley (1997) believes that the facilities manager is the person with the likely authority to tackle all aspects of SBS. They are the professionals that can apply understanding to the problem, which at the moment exists as a complaint, but may become a cause for litigation by building occupants.

Indoor air quality in particular is increasingly causing headaches for commercial landlords. The need to maintain clean ventilation ducts is of such importance that various laws cover the issue, with potentially quite serious consequences if they are neglected. Private litigation against employers by workers who have fallen seriously ill as a consequence of foul air have resulted in punitive financial settlements. One cannot afford to wait for specific SBS regulations and codes of practice during what may be described as the transitional phase between recognition of the problem and the emergence of regulations and official guidelines.

Employment law implications, can be another costly concern. Losing patience with an employee's refusal to work, or his absenteeism, can create grounds for unfair dismissal and, therefore, can create additional liabilities. This should serve as a clear warning for employers not to be too hasty in dealing with complaints.

Legislation clearly lays down the necessity to monitor and efficiently clean air conditioning systems. Such legislation includes:

* Offices, Shops and Railway Premises Act 1963;
* Health and Safety at Work Act 1974;
* Occupiers' Liability Act 1984.

At present, UK legislation does not address the problem of SBS as a separate and identifiable issue/problem, and establishing where liability lies using existing legal principles is by no means an easy task (Tyler, 1991). With lawsuits already being brought in the US for damage resulting from faulty design, construction and maintenance of buildings and plant, it is only a matter of time before the threat of litigation becomes a reality in the UK.

In the event of a prosecution, the onus of proof is placed on the building owner to show that measures taken were reasonable. Proof that symptoms are connected with the building is always going to be difficult and the claimant will need to rely on expert evidence.

In 1972, the Robens Committee reported on health and safety at work. Shortly after this report was published, the Health and Safety at Work Act 1974 became a statutory instrument. This imposed, on employers and occupiers, the duty to ensure the health, safety and welfare at work of employees and visitors to the premises to reasonably practicable standards.

Incidences of ill-health in buildings can probably be evidence that the building owner is in breach of the Offices, Shops and Railway Premises Act 1963.

The Health and Safety at Work Act 1974

2(1) It shall be the duty of every employer to ensure, so far as is reasonably practicable, the health, safety and welfare at work of all his employees.

(2) Without prejudice to the generality of an employers duty under the preceding sections, the matters to which the duty extends includes in particular:

(a) the provision and maintenance of plant and systems of work that are, so far as reasonably practicable, safe and without risk to health ...

(b) the provision and maintenance of a working environment for his employees, that is so far as is reasonably practicable, safe without risks to health, and adequate as regards facilities and arrangements *for* their welfare at work.

Judging what is 'reasonably practicable' depends on the cost-benefit analysis, as defined in *Edwards v NBC* (1949), whereby the inconvenience and expense of alterations is measured against the risk of an event otherwise occurring.

The Act places emphasis upon accident prevention, rather than, as previously, response to events that have already taken place. Under s 2(2), the duties placed upon the employer are expanded to include the working environment. Therefore, if the environment were believed to be producing symptoms of SBS, then provisions of the Health and Safety at Work Act 1974 would be admissible.

Most importantly, the duties of employers do not support civil liability but are, instead, foundations for criminal prosecution and administrative enforcement by the Health and Safety Executive (HSE). Regulations produced as a result of the Health and Safety at Work Act 1974 will support civil liability, unless it is provided otherwise, and therefore will be criminally enforceable (Rostron, 1997).

The Health and Safety at Work Regulations 1992

These Regulations require assessment of risk in the workplace to be carried out (reg 3). The assessment must be sufficiently detailed and must consider the health and safety of all employees. The risk assessment must be reviewed if any significant changes have taken place in matters to which it relates. The assessment must, by definition, consider the possibility of SBS and, if any signs of SBS are recorded, arrangements must be made for its future control.

The Workplace (Health, Safety and Welfare) Regulations 1992

Initially, these Regulations only applied to any new workplace, or new part of a workplace, but, from 1 January 1996, they were made applicable to all workplaces. The Regulations created civil liability. Civil liability can only arise when it can be established that Parliament intended that the breach of any statutory duty should be actionable by any person(s) harmed by the breach of that duty.

It may be, for example, that SBS is linked to deficiencies of a ventilation system which has failed to comply with the Regulation requirements – that systems should be maintained in good working order and be in good repair at all times. Therefore, an individual may have a sound claim in damages against his employer, alleging that the employers breached the duty of care when he knew, or ought to have known, that a risk existed and that significant harm resulted which was reasonably foreseeable.

It is possible that a claim could arise for stress related illness due to a minor yet persistent occurrence. In *Walker v Northumberland CC* (1995) 1 All ER 737 (cited in Raw and Goldman, 1996), the plaintiff settled for approximately £170,000. Mr Walker's employers were held not liable for his first nervous breakdown, which was not reasonably foreseeable, but, when they failed to pay attention to his special needs on his return to work, they were in breach of their duty, because it was reasonably foreseeable that he would succumb again if there was no change in his workload. In 1994, nearly 40% of American companies paid out compensation for work related stress or psychological injury (Goldman, 1996).

It is possible that this reasoning could be applied to stress related illness arising out of the nature of the workplace, especially for SBS. Damages may possibly be awarded by civil courts under negligence to compensate persons affected, where the injury resulted from a failure by those in control of premises to achieve adequate standards. The claim may also be brought under the Occupiers' Liability Act 1957 for breach of the duty to keep the premises safe.

To date, there have been no reported British legal cases on the subject of SBS. However, in the US, it is a completely different story. There, SBS does merit compensation as industrial injury, yet not all cases succeed. It largely depends on the quality of expert evidence. In *Bloomquist v Wapello County* (1989), a group of plaintiffs sued Burlington Industries and were initially awarded $1 million on the basis that the emitted from carpets made in the factory (workplace) sensitised them to other common materials. The judge accepted the plaintiffs' expert's theory of 'clinical ecology', postulating a toxic effect on the immune system caused by chemicals in the working environment. The decision was overturned on appeal, when the defendant's expert managed to convince the court that the theory of 'clinical ecology' had no validity (Raw and Goldman, 1996).

SBS: who is responsible?

From existing UK legislation, it is far from clear where the responsibility lies for preventing the onset of the syndrome, or dealing with it, if it should arise. So, the pending question is, who has to pay the cost for putting the building right? And who is liable for compensating the victims? None of the existing health and safety legislation specifically addresses the problem of SBS.

Under the COSHH Regulations 1988, every employer has a duty to ensure that exposure to substances hazardous to health is either prevented or, where this is not practicable, adequately controlled. The employer also has a duty to assess the risks of substances used in the workplace, which, by definition, includes dust and microorganisms. If an employer has failed in his duty to carry out a COSHH assessment and his staff suffer as a result of this, it will be difficult for the employer to prove compliance with these statutory duties.

If the employer has identified a risk and has controlled it to a level approved in the COSHH Regulations, there may still be employees who react to these low levels. Provided that genuine efforts are made to solve the problem, it is highly unlikely that action against the employer will be taken (Tyler and Brown, 1991).

If the problem arises upon occupation of a new or refurbished building, it is possible that the burden of responsibility may be passed onto the designers, builders and manufacturers of specific component parts. It is even possible for contractors who incorrectly install or operate plant in buildings to be held liable. Under the Health and Safety at Work Act 1974, the contractor must ensure that the erection or installation of an article does not pose any health risks. Therefore, all contractors involved are obliged to anticipate and eliminate the potential risk of SBS symptoms, characteristic of faulty work on their part.

The requirement of actual design of buildings are found in the building regulations 1985, whereby the basic requirement is that 'Any building work shall be carried out with the proper materials and in a workmanlike manner'.

Thus, if SBS symptoms arise a result of faulty design or installation, then it is possible for the designer or contractor to be held liable (Tyler and Brown, 1991).

SBS: insurance matters

SBS has much wider implications than might be immediately perceived when considering insurance.

It is generally understood that exposure to potential sick buildings is a health risk, affecting staff, customers, tenants and visitors. Other parties exposed to risks, include passers-by, and adjacent property and its associated people. Claims arising from such risks include loss of income, denial of access, loss of trading income and loss of business opportunity. The real problem arises when any of the aforementioned parties expects some compensation from another party whom they believe is/are responsible for the problem. This proves to be difficult, costly and time consuming.

So, to conclude, it must be recognised that employees are at liberty to take their skills to another place of work, rather than risk their health by staying where they are. It is therefore more beneficial to bring SBS under control, as opposed to an epidemic of litigation erupting.

Many thousands of claims are brought annually in relation to personal injury suffered as a result of working conditions. Only time will tell if, and how, successful action can be taken to protect those affected by SBS.

THE FUTURE

The future concerning SBS is mixed. On the one hand, some believe that continuing organisational and technological change which affect the way that employees work may be adding further troublesome ingredients to an already unpleasant cocktail of factors affecting employee morale and wellbeing. The Government's decision to shift responsibility for sick pay to the employer is bound to create tighter control over persistent absentees, such as those suffering from the syndrome, who may feel it necessary to return to work, although the work environment could perhaps have been the cause of their illness in the first place.

Another equally valid viewpoint is the current weight of international scientific research effort (Leinster, 1990; Whorton, 1987; Wilson, and Hedge, 1987), may yield the specific cause of the syndrome. It may then be possible to affect a 'cure' and eradicate the serious consequences which SBS currently causes.

Despite much investigation, thought and study over the past 15 years or so, mystery still surrounds the condition which has been given the inappropriate title for an ever increasingly controversial condition (Robertson, 1991) of SBS.

As yet, there is no positive, single cause for SBS, with the term now being used to cover work related complaints. Work related symptoms could be described whereby occupants get symptoms that disappear shortly after they leave the building (MacNeil, 1995). SBS is potentially a serious problem: as well as causing distress among those with the symptoms, it reduces productivity; increases sickness absence; takes up time (the time involved in making and dealing with complaints); and gives a building a bad and lasting reputation.

Due to the uncertainty surrounding SBS, it is difficult to diagnose positively, and even more difficult to find a cause (Rowe, 1994). SBS is undoubtedly at the 'grey' end of the spectrum of occupational diseases; it is not well defined and a major criticism has been frequently reiterated that there is no objective measurement of whether an office workforce truly has a problem or not.

CHAPTER 6

WASTE

HISTORY[1]

Before 1972, there was no legislation concerned primarily with the broad problems of waste disposal; the only controls were the control of waste for public health under the public health legislation. The first preventative legislation was contained in the Town and Country Planning Act 1947, which required any new development, including waste disposal sites or plants, to have planning permission. In 1972, a scare about the dumping of toxic waste led to the Deposit of Poisonous Waste Act. The first extensive legislation controlling waste was the Control of Pollution Act 1974. This made it an offence to dispose of waste on land without a disposal licence. The licence could be rejected on the ground that it may cause water pollution or a danger to public health. However, there was no real development of a waste policy at this time and many of the controls were reactive, rather than preventative.

Policy development

The regulation of waste and the general development of a waste policy was first developed in Europe.[2] Council Directive 75/442 was a basic framework directive, providing for the regulation of waste disposal at a national level without any risk to human health or the environment. It has four mandatory obligations, which have set out the general framework for waste regulation since then. The requirements were: to designate national 'competent authorities' responsible for waste disposal; those waste disposal authorities must draw up waste disposal plans; Impose prior permitting requirements on installations which treat, store or dispose of waste for third parties; the 'polluter pays' principle must apply to waste regulation. It also set out policy

---

1   See Clapp, 1994.

2   In the EU as a whole, over two billion tonnes of waste are produced each year, of which approximately 30 million tonnes can be classified as hazardous. Some 50–60% of the overall solid waste stream is landfilled, though the proportion of landfilled waste varies substantially in individual Member States and ranges from under 30% in Holland and Luxembourg to virtually 100% in Ireland, Portugal and Greece. EU directives on waste have, for the large part, been determined by the EU's various environmental action programmes. In 1989, it drew up a policy document entitled *Waste Management Strategy*, which set long term aspirations with regard to the EU's waste management legislation and activities. Its main principles were prevention of waste by technologies and products; recycling and reuse; optimisation of final disposal; regulation of transport; and remedial action.

goals through encouraging recycling and stating that situation reports should be prepared every three years. Thus, the European Economic Community (EEC) started to develop the concept of the 'waste chain': waste should be minimised, where possible; if not, that waste should be re-used and recycled; if this is not possible, then waste should be incinerated. The least environmentally sound option was to landfill waste. EC waste legislation was substantially revised by the adoption of framework Directive 91/156/EEC[3] (Waste) and Directive 91/689/EEC (Hazardous Waste), which provided a legal framework for the management and disposal of waste as laid out in the Commission's waste management strategy.

These directives provided more rigorous definitions for 'waste' and 'hazardous waste'; they established broad licensing and registration conditions for those who handle, transport, dispose of or recycle waste; and they required the relevant authorities to draw up waste management plans with the aim of achieving 'self-sufficiency'[4] (that is, disposal by Member States of their own waste), allowing the national authorities to control waste movements which do not comply with those plans. The Waste Directive highlighted the following: the importance of the development of clean technology; the importance of recycling and the use of waste in energy production, and self-sufficiency in relation to waste disposal; Best Available Techniques not Entailing Excessive Cost (BATNEEC)[5] should be taken into account; and there should be enhanced planning for the development of waste disposal policies, a full system of regulation including licences and inspections and a new definition of waste – the notion of 'discard' being central to this idea.

The Waste Directive also looked at the development of better final disposal techniques for special waste and stricter requirements on hazardous waste.

On 24 February 1997, the Council adopted a Resolution on a Community strategy for waste management, which was a review of the 1989 strategy. The Resolution underpins the principles of waste prevention first, then recovery and, finally, minimisation of final disposal. It confirms current EU policy on the movement of waste. The Resolution gives precedence to the recovery of materials over energy generation and strongly promotes the principle of producer responsibility.[6]

In England and Wales, these requirements were implemented through Pt II of the Environmental Protection Act, which has been amended by the Environment Act 1995 and the Pollution Prevention Control Act 1999.[7]

---

3   As amended by 96/350/EC.
4   See Jans, 1999, p 121.
5   See below, Chapter 7.
6   See Council Decision 76/431/EEC, setting up a committee on waste management (OJL 115 1.5.76); Council Resolution on a Community Strategy for Waste Management (OJC 076 11.3.97) and Council Resolution on Waste Policy (OJC 122 18.5.90).
7   See Lange, 1999, p 59; Pocklington, 1999, pp 72–75.

The institutional structure

The Environment Agency (EA) has overall control in relation to the regulation of waste.

The waste disposal authorities may operate their own facilities for waste disposal, as well as control waste disposal facilities. However, their main responsibilities are in relation to household waste disposal and they also regulate and enforce operating standards of all waste disposal facilities, including private sites. They can set up local authority waste disposal committees (LAWDCs) or they can tender for contractors. Waste collection authorities have responsibility for the collection of waste. In unitary authorities, the authority will undertake both functions. Waste planning authorities are responsible for identifying areas for waste treatment or deposal; they also have to develop a waste development plan and municipal waste management strategies. There are a number of policy initiatives, such as the National Waste Awareness Initiative and the Parliamentary Sustainable Waste Group.

ENVIRONMENTAL PROTECTION ACT 1990[8]

The duty of care

The regulation of waste is contained in Pt II of the Environmental Protection Act (EPA) 1990. The main aim of Pt II of the Act is to introduce the concept of the 'duty of care' (s 34). This applies to those who produce, import, store, treat, process, transport, recycle or dispose of directive waste.[9] All those dealing with directive waste are required to take reasonable and appropriate steps in relation to it; otherwise, they commit a criminal offence. This includes storing and packaging waste properly; providing a clear description of what it consists of; dealing only with an authorised carrier; providing the carrier with an accurate transfer note; and taking steps to ensure that it is adequately disposed of. The duty of care is broken irrespective of whether harm has been caused.

Everyone in the waste chain is subject to the duty of care, so it is important that waste is disposed of to reputable companies; otherwise, the producer could be prosecuted for fly tipping by another company, breach of the duty of

---

8   As amended by the Environment Act 1995 and the Pollution Prevention Control Act 1999.
9   See the Environmental Protection (Duty of Care) Regulations 1991 (SI 1991/2839).

care may give rise to knowingly permitting the deposit and there may be potential liability under the clean up powers.

The steps that operators should take to comply with the duty of care are set out in a Code of Practice. The main requirements of the duty of care are:

- to prevent, cause or permit; the deposit of controlled waste on land without a waste management licence or in breach of a licence, the keeping, treating or disposal of controlled waste;
- to prevent the escape of waste;
- to ensure that waste is transferred to an authorised person; and
- to ensure that the waste is accompanied by a written description in a transfer note. This must give a description of the waste and details of the parties involved in the transfer. However, it is not necessary if a consignment note is required.

The definition of waste

Defining 'waste' has always been difficult.[10] Section 75 of the EPA 1990 has been repealed by the Environment Act 1995 and the Waste Management Licensing Regulations 1994 (SI 1994/1056). Guidance is to be found in Circular 11/94. Waste that is regulated by the EA is now known as 'directive waste'; the activities under Pt II of the EPA 1990 are now known as 'directive disposal' and 'directive recovery'. 'Directive waste' is defined as any substance or object which the holder discards or intends or is required to discard.

The question that is asked is whether the substance or object has been discarded so that it is no longer part of the normal commercial cycle or chain of utility. Waste recovery operations are distinguished from specialist waste recovery systems. A substance is not considered to be waste just because it has been consigned to a recovery process. Waste recovery operations are listed and cover the recycling or reclamation of a number of substances, including solvents, acids and oils.

Waste consigned to special recovery operations will always be considered to be waste. The phrase 'special recovery operations' is intended to cover operations which re-use substances or objects which are waste. Any materials which are of no further use are, by law, waste, even if they are not considered to be waste in a purchaser's hands.

The Act lays down a chain of utility if an item, other than special waste, is no longer needed for its original purpose. It should be:

- reused;
- repaired;

---

10 See *Mayer Parry Recycling Ltd v EA* (1998) unreported, 9 November.

- recycled; or,
- if none of these is available, then sale or charitable donations may be considered.

Controlled waste is household, commercial and industrial waste. It includes office waste and waste from a house, shop, factory or other business premises. A substance is controlled waste whether it is solid or liquid, and even if it is not hazardous or toxic.

The licensing of waste[11]

Anyone who deposits,[12] recovers or disposes of controlled waste must do so in accordance with the conditions of a waste management licence[13] or licensing exemption and in a way which does not cause pollution of the environment or harm to human health. Activities exempt from waste management licensing are listed in Sched 3 to the 1994 Regulations. An activity may only be exempt from licensing if:

- it is carried out without harm to human health or pollution of the environment;
- the person carrying out the activity has the consent of the occupier or is otherwise entitled to do so on that land; and
- in most cases, if the exempt activity is registered with the EA.

Even if an activity is exempt from the 1994 Regulations, certain activities must still be registered with the EA; it is an offence not to be registered. Under s 33(1)(c), even if an activity is exempt, there is a general requirement to act safely in relation to pollution of the environment or the protection of human health. Guidance notes are prepared by the EA.[14]

---

11 Emissions from incineration are covered under the IIPC Directive; other gaseous emissions are contained in the EPA 1990 and the Clean Air Act 1993. Radioactive waste is covered under the Radioactive Substances Act 1993. Waste water is covered under the Water Resources Act 1991. If waste water or liquid is subjected to recovery or disposal (eg, effluent treatment plants), the DETR has advised that, in its view, this will amount to directive waste and a licence will be required. Under the EPA 1990, s 63 there is residual control over non-directive waste. This may cover the irresponsible disposal of toxic materials. Any person who deposits or knowingly causes or knowingly permits the deposit of any on controlled waste commits an offence if the waste has characteristics of special waste and is not deposited in a accordance with a licence or permission of some description.

12 See *Thomas Waste Management Ltd v Surrey CC* [1997] Env LR 148.

13 See the Waste Management Licences (Consultation and Compensation) Regulations 1999 (SI 1999/481); *R v SOSETR ex p Premiere Environment Ltd* (2000) 9(4) Env LM 10.

14 EA guidance on best practice flaring of landfill gas and on technical competence at waste facilities and on protection of groundwater from waste disposal, Special Waste: a Technical Guidance Note on their Definition and Classification.

Under the Controlled Waste (Registration of Carriers and Seizure of Vehicles) Regulations 1991 (SI 1991/1624), all carriers of waste have to be registered with the EA.[15] The exemptions to this include householders taking waste to a waste site and anyone transporting waste that they have produced, except building and demolition waste. This requirement does not apply to charities and voluntary organisations However, charities do have to register with the EA. Waste dealers and brokers also have to be registered with the EA.

Authorised persons have a duty to stop waste escaping – that is, it has to be stored safely and securely. If the waste goes to someone else, it must be in a suitable container and the person taking away the waste has to be legally authorised to do so. A written description of the waste is needed, along with a transfer note. Both parties must keep copies of the transfer note and the description of the waste for two years. The written description must provide as much information as someone else may need to handle the waste safely.

Section 59 allows for clean-up powers: there is a fine for failure to comply with a notice under this section. There is a defence under s 33(7)(a) where a defendant took all reasonable procedures and exercised all due diligence to avoid the commission of the offence. But it is not enough to rely on procedures. For example, a number of cases seem to cover skips: a skip should be checked every time it is used, to ensure that it complies with the description of waste.

The application process and the definition of 'authorised persons'

A person needs to register[16] as a carrier of waste if, in the course of their business, or in any other way for profit, they transport waste within the UK, either by road, sea or inland waterway.[17]

An application for a licence[18] can be refused (s 36 of the EPA 1990). Authorised persons can include:

---

15 See Control of Pollution (Amendment) Act 1989, which states that a person has to be registered to transport controlled waste; otherwise, it is a criminal offence.

16 If a person is not registered, then an offence is committed. Registration can be refused after a conviction. It is also an offence to give waste to an unlicensed operator. In *R v Hertfordshire CC ex p Green Environmental Industries and Another* (2000) unreported, 22 February, a person who had unlawfully deposited waste without a licence could not refuse to provide information about his activities under the EPA 1990, s 71(2) by a local waste regulation authority on the grounds that his answers may incriminate him or lead to the discovery of evidence that may be used against him in a criminal prosecution.

17 Controlled Waste (Registration of Carriers and Seizure of Vehicles) Regulations 1991 (SI 1991/1624).

18 Planning Compensation Act 1991 (Amendment of Sched 18) Order 1992 in relation to the amount of compensation payable arising from the EPA 1990, s 35A. The amount is assessed in relation to the Waste Management Licences (Consultation and Compensation) Regulations 1999 (SI 1999/481). Section 35 allows the EA to impose licence management conditions which require the licence holder to carry out works or to do other things notwithstanding that he is not entitled to do so.

- council waste collectors;
- registered waste carriers – licensed;
- exempt waste carriers – charities or voluntary organisations;
- holders of waste disposal or waste management licences – these may only be valid for certain kinds of waste/activity;
- persons exempt from the requirements to have waste disposal/waste management licences.

The application may also be rejected if the regulator is satisfied that the rejection will prevent pollution to the environment – pollution is a release or escape of matter capable (by quantity or concentration) of harming humans or any other living organism. There is a right of appeal within six months (s 43 of the EPA 1990).

The procedure for an application is set down in s 36. The regulator consults with the Health and Safety Executive and with other bodies, for example, the fire brigade, and has 21 days to comment (or longer if agreed). The EA is deemed to have rejected the licence if no decision has been issued within four months of receipt. The EA can include any terms/conditions it considers to be appropriate.[19]

It is the duty of the EA to maintain a register[20] containing details of licences, appeals, applications and transfers. Information may be excluded on the grounds of national security or commercial confidentiality.[21]

Part II of the 1990 Act, which replaced the waste disposal licence regime in the Control of Pollution Act 1974, rectified a deficiency in the 1974 Act regime whereby holders of disposal licences could hand in their licences and absolve themselves of further responsibility for landfills and other waste facilities. Under the 1990 Act, a waste management licence remains in force unless it is revoked by the EA or its surrender is accepted (which must be satisfied that environmental pollution or harm to human health is unlikely to be caused).

Since October 1999, waste has been regulated under an integrated pollution prevention and control regime.[22] Section 2 and Sched 1 will also enable the new pollution control system to include requirements similar to those in Pt II of the 1990 Act. Thus, for example, para 5 of Sched 1 will allow provision to be made for restricting the grant of permits to those who are fit and proper persons, a test which is applied under the waste management

---

19 Waste Management Licences (Consultation and Compensation) Regulations 1999 (SI 1999/481).
20 EPA 1990, s 64. The European Commission has produced a draft regulation on the waste management data collection (COM 99) 31 Joint Framework for the Production and Dissemination of Statistical Data on Waste Management.
21 Environment Agency, Environmental Reporting: Guidelines for Company Reporting on Waste March 2000.
22 Pollution Prevention and Control Act 1999.

licensing system. The power to make regulations in this area is necessary in order that 'fit and proper person' provisions may continue to apply to those waste management installations currently regulated under Pt II of the 1990 Act to which the the IPPC Directive applies and which, in future, will be regulated under the new regime, to be set up in the regulations made under s 2 rather than under Pt II.

Similarly, para 8 of Sched 1 allows provisions to be made for regulating the transfer or surrender of permits (matters that are regulated under the waste management licensing system). The Regulations will need to apply such requirements to all installations covered by the IPPC Directive to allow the implementation of the Directive's requirement that appropriate remedial activity takes place following closure of an installation. Section 4 applies to time limited disposal licences issued under Pt I of the Control of Pollution Act 1974, whether converted into time limited waste management licences under Pt II of the 1990 Act or having expired before they could be converted.[23]

Section 4(7) ensures that activities that were not criminal when they were carried out are not criminalised. Under s 4(9), the EA is under a duty to notify licence holders affected by the section of the fact that the licence is affected, and how it is affected.[24]

Enforcement

The offences for waste are contained under s 33(1) of the EPA 1990 and, under reg 1(3) of the Waste Management Licence Regulations 1994 (SI 1994/1056), it is a criminal offence to:

- deposit directive waste in or on land, unless it is in accordance with a waste management licence;

---

23 Section 4(1)–(3) provides that, where certain conditions are fulfilled, 1974 Act disposal licences authorising activities to be carried on in England and Wales which have expired are to be deemed not to have expired but to continue in force until revoked or surrendered under Pt II of the EPA 1990. Similarly, s 4(4) provides that, where certain conditions are fulfilled, extant 1974 Act time limited disposal licences (including those authorising activities to be carried out in Scotland) shall be deemed to have become non-time limited licences, which continue in force until revoked or surrendered. These provisions only apply to licences that were relied upon within the 12 month period before the Act was passed (27 July 1999).

24 Where expired licences are revived, s 4 retrospectively validates things done in reliance upon the expired licence during the period between its expiry and revival. This means that the licence holder will not be subject to criminal prosecution for carrying out activities during this period without an extant licence and that third parties that transferred waste to the licence holder in the belief that the licence was still in force are protected. The section also validates the receipt of any fees paid to the Agencies under the licence and any variation notices, modification, revocation, suspension or transfer of a licence or acceptance of its surrender when it was not in force. These matters are set out in s 4(6), which contains an illustrative list of the effects of s 4(1) and (3).

- treat, keep or dispose of directive waste, unless it is under and in accordance with a waste management licence;
- knowingly cause or knowingly permit either of the above.

The courts have interpreted the word 'knowingly'[25] very strictly: the prosecution need only prove knowledge of the deposit; it is not necessary to show knowledge of the breach of the licence condition which gives rise to the offence. This can be inferred from surrounding events; for example, a company and its senior management, if it knowingly operates a waste site, does not need to be a knowledge of the specific breach of the licence condition, in effect this makes the operators of landfill sites under a strict liability for breaches of waste management licences. There is also a strict liability offence of contravening any condition of a waste management licence s 33(6). Corporate liability is set down in s 157 of the EPA 1990.[26]

If a person is not registered, then an offence is committed. Registration can be refused after a conviction. It is also an offence to give waste to an unlicensed operator.

Planning

Planning permission is required for new waste disposal sites or the extension of existing sites (s 55 of the TCPA 1990). However, any conditions placed on the planning permission have to be for planning purposes, that is, amenity, access, location or visual appearance, rather than for pollution control. They are bad neighbour developments (s 65 of the TCPA 1990).

An environmental assessment may be required before the planning decision is taken. Schedule One where an assessment is mandatory includes storage/disposal of radioactive waste and special waste. Schedule Two where an assessment is discretionary covers controlled waste. The authority need only undertake an assessment if the 'development would be likely to have significant effects on the environment'. There are provisions for consultation with, for example, the EA and the public. There is a right of appeal from the refusal of planning permission.

Waste disposal plans(s 50 of the EPA 1990) set out policies and the intentions for the control and disposal of waste.[27] In September 1999, Planning Policy Guidance Note (PPG 10) on planning and waste management was published. This provides guidance on linking local waste plans to the national waste strategy. Regional planning boards will set up regional technical advisory boards. The guidance allows local authorities to prohibit

---

25 See *Shanks v McEwan (Teesside) Ltd v EA* [1997] Env LR 305.
26 See above, Chapter 2.
27 PPG 23; SI 1994/1056.

certain types of waste facility if the local authority is confident that adequate alternative facilities are available in the area.[28]

THE ISSUES

There are a number of issues of controversy in relation to the disposal and treatment of waste.[29] The first is in relation to how the UK has traditionally disposed of its waste through landfill and the problems that this can cause in relation to contaminated land; the second is the increasing use of incineration causing air pollution problems; the third is in relation to the complexity of the requirements to encourage re-use and recycling in packaging; and the final issue is the concern over the treatment of hazardous waste. Each of these will now be considered.

Contaminated land[30]

In the past, and today,[31] the main way of disposing of waste has been to landfill.[32] Contaminated land presents a number of problems, including groundwater pollution and the production of methane gas.[33] There is a lack of any comprehensive knowledge of where all the contaminated land sites are, as many of them are hidden and have been abandoned in the past by their operators.[34] The requirement for a register of contaminated land was dropped in 1993, when s 143 of the EPA 1990 was scrapped. This has led to a number of recent changes in the law which try to facilitate the clean up of contaminated land. Contaminated land is defined in s 78A(2) of the EPA 1990 as:

> ... land which appears to the local authority in whose area it is situated to be in such a condition, by reason of substances in, on or under land, that significant

---

28 See DETR, *Planning and Waste Management*, 1999; PPGN 10 (waste), September 1999.

29 See Goldsmith and Hildyard, 1986.

30 See Taylor, 2000, p 160.

31 The Contaminated Land (England) Regulations 2000 (SI 2000/227) provide for Pt IIa of the EPA 1990. See DETR, *Limiting Landfill: a Consultation Paper on Limiting Landfill to meet the EC Landfill Directive's Targets for the Landfill of Biodegradable Municipal Waste*, October 1999; DETR, *Contaminated Land: Implementation of Pt IIa of the EPA 1990*, September 1999.

32 Friends of the Earth briefing sheet, 'Don't burn or bury it – alternatives to landfill and incineration', May 1997. See Hencke, 2000b; Hughes and Kellett, 1999; Park, 2000, pp 3–13; Parpworth, 1999, pp 4–6.

33 Ground water pollution is discussed above, Chapter 4. Methane gas can lead to global warming – see above, Chapter 5.

34 For an interesting account of the extent and problems relating to contaminated land, see *The Observer*/Friends of the Earth investigation, *Britain's Buried Poison* (1990) *The Observer (Magazine)*, 4 February, p 11.

harm is being caused or there is a significant possibility of such harm being caused; or pollution of controlled waters is being or likely to be caused.[35]

The regulation of contaminated land has been amended in the Environment Act 1995, which set up the landfill tax (see ss 39–70 and Sched 5 to the Finance Act 1996).[36] The landfill tax credit scheme has been set up with the intention of reflecting the full environmental costs of disposing of waste to landfill and to apply the 'polluter pays' principle. The tax is weight based and is charged per ton of waste. At present, this is £11 and will rise by £1 a year to 2004.[37]

The EC Landfill Directive[38] will have an impact on how waste is disposed of in the UK in limiting landfill. The Government states:

The UK currently disposes of the vast majority of its municipal waste (over 85%) by sending it to landfill, and meeting the targets presents a substantial challenge to this country. The targets in the EC Landfill Directive mean that the UK will have to take action on two levels:

(a) limit the use of landfill to ensure that no more than the allowed amount of biodegradable municipal waste is landfilled by the target dates;

(b) build up alternatives to landfill to deal with diverted waste, encourage the diversion of waste away from landfill towards those alternatives, and encourage initiatives which minimise the amount of biodegradable municipal waste produced.

The Directive on Landfill[39] introduces licence applications and technical requirements for the design, operation, monitoring, shutdown and post-shutdown care for landfills. Under the Directive, landfills are classified according to the type of waste they take in (hazardous, non-hazardous and inert) and operators are required to provide a financial guarantee to cover the costs of site operation. The Directive also stipulates that the relevant authorities must be notified of any adverse environmental effects caused by the landfill. It requires sorting of waste prior to landfilling and bans co-disposal (the mixing of different types of waste in the one site).

---

35 House of Commons Select Committee on Environment, Transport and Regional Affairs 1999–2000, First Special Report, 9 December 1999.

36 This has recently been amended to exempt qualifying material that is used for filling a landfill site or filling existing or former quarries. See Landfill Tax (Qualifying Material) Order 1996 (SI 1996/1528) and the Landfill Tax (Site Restoration and Quarries) Order 1999 (SI 1999/2075).

37 See House of Commons Select Committee on Environment, Transport and Regional Affairs 1998–99, 13th Report, *The Operation of the Landfill Tax*, 14 July 1999, HC 150 1999–2000. See Hencke, 2000b, p 7.

38 Council Directive on the Landfill of Waste (OJL 182 16.7.99). This sets stringent targets for diverting waste away from landfill to more sustainable recovery options, such as recycling, composting and energy recovery.

39 Council Directive 1999/31/EEC.

The Directive sets targets for the reduction of biodegradable municipal waste going to landfill by July 2003 (Art 5). The targets are to reduce biodegradable municipal waste going to landfill by the flowing amounts:

- 75% of the 1995 total by July 2006;
- 50% of the 1995 total by 2009;
- 35% by 2016.

This will mean that the material has to be recycled or composted or some form of energy recovered from it.

The aim of the Directive is to prevent or reduce the negative effects on the environment or human health of the landfill of waste. It provides for a system of permits and a long list of requirements for applying for permits (Art 7), as well as the conditions that can be attached (Art 8). There are also provisions for waste monitoring and aftercare (Arts 11–13). Hazardous and non-hazardous waste have to be landfilled separately and there is a complete ban on some forms of hazardous waste, such as explosives or tyres. There are also provisions for some waste to be treated before landfill.[40]

The Contaminated Land (England) Regulations 2000 (SI 2000/227) govern the remediation of a site. They were passed under Pt IIA of the EPA 1990, as inserted by the Environment Act 1995.[41] The Regulations enacted give guidance to provide for greater consistency across the country. They will prescribe descriptions of land which, if contaminated, will be required to be designated as a special site. Once a site has been designated as such, the EA will regulate the site, rather than a local authority. The Regulations also set out the materials to be included in the remediation notices, particulars to be placed on the public registers, the grounds for appeal against remediation notices and compensation for those to whom they have been required to grant access in order for a remediation notice to be carried out. The extent of remedial works or preventative works would be restricted through guidance of the Secretary of State to those that are necessary, having regard to the use of the site, its location and physical characteristics, the cost and the seriousness of the harm or water pollution being addressed.[42] There is a duty on local authorities to inspect their areas for the presence of contaminated land. If the contamination is serious, the local authority may designate the land as a special site which will then be regulated by the EA. If emergency works are required, the regulatory authority can undertake them and the costs can be received from the appropriate person.

---

40 Limiting Landfill: A Consultation paper on limiting landfill to meet the EC Landfill Directive's targets for the landfill of biodegradable municipal waste. Forster 2000 pp 16–20.
41 This was inserted after the abandonment of the contaminated land registers, provided for in the EPA 1990, s 143.
42 See Sykes, 1999, p 27.

The extent of liability is laid down through the concept of a significant pollutant linkage. This will contain a potential pollutant, a receptor and a potential pathway by which the receptor may be exposed to the potential pollutant. A pollutant linkage that forms the basis for determination of land as contaminated is a significant pollutant linkage. Once this has been identified, liability and costs will be determined. There may be a number of different actions on the same piece of land.

If emergency works are not necessary, the enforcement authority should notify all persons who may be affected by the service of a remediation notice. This includes owners, occupiers and those responsible for the contamination. The enforcing authority will then draw up a scheme to clean up the land. It will set out the costs and timescale and there is then a period of consultation. If the persons agree to clean up the land voluntarily, the enforcement authority is precluded from taking any further action.

If there is no agreement, the enforcement authority will identify everyone who could be responsible for cleaning up the site – these are known as the 'appropriate persons'. The primary responsibility lies with the original polluter. If the original polluter cannot be found, the owner or occupier becomes the appropriate person. The appropriate person is the person who caused or knowingly permitted the substances or any of the substances that have been the cause of the contamination to be in or under the land. There can be joint and severable liability and different remediation notices can require different things to be done. The owner-occupier will not be liable for pollution of controlled waters and there are restrictions on liability for contamination that escapes onto other land. The basic principle here is that the original polluter can be responsible for contamination which has escaped onto other land.

Once everyone has been identified, the enforcing authority excludes less blameworthy persons, the test for whom is laid down in statutory guidance. After these tests have been applied, the costs of carrying out the clean up work are apportioned between those remaining and the authority will consider whether any person would suffer hardship if the costs were to be recovered from them. If that is the case, then a remediation notice cannot be put upon that person. There is the right of appeal within 21 days and, in the event of non-compliance with the remediation notice, there are criminal sanctions. In the case of other contaminated land, there is a maximum daily fine and default powers for the enforcing authority to carry out clean-up works, with the provision for cost recovery. There are three levels of guidance: that which the authorities must act in accordance with; that which the authorities must have regard to; and guidance, which is merely descriptive – this is important if a company wishes to challenge any decision of the enforcement authority on appeal.[43]

---

43   *R v Smith* [1999] Env LR 433, *R v SOSETR ex p Premier Environmental Ltd* [2000] WLR 404.

Recycling and re-use

The recycling and re-use of packaging has been provided for under the European Parliament and Council Directive 94/62/EC of 20 December 1994 on Packaging and Packaging Waste.[44] The introduction of the Directive[45] must be set against the background of the European waste strategy of prevention, increased recovery, safe disposal and the best environmental option, including economic considerations. Other considerations are included in the EU Waste Strategy Document (Com 96/399), which promotes the use of clean technologies, consumer information, Eco labelling, Eco audits and life cycle analysis.

The Packaging Directive aims first, in Art 1(1), to reduce the overall impact of packaging on the environment by reducing packaging at source, eliminating harmful materials in packaging waste, maximising the recovery of packaging waste for reuse, recycling, composting or energy generation, and minimising the quantity going for final disposal. Secondly, it aims to bring national measures closer together in order to remove obstacles to trade and distortions of competition.

The balance between environmental protection and trade freedom is a sensitive one and is open to interpretation by EU Member States. The goal is to balance environmental and single market goals. The conflict that can arise between these two ideals was examined in *Commission v Denmark* [1988] ECR 4608 (the *Danish Bottles* case). This involved Denmark's compulsory requirements for the use of standard returnable containers for beer and soft drinks. The Commission argued that this was disguised discrimination and an impediment to free trade. The Court held that it was permissible to use environmental protection as a reason for discrimination. However, the derogation from the free market had to be proportionate to the end to be achieved – the returnability requirement was acceptable but the licencing requirement on the limited number of container shapes was not. Germany and other countries such as Denmark pioneered waste disposal and waste prevention policy. In relation to paper, cardboard, etc, the German industry has a 93% recycling rate and for glass achieves 81%.

The Directive covers all packaging placed on the market within the EU, whether used at industrial, commercial, office, shop or any other level, and regardless of the material used (Art 2). Packaging is defined as all products made of any materials of any nature to be used for the containment, protection, handling, delivery and presentation of goods, from raw materials to processed goods, from the producer to the consumer. Non-returnable items

---

44 The Commission is in the process of reviewing the Packaging and Waste Directive to reduce the overall recycling target and different targets for packaging material.

45 See Long, 1997, pp 214–19.

used for the same purposes will also be considered to constitute packaging – Art 3 is generally concerned with definitions.

Article 1(2) states that the first priority is prevention. Prevention is important – a reduction in the quantity and harmfulness to the environment of material and substances contained in packaging and in packaging waste at production, marketing, distribution, utilisation and elimination stages, in particular through the use and development of clean products and technologies (Art 3(4)). In addition to the measures to prevent the formation of packaging waste taken in accordance with Art 9, other preventative measures are implemented. Such other measures may consist of national programmes or similar actions adopted, if appropriate in consultation with economic operators, and designed to collect and take advantage of the many initiatives taken within Member States as regards prevention (Art 4). Re-use is promoted. The next two aims are recycling and recovery. The recycling and recovery targets were the most controversial elements during negotiations. Germany, Denmark and the Netherlands voted against adoption of the Directive on the grounds that the targets were not tough enough. They were out-voted by the other nine States, which believed that the targets should be attainable by all. Nevertheless, Greece, Ireland, and Portugal have been given longer to attain the targets; they have until the end of 2005.

Within five years of the Directive being implemented in national law – that is, by 30 June 2001 – between 50% and 65% of packaging by weight must be recovered. Greece, Portugal and Ireland have been given targets of 25%. Between 25% and 45% of packaging by weight must be recycled, with a minimum of 15% of each material being recycled (Art 6).

EU States must ensure that systems are set up to recover packaging from the waste stream so that it can be channelled to the most appropriate method of waste management. Systems must be non-discriminatory for imported packaged goods. Packaging must be clearly marked to indicate the material used in order to help collection, recovery and re-use. The Council must decide on the marking systems within two years of the implementation of the Directive (Art 8). All packaging should comply with the essential requirements of the Packaging Directive in manufacture, re-use and recovery nature (these set down basic levels). Article 9 sets down mandatory requirements. By 1 January 2001, there must have been a review of practical experience and the Council and European Parliament will fix substantially increased targets to be achieved for the second five year period, ending on 30 June 2006. A Member State can go beyond the targets in the Directive, subject to the views of the other Member States, within the framework of the Art 21 Committee and the Commission. However, the Commission must also consider Art 21, which provides that the Commission must avoid distortions of the internal market.

Economic instruments may be used in the absence of relevant Community measures. Since fiscal measures, under current Treaty Articles, have to be passed unanimously, there is little likelihood of EU wide economic instruments being adopted in the foreseeable future (Art 15).

EU governments are required to provide the Commission with information for monitoring purposes. Moreover, they must make sure that the public is aware of: the targets and the systems available to achieve them; packaging users' own role in re-using, recycling and recovering used packaging; the meaning of packaging markings; and the key elements of national schemes for recovery and recycling (Art 13). They must ensure that information databases are harmonised under Art 12: these can be adapted in relation to scientific and technical progress under Art 19 – this also applies to Arts 8(2), Annex 1, Art 10, Art 12(3) and Annex III.

Article 20 allows the Commission to propose specific measures derogating from the general applicable rules in the future: this might be used to deal with technical problems. Article 10 states that the Commission shall promote the preparation of European standards relating to the essential requirements.

The UK implementation of the Directive

In the UK, these measures were implemented through ss 93 and 94 of the Environment Act 1995, which set out producer responsibility obligations and targets for re-use of materials.[46] Industry and the Government in the UK have agreed that the legal obligation for used packaging should be shared by all businesses that have any part in putting packaging on the market. The Regulations therefore affect a broad spectrum of businesses. 'Packaging' is defined as any product that is used to contain and protect goods, or to aid their handling, delivery or presentation. Such products are considered to be packaging at all stages of the process of manufacture and distribution, starting as raw materials and ending when they are delivered to the final user or consumer.

The main obligations are:

- to register with the appropriate agency or join a registered collective scheme;
- to recover and recycle certain percentages of packaging waste for which the producer is responsible;
- to provide data on packaging handled, recovered and recycled.

---

46 See Producer Responsibility Obligations (Packaging Waste) (Amendment) Regulations 1999 (SI 1999/1361): increased recovery targets to 43% and 45% and recycling obligations to 10% and 13%.The Regulations are being phased in over four years. More regulations are likely under the EA 1995, s 93.

Recovery includes a number of processes that result in a net benefit being derived from used packaging. This includes recycling energy recovery from the heat generated during burning and composting of packaging materials. 'Recycling' is a more precise term for the re-processing of used packaging so that the material produced can be re-used for its original, or another, purpose. Composting (organic recycling) is counted as recycling.

The packaging materials on which full obligations are placed from the start are aluminium, glass, paper, plastics and steel. Businesses must report data about packaging made from wood and other materials. Recycling obligations do not apply to wood or other materials.

The Regulations do not cover all businesses. The business must be involved in: manufacturing raw material used for packaging; converting raw materials into packaging; packaging or filling packaging; or selling packaging to the end user (wholesalers were to be included from January 2000 but this has now been withdrawn). The business must produce, handle or supply more than 50 tonnes of packaging materials or packaging each year, including imported but not exported packaging, and it must have a turnover of more than £5 million (although from 2000 business with a turnover of over £2 million will fall under the regulations).

If a business meets all these criteria, then it is legally obliged to recover specific tonnages of packaging waste through methods such as recycling. These recovery obligations are based on the activities which a business is involved in, the volume of packaging it owns and handles over a year and national recovery and recycling targets.

Businesses had until August 1997 to register individually and provide a rough estimate, in tonnes per annum, of packaging handled in 1996, or join a compliance scheme, which takes on the legal responsibility for meeting its members' targets. These compliance schemes must be registered with the EA. A business can meet its obligation either as an individual complier or by joining a collective scheme, that will take on legal obligations in exchange for the company meeting its conditions. An individual complier must register with the EA; provide data on packaging passing through the business each year; once recycling and recovery targets apply, show each year that legal obligations have been met; and pay fees (£750) to the Agency on registration and thereafter annually.

An individual complier has to register individually with the EA. Businesses registering individually are not expected to undertake the recovery and recycling themselves, unless they already have, or plan to develop, the facilities to do this. They can meet their targets by paying waste management companies, specialist reclamation companies and/or reprocessors to undertake the recovery and recycling on their behalf.

A compliance scheme takes on a company's legal obligations, in particular its legal responsibility to meet its recycling and recovery obligations. The

Agency advised businesses to look at the merits of joining a compliance scheme as compared to registering individually. Members of collective schemes must be confirmed as a member of a scheme and meet the scheme's conditions of membership, which will include providing data and payment of the scheme's subscription, levy and other charges. Members of a scheme have no individual legal obligation to meet recovery and recycling obligations, since the scheme assumes this responsibility on behalf of all its members.

Trade associations, waste management and reclamation companies and other organisations with access to packaging waste materials could examine whether there is the opportunity to set up a compliance scheme for their members or customers on a national or regional basis. Any proposed compliance scheme has to produce a detailed operational plan to demonstrate how the recycling and recovery obligations of its members will be discharged and show evidence of adequate financial and technical resources.

The scheme will require approval by the Secretary of State for the Environment and the EA and will also be scrutinised by the Office of Fair Trading. Enquiries on this should be directed to the Agency's Producer Responsibility Registration Unit. Companies cannot split packaging waste between different schemes without registering with one of the Agencies. Companies should have already joined a scheme or have registered with an Agency. Place of registration will depend on the location of a business' or scheme's registered or principal office.

A business must start to reach interim recovery targets and recycling targets for material (packaging which is made from metal, plastics, paper and glass). These interim targets were raised to 45% recovery and 13% recycling of material in 2000. From 2001, businesses must reach full recovery targets of 52% (of which 26% must be through recycling) and recycling targets of 16% of material.[47] A certificate of compliance has to be sent to the EA each year, along with annual fees. Companies will be monitored every three years to ensure that compliance is achieved. It is an offence to fail to take reasonable steps to recycle or recover the statutory targets.

Packaging and packaging materials exported are excluded when calculating a business' obligations, even if the business does not actually export them itself. The business will need to provide proof of the export. An importer of packaging or packaging materials must meet the additional obligations associated with the functions performed prior to import, even where they are the last users of that packaging. For instance, a retailer importing packaged goods must pick up the obligations of the packer/filler, converter and raw materials producer. In the case of imported transit packaging, an importer has 100% of the recycling and recovery obligations.

---

47 Producer Responsibility Obligations (Packaging Waste) (Amendment) Regulations 1999 (SI 1999/1361).

If a company is supplying another business that is the final user of the packaging (in other words, the packaging is not subsequently sold or passed on to another user or consumer), the company becomes the seller/retailer for purposes of the obligation. Thus, if the company is a packaging manufacturer which supplies a food manufacturer with cartons which that company over-wrap with plastic film for transport purposes, that company is deemed to be the packer/filler and the seller/retailer of the film.

If packaging delivered to a company has no further use (and so becomes waste), it is not counted as part of the company's recovery and recycling obligations, as the company is the final user. This applies, for instance, to retail stores, where the packaging used to group individual items together for transit is removed for disposal before goods are sold to customers. However, since it is packaging waste, the company can use it to meet its own obligation by delivering it to a reprocessor.

The targets are that the producer has to meet 6% of the share of the total recovery and recycling target, the converter 9%, the packer/filler 37% and the seller 48%. The activity performed will determine the quantities for which the company is responsible. There are a number of categories which a company can fall into: a producer of materials for packaging; a converter of materials into packaging; a business packing products into or filling packaging; or a seller of packaged goods to the final consumer. These have been defined as the four stages (functions) through which packaging passes on its way along the packaging chain. Each will share in the total target for recovery and recycling. The targets have been specified for each year to 2001. Each business must establish which functions it performs for each element of packaging it handles. It may, under some circumstances, perform more than one function for the same item of packaging.

The recovery obligations can be met by using any packaging material (aluminium, steel, paper (board), plastics, glass and, after 2000, wood and other packaging materials). The recycling target shown is the minimum to be achieved for each material a business handles. Since 2000, the aggregate-recycling rate for all materials handled must be 25%. The amount of material recycled will count towards satisfaction of the overall recovery obligation. Obligations are calculated by multiplying the weight of packaging handled by the appropriate function share and by the recovery and recycling targets in force.

The Regulations state that material that becomes production waste during a business' manufacturing processes may not be counted as packaging or packaging waste for the purpose either of calculating an obligation or of meeting that obligation. This means that it cannot be treated as packaging handled; nor – if it is recovered or recycled – does it count towards meeting an obligation. All packaging is subject to obligations the first time it passes through the packaging chain. Subsequent use attracts no further obligation.

The Producer Responsibility Obligations[48] specified essential requirements that packaging should now meet and limits on heavy metals to be phased in over three years. The 1997 Regulations set down limits for lead, mercury hexavelent chromium and cadmium, with reductions to be made by 30 June 2001. In relation to packaging, the Regulations require that packaging is manufactured so that its volume and weight is limited to the minimum adequate amount to maintain the necessary levels of safety and hygiene and that packaging must ensure that emissions of noxious and other substances are minimised in manufacture. Packaging must also be recoverable through incineration with energy recovery, material recycling or biodegradation or composting and, in general, packaging must be designed, produced and commercialised for re-use. These Regulations cover certain activities involving packaging, from its production as raw material to its supply to the final user.

The EA has the task of ensuring compliance with the Regulations. They will register individual compliers and collective schemes, monitor whether businesses are registered or are exempt, and ensure that registered businesses and schemes meet the compliance requirements. The Agencies are empowered, where necessary, to de-register schemes and bring prosecutions against individual non-compliers. Offences will be dealt with under criminal law and the maximum penalty, on conviction, will be an unlimited fine. The Office of Fair Trading must undertake a competition scrutiny of all schemes before they are registered with the EA. The Director General of Fair Trading advises the Minister – the Secretary of State for Trade and Industry.[49]

Other recycling policies[50]

Recycling and waste minimisation are also promoted through the development of a waste management strategy, which was introduced under s 92 of the Environment Act 1995.[51] The Waste Minimisation Act 1998[52] gives local authorities powers to minimise quantities of controlled waste. However, the Act dies not put any restrictions or requirements on individuals; instead, it is there to promote information on less wasteful products, waste reduction plans or targets in contracts or waste plans.

---

48 The Producer Responsibility Obligations (Packaging Waste) Regulations 1997 (SI 1997/ 648) (Environment Act 1995, ss 93–95) were amended in 1998 by the Packaging (Essential Requirements) Regulations 1998 (SI 1998/1165) and the Producer Responsibility Obligations (Packaging Waste) (Amendment) Regulations 1999 (SI1999/1361). See Environmental Protection (Waste Recycling Payments) (Amendment) (England) Regulations 2000 (SI 2000/831); Council Recommendation Concerning the Re-Use of Waste Paper and of Recycled Paper 81/972/EEC (OJL 355 10.12.81).

49 The Packaging Directive is in the process of review and the targets for 2006 are being considered.

50 See DETR press release 19 April 2000.

51 See EPA 1990, s 44a.

52 See, also, the Energy Conservation Act 1996.

Under the EPA 1990, local authorities are required to publish their plans for the recycling of waste,[53] which is also part of the sustainable development strategy. The main requirements of the strategy are to encourage more public involvement in re-use and recycling; the setting of challenging but realistic targets; a strong emphasis on waste minimisation; changing the perception of the waste hierarchy; and more creative use of economic instruments,[54] for example, the possibility of using landfill tax revenue to fund recycling. Local authorities are also revising the statutory recycling plans under the EPA 1990 to reach Government targets of recovering value from 40% of municipal waste by 2005 and 25% of recycling or composting.[55]

Other areas are also being looked at, such as mineral extraction. Mineral Planning Guidance 6 sets targets for the substitution of recycled or secondary aggregates in place of virgin natural aggregates. The Aggregation Advisory Service advises construction companies about the most effective use of aggregates from all sources.[56] There are proposals for the recycling of other materials, such as batteries,[57] cars and waste from electronic and electrical equipment.

Incineration[58]

There are a number of EC directives which deal with air pollution from incineration.[59] The Government has recently announced that a number of new incinerators may be built in England and Wales.[60] This, it seems, goes against policy developments in the rest of Europe. In an article in *The Guardian*,

---

53 WCAs also have to make plans under the EPA 1990, s 49.

54 Environmental Protection (Waste Recycling Payments) (Amendment) Regulations 1999 (SI 1999/546) under the Environment Act 1995 (Commencement No 14) Order 1999 (SI 1999/803).

55 See Environment Transport and Regional Affairs Select Committee Report, *Sustainable Waste Strategy*, June 1998.

56 www. BRE.co.uk/waste.

57 See the Batteries and Accumulators Containing Certain Dangerous Substances Directive 91/157, which at present only applies to primary and secondary batteries but will soon be extended to all batteries.

58 For a fuller discussion of air pollution problems, see above, Chapter 5.

59 See Directive 89/369 on preventing air pollution from new municipal waste plants; Directive 89/429 on controlling pollution from existing plants; EPA 1990 on IPC; 94/67/EC on incineration of hazardous waste. The Commission has published a draft Directive on non-hazardous waste incineration, which will replace the 1989 Directive. It will look at co-incineration, standards for co-incineration, dioxin limits and biomass exemptions. The European Commission has adopted a proposal (COM 1998 558 Final) for controls on emissions to be extended to a number of waste types not covered by Directive 94/67. This would repeal and replace directives on municipal incineration.

60 For a discussion of the problems of incineration, see Friends of the Earth briefing sheet, 'Up in smoke – why Friends of the Earth opposes incineration', February 1997. See, also, the critical HL Select Committee 1998–99 11th Report, *Waste Incineration*.

Ludwig Kraemer, head of the EU Waste Management Directorate, stated that in many European countries there are no more plans for incinerators to be built, due to concern over public health,[61] traffic congestion and pollution. The EC is drawing up a Waste Incineration Directive. This will merge the provision of the Hazardous Waste Incineration Directive (94/67 EC), although it will continue into force until 2005.[62]

Hazardous and toxic substances

Initially, an exhaustive list of hazardous wastes was to have provided the legally binding definition of 'hazardous waste'. This proved impossible to compile and Directive 94/31/EC postponed implementation of Directive 91/689 from December 1993 until July 1995 to allow for completion of a list. In December 1994, EU environmental ministers approved a core list of wastes which are to be considered hazardous.[63] At the same time, the ministers passed into law the draft Directive governing the incineration of hazardous waste. The hazardous waste list is a key component of the 1991 Hazardous Waste Directive and agreement on the list finally meant that this piece of legislation could be fully implemented. The list contains 200 types of waste, divided into 19 main categories.

Hazardous and toxic substances are defined as special waste.[64] The Directives on Hazardous Waste[65] put strict requirements on the waste and require that competent authorities to be set up and plans approved.[66] Under the Regulations, the offences are disposing of waste other than to a special contractor who holds an appropriate waste management licence or to a carrier registered to carry waste.

Special waste disposal has high penalties for offences, namely, a maximum of five years' imprisonment when sentenced in Crown Court.

Special waste is covered by a consignment note system. These notes have to be kept for three years and the Regulations aim to provide a cradle to grave

---

61 There is a particular concern about a waste incinerator on Tyneside where toxic ash is falling on paths and allotments. The council has ordered 2,000 tonnes of ash to be removed from footpaths and allotments. The ash contains high levels of mercury, cadmium and lead. See Hencke, 2000c.

62 House of Lords Select Committee on the EU 198–99, 11th Report, *Waste Incineration*, 21 July, HL 71.

63 See EC Decision 94/904/EC.

64 Pollution (Special Waste) Regulations 1996 (SI 1996/839); Special Waste (Amendment) Regulations 1997 (SI 1997/251); Controlled Waste Regulations 1992 (SI 1992/2117), as amended; Planning (Hazardous Substances) Act 1990.

65 75/442/EEC; 78/1319/EEC; 91/689/EC; 94/31/EC.

66 See de Sadeleer and Sambon, 1997, pp 9–13; Layard, 1997, pp 16–22.

record of the life of the waste. Operators are also under a duty of care in relation to the waste. 'Special waste' covers a variety of wastes, including liquid wastes, which are either 'controlled waste' or 'special waste' if assessed as exhibiting certain hazardous properties under the Regulations. For the storage of controlled waste produced on the site of storage, no waste management licence is necessary and there are no volume or time limits. Other substances, such as batteries, are also regulated.[67] Poly chlorinated biphenyls (PCBs) may be disposed of by high temperature incineration or by a suitable dechlorination process.[68]

Regarding transport,[69] the Regulations require that the operator:

- identifies the hazards of the goods;

- packages the goods suitably and safely;

- correctly marks and labels the waste;

- provides information on the waste to the vehicle operator/carrier;

- assesses the suitability of vehicles and the training of drivers;

- notifies local authorities and the EA.

At present, the special waste Regulations are under review.[70] The review aims to evaluate the efficiency and effectiveness of the Regulations and to identify possible alternative options for the future regulation of hazardous waste, consistent with the requirements of the Hazardous Waste Directive.[71]

---

67 Regulated Batteries and Accumulators (Containing Dangerous Substances) Regulations 1994 (SI 1994/232); Council Directive 91/157/EEC on Batteries and Accumulators Containing Certain Dangerous Substances (OJL 078 26.3.91, as amended by OJL 5.1.99).

68 The DETR made regulations in 1999 to prohibit (except for the purposes of decontamination or disposal and with special provisions for only slightly contaminated equipment) the holding of PCBs and similar substances. These implement EC Directive 96/59/EC on PCBs.

69 See DETR, *A New Deal for Transport: Better for Everyone*, 1998 on more sustainable methods for transporting waste.

70 DETR, *Review of the Special Waste Regulations*, February 2000.

71 The Planning (Control of Major Accident Hazards) Regulations 1999 (SI 1999/981) change hazardous substances consent legislation and development plan regulations. See Transport of Dangerous Goods Safety Regulations 1999 (SI 1999/257); Carriage of Dangerous Goods (Amendment) Regulations 1999 (SI 1999/303); Transport of Dangerous Goods (Safety Advisors) Regulations 1999 (SI 1999/257); Control of Major Accidents Hazards Regulations 1999 (SI 1999/743).

The import and export of all waste[72]

Council Regulation 259/93/EEC (Supervision and Control of Shipments of Wastes) and EC Directive 97/120[73] came into force on 6 May 1994 and have as their aim the comprehensive regulation of the movement of all waste within, into and out of the EU. The Regulation implements the Basle Convention and OECD Decision on the trans-frontier shipment of waste. The shipment of hazardous waste destined for final disposal to non-OECD countries is prohibited. This is to prevent EU and non-OECD operators from dumping hazardous waste in developing countries.[74] Waste for disposal within the EU requires prior authorisation. The principles of self-sufficiency (disposal by Member States of their own waste) and proximity (local waste disposal) will also apply. The treatment of wastes for recovery operations within the EU will depend on the listing of the wastes in question. Those listed as 'green' will be largely excluded from the Regulation; those listed as 'amber' will be subject to a prior notification requirement; and those listed as 'red' will require prior authorisation.[75]

Regulation 259/93/EEC was amended and extended in February 1997 1998, and 1999 in relation to waste exports out of the EU. The amendment implemented into Community law the decision taken under the Basle Convention to immediately ban exports of hazardous waste destined for final disposal to non-OECD countries, and to ban by January 1998 all exports of hazardous waste destined for recovery in non-OECD countries.[76]

Directive 84/631/EEC requires the use of a detailed consignment note, detailing the source and composition of the waste, the routes by which it will be transported, measures undertaken to ensure safe transportation and the existence of a formal agreement with the consignee of the waste. Transportation cannot take place until the Member States concerned have acknowledged receipt of notification of the shipment. Objections from a Member State must be based on Community law or international agreements concerning environmental protection, public policy, security or health protection. The Directive also includes conditions for packaging and labelling the waste.

---

72 See Kummer, 1999; Commission Proposal Com 1991 1608 final for a Council directive on restrictions on the marketing and use of certain dangerous substances; Commission Proposal Com 1993 638 final proposal for an EP and Council directive relating to the classification, packaging and labelling of dangerous substances; Council Directive 91/689/EEC on hazardous waste (OJL 377 31.12.91, as amended by OJL 168 2.7.94); Council Directive 75/442/EEC on waste (OJL 194 25.7.75, as amended by OJL 243 24.9.96).

73 As amended. See Commission Decision 1999/816/EEC (OJL 316 10.12.99).

74 Tromans, 1998, pp 146–60.

75 EC Amendment Regulation 259/93 on shipments of waste.

76 EC Council decisions on the hazardous waste list (94/904/EEC).

In the UK, the EC Regulations[77] are covered by the UK Management Plan on Imports and Exports of Waste, which Implements the requirements of EC Regulations 259/93 on the shipment of wastes (not radioactive).[78]

The UK Management Plan on Imports and Exports of Waste is in the process of being reviewed.[79] The Consultation Paper sets out the Government's proposed policies on exports and imports into the UK.[80] These are, in brief:

- to ban all exports of waste for disposal, except shipments from Northern Ireland and shipments for trial runs to EC and EFTA countries;

- to allow exports of waste for recovery to Basle Annex VII countries (OECD, EC and Liechtenstein) and of non-hazardous waste to some non-Annex VII countries in accordance with EC controls;

- to ban most imports for waste disposal, except imports for high temperature incineration from Portugal, imports from Ireland to Northern Ireland for high temperature incineration, imports from non-Annex VII countries where they cannot realistically be dealt with in an environmentally sound manner or in closer proximity to the country in question, imports of hazardous waste for high temperature incineration from any country in cases of emergency, and and shipments for trial runs.

- to allow all genuine imports for recovery, including energy recovery, but to prevent imports for disposal under the guise of recovery.

77 Council Regulation 1420/1999/EC establishing common rules and procedures to apply to shipments to certain non OECD countries of certain types of waste (OJL 166 1.7.99); Council Regulation 1547/9199/EC, detailing the control procedures under Council Regulation 259/1993/EC to apply to shipments of certain types of waste to which OECD Decision C(92) 39 final does not apply (OJL 185 17.7.99, as amended by OJL 045 17.2.00); Council Resolution concerning the transfrontier movements of hazardous waste to third countries (OJC 009 12.1.89).

78 See above, Chapter 5 for the disposal of radioactive waste. See, also, Council Decision 94/774 on the requirement for consignment notes and the Transfrontier Shipment of Waste Regulations 1994 (SI 1994/1137); DOE Circular 13/94; EC Amendment to Regulation 259/93 on the shipment of waste. In 1998, these controls were strengthened by Cmnd 4061, which sets out details of the Decision IV/9, clarifying which wastes will be subject to the ban on the exports of hazardous waste to developing countries.

79 Consultation Paper, UK Management Plan on Imports and Exports of Waste, April 2000.

80 See Transfrontier Shipment of Wastes Regulations 1994 (SI 1994/1137) and, in the EC, see the Waste Shipments Regulations 120/97 and 2408/98.

The future[81]

The future for waste has been set out by the Government in *A Way with Waste – A Draft Waste Strategy for England and Wales,* which was published in July 1999.[82] The Government set out seven commitments:

(a) substantial increase in recycling and energy recovery;

(b) engagement of the public in re-use and recycling of household waste;

(c) a long term framework with challenging targets, underpinned by realistic programmes;

(d) a strong emphasis on waste minimisation;

(e) using the waste hierarchy as a guide, not a prescriptive set of rules;

(f) creative use of economic incentives such as the landfill tax;

(g) increased public involvement in decision making.

This strategy has now been replaced by the new *Waste Strategy,* which builds on those policies and provides more details. Its publication followed a series of articles in *The Guardian* on the waste industry. The *Waste Strategy* was published in May 2000.[83]

The proposals in this strategy are as follows:

• to break the link between economic growth and increased waste;

• where waste is created, it should be recycled, composted or used as fuel. By 2015, the Government expects that value can be recovered from two-thirds of household waste and that at least half of that should be through recycling or composting;

• in 1999, the Chancellor announced that the landfill tax would rise from £10 by £1 a year, with a review in 2004;

• the Government is to set up a system of tradeable permits restricting the amount of biodegradable municipal waste that local authorities can send to landfill;

• the report states that, in some cases, local authorities will need to introduce energy recovery facilities, but, if these are needed, the Government believes that they should be adequately sized so that they do not compete with recycling;

• the opportunities of combining waste recovery with combined heat and power should be considered;

---

81 See, also, the EA's *An Action Plan for Waste Management* as part of the EA's strategy for the millennium and beyond.

82 This was preceded by the consultation document *Less Waste More Value – A Consultation Paper on the Waste Strategy for England and Wales 1998.*

83 DETR, *Waste Strategy 2000,* May 2000.

- in relation to incineration of non-hazardous waste where no energy is recovered, this 'is not an option the Government ... would generally wish to encourage';
- however, waste incineration for hazardous waste will still be allowed;
- central to the strategy is the need to curb the growth in waste. The Report sets down a number of targets for waste. Industrial and commercial waste going to landfill is to be reduced to 85% of 1998 levels by 2005. This will focus on recovering value and reducing environmental impacts. The Government has set a target of recovering 45% of municipal waste by 2010 and of recycling or composting 30% of household waste by the same date;
- local authorities are to be set statutory performance standards for recycling;
- there are also proposals for producer responsibility for end of life vehicles and batteries, and electrical and electronic goods are being considered by the EC. The Government also wants to develop a stronger market for recycled materials;
- the Government will set up a waste and resources action programme.

Future developments include a draft EC Directive on civil liability for damage caused by waste.[84] As the Report states, in the future, waste will be disposed of very differently from today through changes such as the ban on certain waste going to landfill, the separating of waste which does not happen at present and the treatment of some waste. The days of putting waste in the ground and forgetting about it are over; the challenge now is to find environmentally acceptable solutions to disposing of waste that do not rely heavily on incineration. This is the challenge for waste in the next 20 years.

CONTAMINATED LAND

The following section deals with the investigation and remediation of contaminated land and the health and environmental hazards associated with landfill sites.These topics are very broad and what follows is a brief and simplified overview, intended to provide the reader with an introduction to the technical aspects of these two subject areas.

The investigation and remediation of contaminated land

The issue of contaminated land in the UK, Western Europe and the US has become increasingly important over the last 30 years or so. During this period,

---

84 Sykes, 1999, p 27; Taylor, 2000, p 160.

the industrial face of Western countries has changed as traditional industries such as mining, shipbuilding and steel and gas manufacture have declined or ceased. Many sites previously occupied by these industries are now vacant and, in many cases, derelict.

The shortage of 'greenfield' sites for new development and the need to preserve quality land has brought about increased pressure to develop old industrial land for commercial, industrial and domestic use. Old industrial sites usually retain below their surface the remains and waste residues from previous uses and occupancy. A site used by successive industries or processes may have layers of waste and contamination present from each.

The Nato Committee on Challenges to Modern Society's definition of contaminated land is as follows:

Land that contains substances which, when present in sufficient quantities or concentrations, are likely to cause harm, directly or indirectly, to man, to the environment, or on occasion to other targets.

In the UK, land contamination is generally considered in the context of redevelopment. Its investigation is usually aimed at determining the extent and degree of any contamination present at a site and the remedial action required to render the site safe for redevelopment.

Physical damage to the land can also be a byproduct of industrial activity. Ground instability due to mining can occur long after the actual mining work has been completed. Contaminated water migrating from abandoned mine workings can pollute watercourses and ground water. Gas emanating from old mine workings can pose a health and safety hazard and old spoil tips can become unstable.

Historically, the real contamination of the land in the UK and Europe began in the 18th century with the expansion of manufacturing industry, and this has continued until recent times. The pollution and contamination of the land and rivers by industrial activity was accepted in the past as being part of the price of progress. Land situated near to industrial activity may be at risk from wind-blown contaminants and the migration of contaminants in surface and ground water. The potential for contamination is therefore not confined to the direct use of a site itself and may reflect the impact of neighbouring uses or activities.

The interest in contaminated land in the modern context began in the mid-1970s, when large areas of land previously used for industrial processes for many years became available for redevelopment. These, the first 'brownfield' sites, were considered valuable for housing development by local authorities.

Formation of the Interdepartmental Committee on the Reclamation of Contaminated Land

When construction on these projects began, the local authorities developing the sites were faced with the problems of ground contaminated by the previous occupancy. In order to provide guidance in these circumstances, the Department of the Environment, in association with the Building Research Establishment and other organisations, formed the Interdepartmental Committee on the Reclamation of Contaminated Land (ICRCL).

The ICRCL was established in 1976, following requests for guidance from local authorities encountering problems with contaminated land when redeveloping old industrial sites for housing. In response, the ICRCL produced a set of guidance notes, which provided the framework upon which contaminated land has been investigated and treated in the UK up to the present time.

The recommendations of the ICRCL

The ICRCL guidance note recommended a systematic approach to the assessment of contaminated land on the basis that each site should be treated individually, on its own merits. In summary, the process advocated by the ICRCL is, first, to study the history of the site in detail; then to take samples of the ground from places of particular interest; and follow this with laboratory analysis of the samples to determine their chemical characteristics. The information obtained from this process is used to assess the degree of ground contamination present and its effect on the proposed end use of the site.

The principal adopted in the UK is to clean up contaminated sites to a degree appropriate to the end use. If, for instance, a contaminated site were to be developed for use as hard standing for vehicle parking, the degree of clean-up would be less stringent than if the site were to be used for a housing development. This is in contrast to the multifunctional approach, in which the site is cleaned up to a high standard irrespective of the end use. The former method is more economical from the point of view of development, but, if the site end use changes in time, it may be necessary to remediate the land again to a higher standard. The multifunctional approach avoids successive remediation work, as the site is cleaned up to a high standard at the beginning, once and for all. From a practical point of view, however, the imposition of high standard clean-up criteria for sites where it is not appropriate to the end use may render these sites uneconomical to develop.

The multifunctional approach to cleaning up contaminated sites has been adopted in Holland. There, the ground water is particularly vulnerable to contamination and the multifunctional approach to remediation is justified. In the UK, however, most of the water-bearing stratum is protected by a thick layer of clay and there is less risk of contamination.

The source-pathway-receptor concept

To illustrate the reasoning behind the end use approach, the previous examples of the hard standing for vehicle parking and housing development will be used. In the former, the contaminated material in the ground will be covered by a concrete slab and the public will have no direct contact with it. In development for housing, on the other hand, the soil will be exposed at the surface in gardens and there will be the potential for direct contact between the contaminated material and the public. In the case of gardens, there is the additional risk of vegetables grown in contaminated soil entering the food chain.

This introduces one of the most important concepts in the assessment of contaminated land – the relationship between the source, the pathway and the receptor:

Source ⟶ Pathway ⟶ Receptor

The source is the contaminant; the pathway is the route or mechanism by which the contaminant can reach or affect the receptor; the receptor is the person, animal, property or object affected by the contaminant.

The principle is that, although contamination may exist and represent a hazard, unless there is a means, mechanism or pathway by which the hazard can affect somebody or something, there is no significant risk. This is illustrated by Cairney and Hobson (1998):

> Metals such as lead and uranium certainly are hazardous to health, particularly if they exist in very high concentrations, yet good quality crystal drinking glasses (with up to 10,000 mg/kg of metals introduced to give different colorations) are used without any concern. The metals are, of course, so locked into glassy silicate compounds that they remain totally insoluble and immobilised, and so cannot harm the users of the crystal glasses.

In this illustration, the source-pathway-receptor link is not established because the pathway does not exist. In judging the risk posed by a contaminant, it is essential to find out whether or not it is capable of being mobilised and whether a pathway exists.

Trigger concentrations

In order to assess the risks involved with different contaminants, the ICRCL devised certain trigger concentrations by which the risk can be assessed in relation to the end use of the site. These trigger values establish certain zones in which different actions are required. This is shown diagrammatically below, Figure 1.

Contaminant concentration below the 'threshold value' is regarded as posing a risk no greater than that normally accepted and the material may be regarded as uncontaminated for the purposes of redevelopment.

Contaminant concentration above the 'action value' is regarded as posing an unacceptable degree of risk and action is required.

Between the 'threshold value' and 'action value' there is a zone in which the concentration of contaminant, although high, may not pose a significantly high risk. The treatment of contaminants in this zone will depend on the intended end use and professional judgment is required to assess the risk and decide the course of action to be taken.

Acceptance criteria

The trigger concentrations for various contaminants in relation to the site end use are given in ICRCL Guidance Note 59/83 (on the assessment and redevelopment of contaminated land). Some of the trigger values given in

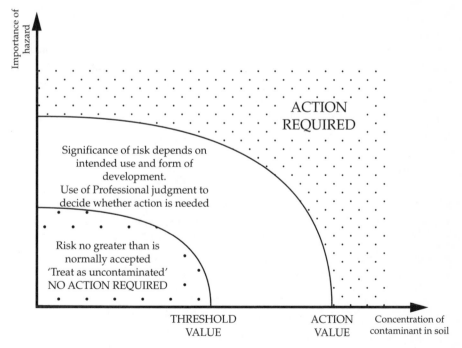

Figure 1: Trigger concentration in relation to hazard

Tables 3 and 4 of Guidance Note 59/83 are indicated below to illustrate the relationship between contaminant, end use and trigger concentration.

Contaminant	Planned uses	Trigger concentrations (mg/kg air dried soil)	
		Threshold	Action
Arsenic	Domestic gardens, allotments	10	*
	Parks, playing fields, open space	40	*
Cadmium	Domestic gardens, allotments	3	*
	Parks, playing fields, open space	15	*
Lead	Domestic gardens, allotments	500	*
	Parks, playing fields, open space	2,000	*
Free cyanide	Domestic gardens, allotments, landscaped areas	25	500
	Buildings, hard cover	100	500

* Values not yet established.

It can be seen that, although the threshold concentration establishing the lower limit of a particular contaminant is given, the action value or the concentration above which action must be taken has not yet been established for some contaminants.

It is important in this context to appreciate that the criteria for determining whether the concentration of a contaminant is acceptable or otherwise cannot hinge on a fixed action value alone. Other factors have to be considered, including the contaminant mobility and pathway.

INVESTIGATION

The investigation of contaminated land normally follows the generally accepted procedure proposed by the ICRCL. This will involve:

- determining the history of the site (desk study);
- establishing the proposed end use for the site;
- planning and executing a site investigation;
- carrying out laboratory analysis on the material recovered;
- carrying out an interpretation of the data obtained and judging the nature and concentration of the contaminants against the acceptance criteria;
- assessing the risks and deciding on the appropriate remedial action.

Desk study

The first step in the investigation is to gather as much information as possible about the site and its history. This is the desk study stage, where information about the site and its history is gathered from current and historical Ordnance Survey maps and from records held at the local library, by the local authority and from other sources. A study of geological maps of the area will give useful information about the nature and depth of the bedrock and the extent of any water-bearing rocks or aquifers. Other geological maps give information about the surface materials overlying the bedrock, such as clay, sand and gravel deposits.

During the desk study stage, a site reconnaissance or 'walk over' visit is carried out. The walk over visit often gives valuable clues as to the previous site use, together with the general feel of the site and the situation and constraints existing at and beyond the site boundaries. Local people can also provide a valuable source of information about their locality not always available from other sources. For example: 'I remember fishing in a pond over there by the trees when I was a boy and then after the War they filled it up with drums of something and covered it over with soil.'

There are many sources of information to draw on in preparing the desk study report on a site. Most are in the public domain and can be obtained free of charge or at little cost. The desk study report should provide a good picture of the site and its history and indicate where the problems are likely to be with regard to contaminants, buried structures, underground tanks, waste storage areas and the like.

When the desk study report has been completed, the prospective developer or purchaser of the site may or may not decide to proceed. Indeed, the desk study is often carried out in order to assess the likely hidden costs and risks involved with the development of a site prior to purchase. A desk study could also be commissioned by a landowner interested in assessing the potential liability involved with ownership.

Field investigation

When the desk study has been completed, the next stage in the investigation is to carry out a physical site investigation to determine the nature, condition and location of any contaminated soil or material at the site. This is often carried out in conjunction with the routine ground investigation for the project normally carried out to provide geotechical information for the design of foundations.

The field investigation usually involves the excavation of pits or the drilling of exploratory boreholes. For small, uncomplicated sites, this may involve a few simple excavations involving a day's work. On large, highly contaminated sites, however, a complex, multi-stage investigation may be required, lasting several months and involving trial pits, boreholes and site monitoring.

Trial pits, which are usually dug by mechanical excavators, have the advantage that they are relatively inexpensive to dig and they expose a fairly large area of the ground for visual inspection and sampling. Trial pits can easily be extended into trenches, from which a particular seam of contamination can be traced. The main disadvantage of trial pits is the limitation on the depth to which they can be excavated, which, with normal equipment, is about four metres.

Boreholes are considerably more expensive to sink but have the advantage that depths of 40 m or so can be reached with conventional cable tool equipment and samples can be recovered from depth. Boreholes are typically 150 mm or 200 mm in diameter and apparatus can be installed in them to monitor ground water and gas. The main disadvantage is the relatively small area of ground they can explore and there is a risk of transferring contamination from one level of the ground to another in the drilling process.

Before commencing the fieldwork, a strategy has to be arrived at to locate the trial pits and boreholes in the most effective positions. If the desk study has identified the areas of the site where contamination is most likely, the field investigation can be concentrated in that area and the trial pits or boreholes targeted accordingly. If the picture is less clear, the pits and boreholes are often arranged in a rectangular grid pattern to gain a preliminary understanding of the site. This might be followed by a more detailed arrangement of sampling points to target specific areas in more detail. As far as the number of sampling points is concerned, the more the better; but the number is usually constrained by cost.

The Draft (British Standard) Code of Practice for the Identification of Potentially Contaminated Land and its Investigation DD 175 (1988) recommended a minimum number of sampling points per hectare (2.5 acres) as follows:

Area of site (hectares)	Minimum number of sampling points
0.5	15
1.0	25
5.0	85

It should be appreciated that 25 boreholes put down on a one hectare site will explore only about 0.005% of the site area. Important technical and commercial decisions as to the degree of contamination and the method of remediation will be based on this very limited amount of information.

The current version of DD 175 (DD 175: 1998) does not continue with this arbitrary method of determining sampling frequency but instead recommends a sampling frequency approach based on the degree of confidence required to identify a certain area of contamination.

During the fieldwork operation, a detailed record is made of the different materials encountered and samples are taken from the ground and stored ready for laboratory testing. The ground conditions, the location of the individual samples and other relevant information is recorded accurately on plan and in elevation, thus enabling it to be positioned in three dimensions.

Laboratory testing and interpretation

The samples of material, groundwater or gas recovered during the fieldwork operation are sent to a specialist laboratory for testing and analysis. Particular care is taken to ensure that the samples are correctly stored and transported to the laboratory to ensure that the material tested is representative of the material in the field.

The range of tests to which the samples are to be subjected, is usually agreed jointly between the organisation carrying out the investigation and the laboratory.

The results of the laboratory analysis will give the range of chemical contaminants present in the materials and liquids together with their concentration. This will be assessed in relation to the adopted acceptance criteria. Considerable experience and judgment is required in interpreting the results of laboratory tests if a realistic assessment of the risks they present is to be made.

Interpreting the results of the investigation

The data obtained from the desk study, fieldwork operation and laboratory analysis is gathered together to provide a three dimensional picture of the site. This will include the surface topography, the location and nature of any made ground, the natural geological strata and the location of the water table and other hydrogeological data. In addition, there will be the location of any contaminated materials and liquids. This, together with the laboratory analysis, will provide the information from which the risk evaluation of the site is carried out and the proposals for remediation determined.

METHODS OF REMEDIATION

There are many methods available for the remediation of contaminated sites. Some methods of treatment are specific to certain types of contaminant. Other methods are more general and can be used to deal with a range of contaminants. Some of the principal methods of remediation are outlined below.

Excavate the contaminated material and remove it from site

This technique involves excavating the contaminated material and transporting it to a repository licensed to receive contaminated waste.

This is currently the cheapest and most popular method of dealing with contaminated land in the UK. Approximately 50% of contaminated land treated in the UK is dealt with in this way. The advantages include the following:

- the contaminated material at the site is dealt with completely, once and for all, and there can be a high degree of confidence in the outcome;
- the method involves the use of well established civil engineering technology and conventional plant and equipment can be used;
- buried structures such as tanks and underground services are exposed in the process and can be dealt with;
- the method provides opportunities for recycling excavated materials.

The disadvantages include the following:

- the contaminated material is not neutralised but transferred to another place, where it will require safekeeping for an indefinite period of time;
- the excavation and transportation of contaminated materials from the site to the repository will create environmental problems, and imported clean material will be required to replace the material taken away.

Reduce the concentration of contamination by mixing

This method is useful in situations where the degree of contamination is not high. It involves diluting the contaminated material with 'clean' material such that the concentration of contamination in the resulting mixture satisfies the acceptance criteria. This technique requires a sufficiently large site area to permit the stockpiling and treatment of the materials prior to replacement. The method could be used in conjunction with an 'excavate and dispose' operation.

Containment

The objective of containment is to prevent contact between the contaminated materials and potential targets by isolating, covering or encapsulating the contaminated material. It can also be used to control contaminant movement and prevent outside agents from affecting the contaminated material. Containment techniques include the installation of vertical barriers in the ground and the installation of horizontal barriers below contaminated material. These techniques use conventional civil engineering plant and equipment. Engineered cover systems incorporating layers of natural clay soil and synthetic material can be used to prevent the upward migration of contaminants and to reduce the infiltration of water from above.

Soil washing

Here, the contaminated material is treated on site by passing it through a mobile washing plant. The contaminants in the soil are leached out by the flushing medium and the cleaned soil is replaced in the ground. The highly contaminated sludge is disposed of at a licensed landfill. The technique is particularly suited to granular soils, such as sand and gravel.

Soil leaching

A technique similar to soil washing, except that the material is treated *in situ*. The leaching fluid, which is infiltrated into the ground using spraying equipment, leaches the contaminants out of the soil. The leachate is then pumped off from a series of wells previously installed in the contaminated ground. The circulatory process of infiltration, leaching and extraction is continued until the concentration of contaminants in the ground has been reduced to the required level. Again, the method is suited to the treatment of granular soils.

Biological methods

The *in situ* biological treatment of contaminated ground uses biological processes to remove, degrade or transform the contaminants present.

Microbial degredation occurs naturally in most soils. The aim of the treatment is to enhance the rate at which the natural processes of degredation occur. The treatment consists of introducing bacteria with nutrients into the affected soil and may be used in conjunction with a water circulating system. The bacteria degrade the contaminants into harmless byproducts. This technique is appropriate in the treatment of certain organic contaminants, such as petrol, diesel, jet fuel and light mineral oil, and works best in granular soils. The process can take a long time to complete.

Soil vapour extraction

This method is used to remove volatile compounds such as petrol from the soil. Air containing the volatile compounds is drawn out through the soil under vacuum from a system of recovery wells installed in the affected area. Fresh air is introduced into the soil through a system of air intake pipes and the process of vaporisation is continued until the volatile compounds have been removed. As with biological methods of remediation, the treatment takes a long time to complete and is best suited to granular soils.

Conclusions

The methods of investigating and treating contaminated land have evolved considerably since the problem came to light in the 1970s. The experience gained by practitioners in the field since then has enabled a coherent approach to the problem to be developed. A great deal of contaminated land remains to be treated and new methods of investigation and treatment will evolve.

HEALTH AND ENVIRONMENTAL HAZARDS ASSOCIATED WITH LANDFILL SITES

Large quantities of commercial, industrial and domestic solid waste are produced each year in the UK. This amounts to some 130 million tonnes every year, an amount that is growing at about 5% per year. The most common method of waste disposal is to landfill: currently, half of the commercial and industrial solid waste produced and nearly all domestic solid waste generated in the UK is disposed of at landfill sites. Some special or hazardous waste is also disposed of to landfill, but this is to sites specifically constructed and licensed to hold special waste safely for an indefinite period of time.

The deposition of waste

The disposal of waste to a landfill involves taking the waste by road or rail to an authorised and controlled pit or repository and tipping it. The waste is then spread and compacted in layers with heavy compaction equipment. At the end of each day's work, the surface is covered with a thin layer of material such as soil or rubble to prevent the surface of the waste from being blown away or scavenged by birds. For the landfill operator, who is now the custodian of the waste, this is the beginning of a long period of involvement and responsibility.

Landfill sites may have a relatively short active life, depending on the rate at which they are filled, and landfill operators are always looking to develop new sites or extend existing facilities to meet demand. Suitable sites meeting the requirements of the planning and environmental authorities are becoming increasingly difficult to find and there is considerable public opposition to this form of development.

The planning and design of landfill facilities

When a site has been identified as a potential landfill facility, a process of consultation is undertaken between the landfill operator, the planning authority, the EA and the Health and Safety Executive.

Apart from the acquisition and planning considerations, a detailed investigation into the geology and hydrogeology of the area is required. The data obtained from this investigation is crucial in assessing the risk the landfill facility will pose to the local community and the environment.

The time taken from the initial planning stage, through the consultation process, geological investigation and design and construction phase, to the beginning of the active operational stage may be in the order of three to five years. The active operational lifespan of the site, during which waste filling takes place, may be five to ten years. Following this active phase, there will be reinstatement and a period of aftercare lasting for 30–50 years. The licence holder's responsibility will continue until there are no further risks associated with the facility. This illustrates the length of the active operational phase of the facility in relation to the pre-operational and post-operational phases and the timespan over which the license holder is responsible for the waste.

Health and environmental hazards

The disposal of waste to landfill creates two main problems: the generation of gas within the waste mass, and the generation of leachate.

Landfill gas is produced by the natural decomposition (biodegradation) of the waste. Leachate is the contaminated liquid collecting at the bottom of the landfill, produced mainly by rainwater percolating through the waste mass and leaching out the contaminants within it.

The generation of landfill gas

The generation of landfill gas is a long process, which takes place in distinct phases.

In the initial aerobic phase of waste decomposition, oxygen is present in the waste mass and organic material such as food residue is broken down by the action of naturally occurring oxygen-requiring bacteria. The byproducts of this activity include carbon dioxide and water. Eventually, as the oxygen in the waste mass becomes exhausted, the aerobic conditions give way to anaerobic, oxygen deficient conditions and bacteria suited to this oxygen deficient environment continue the process of decomposition. The byproducts of the anaerobic phase are principally carbon dioxide and methane. The composition of landfill gas will vary during the life of the landfill but, during the steady production phase, it will consist typically of 55–65% methane and 35–45% carbon dioxide. Other gases, including carbon monoxide, hydrogen, nitrogen and oxygen, are present at various stages in the decomposition process. Eventually, the decomposition of the waste comes to an end, the generation of methane and carbon dioxide decline and aerobic conditions return within the waste mass.

The different phases of gas production extend over a long period of time and a landfill site may produce gas for a period of 30 years or more. On the basis of ideal conditions existing within the waste mass, it has been estimated that, over the whole period of decomposition, one ton of dry waste could theoretically produce 400 m^3 of landfill gas. In practice, however, it has been found that about half of this amount of gas is generated.

Landfill gas is a toxic asphyxiant and may be heavier or lighter than air, depending on the relative proportions of methane and carbon dioxide present. The flammability of landfill gas also depends on the proportions of methane and carbon dioxide present. Mixtures of landfill gas and air are potentially flammable and explosive. The venting of landfill gas into the atmosphere is undesirable from an environmental point of view, as the methane it contains is a potent greenhouse gas. Modern landfill sites usually incorporate a gas collection system within the waste, from which the gas can be flared off safely at points around the site. Although this will release carbon dioxide into the atmosphere, the more potent methane will have been destroyed in the process.

A more favourable alternative is to recover energy from the gas by burning it and generating electricity. Many landfill facilities have an energy recovery plant, where electricity is produced from landfill gas on a commercial basis.

The migration of landfill gas

The principal concern over landfill gas is the risk of the gas migrating away from the repository. Depending on the local geological conditions and the construction and maintenance of the landfill repository, there may be potential for the gas to escape and migrate through the ground beyond the repository and collect in confined spaces, such as service ducts, underground chambers and basements, some distance away. Migration may be initiated when the site is capped and the gas is prevented from venting to the atmosphere naturally. In these circumstances, the gas under pressure may find migratory escape routes through porous or disturbed ground.

An example of this was the explosion at 51 Clarke Avenue in Loscoe, Derbyshire, in 1986. Landfill gas had migrated from a nearby landfill site through permeable and fractured rock. Having reached the surface, it collected in the space beneath the suspended ground floor of a bungalow. The explosion was assumed to have resulted from the gas being ignited when the central heating boiler switched on automatically in the morning. The investigation following the Loscoe incident showed that an old quarry, the Loscoe 'brick pit', was situated some 100 m away from 51 Clarke Avenue. The pit, which had been worked for brick, clay, stone and coal from before 1879, had been used as a landfill site for the disposal of domestic waste from 1977–82. The quarry was originally excavated through coal measures strata consisting of interbedded layers of sandstone and coal. Prior to its use as a landfill facility, no preparation or lining of the pit was carried out. When the quarry was completely filled with waste, it was capped with a layer of clay.

The investigation into the incident carried out by the British Geological Survey showed that inclined beds of permeable sandstone provided the pathway by which landfill gas migrated from the landfill site to the surface in the area of 51 Clarke Avenue. Figure 2 shows a diagrammatic cross section through the site indicating the geological conditions and the gas migration pathway.

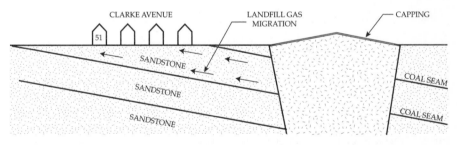

Figure 2: Diagrammatic cross section through Loscoe landfill

The incident at Loscoe illustrates the nature of the risks associated with landfill gas. It can travel long distances through permeable ground and through natural weaknesses and discontinuities in rock. The report on the incident produced by the British Geological Survey emphasised the need for a thorough understanding of the geology and hydrogeology in the area of existing or proposed landfill facilities if accidents similar to the Loscoe explosion are to be prevented.

The generation of leachate

During landfilling operations, rainwater will percolate through the waste mass and become contaminated by the materials it comes into contact with. Typical waste material will include food residue, oils, paint, cloth, paper, newsprint, plastics, corroding food cans and metals, batteries and soluble and leachable industrial waste. The contaminated liquid or leachate will gather at the bottom of the landfill. If the pit is unlined and the natural material at the base is permeable, the leachate will migrate away from the landfill repository. Depending on the geological conditions in the area, the migration of the contaminated fluid may have the potential to pollute rivers, watercourses and groundwater in the area.

Depending on the nature of the waste, leachate may contain a wide range of contaminants, including metals and heavy metals. In the early phase of waste decomposition, the leachate is likely to be slightly acidic and, in the later phase, slightly alkaline. Leachate is toxic as far as plant, aquatic and animal life is concerned.

In the case of modern, engineered landfill facilities, where the base of the pit is made impermeable by virtue of the natural strata or by the provision of an impermeable lining system, the leachate will be contained and migration prevented. It can then be pumped away to holding tanks at the facility for treatment, prior to being discharged into the sewer.

THE DESIGN AND CONSTRUCTION OF LANDFILL FACILITIES

Earlier landfill sites generally utilised the void space provided by disused quarries, pits and other surface depressions and were developed with little attention to the risk of gas and leachate migration. Landfill facilities were not 'designed', in the modern sense of the word. The incident at Loscoe raised public and government awareness of the risks associated with landfill facilities and brought about changes in the way that these facilities are designed and constructed.

In terms of gas generation, landfill prior to the 1960s produced less gas than modern facilities because of the nature of the waste content. Prior to 1960, typical domestic waste included a high proportion of ash and inert material, with little food residue and paper. Since then, however, the nature of domestic waste has changed considerably to include progressively more paper and putrescible material, such as food residue, and far less inert material. This means that modern waste has a much greater potential for producing landfill gas.

Before a modern landfill facility is designed, a very detailed geological and hydrogeological investigation of the site and its environs is carried out and the consequences of a leak of gas or leachate from the facility are carefully evaluated. The design and construction of the landfill repository will reflect this risk evaluation.

Large landfill facilities are normally developed progressively as a series of cells. As one pit or cell is being filled, another might be under construction or being prepared to receive waste, whilst a third may be full and undergoing capping and restoration.

The design and construction of a landfill cell

The construction of the pit or cell will usually involve the excavation of a wide, smooth sided trench with side slopes of about 25°–30°. The depth of the cell will depend on the geological conditions, but will usually be in the range of 5–20 m. The materials used to line the bottom and sides of the cell will depend principally on the nature of the ground into which the cell is excavated and the nature of the risk associated with any leakage of gas or leachate from it.

If the site is situated in an area where the natural geology consists of low permeability clay, for instance, the risk of gas or leachate migration will be low. In these circumstances, it may be sufficient to line the bottom and sides of the cell with a layer of the local clay material, reworked and engineered to form a barrier of consistent thickness, density and permeability. On the other hand, if the site were situated on highly permeable ground, such as sand and gravel, there would be a high risk of gas and leachate migration. In these circumstances, where the migration risk is high, it may be necessary to install a complex, multiple layer lining system, incorporating layers of engineered natural materials such as clay in conjunction with synthetic materials such as high density polyethylene or polypropylene. The installation of the cell lining is carried out to a high specification and is subjected to rigorous quality control and testing in order to minimise the possibility of leakage.

The base of the cell is usually formed with a slight slope, so that leachate collecting at the bottom of the waste will be directed to a sump situated in the floor of the cell. A pumping well is constructed incrementally as the waste level rises, allowing access to the sump so that the leachate can be pumped away from the cell as required.

Monitoring the site

In granting a waste licence, the EA will require the site to be monitored and maintained until it can be shown that there is no further risk associated with it. The monitoring of landfill gas is routinely carried out from gas sampling probes or gas monitoring boreholes situated within the landfill cells. Samples of the gas are taken at regular intervals in order to determine its pressure and composition. Similar arrangements are provided for the monitoring of leachate; its composition and level within the cell.

Monitoring facilities are also provided outside the landfill cells in order to detect gas migration. The detection of landfill gas by monitoring equipment situated outside the landfill cell might be indicative of a leak in the cell lining system.

The protection of buildings situated close to landfill facilities

Buildings situated close to landfill facilities are potentially at risk from the migration of landfill gas. Depending on the geological conditions involved, those situated close to older sites may be at greater risk than those near modern sites where thorough geological appraisal has been carried out and where properly engineered lining systems are in place.

The migration of gas from a landfill site or other gassing source can be contained by the installation of vertical barriers in the ground. In principle, this will involve excavating a deep vertical trench across the migration pathway and filling it with a material that will impede the transmission of the gas. Typical construction might involve a cement-bentonite slurry fill to the trench, with the inclusion of a high density polyethylene membrane. Other techniques are available for the construction of barriers, all of which use conventional civil engineering technology.

In some situations, a gravel filled trench is constructed across the migration pathway to intercept the gas and allow it to vent off into the atmosphere. This technique can be used in conjunction with vertical barriers. Similar techniques can be used to contain migrating leachate and techniques are available by which horizontal barriers can be installed at depth beneath the waste to prevent the downward migration of leachate.

In situations where a new development is proposed close to a landfill facility, planning consent will normally require some protection against gas migration to be included in the construction to satisfy the requirements of the Building Regulations.

The protection of buildings

Gas protection might include the incorporation of continuous horizontal gas proof membranes in the ground floor construction of the buildings and the cross-ventilation of the space beneath the ground floor. The ventilation of the underfloor space can be provided either by passive, natural ventilation or by active, forced ventilation, using electrically operated fans. Gas activated alarm systems can also be installed and linked to active venting systems.

The future development of land used for landfilling

When filling operations come to an end and the landfill cell is full, the surface of the waste is capped. The terms of the waste licence will require the operator to return the site to an acceptable condition after the completion of filling and this will normally involve landscaping and planting. The management of landfill gas will continue for a long period of time, but the generation of leachate will reduce substantially after the waste surface is capped.

Restoration

Although restoration tends to be site specific, in general it will involve capping the surface of the waste and covering it with agricultural soil in preparation for planting and screening. The land will eventually be returned to beneficial use: an agricultural or public amenity, such as woodland. The continuing generation of landfill gas and surface settlement will continue for a long period and will normally preclude hard development for an indefinite period of time.

The capping system will typically include a gas collection system located immediately above the surface of the waste. This will consist of a layer of granular material containing a system of perforated pipes designed to intercept and collect the gas. Above this will be a thick layer of relatively impermeable material, such as compacted clay, and then a thick layer of subsoil containing a land drainage system. A surface layer of topsoil will complete the capping system.

The capping system may be modified or improved by the inclusion of synthetic materials. The total thickness may be in the order of two metres.

Surface settlement

The waste material in the landfill will compact under the effects of its own self weight and, in addition, its decomposition will create voids in the waste mass. These two effects in combination will result in the surface of the waste settling, and, in time, this may amount to some 25% of the waste thickness (Meyerhof, 1951).

Although most of the self-weight settlement of the waste will occur within about five years of being placed, some additional long term settlement will continue for many years. By monitoring the surface of a site over a period of time, its settlement trend can be determined. From this, an estimate can be made of the final amount of settlement likely to occur and the timescale involved. Additional loading applied to the surface of the waste will bring about a rapid increase in settlement and permanent hard development at the surface of waste is not normally a practical proposition unless ground improvement work is carried out first.

Conclusions

Current Government policy is to reduce the amount of waste sent to landfill sites for disposal. Until practical alternative methods of reducing and managing waste are in place, however, landfill will remain the principal method of waste disposal in the UK for the foreseeable future.

Given the continuing need to develop new landfill sites, there will be increasing environmental pressure in the future to ensure that their design, construction and operation is safe and environmentally acceptable.

CHAPTER 7

INTEGRATED POLLUTION PREVENTION AND CONTROL

BACKGROUND

Releases from the major polluters have traditionally been controlled by three distinct control regimes. The Fifth Report of the Royal Commission on Environmental Pollution (Cmnd 6371, 1976) proposed that polluting releases should be directed to the environmental medium where the least environmental damage would be done. This proposal was accompanied by the recommendation that a body be created with responsibility for ensuring that wastes were disposed so as to minimalise effects in all three environmental media, thus achieving the optimum environmental solution overall.

These recommendations were reinforced by a Cabinet Efficiency Unit Report in 1986 which stated that, as a long as the three environmental media were treated separately, there was a danger that the allocation of resources would not reflect an overall view of where the problems were most severe; and that the end result would be a haphazard disposal of pollutants unrelated to an overall assessment of the optimum solution for the environment as a whole.[1] The Environmental Protection Act (EPA) 1990, as amended by the Environment Act 1995 and the Pollution Prevention and Control Act 1999 are the primary pieces of legislation which affect integrated pollution prevention and control (IPPC).[2]

The agencies responsible for IPPC are:

- the Environment Agency (EA);
- local authorities.

The main objectives of IPPC are:

- to prevent or minimalise the release of prescribed substances and to render harmless any such substances that are released;
- to develop an approach to pollution control that considers discharges from industrial processes to all media in the context of the effect on the environment as a whole.

---

1   *R v EA ex p Glosan Laom Seller (No 2)* [1999] Env LR 73; *Dudley MBC v Henley Foundries Ltd* [1999] Env LR 895; Purdue, 1991, p 534; Waite, 1992, p 2; Lea, 1998, pp 913–18.
2   See Mehta and Hawkins, 1998, pp 61–75.

It has the following additional aims:

- to improve the efficiency and effectiveness of the EA;
- to streamline and strengthen the regulatory system, clarifying the roles and responsibilities of the EA, other regulatory authorities and the firms they regulate;
- to contain the burden on industry by providing for a 'one stop shop' on pollution control for the potentially most serious polluting processes;
- to maintain public confidence in the regulatory system by producing a clear, transparent system that is accessible and easy to understand and clear and simple in operation;
- to ensure that the system will respond flexibly, both to changing pollution abatement technology and to new knowledge on the effects of pollutants;
- to provide the means to fulfil international obligations relating to environmental protection.

THE EPA 1990

Part I of the 1990 Act contains the IPC and LAPC regimes. Both are concerned with regulating pollution from industrial processes. The first is concerned with preventing or minimising pollution of the environment due to the release of substances into the air, water or land, and the second is concerned with preventing or minimising air pollution and applies to those industrial processes that are not considered to give rise to significant pollution of water or land. Central to both regimes is the requirement that the 'best available techniques not entailing excessive cost' (BATNEEC) should be used to prevent or minimise pollution. In addition to these regimes, Pt II of the 1990 Act contains the waste management licensing system, which is concerned with regulating the deposit, disposal or recovery of waste.

IPC applies to certain processes and substances. *Prescribed processes* are separated into two parts: Pt A processes and substances are subject to IPC; and Part B governs those that are covered by other agencies. There are some exemptions:

- emissions which are too trivial to do any harm;
- emissions which are too trivial to do any harm when released to the land;
- processes undertaken at a working museum, demonstrating an industrial process;
- processes undertaken at a school or educational institution;
- engines used to propel aircraft, vehicles, ships, etc;
- processes carried out as a domestic activity at a private dwelling.

A 'process' includes all operations undertaken by the same person (that is, the authorisation holder) at the same location, including operations related to the main process.

There are three separate lists of *prescribed substances,* according to whether the substance is to be controlled in relation to air, water or land.

All IPC processes under Pt 1 of the Act are subject to BATNEEC. This is only one of the objectives set out in s 7 of the Act, and all of these have to be met. BATNEEC can be looked at as two parts: BAT and NEEC.

- Best available technique:
  - best – the best technique is the most effective in preventing, minimising or rendering harmless any polluting emissions. There may be more than one set of techniques that achieve comparable effectiveness – that is, there may be more than one set of best techniques;
  - available – techniques should be procurable by the operator of the process in question. This does not imply that the technique is in general use, but it does require accessibility. It includes a technique which has been developed (or proven) at a scale which allows its implementation in the relevant industrial context with the necessary business confidence. It does not imply that sources outside the UK are unavailable, nor does it imply a competitive supply market. If there is a monopoly supplier, the technique counts as being available, provided that the operator can procure it;
  - technique – this includes both the process and how the process is operated. It includes matters such as numbers and qualification of staff, working methods and training and design, construction, layout and maintenance of buildings.
- Not entailing excessive cost.

There are two standards in relation to new processes and old processes. BATNEEC can be expresses in technological terms, that is, in relation to hardware or emissions or as a performance standard. The EA will normally express BATNEEC in terms so as to constrain the development of cleaner techniques or to restrict the operator's choice in achieving a given standard.

The EA has produced a number of guidance notes to guide businesses in relation to the operation of these various standards. These aim to ensure consistency in decision making. There are integrated pollution control guidance notes on waste disposal and recycling. There is a technical guidance note in relation to BPEO for IPC in two volumes. The first covers the principles and methods to be used, including guidance for assessing harm, compiling options of specific industrial processes and economic information required to gauge the practicality of process options. The second contains the technical data and environmental assessment levels.

Application procedures

The Environmental Protection (Applications, Appeals and Registers) Regulations 1991 (SI 1991/507) establish a detailed procedure for applications for IPC authorisations. The application should point out clearly any information that the applicant wishes to be withheld from public registers on the grounds of national security or commercial confidentiality. Section 22 of the Act allows information to be excluded on the grounds of commercial confidentiality. There are also consultation procedures with statutory consultees, who are notified within 14 days of the application and have 28 days in which to respond, unless the application contains information that may be commercially confidential or a risk to national security, in which case the time runs from when these issues are finally determined. The public also has the right to be consulted and the application must be published in a local newspaper.

The time limit for determining the application is four months, either from the date the application is received or when the issues of commercial confidentiality, etc, have been resolved. The application can be refused, varied or agreed.

Enforcement

- Penalties (s 145 of the EPA 1990) – a £20,000 fine and/or three months' imprisonment on summary conviction and, on indictment, an unlimited fine and/or two years' imprisonment. Under s 217 of the EPA 1990, liability is set down in relation to the directors and senior managers of a company. Section 90(6), as inserted by the Environment Act 1995, provides for the serving of enforcement notices in relation to water pollution offences.

- Enforcement notice – this can be served on an operator whom the EA believes is contravening, or likely to contravene, any of the conditions in the authorisation. The enforcement notice will specify the matters constituting the contravention and require specific steps to be taken, in a specified period, to remedy the situation.

- Prohibition notice – this can be served on an operator where the EA believes that there is an imminent risk of serious pollution. The notice will specify the risks, the steps that must be taken to remove it and the time by which this must be done. It also suspends the authorisation for whatever aspects of the operation were causing the risk and, in addition, can impose conditions relating to any part of the process for which the authorisation was not suspended.

- Revocation of authorisation – written notice has to be given before a licence can be revoked. Authorisation may be revoked in cases where there has been a persistent failure to comply with conditions.

In all of these cases, the Secretary of State has a reserve power of direction.

The Pollution Prevention and Control Act 1999[3]

This Act, for the first time, takes into account other environmental factors such as noise, use of raw materials, accident prevention, site restoration and energy efficiency. It implements the requirements of the Directive on Integrated Pollution Control (1996/61/EC). It must be brought into effect by October 1999 for new processes or those which are subject to significant change; existing processes must be brought within the scheme before October 2007. The Act implements these requirements by repealing Pt 1 of the EPA 1990.

The Act is really a framework Act, leaving much of the detailed implementation to regulations, which can be made by the SOSETR.[4] The main purpose of ss 1 and 2 and the Schedules to the Act is to enable a single, coherent pollution control system to be set up by regulations which will apply to all of the installations to which the IPPC Directive applies, and to those installations currently regulated under Pt I of the 1990 Act but to which the Directive does not apply. Section 2 and Sched 1 also provide for regulations to be made under the Act to cover various ancillary matters connected with the prevention or control of pollution. An example would be the collection of information about emissions, energy and waste for inclusion in a pollution inventory.[5]

---

3   See Long and Mereu, 1999, pp 180–84.

4   See EA, *IPPC Directive – Regulatory Package Consultation*, May 2000 .

5   Section 1 of the Act sets out the general purpose for which regulations may be made under s 2 of the Act, including, in particular, implementing the IPPC Directive. The new system will need to incorporate the concepts and principles used in the Directive (such as BETs and the general principles concerning energy efficiency, the control of waste production and site restoration) insofar as the installations covered by the Directive are concerned. The Directive's requirements will, however, where appropriate, be modified or disapplied for the purposes of applying the new control regime to installations not covered by the Directive. Section 2 confers power on the Secretary of State to make regulations creating a regime of pollution control for the purpose set out in s 1 and to the extent provided for in Sched 1. Schedule 1 provides that the regulation making power in s 2 may be used to establish a system of pollution control requiring operators of specified installations or plants, or those carrying out specified activities, to hold permits (para 4); for those permits to contain conditions (para 6) which are to be reviewed by the regulator (para 7); for publicity to be given to specified matters (eg, to applications for permits); for information on emissions, energy and waste to be supplied (for inclusion, eg, in public registers, the EA's Pollution Inventory and any future European polluting emissions register) (paras 11 and 12); for regulators to take enforcement action (para 15); for the creation of offences (eg, failure to comply with permit conditions) (para 17); and for rights of appeal (para 19). Schedule 1, para 2 will enable the regulations to determine the authorities that will exercise the functions under the new pollution control system. As under Pt I of the 1990 Act, it is intended that the role of granting and updating permits, taking enforcement action, etc, will be divided between the EA and local authorities in England and Wales.

Thus, ss 1 and 2 of the Act confer on the Secretary of State power to make regulations providing for a new pollution control system to meet the requirements of the IPPC Directive (96/61/EC) and for other measures to prevent and control pollution. Schedule 1 lists the purposes for which the powers under s 2 can be used.

Section 3 is concerned with the use and discharge of chemicals from oil and gas installations, whilst s 4 addresses a problem arising under the transitional provisions in Pt II of the EPA 1990 by removing time limits applying to waste disposal licences.[6]

The IPPC Directive was implemented by the UK in 1999. It requires a range of industrial installations to be regulated by a system of integrated pollution control (that is, a system in which emissions to air, water and land, plus other environmental effects, are considered together and conditions set so as to achieve a high level of protection for the environment as a whole). Permit conditions must be based on the use of the BATs, which is a very similar concept to BATNEEC in Pt I of the 1990 Act. Both concepts are designed to provide for a flexible, case by case approach to regulation that balances cost with environmental benefit. Around 7,000 installations in the UK will be covered by the Directive, including: most of those regulated at present under the IPC regime in Pt I of the 1990 Act; some 1,500 of the 13,000 regulated at present under the LAPC regime in Pt I of that Act; over 1,000 of the installations regulated under the Waste Management Licensing regime contained in Pt II of that Act; and significant numbers of installations which are at present unregulated by Pts I or II of the 1990 Act. This latter category mainly comprises large, intensive pig and poultry installations, plus large installations for the manufacture of food and drink products.[7]

The Government's proposals for the implementation of the IPPC Directive have been the subject of three consultation papers: *UK Implementation of EC Directive 96/61 on Integrated Pollution Prevention and Control: Consultation Paper*, issued in July 1997; *UK Implementation of EC Directive 96/61 on Integrated Pollution Prevention and Control: Second Consultation Paper*, issued in January 1998; and *Third Consultation Paper on the Implementation of the IPPC Directive*, which was issued in December 1998. A fourth consultation paper, including a draft of the regulations that the Secretary of State proposes to make under the Act, was published in August 1999. The Report on the responses to the fourth

---

6 See above, Chapter 6.

7 As under the present regimes under Pt I of the 1990 Act, fees will be payable to regulators in relation to the exercise of some of their functions (eg, in relation to the determining of applications for the grant of a permit and for the variation of the conditions of a permit). Schedule 1, para 1 enables the regulations to establish standards, objectives, requirements and limits and in relation to emissions.

consultation paper on implementation of the IPPC Directive was published in April 2000.[8]

Guidance notes will be published. The importance of IPC was highlighted by the *Observer*/Friends of the Earth survey into the pollution from some of the largest factories in England and Wales. Friends of the Earth want the amount of pollution to be cut by 80% by 2005.[9] New installations and those undergoing substantial change will be regulated under the new regime set up under the Act from the date on which the new regime comes into force. Existing installations will be phased into the new regime, generally on a sectoral basis, before the 31 October 2007 deadline specified by the IPPC Directive.

Recent changes

A number of guidance notes have been written by the EA to guide businesses in relation to the operation of these various standards. These ensure consistency in decision making. The EA is also developing operator and pollution risk appraisal (OPRA) for assessing pollution risks from major industrial process. This is based on an analysis of the inherent level of environmental risk involved in a particular industrial process and the performance of the operator in managing that risk. The results will be used in annual work planning to set target inspection frequencies for sites. This does not, however, mean that the lower risk sites will be forgotten, as a minimum inspection rate will be set; OPRA will also help operators to identify where the most effective improvements can be made, by highlighting the major factors contributing to the environmental risk of a particular process. Areas which will be looked at include: evaluating attributes of the operator's performance (for example, maintenance, training and operation) and the process pollution risk (for example, the presence of hazardous materials, scale and frequency of hazardous operations); and a more systematic method for evaluating process pollution risk, based on selecting a representative hazardous substance for the process. The selected substance will be the one with the highest environmental risk. The inspector must also, however, consider the other substances used on a site during the assessment; the attainment of certified environmental management systems (ISO 14001) is recognised, but a high overall operator performance rating depends on direct evidence of, for example, good

8   The Report looked at issues such as the charging scheme, transitional provisions and the meaning of 'installation', as well as issues such as noise regulation, guidance notes, the trivial environmental impact exemption, review periods, substantial changes leading to standard terms and the relationship between local authorities and the EA in relation to minimum water conditions.

9   The Report looks at acid rain, the worst site being National Power's Drax power station; the worst for cancer causing chemicals to air is Associated Octel near Ellesmere Port; for dioxins, the worst offender is British Steel in Llanwern. See Alridge, 1999, p 7.

maintenance and operation. The pollution risk appraisal considers both the real risk of harm to the environment arising from hazardous chemicals and the perceived risk from the process due to offensive characteristics such as visible or odorous emissions.

This risk appraisal method may also have other applications. The EA is considering extending the OPRA concept to other areas of its environmental protection functions, such as waste regulation

Energy

Energy policy was examined in Chapter 5, above. However, energy efficiency is now an important requirement under IPPC. In the *Third Consultation Paper on the Implementation of the IPPC Directive* January 1999, the Government set out its regulatory proposals in relation to energy efficiency. It states that the Government expects that the Directive's requirements in relation to energy efficiency will be met through site specific permit conditions, based upon a list of technologies and benchmarks of cost effective energy efficiency. Sector-specific guidance notes will be issued, which will discuss the energy efficiency improvements that may be reasonably required from installations in each sector. The industry may also reach sectoral agreement as an alternative to imposing a permit condition. A charging scheme will also be introduced. Part L of the Building Regulations, which has been reviewed, shows a wide range of options for improving the energy efficiency of buildings.[10]

Noise controls[11]

Whilst the new Pollution Prevention Control Act covers noise from those premises subject to IPC, there are also some other Acts which control noise. The main control is through an action for statutory nuisance under Pt III of the EPA 1990.[12] The Noise and Statutory Nuisance Act 1993 expanded the categories of nuisance to include noise that is prejudicial to health or a nuisance and is emitted from, or caused by, a vehicle, machinery or equipment in a street (s 79(1)(g)(a)). If noise is emitted which is judged to be a statutory nuisance (that is, prejudicial to health or a nuisance), a local authority must serve an abatement notice. This may require that the noise be stopped or that

---

10 Energy use in buildings is responsible for 40–50% of the UK's emissions of carbon dioxide, one of the greenhouse gases.

11 Penn, 1995.

12 See DETR leaflet, *NOISE: How to Keep Peace with your Neighbours*; DETR information note on noise, 1 June 1999. See www.detr.gov.uk.

it be limited to certain times during the day.[13] A notice must be served on the person or the owner/occupier or the offending vehicle, machinery or equipment. There is the right of appeal within 21 days for the person who has been served with the notice. Failure to comply with a notice without reasonable cause can be fined.

Local authorities can gain entry to premises to abate a nuisance, for example, burglar alarms. They can also enter vehicles, machinery or equipment if the owner cannot be found. Under the Noise Act 1996, local authorities can seize noise making equipment and apply for forfeiture.[14] A local authority can also apply for an injunction if it feels that summary proceedings would not provide an adequate remedy. Courts can also have regard to codes of practice when considering the BPM defence; these give advice about minimising potentially noisy problems and deal with a wide variety of matters,[15] including construction sites and non-industry specific noise, such as alarms,[16] model aircraft, pop concerts and ice cream vans.

Under s 82 of the EPA 1990, an individual can take an action to the court. Three days' notice must be given to the maker of the noise and details have to be given of the complaint. Evidence will also be needed. An action can also be brought under the common law action of nuisance for an injunction or damages for loss.

The Noise Act 1996 was passed to minimise night time noise nuisance. The local authority or the Secretary of State must say that it applies in a particular area. A person has to make a complaint about noise before the local authority will act. If noise emitted from a dwelling is above a permitted level between the hours of 11 pm and 7 am, then the local authority may serve a warning notice on the person responsible. Failure to comply with the notice may result in a fixed penalty notice or court proceedings.

Under the Noise and Statutory Nuisance Act 1993 and the Control of Noise (Code of Practice on Noise from Audible Intruder Alarms) Order 1981 (SI 1981/182), audible alarms on buildings should be constructed so that they turn off after a period of 20 minutes. A local authority may serve an abatement notice if the noise from an audible alarm is considered to be a statutory

---

13 For the requirements to be stated in the notice, see *Budd v Colchester BC* (1999) *The Times*, 14 April; *Kirklees MBC v Firled* (1997) 96 LGR 151; *R v Kennet DC ex p Somerfield Pty Co Ltd and Somerfield Stores* [1999] JPL 361. Whether the court should consider the facts at the date of the service or at the appeal was looked at in *SFI Group (Formerly Surrey Free Inns plc) v Gosport BC; R v Knightsbridge CC ex p Cataldi* (1999) *The Times*, 5 April. See, also, the Environmental Protection (Statutory Nuisance) (Appeals) Regulations 1995 (SI 1995/2644); *Sovereign Rubber Ltd v Stockport MBC* [2000] ELM 27.

14 Forfeiture is where the person who has caused the nuisance has to give up their interest in the property to the injured party.

15 Bylaws may also prevent noise in a particular area.

16 In London, under the London Authorities Act 1991, local authorities have additional powers in relation to alarms.

nuisance. Where a London borough has adopted the provisions of the 1991 Act, a local authority officer may enter the premises to turn off the alarm if it sounds for a period longer than one hour. If forcible entry is required, a warrant can be obtained from a magistrates' court, authorising an environmental officer to turn the alarm off. Similar powers for authorities outside London under the 1993 Act have yet to come into force. The Control of Pollution Act 1974, as amended by s 8 of the 1993 Act, limits the hours during which a loudspeaker may be operated in the street.

There are a number of provisions in relation to noise from motor vehicles. Under the Road Traffic Act 1988, it is an offence to operate a motor vehicle horn between the hours of 11 pm and 7 am. In relation to commercial vehicles, reversing alarms must not be strident (Road Vehicles (Construction and Use) Regulations 1986 (SI 1986/208).

The general policy under the Road Traffic Act 1988 and Road Vehicles (Construction and Use) Regulations 1986 is to maintain vehicles in good working order so as to minimise noise emissions. The Road Traffic (Vehicle Emissions) (Fixed Penalty) Regulations 1997 (SI 1997/3058) empower seven trial local authorities to carry out roadside checks for the prevention of noise or of exhaust emissions. These Regulations require every exhaust system and silencer to be maintained in good and efficient working order. It is also an offence under the Regulations to use a vehicle on the road in a way that causes excessive noise. Theft alarms fitted to vehicles must turn off after five minutes under the Road Vehicles (Construction and Use) Regulations 1986. It is an offence to operate an alarm that does not turn off after five minutes.

The 1986 Regulations require the driver of a vehicle, when it is stationary, to stop the action of any machinery attached to or forming part of the vehicle (including the engine) as far as this may be necessary to prevent noise. The requirement does not apply if the vehicle is stopped in traffic; if it is necessary to examine the machinery due to its failure or derangement; if the machinery is not used for driving the vehicle; or if the vehicle is propelled by gas produced in plant carried on the vehicle.[17]

A local authority may serve an abatement notice if it judges noise from these sources to be a statutory nuisance. There are special procedures for serving a notice where the person responsible for the vehicle, machinery or equipment cannot be found and special powers for entry for local authorities to de-activate car alarms. An individual may also apply to the magistrates' court for an abatement order. Failure to comply with a notice or order is an offence. There is a right of appeal against both.

Aircraft noise is covered under the Civil Aviation Act 1982. The Secretary of State sets maximum levels for noise emitting from UK airports. He can also specify the maximum number of times that planes can land and take off, or

---

17   See *CBT Committee v FTA* [1991] 3 WLR 828; *R v LB Greenwich* (1996) 255 ENDS Rep 49.

specify a period when they cannot do so. Under the Act, grants may be available for insulating homes.[18]

In relation to noise from construction sites, noise must also be minimised so as not to cause a nuisance.[19] A contractor may apply under s 61 of the Control of Polution Act 1974 to a local authority, or the authority may specify by notice acceptable noise levels, hours of operation, etc, of construction works. Such consent does not prevent subsequent action under the statutory nuisance legislation in the 1990 Act. Failure to comply with a notice is an offence but there is a right of appeal. Individuals can take action under s 82 of 1990 Act.

Noise abatement zones are provided for under Pt III of the Control of Pollution Act 1974. Within these zones, local authorities set targets to reduce or prevent an increase in the ambient noise level. The local authority can also issue noise reduction notices to reduce noise which is reasonably practicable and would secure a public benefit under s 66(4).[20]

The Noise and Nuisance Policy Unit is part of the DETR's Air and Quality Environment Unit. It develops policies and initiatives and co-ordinates UK policy towards EC proposals[21] on environmental noise.[22] The DETR is undertaking research into developing better measurements of environmental noise and the effectiveness of noise mitigation processes.

Planning

Development plans have a role to play in noise reduction and minimisation by zoning, whilst noise levels are a material consideration for planning authorities. Noise may well be an issue for large developments, such as roads and airports, and may feature in planning inquires, such as that into the third London airport. The Highway Authority must publish details of new roads and the public can object on any grounds, including noise. There may be a public inquiry. The issue of zoning has also been looked at by the European Community in the Second and Fourth Action Plans.[23]

---

18 DETR, *Noise Limits on Aircraft Leaving Heathrow, Stanstead and Gatwick,* March 1999; see, also the Aeroplane Noise Regulations 1999 (SI 1999/1452).

19 Control of Pollution Act 1974, s 60. See Code of Practice (BS 5228) BSI reducing noise at construction sites and other open sites.

20 Commission Proposal COM (1998) 046.

21 EC draft Noise Directive.

22 Other useful organisations include the Building Research Establishment, National Physical Laboratory, Institute of Sound and Vibration Research, National Society for Clean Air and the Heathrow Association for the Control of Aircraft Noise.

23 Specific controls have also been introduced, eg, EC action on lawnmowers (84/538/EEC) and household appliances (6/594/EEC).

Building control[24]

The Building Regulations 1991[25] (as amended) ensure the health and safety of people in and around buildings by providing functional requirements for building, design and construction. Environmental issues relevant to the construction industry are promoted through the Regulations for, for example, improving energy efficiency. Failure to comply with the Building Regulations when constructing a new building, or materially altering an existing one, is an offence and the local authority may remove or alter the offending work.

In relation to general building work, products used in building and civil engineering works must: be safe to use; safe in case of fire; not be a threat to health and hygiene (that is, not give off toxic gas, etc); be economical with the amount of energy used; and be designed to keep noise levels to a minimum. In relation to buildings, the 1991 Regulations include provisions that buildings are constructed so as to ensure that noise is not transmitted between buildings or flats.[26] Some local Acts also contain building control provisions.

NOISE TECHNOLOGY

Noise is generally defined as 'unwanted sound'. Although there is general agreement about some forms of sound as being 'unwanted', it can also be subjective. Church bells, for example, are appreciated by some and not by others.

Noise can be 'unwanted' for several reasons, and these are used as criteria for noise assessment by, for example, the British Standard BS 4142. They include:

- physical damage to the ear;
- speech interference;
- annoyance.

The normal human frequency range for hearing is from about 20 Hz to 20,000 Hz. This varies with age: the range of hearing becoming less as one gets older. At the low frequency end, several people are significantly bothered by noise with frequencies below 20 Hz, although this may have more to do with the vibration than the noise of these frequencies.

---

24 For a discussion of general building controls, see McManus, 1994, Chapter 10.
25 Made under the Building Act 1984, s 1.
26 See *City of London Corpn v Bovis Construction Ltd* [1992] 5 All ER 697.

The decibel

Humans can detect fairly low noise levels and are also subject to much louder noises. In order to measure this range of noise intensity on a reasonable scale, the logarithm of noise is measured. The 'unit' used for noise measurement is the decibel (dB), although it should be noted that it is not truly a 'unit', but a ratio. The scale is defined such that 0 dB corresponds to a noise level at the bottom end of the human hearing range (just audible, but only just). The sound pressure level of various noises is shown below:

Noise	Approximate sound pressure level (dB(A))
Jet engine 25 m away	140
Submarine engine room	120
Pneumatic drill 7 m away	90
Vacuum cleaner	80
Inside car	70
Quiet bedroom	35

The scale used for measurement of the noise levels is the dB(A) scale. This is simply the decibel scale, with adjustments made to accommodate the characteristics of human hearing. Humans hear sound in the frequency range 1,000–5,000 Hz well, and so no adjustment is needed in that region. However, humans hear less well as the frequency rises above 5,000 Hz or below 1,000 Hz. Noises at the limit of our frequency range bother us less, because we hear them less well. The A weighting takes this into account by subtracting an amount from the measured level. This is done to convert meter readings (a meter will detect the pressure of the sound wave, no matter what the frequency of the sound) into readings which approximate to the response of the human ear, which does vary with frequencies.

There are other adjustment weighting scales, but the only other scale in common use is the C weighting scale. This makes slightly different adjustments but works on the same principle. The A weighting is used most often, and is the one required by legislation in the UK.

The fact that the dB scale is logarithmic means that noise levels cannot be added simply. Two noises, each with a sound level of 50 dB, will not have a sound level of 100 dB when running together. The sound level would be 53 dB. The sound level rises by 3 dB for each doubling of the noise. Thus, if the sound pressure level of one lawnmower is 75 dB, and four lawnmowers are run in approximately the same place, the resulting sound pressure level will be 81 dB (add 3 dB twice, doubling from one to two lawnmowers, and again from two to four).

In practice, one consequence of this is that a difference in sound pressure levels of only 10 dB means that the lower sound level is insignificant. Thus, when predicting sound levels, any noise sources which are at least 10 dB quieter than the noisiest source can be ignored in the calculation.

The other useful figure when calculating the effect of noise is that which results from distance. Sound propagates spherically from its source (provided that its line of movement is not restricted) and the sound energy radiates out in this spherical form. The same amount of energy occupies a small sphere close to the sound source, but a larger sphere further away. Thus, the amount of sound energy received at a greater distance is less, because it represents a smaller proportion of the radiating sphere. This principle is applied to the logarithmic decibel scale, and the conclusion is that the sound pressure level (that sound level recorded by a receiver) reduces by 6 dB for each doubling of distance.

NOISE MONITORING

Noise monitors measure the sound intensity, and convert this to the dB(A) (or dB(C)) scale. Noise monitors are small instruments and are generally hand held. They come in a variety of accuracy ranges – it is important to use as high a standard of instrument as need dictates.

Measurement of unsteady noise can be done several ways. The noise indices in common use are:

L_{Aeq}
L_{A10}
L_{A90}
SEL

L_{Aeq} is a measurement of the equivalent steady noise which would have given the same sound pressure level as the measured varying noise. If the varying noise level was plotted on a graph (sound pressure level against time), then the area underneath that graph is the same as that under the equivalent horizontal line of L_{Aeq}.

An alternative way of measuring noise is to take spot measurements, equally spaced in time. L_{A10} is the sound pressure level exceeded for 10% of the time (which means that it is exceeded by 10% of the measurements). It thus represents a peak noise level.

L_{A90}, in the same way, represents the noise level exceeded for 90% of the time. This is often used for measurement of background noise levels.

In general, if all three readings were taken of the same noise over the same time, L_{A10} would be highest, L_{Aeq} would be the middle reading and L_{A90} would be the lowest. However, this is not always true. In particular, a loud, infrequent noise may occur for less than 10% of the time, in which case it would not be picked up by L_{A10}. In that case, the L_{Aeq} may be higher.

The SEL is the single event level, or sound exposure level, which would give as much noise energy in one second as that contained in the single noise event. It is most useful for measuring noise from discrete events such as aircraft, trains and sirens.

Noise legislation varies with the noise source, and different legislation requires different types of measurements, as described above.

Reduction of noise at source

Noise is best dealt with by reduction at source, and there is a commitment within the Health and Safety at Work Act 1974 that attempts should be made to do this for sound levels in excess of 85 dB(A). There are a variety of ways in which noise can be reduced at source.

Noise can generally be regarded as coming from one of three sources: vibration; aerodynamic noise from disturbance of a fluid such as air or water; and impact (which may also cause secondary vibration). Noise can be caused unnecessarily by poor maintenance of machinery. Good maintenance and lubrication are therefore the first steps in reducing noise. High quality parts are machined to close tolerances, and this leads to less noise as parts (such as gears) move less against each other. Better balancing of rotating parts also reduces noise levels.

Resonance (vibration at the natural frequency of the structure or part) can result in very high vibration amplitudes, and hence high levels of noise. Resonance can also be damaging to the parts and is generally undesirable. Minimisation of noise requires a minimisation of resonance, but it can be difficult to avoid altogether. Vibration can be reduced by altering the stiffness of the material or by isolation using materials such as rubber, cork or plastic which can take the energy out of vibration before it reaches the noisy part. Damping can reduce the length of time of vibration, and hence reduce the time of exposure to high noise levels.

Silencers can be used on machinery with a localised exhaust system, such as motor vehicles or pumps. They can be either dissipative or reactive. A dissipative silencer works by converting the noise energy into heat energy, and is effective at high and medium frequencies. However, it works less well at low frequencies. A reactive silencer works by bouncing the sound back towards the source, where it interferes with the outgoing noise. This is effective with noises which have a dominant frequency, as their effect can be reduced by the interference from the returning frequency.

Further improvements at source can be made by changing the process. Impact noise can be removed by changing away from an impact process. For example, concrete can be broken by a bending action, rather than by direct blows, and rivets can be squeezed into metal, rather than hammered.

ACTIVE NOISE CONTROL

The principle behind active noise control is that more noise is made, but it is made out of phase with the original noise, and hence the two cancel out. Sound propagates as a wave, and these waves add. So, if two sounds are produced, one which goes through the positive part of its cycle and the other going through the negative part, the two together will cancel, producing (in theory) no sound at all. In practice, this is impossible to achieve. However, it can be useful for noise sources which are heavily dominated by a noise of one known frequency. A significant reduction can be made by an out of phase counter noise. This is particularly true of low frequency noise, where the wavelength is sufficiently long for minor errors in the anti-phase noise to be insignificant.

Active noise control is more difficult to apply to broad band noise, particularly if it varies unpredictably. It requires, then, a feedback mechanism, and this cannot work at infinite speed. The anti-phase noise is therefore always slightly late, which reduces its effectiveness considerably.

Enclosure

Noise can be enclosed in order to reduce its impact outside the enclosure. Enclosure could be by a room, or by a small piece of enclosing material around the machine in question. A discotheque, for example, can be noisy inside the room but reasonably quiet outside. However, this is at the expense of the people in the room, as some of the noise is bounced back into the room. Enclosures are only as good as their complete make-up. A hole in an enclosure can render it much less effective. Most enclosures have holes of some sort: a door or window in a noisy room, or a space for an electric lead going to a machine. The sound reduction by the enclosure will increase significantly if these gaps are minimised or filled.

Within a room, the noise level can be reduced by the use of sound absorbing material. The ultimate in this respect is the anechoic chamber, which is a room covered by absorbing material, usually wedge shaped. These absorbers prevent the reflection of sound so that noise in the room is only caused by the noise source, and does not include the additive effects of reflection. In practice, anechoic chambers are expensive and would be used only for noise experimentation. However, the principle can be applied to all rooms and provision of sound absorbing materials can seriously improve the noise levels in a room. Curtains, carpets and soft furnishings are easy ways of reducing reflected noise.

Use of barriers

Noise levels can be reduced by placing a barrier between a noise source and the receiver. This method is commonly in use along stretches of road, such as motorways. Barriers can be thin, as in a wall, or thick, as in an earth bund. Noise travels in straight lines, so a barrier might be thought to remove noise altogether. However, although the direct line of sight is removed, what does happen is that the noise diffracts over the top of the barrier. Nevertheless, a significant reduction in sound level can be achieved with barriers. Added to this is the psychological effect of not being able to see the sound source; an effect which is considered to be significant. The length of the barrier is also relevant, as sound can also diffract around the end. Too short a barrier is therefore ineffective. In practice, noise levels can be reduced by up to 25 dB by the use of barriers.

Ear protectors

It is recognised that reduction of noise is not always possible, and that workers may need to enter noise enclosed areas for a variety of reasons. The final line of defence for such a person is the use of ear protectors. These may be small devices put directly into the ear, or ear muffs.

BUILDINGS AND THE ENVIRONMENT

Various approaches may be employed to assess the environmental impact of a building and to limit the adverse effects. An environmental policy may be constructed for a particular building or use may be made of a proprietary assessment method. An environmental strategy needs to be adopted. In some schemes, the appointment of a consultant purely to deal with such concerns is made in the initial stages of design. Then, a policy is formulated which the consultant monitors throughout the whole construction process. Rather than start from scratch, however, it is usually more convenient to use one of the assessment methods already developed. At the forefront of much work is the Building Research Establishment (BRE), which over the past 20 years has developed a number of assessment tools. The Building Research Establishment Environmental Assessment Methods (BREEAMs) deal with the whole building. The first version was published in 1990 and the original rudimentary scheme has been developed into a sophisticated tool. The original version dealt with new office design. Its stated main objectives were:

- to provide recognition for buildings that are friendlier to the global environment than normal practice and so help to stimulate a market for them;
- to improve the internal environmental quality and occupant health;
- to raise awareness of the dominant role that the use of energy in buildings plays in global warming through the greenhouse effect, and in the production of acid rain and the depletion of the ozone layer;
- to reduce the long term impact that buildings have on global environmental hazards;
- to provide a common set of targets and standards, so that false claims of environmental friendliness are avoided;
- to encourage designers to achieve environmentally sensitive buildings.

The issues that it felt competent to deal with included the global ones relating to the emission of carbon dioxide and CFCs, timber and timber products and the recycling of materials. In the case of neighbourhood effects, Legionnaires' disease, local wind effects and the reuse of an existing site were considered. On the indoor front, the issues examined in addition to the threat of Legionnaires' disease were air quality, hazardous materials and lighting. It was recognised that there was a whole host of issues, such as embodied energy, for which insufficient information was available at the time. It is a sign of the progress made that most of the issues are now included in the latest schemes.

The second scheme related to new superstores and supermarkets and was mainly sponsored by J Sainsbury, the supermarket. BREEAM 2/91 addressed similar global and indoor effects as BREEAM 1/90. In the case of neighbourhood effects, as well as including re-use of an existing site and Legionnaires' disease, the list included petrol vapour recovery, the overshadowing of other buildings and land and water economy.

The third version, BREEAM 3/91, is an environmental assessment for new homes. Version 4/93 of BREEAM dealt with existing office buildings, giving credits in the following areas:

- Global issues and use of resources:
  - global warming – carbon dioxide emissions;
  - ozone depletion – CFCs, HCFCs and halons;
  - use of resources – building maintenance.
- Local issues:

- o Legionnaires' disease arising from wet cooling towers;
- o noise from the building.
- Indoor issues:
  - o lighting;
  - o air quality;
  - o hazardous material;
  - o Legionnaires' disease arising from domestic hot water systems;
  - o healthy building indicators.

BREEAM was always designed to evolve. BREEAM 98 for new offices has now replaced the two earlier versions which treated new and existing offices separately. The new version is the result of a major review of BREEAM issues, improved industry practice and design options that can lead to further improvement. The scheme consists of a core assessment of the building fabric and services, with two optional parts relating to the quality of the design/procurement and management/operating procedures. In the core assessment, the issues dealt with give a comparative estimate of the building's potential environmental impacts in operation. It enables an index of environmental performance to be calculated. Issues not previously dealt with are included where knowledge has become available. These include materials specification and consideration of commuter transport. In previous schemes, a summary of credits obtained for the various issues was given, but here, a weighting system has been introduced to determine objectively an overall rating for the building. The result is the replacement of the former three main classes with a set of assessment categories that the authors believe are more in line with both environmental impacts and the concerns of industry.

CHAPTER 8

RURAL AREAS AND NATURE CONSERVATION

HISTORY

First, to put the use of rural land into its historical context, it is important to realise that the use of rural land has always been tied into property rights.[1] Before the Norman Conquest, other invaders (for example, the Romans) had not bothered to take control of the land. However, the men that William the Conqueror brought with him to England were skilled and expected to be rewarded for their services. William immediately put England under the heel of a land owning class of knights and claimed all the land for the monarchy. After this, any land would only be owned with permission from the King. William also left the legacy that this group of landowners would enjoy a privileged status and a passion for hunting. Forests did have some protection during this time, until the 14th century, when the Crown saw them as a way of raising money. Before then, the royal forests had covered one-quarter of England. By 1330, the area of royal forest had shrunk to two-thirds of what it had been in 1250.

The way in which the countryside and rural land is controlled today found its roots at this time. So much of the English landscape was changed from very early times, with the need for wood for building and other purposes that led to massive deforestation; also, the land was seen as a reward for loyalty and a way of acquiring wealth. Many of the restrictions on the use of land in relation to commoners, as well as the types of activities undertaken, were fixed after the Norman Conquest and are still evident today. This led to restrictions being placed on the use of this land by commoners who had enjoyed many rights over it. It also meant that animals and plants were often protected, as property and game law in England had harsh sentences, often of death or transportation. It also meant that many of the protections that were eventually placed on the rural environment were voluntary. This was because, historically, a lot of land has been held by very wealthy and influential owners and there were few restrictions placed on its use, especially when owning property was a requirement to vote.[2]

However, modern law emerged after the Second World War with the growth of towns, increased leisure use and the loss of farmland to other developments, especially housing. There was a belief in planning and that

---

1   See Goldman, 1998, for an international perspective on the commons. In relation to the UK, see Rackham, 1997; Thomas, 1983; Shoard, 1997.

2   Hil, 1996.

those who had returned from the War wanted to live in a better society with increased access to the countryside and the development of national parks.

Agriculture had already gone through massive changes in relation to the enclosure movements that began in Tudor times and which had already led to farms increasing in size and production increasing. However, in general, agriculture has become an industry since the Second World War and this has led to a massive change in the rural landscape, with the increased use of fertilisers and pesticides. To increase yields, farming was industrialised and problems began to emerge in relation to the loss of hedgerows, plant and animal species and water pollution.[3]

Agriculture is not the only development to have an impact on the countryside: the increasing urban sprawl has led to the loss of countryside and farmland; the building of roads and out of town developments, along with changing lifestyles, have all led to an increased pressure on the countryside. Mining and forestry also have an impact on the rural landscape.

These developments have led to a widespread destruction of the countryside since 1945. 95% of hay meadows have been destroyed; half of the remaining 5% have been damaged; 99% of lowland heaths have vanished; and, from 1979–90, 109,000 miles of hedgerows have been destroyed; there has been a 30% decline in plant species in arable land and 14% in meadows/grassland.[4] Since 1947, 109,000 miles of hedgerows have been destroyed This is enough to go round the world four times.[5]

At the present time, 76% of land in the UK is used for agriculture and forestry covers 10%. Land in urban use is projected to increase from 10% of the total land area in 1981 to just under 12% in 2016.

Administrative bodies

There are a number of bodies involved in the regulation of rural areas. The main Government departments are the Department for the Environment, Transport and the Regions (DETR) and the Ministry for Agriculture, Farming and Fisheries (MAFF). The Farming and Rural Conservation Agency replaced the Agricultural Development and Advisory Service (ADAS). It is the contact point for planning authorities in relation to plans, individual planning applications and other issues concerning agriculture. It also undertakes work in relation to the rural economy, land use planning, milk hygiene, environmental protection, environmental schemes and wildlife management.

---

3   See Harvey, 1998.
4   For the state of ponds, see DETR press release 604, 20 July 1998.
5   From Nature Conservancy Council, *Conservation of Nature in England and Wales*, Cmnd 7122.

Statutory control is also exercised by English Nature[6] (EN) (formerly the Nature Conservancy Council), the Countryside Agency, the National Parks Committee, the Sports Council, the Forestry Commission, the Environment Agency (EA) and local authorities. The Countryside Agency,[7] set up under s 35 of the Regional Development Agencies Act, amalgamated the Countryside Commission and Rural Development Commission. Regional Development Agencies were established in 1999. These have been set up to promote the economic development and improve the competitiveness of the English regions. They also have a purpose of contributing to achieving sustainable development, where it is relevant in their area to do so.

Local authorities have responsibility for planning and protecting green spaces in urban areas, as well as for making tree preservation orders. They also have other powers relevant to the countryside in relation to traffic, waste and pollution control.

There is also a large number of interest groups which influence policy making, either through lobbying or through their participation in informal governmental and other bodies. These include the National Farmers' Union, the Countryside Alliance, the Country Landowners' Association, the Council for the Protection of Rural England, the Open Spaces Society, Friends of the Earth, Greenpeace, RSPB, RSPCA, and various sporting bodies.

Nature conservation[8]

Planning

Planning policy guidance of nature conservation (PPG 9)[9] advises on how government policies for the conservation of our natural heritage are to be reflected in land use planning and contains the commitment to sustainability and to conserving the diversity of our environment.[10] The main objectives of

---

6   EN has published a number of position statements on: Access to the Countryside and Urban Greenspace, February 2000; Aggregate Extraction and Nature Conservation, June 1998; Environmentally Sensitive Agriculture and Nature Conservation, May 1997; Environmentally Sustainable Forestry and Woodland Management, November 1994; Genetically Modified Organisms, February 2000; Road and Nature Conservation, January 1997; Sites of Special Scientific Interest, February 2000; Sites of Importance for Nature Conservation, January 1995; Sustainable Development, April 1999; and Waste Management, May 1997.

7   House of Commons Select Committee on Environment, Transport and Regional Affairs 1998–99 Fourth Report, *The Countryside Agency*, 28 January 1999, HC 6.

8   Last, 1999, pp 15–33; Marshall Smith, 1999, pp 691–706; Garner and Jones, 1993, 1997; Gregory, 1994; Fry, 1995; Kirby, 1995; Lowe and Cox, 1989; Gregory, 1994; Reid, 1992, pp 231–56; Reid, 1994; Rodgers, 1996.

9   See PPG 9 on nature conservation and Circulars 24/82, 27/87.

10 See 'Natures place' (1995) 8 English Nature.

the policy note are to ensure that its polices contribute to the conservation of the abundance and diversity of British wildlife and its habitats; minimise the adverse effects on wildlife where conflicts of interest are unavoidable; and meet the UK's international responsibilities and obligations for nature conservation. Under the Town and Country Planning Act 1990, plans must take into account key wildlife sites of importance and the presence of a protected species, such as bats, is a material consideration for a local planning authority (LPA) when determining a development proposal which, if carried out, would harm the species or its habitat. EN must be consulted before planning permission is granted.

The national park authorities develop and implement policies for the parks in accordance with the statutory purposes of their designation and determine planning applications.[11]

COUNTRYSIDE PROTECTION

International controls

International criteria for designation of national wilderness areas[12] are that they must be extensive natural landscapes of great beauty/special scientific interest, which have not been materially altered by human occupation/exploitation. They must be owned by the Government primarily for the purpose of conservation, with strict conditions on their public enjoyment. There are no wilderness areas in the UK. The other international designation is that of 'World Heritage Site'. The International Convention Concerning the Protection of the World Cultural and Natural Heritage was signed in 1972 and provides protection for sites of outstanding universal value. Where a site is accepted, it must be protected and conserved from all threats. There are a number of World Heritage Sites in the UK.

The Ramsar Convention

Under the Convention, the contracting parities have to ensure that wetland conservation should be considered when developing their national land use planning. They should formulate the wise use of wetlands as far as possible. Each contracting party has to specify at least one wetland site that is of

---

11 National Parks and Access to the Countryside Act 1949; Planning in National Parks Act 1949, as amended by the Environment Act 1995.

12 Rutherford, 1993, pp 369–84.

international importance, based on ecology, botany, biology or hydrology. This is then included in the International List of Wetlands of International Importance. Conservation of wetlands is to be promoted through the use of nature reserves under the Convention. There have been 154 proposed Ramsar sites identified by EN.

The Bern Convention on the Conservation of European Wildlife and Natural Habitats 1979

This aims to ensure conservation and protection of all wild plants and animal species, to increase co-operation between States and to afford special protection to the most vulnerable or threatened species. It led to the EC Habitats and Wild Birds Directives and the Wildlife and Countryside Act (WCA) 1981.[13]

The Bonn Convention on the Conservation of Migratory Species of Wild Animals [14]

The Bonn Convention) arose from a recommendation of the 1972 United Nations Conference on the Human Environment which recognised the need for countries to co-operate in the conservation of species that migrate across national boundaries or between areas of national jurisdiction and the high seas. A number of threats can affect migrating species, including hunting, loss of habitat and degradation of feeding sites. Conferences of the parties to the Convention are held every three years. In 1985, a Standing Committee was established to provide guidance on the implementation of the Convention. It comprises one elected party from each of the five major geographic areas (Africa, America, Asia, Europe and Oceania). There are two appendices to the Convention. Appendix I lists species in danger of extinction throughout all, or a significant proportion of, their range, and so given full protection from hunting, fishing, capturing, harassing and deliberate killing.

Conservation measures also have to be taken by range States (countries that exercise jurisdiction over any part of a species distribution). The range States have to protect habitat and counter factors that might endanger the species or impede their migration. Under Appendix II, there are two forms of agreement: an agreement intended to benefit migratory species, especially those with an unfavourable conservation status over their entire range; or an agreement encouraged for populations of species that periodically cross national jurisdictional boundaries but are not necessarily migratory under the

---

13   DETR website, available at www.detr.gov.uk.
14   See www.wcmc.org.uk/cms.

definition provided by the Convention. Agreements that have been reached include the Agreement on the Conservation of Bats in Europe, which came into force on 16 January 1994 and aims to encourage co-operation within Europe to conserve all of its species of bats. It restricts the killing or capture of bats, protects their habitat, co-ordinates research and increases public awareness of bat conservation. The Agreement on the Conservation of Small Cetaceans of the Baltic and North Sea entered into force on 29 March 1994 and sets out measures to conserve over 30 species of small cetaceans. The African-Eurasian Waterbird Agreement aims to create a legal basis for the conservation policy of 116 range States for all migratory waterbird species and populations, individuals of which migrate in the Western Palearic and Africa. It covers 170 species, with 417 separate population sites and spans an area of 60 million km^2 (almost 40% of the Earth's surface).

The Convention on International Trade in Endangered Species of Wild Flora And Fauna (CITES)

The main legislation that protects endangered species is CITES, which covers some 34,000 plants and animals and also regional agreements in relation to either particular areas or to a particular species. CITES was signed in 1973 and regulates international trade and prohibits the trade of animals which are threatened with extinction (Appendix I). It also allows some controlled trade in species that are not yet endangered but may become so (Appendix II). Appendix III is a mechanism which allows a country to introduce domestic legislation regulating the export of species not in either of the above categories, and the country can then seek the support of other countries in enforcing its own domestic legislation. CITES operates a permit system, which has to be overseen on a domestic level by a management and scientific authority.[15]

In the UK, CITES is administered by the Department of the Environment, through its wildlife trade licensing branch.[16]

The Habitats Directive (92/43/EC)[17]

Under this Directive, each Member State must compile a list of areas containing the habitat types and species listed in the Directive. It sets out the scientific criteria for doing this. Special Areas of Conservation (SACs) have to

15 Council Regulation 338/97 on the protection of species of wild fauna and flora by regulating trade (OJL 061 3.3.97, as amended by OJL 171 7.7.99 and 939/97 OJL 140 30.5.97).

16 Harte, 1997, pp 139–80; Nollkaemper, 1997, pp 271–86; Harrop, 1997, pp 287–302; Ong, 1998, pp 291–314.

17 The Conservation (Natural Habitats, etc) (Amendment) (England) Regulations 2000 (SI 2000/192) amend the 1994 Regulations (SI 1994/2716), which implemented Council Directive 92/43/EC on the Conservation of Natural Habitats and of Wild Flora and Fauna (OJL 206 22.7.92, as amended by OJL 305 8.11.97).

be designated by 2004.[18] SACs will be those 'which make a significant contribution to the conservation of the habitats and species identified by the Directive. These will be the best area to represent the range and variety of those habitats and species'. These flora and fauna are given strict protection which prohibits their deliberate capture, killing, destruction, disturbance or sale. Other less threatened species may be managed or taken from the wild, provided that this can be done sustainably, that is, without threat to the conservation of the species. The Habitats Directive has been implemented in the UK by the Conservation (Natural Habitats, etc) Regulations 2000 (SI 2000/192). This requires all statutory bodies to act in accordance with the Directive.

Statutory controls

Under s 11 of the Countryside Act 1968,[19] ministers and other public and statutory bodies must have regard to the desirability of conserving the natural beauty and amenity of the countryside. Under the Conservation (Natural Habitat, etc) Regulations 2000, the competent authorities must have regard to the requirements of the Habitat Directive in exercising their functions. The WCA 1981 was introduced by the then Government to meet the UK's obligations under the Birds Directive 1979 to protect the habitat of certain species. The National Parks and Access to the Countryside Act 1949 set up the national parks and provided access to the countryside, whilst the Land Drainage Act 1994 allows ministers to intervene to save wetlands from drainage in the event of being threatened by an internal drainage board. Part III of the Environment Act 1995 amended the purposes of national parks and set up the national parks authorities.

Habitat protection[20]

- National parks were established in 1949.[21] These are areas designated by the Countryside Commission and confirmed by the SOSETR as national parks. They are administered by national park authorities.[22] The park authority has all the powers of an LPA in its area.[23] National parks cover

---

18 See DETR press release 219 ENV 20 March 1987 on more sites to be entered as SACs.

19 See DETR, *SSSI: Better Protection and Management*, 10 September 1998.

20 *Conservation of Nature in England and Wales*, Cmnd 7122.

21 National Parks and Access to the Countryside Act 1949, as amended.

22 Environment Act 1995: see Circular 12/96; Environment Act 1995, Pt III – National Parks.

23 See PPGN 7 countryside – environmental quality and economic and social development.

exceptionally fine stretches of relatively wild countryside. The object of designating them is to preserve and enhance their natural beauty, wildlife and cultural heritage and to promote opportunities for public understanding and enjoyment of the special qualities of their areas. If there is conflict, conservation takes precedence. Development is very strictly controlled;[24] however, this does not prevent all development. For example, farming and quarrying often take place in national parks. The national parks include Dartmoor, Exmoor, the Lake District, Northumberland, the North York Moors, the Peak District, the Yorkshire Dales, the Broads, the Brecon Beacons, the Pembrokeshire coast, Snowdonia and, more recently, the New Forest. The South Downs are in the process of being designated.

- Areas of outstanding natural beauty (AONBs) are normally smaller areas of land than national parks and are considered to be areas of fine landscape quality. They are designated by the Countryside Agency and confirmed by the SOSETR.[25] Designation is intended to assist sound planning and development by giving clear official recognition to the importance of preserving the attractiveness of the areas. The LPA decides planning applications. The Countryside Agency promotes the practical management of AONBs, although overall responsibility rests with the relevant local authority. Work carried out on such sites must be done with its advice. There are 41 AONBs in England and Wales: the first was the Gower in Wales and the most recent was the Tamar Valley in 1995.

- Sites of special scientific interest (SSSIs)[26] are areas that have special scientific interest for flora, fauna or geological or physio-geographical features.[27] These are designated by EN and the landowner is told of the restrictions on the use to which the land can be put.[28] Management agreements are then drawn up. When land is designated as an SSSI, EN notifies the owners and occupiers, the LPA and the Secretary of State. Site owners and occupiers receive a site map; a description of the site's special interest; a letter detailing their legal obligations; and a list of operations likely to damage the site's conservation interest.[29] These details are notified to owners and occupiers, LPAs and the Secretary of State by the statutory nature conservation body. Decision makers must consult EN and take special interest into account when considering development proposals. The LPA must review extant planning permissions and take any

24 Development has to be in the public interest, good for the local economy and must take account of the extent to which any detrimental effects can be mitigated.
25 Areas of outstanding natural beauty: 1949 Act, ss 87(1), 88(2); TCPA 1990, s 106.
26 *Op cit*, DETR, fn 19; NCC Guidelines for selection of Biological SSSIs 1989.
27 SSSIs – WCA 1981, s 28.
28 See *Southern Water Authority v NCC* [1992] 2 All ER 481.
29 Fry, 1993, pp 109–20; Harte, 1991, pp 293–309.

appropriate action if they believe that they will have a significant effect on the site.[30]

- Nature conservation orders (NCOs) are stringent safeguards which include the power of compulsory purchase. A site of national importance may be further protected through a nature conservation order under s 29 of the WCA 1981, which provides protection against certain operations and applies to all persons, not just owners and occupiers. The Countryside Agency can compulsorily purchase land or demand its restoration, if damaged, and issue stop orders. Compensation may be payable when an NCO is made.

- National nature reserves are managed especially for the study of fauna and their habitats or for the study of the physical characteristics of the land – this is through agreement with the landowner. They were set up under the National Parks and Access to the Countryside Act 1949.

- Local nature reserves were set up under the National Parks and Access to the Countryside Act 1949 to provide opportunities for the study and research into matters of flora and fauna and its conservation. Bylaws can be passed to exclude all visitors from the area and management agreements can be entered into.

- Non-statutory nature reserves are established and maintained by a variety of public and private bodies.

- Sites of importance for nature conservation are designated by local authorities for planning purposes.

- Marine nature reserves are areas of land covered by tidal areas. These are then controlled through bylaws.

- Heritage coasts are controlled by the Heritage Coast programme, which applies to England and Wales. It covers coastlines considered to be of exceptionally fine scenic quality which are substantially undeveloped and contain features of special significance and interest. Although these areas do not have any statutory protection, management plans are developed with local authorities and they are indicated on planning documents. Their management is supported by Heritage Coast officers and much of the land is in private ownership.

- Limestone pavements are protected through limestone pavement orders.[31] These prohibit the removal or disturbance of limestone.

- Management agreements are voluntary. A management agreement is a contract between EN and landowners to manage the land for nature conservation. The 1990 Wildlife Enhancement Scheme provides

---

30 See *op cit*, DETR, fn 19; Planning and Environment Reform Working Group Report [1999] JPL September, 789.

31 Limestone pavements – WCA 1981, s 34.

compensation[32] and it covers activities such as hedge laying and water control.

- County parks are specifically designated for public enjoyment under the Countryside Act 1968.[33]

- The Norfolk and Suffolk Broads is the area designated by the SOSETR. The area has similar status and purposes to the national parks, with additional responsibilities for navigation. It is administered by the Broads Authority, which is also the LPA for the area. The Broads Authority develops and implements policies for the area in accordance with its statutory remit set out in the Norfolk and Suffolk Broads Act 1988, which is designed to address specific environmental needs. It is an offence to carry out works likely to damage flora or fauna without permission.

- The Natura 2000 network covers SSSIs through the Conservation (Natural Habitats, etc) Regulations 1994 (SI 1994/2716). This covers European sites which are designated special[34] protection areas[35] under the Birds Directive[36] and special conservation areas under the Habitats Directive on the Conservation of Natural Habitats of wild Fauna and Flora.[37] Management agreements are central to these sites and the permitted development order can be changed at any time. If an owner wishes to undertake any activity, EN must give consent, unless there is a reasonable excuse, such as planning permission. If there is a danger that the plan or project will damage the site, permission can only be granted by the SOSETR if there are no alternative solutions and the plan or project has to be carried out for imperative reasons of overriding public interest, including those of a social or economic nature.

Biodiversity[38]

In June 1992, at the United Nations Conference on Environment and Development, the Biodiversity Convention was signed by 150 countries, Art 2 of which states that biodiversity is:

---

32 See *Thomas v Countryside Commission for Wales* (1993) 5 ELM 191, QB.

33 Countryside Act 1968, ss 6–10.

34 Case C 3/96 *Commission v Netherlands* [1999] Env LR, as reported in Gillies, 1999, pp 125–32. See, also, *World Wide Fund for Nature Ltd and RSPB v SOS* [1997] 1(2) Env LR 133.

35 See Case C 44/95 *R v SOS for the Environment ex p RSPB* [1997] QB 206. It was held that, when designating SPAs, the body had some discretion; however, it had to be based on ornithological criteria, not economic considerations.

36 79/409/EEC (OJL 103/1).

37 92/43 EEC (OJL 206/7).

38 See Reaka-Kudla *et al*, 1996; De Klem and Shine, 1993; Swanson, 1997; Kameri-Mbote and Cullet, 1999.

The variability among living organisms from all sources, including, *inter alia*, terrestrial, marine and other aquatic ecosystems and the ecological complexes of which they are part; this includes diversity within species, between species and of ecosystems.

Article 6(a) of the Convention on Biological Diversity states that each contracting party should 'develop national strategies, plans or programmes for the conservation and sustainable use of biodiversity'.

The UK Government's biodiversity strategy was laid down in *Biodiversity – the UK Action Plan* (1994).[39] The goals are to:

- conserve and, where practicable, enhance:
  - the overall population and ranges of native species and the quality and range of wildlife habitats and ecosystems;
  - internationally important and threatened habitats, ecosystems and species;
  - species, habitats and natural and managed ecosystems that are characteristic of local areas;
  - the biodiversity of natural habitats, where this has been diminished over recent decades;
- to increase public awareness and involvement in conserving biodiversity; and
- to contribute to the conservation of Biodiversity on a European and Global scale.

The UK will report on implementation of the Action Plan in 2001. Action plans have been prepared for 391 priority species and 45 priority habitats. There are also local biodiveristy action plans and PPG 9 on nature conservation is soon to be revised. In 1996, a UK Biodiversity Group was established, whose members included representatives from Government, local government, statutory agencies, business, commerce, land management and voluntary conservation agencies. Its terms of reference are to co-ordinate and oversee the implementation of the UK Biodiversity Action Plan to monitor and evaluate national biodiversity targets, report on progress and to advise Government.[40]

---

39 House of Lords Select Committee on the European Union 22nd Report, *Biodiversity in the European Union* (final report) HC 120, 9 November 1999; House of Lords Select Committee on the European Union 22nd Report: *Biodiversity I the European Union Final report: international Issues*, 11 January 2000, HL.

40 See DTR press release 342 ENV 5 May 1998 of the Fourth meeting of the Conference to the Parties.

The protection of plants and trees

Plants

Under the WCA 1981, it is an offence to pick, uproot or destroy any listed wild plant. In addition, it is an offence to uproot any wild plant. It is a defence to show that the act was an incidental result of a lawful operation and could not have been reasonably avoided.

Trees[41]

LPAs can protect trees through tree preservation orders,[42] which make it an offence to cut down, top, lop, uproot, wilfully damage or destroy a tree without the LPA's consent. It covers hedgerow trees but not bushes, hedges or shrubs and can cover anything from a single tree to woodland. Details of confirmed and provisional orders are kept in the local land charges register. The LPA can modify the order. The LPA has to give notice to the owner and other interested parties that it is serving the notice making the order, and it has to be left at a convenient place for public inspection. Objections must be made within 28 days of serving the notice, giving reasons for the objection and details of the relevant trees. The LPA will take these comments into account when it decides whether to confirm the order and it may hold a local inquiry. The owner has responsibility for looking after the trees but must be given permission to carry out work on them, unless they are dying, dead or dangerous. Except in an emergency, five days should be given as notice before a tree which is dying, dead or dangerous is cut down. If the LPA thinks that unauthorised work has been carried out, the owner can be prosecuted. Trees will have to be replanted if a tree is cut down or destroyed in breach of an order

If the Forestry Commission has given a grant, a tree preservation order can only be made if there is no current plan of operations, and only then with the Forestry Commission's consent. The Forestry Commission may give a felling licence, the exceptions to which are set out in the Forestry Act 1967 and regulations. If a felling licence is refused, compensation may be granted.

The Town and Country Planning (Trees) Regulations SI 1998/290 came into force in 1999. For trees in conservation areas, persons must give the LPA six weeks' notice before topping or lopping. If trees have to be cut down, replacement planting is mandatory.[43] Hedgerows, bushes and shrubs will not be covered, although coppice woodlands can be covered. The LPA has a duty

---

41 See, DETR (Rural Development Division), *Research for Amenity Trees*, 10 May 2000.
42 Information available at: www.wildlife-countryside.detr.gov.uk/tpo/leaflet/index.htm.
43 Town and Country Planning Act 1990, ss 198, 206, 211.

to ensure that appropriate provision is made for conserving or planting tress when granting planning permission. A tree survey may be undertaken and trees have to be protected during development.

Hedgerows[44]

The Hedgerows Regulations 1997 (SI 1997/1160) were made under s 97 of the Environment Act 1995.[45] The Regulations state that permission is required from the appropriate LPA for the removal of most countryside hedgerows through a hedgerow removal notice. If the authority believes that the hedgerow is important, this must be established using a set of statutory criteria and it may then refuse consent to the removal and issue a hedgerow retention notice. It is an offence to deliberately remove a hedgerow without prior permission. The LPA may also require the replacement of an illegally removed hedgerow through a hedgerow replacement notice.[46]

THE PROTECTION OF BIRDS AND WILD ANIMALS[47]

Birds

European law provides for the protection of birds.[48] The EC Directive on the Conservation of Wild Birds (79/409/EEC) emphasises the need to protect not just birds, but also their habitat. There are measures to protect vulnerable birds and all migratory birds through a network of special protection areas, of which 218 have been proposed.[49]

Wild birds are given a degree of protection under the WCA 1981. They are defined by s 27(10) of that Act as 'any bird of a kind which is ordinarily resident in or is a visitor to Great Britain in a wild state, not including any birds that have been bread in captivity or poultry or game birds'. 'Poultry' includes domestic fowls, geese, ducks, guinea fowls, pigeons, quails and turkeys, while 'game birds' includes pheasant, partridges, etc. Except for offences involving the illegal use of weapons and articles, the WCA 1981 does not cover the following game birds: pheasant, partridge, black grouse, red

---

44　See DETR, Effect of Agricultural Practices on Hedges, 1997; Brown, 1998; Holder, 1999, pp 100–14.

45　See *Bullock v SOS Environment* (1980) 40 P & CR 246.

46　See DETR, *Review of the 1997 Hedgerow Regulations*, 1998.

47　See Brooman and Legge, 1997; Reid, 1994.

48　See Wils, 1994, pp 219–42. EC Directive on the Conservation of Wild Birds (79/409/EEC); Council Directive 79/409 (OJL 103 25.4.79) on the Conservation of Wild Birds, amended by OJL 223 13.8.97; see, also, Council Resolution OJC 103 25.4.79.

49　Bowman, 1999, pp 281–300.

grouse and ptarmigan. Birds are protected in a number of Schedules to the WCA 1981. The main offence is found in s 1: it is an offence to intentionally kill, injure or take any wild bird, or to take or destroy the nest or eggs. An offence is also committed under s 1 of the WCA 1981 if a person has in their possession or control any live or dead wild bird or any part of, or anything derived from, such a bird, including the eggs.

There are two defences: the first is where the defendant can show that the bird or egg was sold to them otherwise than in contravention of the legislation; and, secondly, where the bird or egg had not been taken in contravention of the Act. It is also an offence to keep wild birds unless they are registered and ringed (this does not include owls or vultures). It is also an offence to disturb a bird when it is building a nest or breeding, or to disturb young birds.

Wild animals

The provisions covering wild animals parallel those for birds. Section 9 of the WCA 1981 gives protection to certain wild animals: it is an offence to intentionally kill, injure or take any wild animal included in Sched 5. It is also an offence to have in one's possession or control any live or dead wild animal included in Sched 5 or any part of, or anything derived from, such an animal. The defences are set out in sub-s 3: these include that the animal had not been killed or taken, or had been killed or taken otherwise than in contravention of the relevant provisions; or it had been sold to the person in contravention of the WCA 1981 and the Conservation of Wild Creatures and Wild Plants Act 1975. The habitat of animals is protected in sub-s 4 and sub-s 5 covers the selling of wild animals, which is an offence. Section 10 sets out the exceptions to s 9. These include that the action was undertaken by the Minister of Agriculture, Fisheries and Food or the SOSETR under s 98 of the Agriculture Act 1947.

Individual species protection[50]

Some animals have special protection under the law,[51] for example, badgers and deer.

---

50 For a general discussion on the issues of wild animal welfare, see Brooman and Legge, 1997; Kirkwood, 1992, pp 139–54; Garner, 1995, pp 114–29; Clark, 1979, pp 171–88; Rodman, 1977, pp 83–45. On the Wild Mammals Protection Act 1996, see Radford, 1991, p 146.

51 Conservation of Seals Act 1970; Conservation of Seals Order 1993 (SI 1993/2876); Salmon and Freshwater Fisheries Act 1975; Salmon Act 1986.

Badgers

In the Badgers Act 1992, it is an offence under s 1 to take, injure or kill badgers. Section 1(1) states that a person is guilty of an offence if, except as permitted by or under this Act, he wilfully kills, injures or takes, or attempts to kill, injure or take, a badger. Section 3 covers possession of any dead badger or any part of, or anything derived from, a dead badger. The defences are contained in s 4. Section 3 also concerns interfering with badger setts by damaging all or part of a sett; destroying a sett; obstructing access to, or any entrance of, a badger sett; causing a dog to enter a badger sett; disturbing a badger when it is occupying a badger sett; and intending to do any of those things or being reckless as to whether one's actions would have any of those consequences.

Foxes

Foxes are also protected under the WCA 1981. The use of self-locking snares is illegal and snares set to catch foxes must be inspected at least once every 24 hours. It is an offence to set snares for, or to otherwise to try to kill, foxes without taking all precautions to prevent the capture of other, more protected species, such as badgers. Foxes may also be protected under the Protection of Animals Act 1911, which prohibits the use of poisonous substances.[52]

Deer

Under the Deer Act 1991, it is an offence to take deer in the closed season. There are also prohibitions on the type of weapons that can be used to kill deer. Certain exceptions to the Act are provided for, including any act done by any person to prevent the suffering of any injured or diseased deer. There is also a defence for occupiers of land if the person had reasonable grounds to believe that the deer were damaging crops.

Bats

All species of British bats are protected against intentional killing, injury, sale or disturbance. It is an offence to disturb a protected bat while it is occupying a structure that it uses for shelter or protection.

The Wild Mammals Protection Act 1996

The problems of protecting wild animals under the Protection of Animals Act 1911 were outlined in the case of *Rowley v Murphy*.[53] In this case, a wild stag,

---

52 There are also other controls placed on the killing of foxes under, eg, the Pests Act 1954.
53 [1964] 2 QB 43; [1964] 1 All ER 50; [1963] 3 WLR 1061.

which was being hunted, jumped over the hedge of a field onto a main road, slipped on its tarmac surface and went under a stationary van, between its front and rear wheels. The stag was dragged from beneath the van and killed with a knife. They were charging with cruelly terrifying an animal by cutting its throat with a knife, contrary to the Protection of Animals Act 1911. However, the Act only protects animals in captivity and it was held that a mere temporary inability to get away was not a state of captivity.[54]

Due to concern that cases of cruelty were occurring with no legal redress, the Wild Mammals Protection Act was passed in 1996. Section 1 states:

> If, save as permitted by this Act, any person mutilates, kicks, beats, nails or otherwise impales, stabs, burns, stones, crushes, drowns, drags or asphyxiates any wild mammal with intent to inflict unnecessary suffering, he shall be guilty of an offence.

Section 2 provides the exemptions, which include mercy killings; killings conducted in a reasonably swift and humane manner of any wild mammal if the defendant shows that the wild mammal had been injured or taken in the course of lawful shooting, hunting, coursing or pest control activity; doing anything which is authorised under any enactment; any act made unlawful under s 1 if the act was done by means of any snare, trap, dog or bird lawfully used for the purpose of killing or taking any wild mammal; or the lawful use of any poisonous or noxious substance on any wild mammal.

Enforcement

Each police force has an appointed Wildlife Liaison Officer or some identified person responsible for the enforcement of wildlife legislation. The police are the main enforcers of wildlife legislation, along with the RSPB, RSPCA and other wildlife groups.[55]

---

54 See, also, *Hudnott v Campbell* (1986) *The Times*, 27 June.

55 See Partnership for Action against Wildlife Crime (PAW) Enforcement Plan 2000–03. This is a national wildlife crime unit to coordinate the police, HM Customs and Excise and voluntary organisations. PAW will try to raise awareness of wildlife crime amongst the judiciary and police and encourage partnership at a local and regional level.

AGRICULTURAL CONTROLS[56]

General policies

The Agricultural Act 1947 introduced tariffs, quotas and a system of guaranteed minimum prices for farm products. In 1951, production grants were introduced, but these were replaced by European farm capital grant schemes. The Common Agricultural Policy (CAP) revoked previous schemes. However, CAP still supported minimum prices and in 1992 there were a range of agri-environmental measure introduced.[57]

In 1997, the European Commission presented its Communication Agenda 2000. In June 1998, the Cardiff Summit agreed a process of integration of the environment into other sectors, including agriculture, and, in December 1998, the Vienna Council called for a comprehensive strategy for agriculture. In February 1999, the Commission produced a Communication to the Council and the Parliament on *Directions towards Sustainable Agriculture*. The Agenda 2000 reform of the CAP has as its aim a balanced, sustainable agricultural policy. The Commission will draw up regulations for many of the details of the reform and Member States will have to draw up rural development plans, consider proposals to make use of environmental cross-compliance mechanisms, devise indicators as to how they can monitor and report on these plans and measures and consider how they can develop proposals in the long term. Agenda 2000 states that forestry and agri-environmental forestry payments will be brought together, with structural measures and farm capital grants as a single rural policy.[58] The England Rural Development Plan was submitted to the European Commission in January 2000. This sets out the Government's plans for assisting agriculture and the rural economy over the next seven years.[59]

In the UK, MAFF has published a number of consultation papers as part of its review of agricultural policy.[60] *A New Direction for Agriculture* (1999) sets out a national strategy for agriculture and implementing Agenda 2000 Cap Reform.

In December 1999, MAFF announced that farm spending would be switched from production aids to supporting the rural economy. This involved increasing expenditure under EU Rural Development Regulation,

---

56 Hawke and Kovaleva, 1998; Rogers, 1998; Hough, 1998.

57 See UK Round Table on Sustainable Development's Report – *Aspects of Sustainable Agriculture and Rural Policy*, July 1998, p 2.

58 *Ibid.*

59 See MAFF website: www.maff.gov.uk/farm/ag2000.htm.

60 See DETR, *The Rural Development Regulation*, 10 May 2000.

which is the second pillar of the CAP. It aims to advance environmentally friendly farming practices, to modernise and restructure farming and to support off farm rural development. There may be direct payments for environmental improvement, as all rural development plans need to take into account the requirements of the environment so that there is aid for training, diversification, restructuring, agri-environmental measures, etc.

Planning[61]

The use of planning controls is limited, as s 55(2) of the Town and Country Planning Act 1990 exempts the use of land for agriculture/forestry from planning controls. The General Permitted Development Order (GPDO)[62] provides that many agricultural developments are granted permitted development rights, so no planning permission is required to change use between agriculture forestry or horticulture to cease or begin agricultural activity. The GPDO allows planning permission for building and engineering development for agricultural purposes, subject to limits.[63]

Genetically modified crops

Genetically modified crops have become one of the most controversial areas[64] of food production.[65] Public concern led to the Government changing its policy on genetically modified organisms (GMOs).[66] There are health concerns,[67] and also environmental concerns in relation to wildlife[68] and habitat.[69]

---

61 For general planning procedure, see above, Chapter 3.
62 See Appendix B
63 See Appendix B.
64 Monsanto Annual Report (Novartis). See, www.monsanto.co.uk.
65 See 'The Monsanto files – can we survive genetic engineering?' (1998) 28(5) *The Ecologist* (special issue).
66 See Environment Audit Committee 1998–99, Fifth Report, *GMOs and the Environmental Co-ordination of Government Policy*, May 1999.
67 Genetically Modified and Novel Foods (Labelling) (England) Regulations 2000 (SI 2000/768). These provide for the enforcement of Council Regulation 1139/98/EC concerning the compulsory labelling of food containing GMOs of particulars other than those provided for in Directive 79/112/EEC and the labelling requirements in Council Regulation 258/97/EC, Art 8(1), concerning novel foods and novel food ingredients.
68 ACRE Consultation Paper on the Commercial Use of GM Crops in the UK – The Potential Wider Impact on Farmland Wildlife 1999.
69 House of Lords Select Committee on the European Communities 1998–99, Second Report, *EC Regulation of Genetic Modification in Agriculture*, January 1999.

The EC has set down criteria for procedures to allow the deliberate release into the environment of GMO plants and for their contained use. The EC regulation of GMOs is to change.[70]

In the UK, GMOs are regulated under Pt VI of the Environmental Protection Act 1990.[71] There are a number of bodies involved in the regulation of GMOs, including the Advisory Committee on Releases to the Environment,[72] the Human Genetics Commission, the Agriculture and Environment Biotechnology Commission and the Food Standards Agency, which will consider food issues more widely.

The Seeds (National List of Varieties) Regulations 1982 (SI 1982/1615) require that new varieties of plants must be put through trials before farmers can use them under the National Lists scheme for the EC Common Catalogue. In relation to the trials, there was to be a voluntary agreement between the Government and the industry on the conduct of the evaluations. This meant that there was supposed to be no general unrestricted cultivation of GM crops until the trials had finished. The scientific steering committee[73] will decide whether further trials should take place.[74]

Trials for GM crops began in 1999 but were subject to a number of direct actions to remove them.[75] This led to a number of cases, including *Monsanto v Tilley and Others* ((1999) *The Times*, 30 November). In this case, Monsanto sought injunctions restraining the defendants from trespassing on certain land and uprooting and damaging crops belonging to Monsanto. The defendants based their defence on a plea of necessity or acting to protect third parties in the public interest. Monsanto appealed and the Court of Appeal held that the defences were not available in this case because of the absence of an emergency and the presence of a public licensing authority.

Greenpeace volunteers have also been charged with criminal damage after destroying a field of experimental crops of genetically modified maize. They were initially acquitted on a charge of theft but the court did not reach a verdict on the criminal damage charge. On 2 May 2000, the CPS stated that it would seek a re-trial.[76]

---

70 Proposed amendment of Directive 90/220 on deliberate releases of GMOs [1998] OJL 139/1.

71 Genetically Modified Organisms (Risk Assessment) (Records and Exemptions) Regulations 1996 (SI 1996/1106); Genetically Modified Organisms (Deliberate Release) Regulations (SI 2000/347); Genetically Modified (Contained Use) Regulations 1999 (SI 1999/14).

72 ACRE Annual Report No 5, 1998, March 1999.

73 It produces a yearly report: see DETR press release 1089, 11 November 1999.

74 See DETR press release 1057, 5 November 1999.

75 See Vidal, 1998.

76 See Greenpeace news release 2 May 2000, available at: www.greenpeace.org.uk.

There has also been concern from organic farmers about cross-contamination. This led to the case *R v Secretary of State for the Environment ex p Watson* ([1998] EGCS 122, CA), which was a judicial review action of the Government's decision to allow GM crops to be planted next to Watson's organic farm. The farmer failed. However, guidelines have been drawn up by the industry to reach agreement with neighbouring farmers on planting GMO crops.

Concerns have also arisen in relation to whether the regulations have been complied with. In *R v Secretary of State for the Environment ex p Friends of the Earth* ((1999) Env B, 23 September, p 6), leave was granted to Friends of the Earth to test the legality of the Government's approach in relation to an application by AgrEvo UK Ltd to proceed with trial planting of GM oil seed rape under its existing licence.

In May 2000, concern arose over GM seeds being planted on farms. Advice was given by the Advisory Committee on releases to the environment to the Secretary of State and MAFF under s 124 of the EPA 1990.[77] This was issued in relation to the concern that GM and non-GM seed had been found together in relation to oil seed rape which had already been sown by farmers The non-GM seed had been contaminated with 1% of GM seeds. ACRE considered the risk to the environment and human health to be low. However, the DETR took a precautionary step, advising that the situation should be independently monitored. It seemed clear that the farmers would have to either re-plant with an alternative eligible crop or grow the crop and harvest it. However, it would have to be disposed of, as there is no marketing consent for the GM part of the crop. The Government expects the farmers to pursue compensation claims with the seed supplier.

The Government has announced that new safeguards will be placed over GM crops,[78] including greater notice to local people of farm trials – from 10 days to two months. New trials will also be decided individually, looking at such factors as wind and geography on any potential contamination. The Government will also consider the possibility of barrier crops around the sites and the present isolation zone will be extended.[79]

On 29 January 2000, the Biodiversity Protocol was agreed. This adopts a precautionary approach to transboundary movements of living modified organisms(LMOs). Any countries exporting LMOs will have to provide the importing country with an advanced information agreement on the nature of the products.

---

77   MAFF press release 17 May 2000.

78   Fifth special report, 16 May 2000, HC 481 Reply by the Government to the Third Report (7 March 2000 HC71) from the Agriculture Committee.

79   See Ahmed, 2000.

The control of pesticides[80]

Pesticides are mainly controlled through the Food and Environmental Protection Act 1985.[81] This protects human and plant health and the environment. It aims to secure a safe and efficient means of controlling pesticides, as well as making information about pesticides publicly available. The Act states that no pesticide can be made, imported, sold, supplied, stored used or advertised without approval. Enforcement powers include powers of seizure, disposal and remedial action by MAFF. Buffer zones have been introduced to protect water[82] and fields,[83] margins. MAFF also monitors pesticide levels[84] and random samples may be taken. There are a number of codes of practice for sellers and users. The Pesticide Forum[85] brings together agro-chemical, farming, retailing, environmental and consumer interests.[86] Plant protection products are approved by the Pesticide Safety Directorate (part of MAFF). Future regulations will apply to biocidal products.[87]

Organic farming

Organic farming makes up only 3% of the agricultural area in the UK.[88] It is regulated under the Agri-Environment Regulation (2078/92/EC), which has been implemented in the UK by the Organic Farming Regulations 1999 (SI 1999/590). These provide for grants for organic farming.[89] Council Regulation 2092/91/EC on Organic Production of Agricultural Products and Indicators[90] sets strict standards before agricultural products may be marketed as organic. In the UK, there is a certification and inspection scheme run by the Register of Organic Food Standards.[91] The organic farming scheme replaces the organic

---

80   See Carson, 1962.

81   The Pesticide Act 1998 amends the Food and Environmental Protection Act 1985 in relation to the regulation and enforcement of pesticides.

82   DETR, *Economic Instruments for Water Pollution*, 1997, looked at economic instruments to reduce pesticide use.

83   There are also controls over spraying and groundwater.

84   Pesticides (Maximum Residues in Crops, Food and Feeding Stuffs) (Amendment) Regulations 1999 (SI 1999/1109).

85   The Pesticides Trust publishes *Pesticides News*, which also has a record of cases.

86   See *op cit*, UK Round Table on Sustainable Development, fn 57, pp 23–25.

87   See the Plant Protection Product Directive 91/414/EEC (OJL 230/1) and the Regulations made to implement it: Commission Regulation 1199/97/EEC (OJL 170).

88   See www.englishnature.org.uk.

89   The Organic Farming (Wales) Regulations 1999 (SI 1999/2735) (as amended) provide for the payment of aid to farmers who undertake to introduce organic farming methods to comply with Council Regulation 2078/92/EEC (OJL L215 30.7.92).

90   As amended by Commission Regulation 1999/98/EC.

91   House of Lords Select Committee on the European Union 16th report, *Organic Farming and the EU*, 29 July 1999, HL 93.

aid scheme; this is voluntary and offers financial help to convert from non-organic to organic farming. Certain environmental management operations have to be undertaken and the farmer has to be registered as an organic producer under EC Regulation 2092/91. It is illegal to sell food as organic unless it complies with the Regulation.

Agri-environmental schemes[92]

There are a number of schemes to improve the environmental protection of the countryside from intensive farming, including:

- the arable stewardship scheme, which aims to benefit wildlife in arable areas;
- the farm biodiversity plans;
- the countryside access scheme, which aims to increase the benefits for land which is set aside under the arable area payments scheme and offers farmers incentives to improve public access. The scheme is voluntary and aims to encourage farmers to provide public access to suitable set aside land;
- the countryside stewardship scheme which aims to protect, enhance, restore and re-create landscapes;[93]
- environmentally sensitive areas were first set up in 10 designated areas in 1987 and 1988. The scheme has been expanded into 12 new areas and provide incentives for farmers to enhance and protect the landscape, wildlife and historic interests. Environmentally sensitive areas are particularly high landscape or historic value which are threatened by changes in farming practice, incentives are offered to farmers to protect the environment and improve public access. Environmental objectives are set for 5 or 10 year management agreements;[94]
- the farm woodland premium scheme encourages farmers to plant trees on agricultural land. Grants are available from the Forestry Commission under the scheme;
- the habitat scheme encourages farmers to create or improve wildlife habitats over 10 or 20 years by taking land out of production, introducing intensive grazing and managing it for the benefit of wildlife. It targets water fringes, coastal saltmarsh and land formerly in the five year set aside

---

92 See MAFF, *Countryside Access, Countryside Stewardship and Environmentally Sensitive Areas in England*, 1998.

93 The Countryside Stewardship (Amendment) Regulations 1999 (SI 1999/1177).

94 House of Commons Select Committee on Agriculture Fourth Report, *Environmental Regulation and Farming*, 17 March 2000, HC 212.

schemes. The habitat scheme is to be incorporated into the countryside stewardship scheme;

- the moorland scheme aims to protect and improve moorland environment and to encourage upland farmers to graze fewer sheep.

Forestry

This has also changed from being a country activity to a large scale industrial concern. It has led to acidification of rivers and soil erosion, as well as a loss of habitat for many species.[95] 10% of the UK is covered by forest and the Government would like to see a doubling of forest over the next half century. Only 1.4% of Great Britain is covered by ancient semi-natural woodland; two-thirds of the forest is conifer and one third broad leafed.

Agencies

The Forestry Commission advises ministers on policy issues.[96] It has a statutory Board of Commissioners and two executive agencies – Forest Enterprise and Forest Research – which work to targets set by the Commissioners and ministers. Forest Enterprise is responsible for the management of forests and woodland and Forestry Research undertakes research to promote forestry and sustainable forestry management.[97]

However, forestry does not count as development for the purposes of the planning system.[98]

Grants

Forestry grants[99] include the woodland grant scheme, for planting and looking after woodland, and the farm woodland premium scheme. Grants are

---

95 Under the Forestry Act 1991, regional advisory committees have been set up. Under the Wildlife and Countryside (Amendment) Act 1985, there is a duty on the Forestry Commission to balance afforestation with flora and fauna.

96 Plant Health (Forestry) (GB) Amendment (No 2) Order 1998 (SI 1998/3109) and Council Resolution on a forestry strategy for the EU (OJC 056 26.2.99). Council Regulation 2158/92/EEC on the protection of Community forests against fire (OJL 217 31.7.92, implemented by OJL 203 3.8.99).

97 See www.forestry.gov.uk.

98 Town and Country Planning (Trees) Regulations 1999 (SI 1999/1892); Environmental Impact (Forestry) Regulations (England and Wales) 1999 (SI 1999/2228).

99 See Reid, 1996, p 59. The 1998 Regulations state that the formal consent of the Forestry Commission is need before work starts on initial afforestation projects where they are likely to have an effect on the environment.

not available for operations which could damage SSSIs. The Forestry Commission consults the conservation agencies on all applications for forestry grants and felling proposals in SSSIs and no work is approved without their agreement. The regulations that govern both the woodland grant scheme and provisions for felling licences are set out in the Forestry Act 1967.

Felling

A felling licence is needed for felling trees. This is obtained from a Forestry Commission conservancy office. Everyone involved in the felling of trees must ensure that the licence has been obtained and that the conditions are adhered to. This is strictly controlled and the owner must usually re-plant the felled area. It is an offence to undertake felling without a licence, unless it is covered by the exceptions.[100] A register lists details of felling and planting, giving locations and details of this work, as well as the work that Forest Enterprise does. Forest Enterprise must have permission from the Forestry Authority to undertake any work and woodland officers visit the site of any proposed felling. After the information has been on the register for four weeks and all comments have been received, the Forestry Commission formally approves the work and a contract is signed with the applicant.

Breeding

The Forestry (Reproductive Material) Regulations 1977 (SI 1977/308) control the quality of seeds, plants and cuttings marketed for forestry purposes. The Forestry Commission maintains a register of the seed strands and poplar beds which meet the regulatory standards. Applications can be made to the Tree Improvement Branch to have a source entered. Certificates of provenance are issued to provide the customer with details of the provenance and origin of the collection. An application can be made to the EC for permission for the marketing of stock from unregistered sources if there is a shortage of material.

Conservation

Responsible forestry has also been developed by the Soil Association, through the responsible forestry programme established in 1992 and. The Association has devised the responsible forestry standards and the Woodmark certification scheme, which also embodies the principles and criteria of the Forest Stewardship Council. If the Forestry Commission is selling land of

---

100 See *Tree Felling*, Forestry Commission Booklet.

conservational importance, that land should first be offered to conservation bodies at the district valuer's price.[101]

Mining[102]

Mining causes problems in relation to the countryside and access,[103] as it can have an impact on visual amenity though open cast sites[104] or spoil heaps[105] and other waste,[106] as well as through water pollution problems[107] and land subsidence.[108] There are planning controls[109] on mining to protect nature conservation.[110] Section 53 of the Coal Industry Act 1994 imposes an environmental duty on the coal industry. Mining is governed by s 55(4) of the TCPA.[111] The Mineral Planning authorities have to draw up a mineral local plan. There should be co-operation with the Coal Authority, the Sand and Gravel Association and representatives of other extractive industries, and, in relation to after use, MAFF, the Forestry Commission, the Countryside Agency, English Heritage and EN, where this is appropriate. An EIA[112] will be needed if the development is likely to have a significant effect on the environment and will be mandatory for all proposals for open cast mining where the surface area exceeds 25 hectares.[113] There are also a number of mineral planning guidance notes (MPGs).

---

101 See EIA (Forestry) (England and Wales) Regulations 1999 (SI 1999/2228).

102 See above, Chapter 5 on energy policy, particularly the policy document *Conclusions of the Review of Energy Sources from Power Generation* (Cmnd 4071, October 1998).

103 See the Mines (Working Facilities and Support) Act 1966.

104 Opencast Coal Act 1958.

105 The Mines and Quarries (Tips) Act 1969 covers spoil heaps.

106 Coal Industry Act 1994; Waste Management Licensing Regulations 1994 (SI 1994/1056).

107 Water Resources Act 1991, as amended by the EA 1995, which removes statutory protection for mine owners to just abandon mining sites and in relation to water pollution from mines. See, also, the Opencast Coal (Compulsory Rights, Drainage and Rights of Way) (Forms) Regulations 1994 (SI 1994/3097); Groundwater Regulations 1998 (SI 1998/2746).

108 The Coal Mining Subsidence Act 1991 provides remedies for subsidence.

109 See Town and Country Planning (Minerals) Regulations 1995 (SI 1995/2863).

110 Wildlife and Countryside Act 1981; Council Directive 79/409/EEC on the Conservation of Wild Birds; Council Directive 92/43/EEC on the Conservation of Natural Habitats and of Wild Fauna and Flora.

111 Town and Country Planning (General Permitted Development) Order 1995 (SI 1995/418); Town and Country Planning (Minerals) Regulations 1995 (SI 1995/2863).

112 *R v North Yorkshire CC ex p Brown and Another* (1999) *The Times*, 12 February. In this case, the House of Lords stated that the imposition of conditions on an old mining consent is a development consent within the meaning of Directive 85/337/EEC; therefore, an EIA would be needed if the characteristics of the decision in question required one.

113 Town and Country Planning (Environmental Impact Assessment) (England and Wales) Regulations 1999 (SI 1999/293); and Circular 2/99.

Current MPGs

MPG1:   General considerations and development plan system;

MPG2:   Applications, permissions and conditions;

MPG3:   Coal mining and colliery spoil disposal;

MPG4:   Revocation, modification, discontinuance, prohibition and suspension orders.

MPG5   Instability in surface mineral workings;

MPG6:   Guidance for aggregates provision in England;

MPG7:   The reclamation of minerals workings;

MPG8:   Planning and Compensation Act 1991: interim development permissions (IDOs) – statutory provisions and procedures;

MPG9:   Planning and Compensation Act 1991: IDOs – conditions;

MPG10:   Provision of raw materials for the cement industry;

MPG11:   The control of noise at surface mineral workings;

MPG12:   Treatment of disused mine openings and availability of information on mined ground;

MPG13:   Guidelines for peat provision in England, including the place of alternative materials;

MPG14:   Environment Act 1995: review of mineral planning permissions;

MPG15:   Provision of silica sand in England.

The DETR's *Opportunities for Change* (February 1998) set out the objectives of sustainable development[114] in relation to minerals planning:

- to conserve minerals whilst ensuring an adequate supply to meet the needs of society;

- to minimise the production of waste and to use material efficiently, including recycling;

- to encourage sensitive working practices for mineral extraction and to preserve and enhance the overall quality of the environment once the extraction has finished;

- to protect areas of nature conservation and landscape protection, other than in exceptional circumstances where it has been demonstrated that development is in the public interest;

- to minimise impacts from the transport of mineral.[115]

---

114 MPG has been revised on coal mining and colliery disposal. On the materiality of other sites, see *Secretary of State for the Environment v PG Edwards and Breckland DC* [1994] JPL B110; *Pioneer Aggregates (UK) Ltd v Secretary of State for the Environment* [1985] 1 AC 132. See, also, *Trust House Forte Hotels Ltd v SOS for the Environment and Northavon DC* [1986] JPL 834.

115 See DETR MPG 3 (revised), *Coal Mining and Colliery Spoil Disposal*, March 1999.

THE FUTURE

General countryside protection and planning

Policy developments in relation to the countryside cannot be seen in isolation with other policies such as transport, energy, water and waste. Neither can they be separated from urban policies, as these have an impact on the protection of the countryside. The main method of protection for the encroachment of urban living onto the countryside is through greenbelts.[116]

Greenbelts

There is a presumption against the development in greenbelts, except in special circumstances.[117] 13% of England was designated greenbelt in 1997. There are now 14 Greenbelts in England. Within a greenbelt, approval should not be given for development or change of use for purposes other than agricultural, forestry, agricultural sport or other uses appropriate to rural areas. PPGN 2 exceptions may include power stations and mining, if they are needed to fulfil specific operational requirements or are in the national interest. Local circumstances will be taken into account. The boundaries of greenbelts can change but permanence is the general rule.

The general aims of greenbelts are to:

- check urban sprawl;
- safeguard the countryside from further encroachment;
- protect neighbouring towns from merging;
- preserve the special character of historic towns;
- assist in urban regeneration;
- enhance and improve the natural beauty of the countryside;
- increase opportunities for its quiet enjoyment.

The problems of greenbelts are as follows:

- they are weak instruments of regional/strategic planning;
- they have forced too much growth on towns/villages beyond the greenbelt;

---

116 See DETR press release, Land Use Change in England, 8 December 1999, which states that the percentage of new dwellings built on previously developed land was 52% in 1997. From 1989–97, dwellings were built at a density of 28 dwellings per hectare. 13% of land was covered by greenbelts in 1997.

117 See PPGs 2 and 3; Circulars 14/84, 16/87, 27/87, 7/91 (revised March 1992).

- they have done little to improve the appearance of open land or to promote recreation;
- other policies have been just as important as greenbelts in controlling development in the countryside;
- they are seen as different things to different people.

Rural regeneration

The Countryside Agency's publication, *Tomorrow's Countryside – 2020 Vision*,[118] highlights the fact that there are different problems facing different rural communities, just as is the case in urban communities. However, some are in fact the same: for example, transport problems, pollution and loss of green space. Its strategy is to provide a countryside of:

- diverse character and outstanding beauty;
- prosperous and inclusive communities;
- economic opportunity and enterprise;
- sustainable agriculture;
- transport which serves everyone and does not destroy the environment;
- recreational access for local people and visitors.

The Countryside Agency's Report, *The State of the Countryside 1999* (April 1999), provides many interesting facts about the countryside, some of which include the following:

- the population is older than the national average;
- over half of the population expresses a desire to live in the countryside;
- the amount of land that has been developed from rural to urban use increased from 29% in 1985 to 41% in 1993;
- between 1984 and 1993, 158,000 km of hedges were lost – about one-third of the total that existed in 1984;
- there is a marked decline in the number of farm and woodland species of birds;
- there has been a fluctuating decline in farm income;
- in June 1998, 7% of agricultural land in England was covered by one or more agri-environmental schemes – 72% of these are Environmentally Sensitive Areas and 19% are under the countryside stewardship scheme;
- 20% of England total housing stock is in rural areas and this has grown by 5%, compared to 3% in urban areas. It is expected to grow by 25% from 1991 to 2011. Most of this is internal immigration, except for the south

118 See www.countryside.gov.uk.

coast, where it is due to people moving, particularly out of London. 58% of second homes are within rural areas but 0.4% of all rural homes are second homes;

- tourism and recreation are also looked at. The average journey a visitor makes to get to the countryside is 16 miles. Half include a round trip of five miles or less. 55% of trips are made by car; 38% walking; 4% bicycle; and 1% bus and coach. The rest make up less than 1%, including trains.

It is interesting to note that the number of journeys made by rural and urban dwellers is roughly the same, although rural travellers travel longer distances. However, there is a real lack of public transport: 75% of rural parishes in 1997 had no daily bus service and 65% had no six days per week bus service. 44% of all parishes have no buses before 9 am and 77% no buses after 7 pm. 93% of rural parishes have no rail service. However, 21% of parishes had a community minibus scheme. 80% of rural journeys to work are made by car, compared to 66% nationally. Traffic has been growing faster on rural roads: from 1981–97, the increase in vehicle flows in urban areas was 23%, whilst in rural areas it has been 75%. The majority of deaths are on rural roads.

The Rural England Discussion Document[119] sets out the aims and objectives of the proposed Government White Paper on Rural England:

> The White Paper will look at the longer term future for the English countryside and at how policies on the economy, health, transport, education, the environment, crime, agriculture, planning and many other areas will support a sustainable countryside and rural communities in the future. It will consider how the prosperity and competitiveness of rural economies can be strengthened; how development and regeneration policies can assist rural areas which have concentrations of problems or disadvantage; and how to make sure that all rural people have the opportunity to participate fully in society. It will examine ways of conserving and enhancing the countryside for us all. And it will look at how social, economic and environmental objectives can be integrated to ensure that there is sustainable development in rural areas.

The Government wants to ensure:

- economic vitality;
- sustainable development;
- strong communities;
- a fair and inclusive society;
- working in partnership.[120]

---

119 DETR, *Rural England – A Discussion Document*, Feb/Nov 1999; House of Commons Select Committee on Environment, Transport and Regional Affairs 1999–2000, Seventh Report, *Rural White Paper*, 17 May 2000, HC 32.

120 RDA, *Guidance on Rural Policy*, 17 December 1998; Cabinet Office, *Rural Economies Report*, December 1999; *op cit*, UK Round Table on Sustainable Development, fn 57.

Rural England – A Discussion Document will lead to a rural White Paper. This consultation paper really just raises some of the principles that the Government will follow in its rural White Paper, rather than providing an imaginative starting point for debate, as is the case in the urban development report.

There are also other initiatives in relation to rural England. These include:

- village appraisals and design statements;
- parish paths partnership;
- PPG 7 on the countryside – environmental quality and economic and social development;
- regional development agencies and regional planning guidance, which will contain a sustainability appraisal.

The Countryside (Amenity and Conservation) Bill 2000[121]

A new policy for the countryside is being developed in the Countryside (Amenity and Conservation) Bill 2000. The Bill proposes a new statutory right of access[122] to mountain, moor, heath, downs, and registered common land. However, it does not cover coasts, woodland, gardens, parks or cultivated land. It does not include cycling, horse riding or driving vehicles and all dogs must be kept on leads during the spring. Landowners will be able to close the land for 28 days a year for shooting or other reasons, and for longer if they can convince committees of local interest groups that they have good reason. If landowners put up bogus notices, they will be fined.[123]

Local authorities will have to draw up plans to improve rights of way, including providing recreational circular walks. Some rights of way will be made public highways. At present, the law is that rights of way must not be stopped up, obstructed or damaged and that owners and occupiers of land must reinstate rights of way after ploughing and ensure that crops do not make the highway inconvenient to use. There are already controls in relation to motor vehicles that must not, without lawful authority, be driven over any footpath or bridleway and the use of cycles, horses and motor vehicles on a public footpath may be trespass or may constitute a public nuisance.[124]

The Bill aims to strengthen the protection of SSSIs, and measures to prevent damage will be reinforced through tougher penalties. EN will be able to prevent neglect and force landlords to restore damaged sites. If there is a

---

121 See Sculthorpe, 1993.
122 Rights of Way and Access to Mountains Act 1939; National Parks and Access to the Countryside Act 1949.
123 See Shoard, 1999.
124 Highways Act 1980, as amended by the WCA 1981 and Rights of Way Act 1990.

breakdown in negotiations, the sites may be compulsorily purchased or restored at the owner's expense. There will also be a statutory duty for public bodies to further the conservation and management of SSSIs.

The Bill will give extra powers for the prosecution of wildlife criminals, including custodial sentences.[125] It will create a new offence of reckless disturbance, the police will have more powers to enter premises to check species sales and take DNA evidence, the courts will be given powers to impose higher penalties for all wildlife offences and it will amend the WCA 1981 and the Conservation (Natural Habitats, etc) Regulations 1994 (SI 1994/2716).

Common land

The Countryside (Amenity and Conservation) Bill[126] will look at access to common land.[127] Common land[128] includes village and town greens.[129] In the recent case of *R v Oxfordshire CC ex p Sunningwell PC*,[130] the designation of 'town and village greens' was simplified. To register a town green, it must be shown that persons have used the land for 20 years for sports and pastimes as of right.[131] The case stated that use and enjoyment included modern pursuits, such as walking the dog, and did not necessarily limit it to playing cricket or maypole dancing. Recently, 'Millennium greens' have been set up and managed by the Countryside Agency – these are areas of open space which are to be enjoyed by the community permanently.

Under s 194 of the Law of Property Act (LPA) 1925, the erection of any building or fence, or the construction of any work which prevents or impedes access to the land, is unlawful unless the Secretary of State's consent is obtained. This includes common land and town and village greens. Under s 193 of the LPA 1925, the public enjoys the right of access for air and exercise on urban and metropolitan commons, but not rural ones. Under s 194(2) of the

---

125 See www.wildlife-countryside.detr.gov.uk.

126 This was preceded by a number of consultation documents, including DETR, *SSSIs: Better Protection and Management*, September 1998; DETR, *SSSIs: Better Protection and Management – the Government's Framework for Action – Outcome of the Consultation Exercise*, August 1999.

127 See DOE press release 437, 1998.

128 See the Open Spaces Society at www.oss.org.uk.

129 See DETR, *Greater Protection and Better Management of Common Land in England and Wales*, February 2000. See, also, Rowe, 2000. For a comprehensive look at the law in relation to commons, see Rodgers, 1999, pp 231–55.

130 (1999) *The Times*, 25 June, HL.

131 See Open Spaces Society, *Getting Greens Registered: A Guide to Law and Procedure for Town and Village Greens*, 1995. The main obstacle to the registration of greens is the locality issue, ie, the green must be used for a specific locality, not by the public in general. This is decided on a case by case basis but it needs a clearer definition.

LPA 1925, the council or any other interested person can make an application to the county court for the removal of work unlawfully carried out on common land or town or village greens and the restoration of the land to the condition it was previously in. Village greens are also protected under s 12 of the Enclosure Act 1857 and s 239 of the Commons Act 1876.

Urban regeneration

The Government's strategy for urban development has been developed. Towards an Urban Renaissance: 1999 and the aim of the Report was to 'identify causes of urban decline in England and recommend practical solutions to bring people back into our cities, towns and urban neighbourhoods'.

The Report states that:

> ... on current policy assumptions, the Government is unlikely to meet its own target that 60% of new dwellings[132] should be built on previously developed land. Achieving this target is fundamental to the health of society. Failure to do so will lead to fragmentation of the city and erosion of the countryside. It will also increase traffic congestion and air pollution, accelerate the depletion of natural resources, damage biodiversity and increase social deprivation.

The Report made over 100 recommendations for change. It provides an urban fact-file – some of its findings are listed below:

- urban areas in England account for 90% of population, 91% of economic output and 89% of all jobs;
- Government projections estimate that 3.8 million extra households will form, between 1996 and 2012, a 19% increase;
- car traffic is predicted to grow by one-third in the next 20 years and average commuting time is 40% higher than 20 years ago;
- around 1.3 million residential and commercial buildings are currently empty.

The Report highlights the following policies:

- limit building on greenfield sites;
- require public bodies and utilities to release redundant urban land and buildings for regeneration;
- launch a campaign to ensure that all contaminated land is brought back to beneficial use by 2030;
- introduce an empty property strategy;

---

132 White Paper, *Planning for the Communities of the Future,* February 1998. This set out a new approach to planning for household growth at regional and local levels and established a 60% target for use of recycled land.

- harmonise VAT on new buildings and residential conversions;
- improve urban design;
- ensure that developments are built at an appropriate density;
- target 65% of transport expenditure towards public transport and cyclists and pedestrians;
- create 'home zones' which put pedestrians first in residential areas;
- change the planning system and devolve decision making to the community level;
- strengthen the strategic management and enforcement roles of local authorities over the whole urban environment;
- create neighbourhoods of mixed tenures and incomes;
- introduce regional resource centres for urban development;
- introduce urban priority areas;
- establish a renaissance fund for local groups to improve their own neighbourhoods;
- put local transport plans on a statutory footing, with targets to increase the number of journeys by public transport, walking and cycling;
- set a maximum standard of one car parking space per household.

These policies are set out in more detail in the Report, which had some interesting and innovative ideas that could be included in a Government White Paper. The Report sets itself goals for 2021. Some of these include the following:

- the main urban indicators will all show an improvement;
- there will be a balanced economy within cities, between cites and between regions;
- greenfield land use will have decreased as more brownfield land is used;
- urban de-population will have been reversed;
- at least five major English cites will be in the European top 50, with none in the bottom third;[133]
- people will enjoy living in cities and will view them as safe and attractive.

The second policy development is the new PPG 3 on housing. PPG 3 states that 60% of new homes should use recycled land or buildings, as compared to the previous target of 50%. 70% of new households in the next 20 years will be single households. The priority is to develop brownfield sites first and to use land efficiently, as well as providing affordable homes. There is also a plan to promote mixed use developments and these principles will be embodied in

---

133 See www.regeneration.detr.gov.uk. The urban exchange initiative is a framework of inter-governmental meetings with European ministers responsible for urban policy.

regional planning guidance, the first of which is being drawn up for the South East of England. The Government has stated that it will move away from the 'predict and provide' approach to plan, monitor and manage housing.[134]

The Council for the Protection of Rural England (CPRE) states that it makes four important changes:[135]

(a) PPG 3 ends the predict and provide planning for housing based on a 20–25 year trend, and instead focuses on annual building rates over a five year period;

(b) it encourages the re-use of urban sites before building on rural ones;

(c) it emphasises good house design and the avoidance of low density housing – developments need to be greater than 30 dwellings per hectare (at present, the current average is 25);

(d) PPG 3 prefers urban extension to new settlements where greenfield development is necessary.

However, CPRE points to two 'unfortunate' weaknesses of PPG 3:

(a) it does not give local authorities sufficient powers to require affordable housing as part of any new development or to require that the type and size of housing meets the needs of single and elderly people;

(b) it does not address the implications of housing developments for water resources[136] or for construction materials.

The third policy development is in relation to improving the green spaces that are in urban areas. The findings of the Environment, Transport and Regional Affairs Select Committee's *Report on Town and Country Parks,* January 2000, included:

- the Countryside Agency should review its funding to country parks;

- local authorities should improve their knowledge of their parks;

- the Government should come up with an effective research programme as part of its urban White Paper;

- municipal parks could be developed for informal and formal games and city farms and wildlife areas have an important part to play;

- parks should be made safe;

- decline should be arrested – there was a concern that English Heritage had neglected parks and that there was a need for more funding for parks;

- green flag awards and friends schemes should be encouraged;

---

134 See PPG 3 Housing Statement by the Deputy Prime Minister, DETR press release, 7 March 2000.

135 Information from CPRE website: www.greenchannel.com/cpre/.

136 See above, Chapter 4.

- a new agency, the Urban Parks and Greenspaces Agency, should be developed.

In the Government's *Response to the Environment, Transport and Regional Affairs Select Committee's Report on Town and Country Parks*, January 2000, it stated that:

- PPG 17 on sports and recreation will be revised;

- the heritage lottery fund and English Heritage are surveying historic parks and gardens;

- the Government does not feel that there is a compelling case for a new agency.

The future

Urban policies and rural policies[137] have to be looked at together. If urban areas are not pleasant places to live in, more people will wish to move to the countryside to live and work. There are a number of ways in which urban areas can provide green spaces: through redevelopment and the planning system, conservation areas, allotments[138] and designating land as green space, town and country parks can be protected and improved.[139] The Government's projected housing plans are a step in the right direction, in that they encourage building on brownfield rather than greenfield sites.[140]

The UK Round Table on Sustainable Development's Report,[141] *Aspects of Sustainable Agriculture and Rural Policy*, July 1998, outlines a definition of 'sustainable agriculture':[142]

Farming policies and practices which ensure an adequate supply of safe, nourishing and affordable food; and whose direct, indirect, upstream and downstream and future impacts sustain and nurture the soil, air and water and their productive capacity; provide jobs; protect and enhance wildlife, landscape, historic and cultural features; and minimise the use of non-renewable resources[143] ... the current reappraisal of the objectives of MAFF should lead to the establishment of a new set of priorities and a new

---

137 Fairlie, 1999, pp 82–84; Holliday, 1999, pp 128–32.

138 See Crouch and Ward, 1997.

139 House of Commons Select Committee on Environment, Transport and Regional Affairs 1998–99, 20th Report, *Town and Country Parks*, 6 November 1999, HC 477.

140 House of Commons Select Committee on Environment, Transport and Regional Affairs 1998–99, 17th Report, *Housing PPG3*, 1 September 1999, HC 490.

141 UK Round Table on Sustainable Development, *Integrating Biodiversity into Environmental Management Systems*, May 1998; UKRTSD, *Aspects of Sustainable Agriculture and Rural Policy*, July 1998.

142 MAFF, *Development of a Set of Indicators for Sustainable Agriculture in the UK: a Consultation Document*, 22 June 1998.

143 *Ibid*, fn 141, p 4, para 10.

development mission, strengthening its competencies on issues of rural development and rural environmental concerns.[144]

The Report also looks at planning:

> ... the lack of clarity of current planning controls over agricultural buildings and over the carrying out of excavations or engineering operations for the purpose of agriculture, and the general inconsistency of approach in comparison to planing requirements which apply to other industries, is unjustifiable. It is important that controls do not stifle legitimate diversification in the economy of rural areas. But all development should be subject to proper control.[145]

The Report states that a duty of care in respect of wildlife landscape and natural features should be put upon landowners and managers of all agricultural and undeveloped land in rural areas.[146]

It seems clear that the changes to agriculture have to be seen in the wider context of rural policy and the diversification that is taking place in rural life. The challenge for both urban and rural regeneration is to ensure sustainable development through imaginative, coherent, long term planning, with the courage to take what are sometimes difficult decisions in an open and accountable way.

---

144 Recommendation 6, p 15.
145 *Op cit*, UK Round Table on Sustainable Development, fn 141, p 19, para 70.
146 Recommendation 11, p 26.

THE TOWN AND COUNTRY PLANNING (USE CLASSES) ORDER 1987 (SI 1987/764) (AS AMENDED)

[Dated 28 April 1987. Made by the Secretary of State for the Environment under ss 22(2)(f) and 287(3) of the Town and Country Planning Act 1971, now ss 55(2)(f) and 333(3) of the Town and Country Planning Act 1990.]

Citation and commencement

1   This Order may be cited as the Town and Country Planning (Use Classes) Order 1987 and shall come into force on 1st June 1987.

Interpretation

2   In this Order, unless the context otherwise requires—

'care' means personal care for people in need of such care by reason of old age, disablement, past or present dependence on alcohol or drugs or past or present mental disorder, and in class C2 also includes the personal care of children and medical care and treatment;

'day centre' means premises which are visited during the day for social or recreational purposes or for the purposes of rehabilitation or occupational training, at which care is also provided;

'industrial process' means a process for or incidental to any of the following purposes:

(a) the making of any article or part of any article (including a ship or vessel, or a film, video or sound recording);

(b) the altering, repairing, maintaining, ornamenting, finishing, cleaning, washing, packing, canning, adapting for sale, breaking up or demolition of any article; or

(c) the getting, dressing or treatment of minerals;

in the course of any trade or business other than agriculture, and other than a use carried out in or adjacent to a mine or quarry;

'Schedule' means the Schedule to this Order;

'site' means the whole area of land within a single unit of occupation.

Use classes

3.—(1) Subject to the provisions of this Order, where a building or other land is used for a purpose of any class specified in the Schedule, the use of that building or that other land for any other purpose of the same class shall not be taken to involve development of the land.

(2) References in paragraph (1) to a building include references to land occupied with the building and used for the same purposes.

(3) A use which is included in and ordinarily incidental to any use in a class specified in the Schedule is not excluded from the use to which it is incidental merely because it is specified in the Schedule as a separate use.

(4) Where land on a single site or on adjacent sites used as parts of a single undertaking is used for purposes consisting of or including purposes falling within any two or more of classes B1 to B7 in the Schedule, those classes may be treated as a single class in considering the use of that land for the purposes of this Order, so long as the area used for a purpose falling either within class B2 or within classes B3 to B7 is not substantially increased as a result.

(5) No class specified in the Schedule includes any use for a purpose which involves the manufacture, processing, keeping or use of a hazardous substance in such circumstances as will result in the presence at one time of a notifiable quantity of that substance in, on, over or under that building or land or any site of which that building or land forms part.

(6) No class specified in the Schedule includes use—

(a) as a theatre,

(b) as an amusement arcade or centre, or a funfair,

(c) for the washing or cleaning of clothes or fabrics in coin-operated machines or on premises at which the goods to be cleaned are received direct from the visiting public,

(d) for the sale of fuel for motor vehicles,

(e) for the sale or display for sale of motor vehicles,

(f) for a taxi business or business for the hire of motor vehicles,

(g) as a scrapyard, or a yard for the storage or distribution of minerals or the breaking of motor vehicles.

Change of use of part of building or land

4.—In the case of a building used for a purpose within class C3 (dwellinghouses) in the Schedule, the use as a separate dwellinghouse of any part of the building or of any land occupied with and used for the same purposes as the building is not, by virtue of this Order, to be taken as not amounting to development.

Revocation

5.—The Town and Country Planning (Use Classes) Order 1972 and the Town and Country Planning (Use Classes) (Amendment) Order 1983 are hereby revoked.

SCHEDULE
PART A

Class A1. Shops

Use for all or any of the following purposes—

(a) for the retail sale of goods other than hot food,

(b) as a post office,

(c) for the sale of tickets or as a travel agency,

(d) for the sale of sandwiches or other cold food for consumption off the premises,

(e) for hairdressing,

(f) for the direction of funerals,

(g) for the display of goods for sale,

(h) for the hiring out of domestic or personal goods or articles,

(i) for the reception of goods to be washed, cleaned or repaired,

where the sale, display or service is to visiting members of the public.

Class A2. Financial and professional services

Use for the provision of—

(a) financial services, or

(b) professional services (other than health or medical services), or

(c) any other services (including use as a betting office) which it is appropriate to provide in a shopping area,

where the services are provided principally to visiting members of the public.

Class A3. Food and drink

Use for the sale of food or drink for consumption on the premises or of hot food for consumption off the premises.

PART B

Class B1. Business

Use for all or any of the following purposes—

    (a) as an office other than a use within class A2 (financial and professional services),

    (b) for research and development of products or processes, or

    (c) for any industrial process,

being a use which can be carried out in any residential area without detriment to the amenity of that area by reason of noise, vibration, smell, fumes, smoke, soot, ash, dust or grit.

Class B2. General industrial

Use for the carrying on of an industrial process other than one falling within class B1 above or within classes B3 to B7 below.

[Class B3. Special Industrial Group A

This class which was special industrial group A, is now excluded from the order by SI 1992 No 610.]

Class B4. Special Industrial Group B

Use for any of the following processes, except where the process is ancillary to the getting, dressing or treatment of minerals and is carried on in or adjacent to a quarry or mine—

    (a) smelting, calcining, sintering or reducing ores, minerals, concentrates or mattes;

    (b) converting, refining, re-heating, annealing, hardening, melting, carburising, forging or casting metals or alloys other than pressure die-casting;

    (c) recovering metal from scrap or drosses or ashes;

    (d) galvanizing;

    (e) pickling or treating metal in acid;

    (f) chromium plating.

Class B5. Special Industrial Group C

Use for any of the following processes, except where the process is ancillary to the getting, dressing or treatment of minerals and is carried on in or adjacent to a quarry or mine—

(a) burning bricks or pipes;

(b) burning lime or dolomite;

(c) producing zinc oxide, cement or alumina;

(d) foaming, crushing, screening or heating minerals or slag;

(e) processing pulverized fuel ash by heat;

(f) producing carbonate of lime or hydrated lime;

(g) producing inorganic pigments by calcining, roasting or grinding.

Class B6. Special Industrial Group D

Use for any of the following processes—

(a) distilling, refining or blending oils (other than petroleum or petroleum products);

(b) producing or using cellulose or using other pressure sprayed metal finishes (other than in vehicle repair workshops in connection with minor repairs, or the application of plastic powder by the use of fluidised bed and electrostatic spray techniques);

(c) boiling linseed oil or running gum;

(d) processes involving the use of hot pitch or bitumen (except the use of bitumen in the manufacture of roofing felt at temperatures not exceeding 220°C and also the manufacture of coated roadstone);

(e) stoving enamelled ware;

(f) producing aliphatic esters of the lower fatty acids, butyric acid, caramel, hexamine, iodoform, napthols, resin products (excluding plastic moulding or extrusion operations and producing plastic sheets, rods, tubes, filaments, fibres or optical components produced by casting, calendering, moulding, shaping or extrusion), salicylic acid or sulphonated organic compounds;

(g) producing rubber from scrap;

(h) chemical processes in which chlorphenols or chlorcresols are used as intermediates;

(i) manufacturing acetylene from calcium carbide;

(j) manufacturing, recovering or using pyridine or picolines, any methyl or ethyl amine or acrylates.

Class B7. Special Industrial Group E

Use for carrying on any of the following industries, businesses or trades—

Boiling blood, chitterlings, nettlings or soap.

Boiling, burning, grinding or steaming bones.

Boiling or cleaning tripe.

Breeding maggots from putrescible animal matter.

Cleaning, adapting or treating animal hair.

Curing fish.

Dealing in rags and bones (including receiving, storing, sorting or manipulating rags in, or likely to become in, an offensive condition, or any bones, rabbit skins, fat or putrescible animal products of a similar nature).

Dressing or scraping fish skins.

Drying skins.

Making manure from bones, fish, offal, blood, spent hops, beans or other putrescible animal or vegetable matter.

Making or scraping guts.

Manufacturing animal charcoal, blood albumen, candles, catgut, glue, fish oil, size or feeding stuff for animals or poultry from meat, fish, blood, bone, feathers, fat or animal offal either in an offensive condition or subjected to any process causing noxious or injurious effluvia.

Melting, refining or extracting fat or tallow.

Preparing skins for working.

Class B8. Storage or distribution

Use for storage or as a distribution centre.

PART C

Class C1. Hotels and hostels

Use as a hotel, boarding or guest house or as a hostel where, in each case, no significant element of care is provided.

Class C2. Residential institutions

Use for the provision of residential accommodation and care to people in need of care (other than a use within class C3 (dwelling houses)).

Use as a hospital or nursing home.

Use as a residential school, college or training centre.

Class C3. Dwellinghouses

Use as a dwellinghouse (whether or not as a sole or main residence)—

(a) by a single person or by people living together as a family, or

(b) by not more than 6 residents living together as a single household (including a household where care is provided for residents).

PART D

Class D1. Non-residential institutions

Any use not including a residential use—

(a) for the provision of any medical or health services except the use of premises attached to the residence of the consultant or practitioner,

(b) as a crêche, day nursery or day centre,

(c) for the provision of education,

(d) for the display of works of art (otherwise than for sale or hire),

(e) as a museum,

(f) as a public library or public reading room,

(g) as a public hall or exhibition hall,

(h) for, or in connection with, public worship or religious instruction.

Class D2. Assembly and leisure

Use as—

(a) a cinema,

(b) a concert hall,

(c) a bingo hall or casino,

(d) a dance hall,

(e) a swimming bath, skating rink, gymnasium or area for other indoor or outdoor sports or recreations, not involving motorised vehicles or firearms.

THE TOWN AND COUNTRY PLANNING (GENERAL PERMITTED DEVELOPMENT) ORDER 1995 AS AMENDED (ABRIDGED VERSION)

Brought into Force: 3rd June 1995

ARTICLE 3
SCHEDULE 2

PART 1
DEVELOPMENT WITHIN THE CURTILAGE
OF A DWELLINGHOUSE

Class A

Permitted development

A.—The enlargement, improvement or other alteration of a dwellinghouse.

Development not permitted

A.1—Development is not permitted by Class A if—

(a) the cubic content of the resulting building would exceed the cubic content of the original dwellinghouse—

    (i) in the case of a terrace house or in the case of a dwellinghouse on article 1(5) land, by more than 50 cubic metres or 10 %, whichever is the greater,

    (ii) in any other case, by more than 70 cubic metres or 15%, whichever is the greater,

    (iii)in any case, by more than 115 cubic metres;

(b) the part of the building enlarged, improved or altered would exceed in height the highest part of the roof of the original dwellinghouse;

(c) the part of the building enlarged, improved or altered would be nearer to any highway which bounds the curtilage of the dwellinghouse than—

    (i) the part of the original dwellinghouse nearest to that highway, or

(ii) any point 20 metres from that highway,

whichever is nearer to the highway;

(d) in the case of development other than the insertion, enlargement, improvement or other alteration of a window in an existing wall of a dwellinghouse, the part of the building enlarged, improved or altered would be within 2 metres of the boundary of the curtilage of the dwellinghouse and would exceed 4 metres in height;

(e) the total area of ground covered by buildings within the curtilage (other than the original dwellinghouse) would exceed 50% of the total area of the curtilage (excluding the ground area of the original dwellinghouse);

(f) it would consist of or include the installation, alteration or replacement of a satellite antenna;

(g) it would consist of or include the erection of a building within the curtilage of a listed building; or

(h) it would consist of or include an alteration to any part of the roof.

A.2—In the case of a dwellinghouse on any article 1(5) land, development is not permitted by Class A if it would consist of or include the cladding of any part of the exterior with stone, artificial stone, timber, plastic or tiles.

Interpretation of Class A

A.3—For the purposes of Class A—

(a) the erection within the curtilage of a dwellinghouse of any building with a cubic content greater than 10 cubic metres shall be treated as the enlargement of the dwellinghouse for all purposes (including calculating cubic content) where—

(i) the dwellinghouse is on article 1(5) land, or

(ii) in any other case, any part of that building would be within 5 metres of any part of the dwellinghouse;

(b) where any part of the dwellinghouse would be within 5 metres of an existing building within the same curtilage, that building shall be treated as forming part of the resulting building for the purpose of calculating the cubic content.

Class B

Permitted development

B.—The enlargement of a dwellinghouse consisting of an addition or alteration to its roof.

Development not permitted

B.1—Development is not permitted by Class B if—

(a) any part of the dwellinghouse would, as a result of the works, exceed the height of the highest part of the existing roof;

(b) any part of the dwellinghouse would, as a result of the works, extend beyond the plane of any existing roof slope which fronts any highway;

(c) it would increase the cubic content of the dwellinghouse by more than 40 cubic metres, in the case of a terrace house, or 50 cubic metres in any other case;

(d) the cubic content of the resulting building would exceed the cubic content of the original dwellinghouse—

   (i) in the case of a terrace house by more than 50 cubic metres or 10%, whichever is the greater,

   (ii) in any other case, by more than 70 cubic metres or 15%, whichever is the greater, or

   (iii) in any case, by more than 115 cubic metres; or

(e) the dwellinghouse is on article 1(5) land.

Class C

Permitted development

C.—Any other alteration to the roof of a dwellinghouse.

Development not permitted

C.1—Development is not permitted by Class C if it would result in a material alteration to the shape of the dwellinghouse.

Class D

Permitted development

D.—The erection or construction of a porch outside any external door of a dwellinghouse.

Development not permitted

D.1—Development is not permitted by Class D if—

(a) the ground area (measured externally) of the structure would exceed 3 square metres;

(b) any part of the structure would be more than 3 metres above ground level; or

(c) any part of the structure would be within 2 metres of any boundary of the curtilage of the dwellinghouse with a highway.

Class E

Permitted development

E.—The provision within the curtilage of a dwellinghouse of any building or enclosure, swimming or other pool required for a purpose incidental to the enjoyment of the dwellinghouse as such, or the maintenance, improvement or other alteration of such a building or enclosure.

Development not permitted

E.1—Development is not permitted by Class E if—

(a) it relates to a dwelling or a satellite antenna;

(b) any part of the building or enclosure to be constructed or provided would be nearer to any highway which bounds the curtilage than—

    (i) the part of the original dwellinghouse nearest to that highway, or

    (ii) any point 20 metres from that highway,

whichever is nearer to the highway;

(c) where the building to be constructed or provided would have a cubic content greater than 10 cubic metres, any part of it would be within 5 metres of any part of the dwellinghouse;

(d) the height of that building or enclosure would exceed—

    (i) 4 metres, in the case of a building with a ridged roof; or

    (ii) 3 metres, in any other case;

(e) the total area of ground covered by buildings or enclosures within the curtilage (other than the original dwellinghouse) would exceed 50% of the total area of the curtilage (excluding the ground area of the original dwellinghouse); or

(f) in the case of any article 1(5) land or land within the curtilage of a listed building, it would consist of the provision, alteration or improvement of a building with a cubic content greater than 10 cubic metres.

Interpretation of Class E

E.2—For the purposes of Class E—

'purpose incidental to the enjoyment of the dwellinghouse as such' includes the keeping of poultry, bees, pet animals, birds or other livestock for the domestic needs or personal enjoyment of the occupants of the dwellinghouse.

Class F

Permitted development

F.—The provision within the curtilage of a dwellinghouse of a hard surface for any purpose incidental to the enjoyment of the dwellinghouse as such.

Class G

Permitted development

G.—The erection or provision within the curtilage of a dwellinghouse of a container for the storage of oil for domestic heating.

Development not permitted

G.1—Development is not permitted by Class G if—

(a) the capacity of the container would exceed 3,500 litres;

(b) any part of the container would be more than 3 metres above ground level; or

(c) any part of the container would be nearer to any highway which bounds the curtilage than—

(i) the part of the original building nearest to that highway, or

(ii) any point 20 metres from that highway,

whichever is nearer to the highway.

Class H

Permitted development

H.—The installation, alteration or replacement of a satellite antenna on a dwellinghouse or within the curtilage of a dwellinghouse.

Development not permitted

H.1—Development is not permitted by Class H if—

(a) the size of the antenna (excluding any projecting feed element, reinforcing rim, mountings and brackets) when measured in any dimension would exceed—

   (i) 45 centimetres in the case of an antenna to be installed on a chimney;

   (ii) 90 centimetres in the case of an antenna to be installed on or within the curtilage of a dwellinghouse on article 1(4) land other than on a chimney;

   (iii)70 centimetres in any other case;

(b) the highest part of an antenna to be installed on a roof or a chimney would, when installed, exceed in height—

   (i) in the case of an antenna to be installed on a roof, the highest part of the roof;

   (ii) in the case of an antenna to be installed on a chimney, the highest part of the chimney;

(c) there is any other satellite antenna on the dwellinghouse or within its curtilage;

(d) in the case of article 1(5) land, it would consist of the installation of an antenna—

   (i) on a chimney;

   (ii) on a building which exceeds 15 metres in height;

   (iii)on a wall or roof slope which fronts a waterway in the Broads or a highway elsewhere.

Conditions

H.2—Development is permitted by Class H subject to the following conditions—

(a) an antenna installed on a building shall, so far as practicable, be sited so as to minimise its effect on the external appearance of the building;

(b) an antenna no longer needed for the reception or transmission of microwave radio energy shall be removed as soon as reasonably practicable.

Interpretation of Part 1

I.—For the purposes of Part 1—

'resulting building' means the dwellinghouse as enlarged, improved or altered, taking into account any enlargement, improvement or alteration to the original dwellinghouse, whether permitted by this Part or not; and

'terrace house' means a dwellinghouse situated in a row of three or more dwellinghouses used or designed for use as single dwellings, where—

(a) it shares a party wall with, or has a main wall adjoining the main wall of, the dwellinghouse on either side; or

(b) if it is at the end of a row, it shares a party wall with or has a main wall adjoining the main wall of a dwellinghouse which fulfils the requirements of sub-paragraph (a) above.

PART 2
MINOR OPERATIONS

Class A

Permitted development

A.—The erection, construction, maintenance, improvement or alteration of a gate, fence, wall or other means of enclosure.

Development not permitted

A.1—Development is not permitted by Class A if—

(a) the height of any gate, fence, wall or means of enclosure erected or constructed adjacent to a highway used by vehicular traffic would, after the carrying out of the development, exceed one metre above ground level;

(b) the height of any other gate, fence, wall or means of enclosure erected or constructed would exceed two metres above ground level;

(c) the height of any gate, fence, wall or other means of enclosure maintained, improved or altered would, as a result of the development, exceed its former height or the height referred to in sub-paragraph (a) or (b) as the height appropriate to it if erected or constructed, whichever is the greater; or

(d) it would involve development within the curtilage of, or to a gate, fence, wall or other means of enclosure surrounding, a listed building.

Class B

Permitted development

B.—The formation, laying out and construction of a means of access to a highway which is not a trunk road or a classified road, where that access is required in connection with development permitted by any Class in this Schedule (other than by Class A of this Part).

Class C

Permitted development

C.—The painting of the exterior of any building or work.

Development not permitted

C.1—Development is not permitted by Class C where the painting is for the purpose of advertisement, announcement or direction.

Interpretation of Class C

C.2—In Class C, 'painting' includes any application of colour.

PART 3
CHANGES OF USE

Class A

Permitted development

A.—Development consisting of a change of the use of a building to a use falling within Class A1 (shops) of the Schedule to the Use Classes Order from a use falling within Class A3 (food and drink) of that Schedule or from a use for the sale, or display for sale, of motor vehicles.

Class B

Permitted development

B.—Development consisting of a change of the use of a building—

(a) to a use for any purpose falling within Class B1 (business) of the Schedule to the Use Classes Order from any use falling within Class B2 (general industrial) or B8 (storage and distribution) of that Schedule;

(b) to a use for any purpose falling within Class B8 (storage and distribution) of that Schedule from any use falling within Class B1 (business) or B2 (general industrial).

Development not permitted

B.1—Development is not permitted by Class B where the change is to or from a use falling within Class B8 of that Schedule, if the change of use relates to more than 235 square metres of floor space in the building.

Class C

Permitted development

C.—Development consisting of a change of use to a use falling within Class A2 (financial and professional services) of the Schedule to the Use Classes Order from a use falling within Class A3 (food and drink) of that Schedule.

Class D

Permitted development

D.—Development consisting of a change of use of any premises with a display window at ground floor level to a use falling within Class A1 (shops) of the Schedule to the Use Classes Order from a use falling within Class A2 (financial and professional services) of that Schedule.

Class E

Permitted development

E.—Development consisting of a change of the use of a building or other land from a use permitted by planning permission granted on an

application, to another use which that permission would have specifically authorised when it was granted.

Development not permitted

E.1—Development is not permitted by Class E if—

(a) the application for planning permission referred to was made before the 5th December 1988;

(b) it would be carried out more than 10 years after the grant of planning permission; or

(c) it would result in the breach of any condition, limitation or specification contained in that planning permission in relation to the use in question.

Class F

Permitted development

F.—Development consisting of a change of the use of a building—

(a) to a mixed use for any purpose within Class A1 (shops) of the Schedule to the Use Classes Order and as a single flat, from a use for any purpose within Class A1 of that Schedule;

(b) to a mixed use for any purpose within Class A2 (financial and professional services) of the Schedule to the Use Classes Order and as a single flat, from a use for any purpose within Class A2 of that Schedule;

(c) where that building has a display window at ground floor level, to a mixed use for any purpose within Class A1 (shops) of the Schedule to the Use Classes Order and as a single flat, from a use for any purpose within Class A2 (financial and professional services) of that Schedule.

Conditions

F.1—Development permitted by Class F is subject to the following conditions—

(a) some or all of the parts of the building used for any purposes within Class A1 or Class A2, as the case may be, of the Schedule to the Use Classes Order shall be situated on a floor below the part of the building used as a single flat;

(b) where the development consists of a change of use of any building with a display window at ground floor level, the ground floor shall not be used in whole or in part as the single flat;

(c) the single flat shall not be used otherwise than as a dwelling (whether or not as a sole or main residence)—

(i) by a single person or by people living together as a family, or

(ii) by not more than six residents living together as a single household (including a household where care is provided for residents).

Interpretation of Class F

F.2—For the purposes of Class F—

'care' means personal care for people in need of such care by reason of old age, disablement, past or present dependence on alcohol or drugs or past or present mental disorder.

Class G

Permitted development

G.—Development consisting of a change of the use of a building—

(a) to a use for any purpose within Class A1(shops) of the Schedule to the Use Classes Order from a mixed use for any purpose within Class A1 of that Schedule and as a single flat;

(b) to a use for any purpose within Class A2 (financial and professional services) of the Schedule to the Use Classes Order from a mixed use for any purpose within Class A2 of that Schedule and as a single flat;

(c) where that building has a display window at ground floor level, to a use for any purpose within Class A1 (shops) of the Schedule to the Use Classes Order from a mixed use for any purpose within Class A2 (financial and professional services) of that Schedule and as a single flat.

Development not permitted

G.1—Development is not permitted by Class G unless the part of the building used as a single flat was immediately prior to being so used used for any purpose within Class A1 or Class A2 of the Schedule to the Use Classes Order.

PART 6
AGRICULTURAL BUILDINGS AND OPERATIONS

Class A Development on units of 5 hectares or more

Permitted development

A.—The carrying out on agricultural land comprised in an agricultural unit of 5 hectares or more in area of—

(a) works for the erection, extension or alteration of a building; or

(b) any excavation or engineering operations,

which are reasonably necessary for the purposes of agriculture within that unit.

Development not permitted

A.1—Development is not permitted by Class A if—

(a) the development would be carried out on a separate parcel of land forming part of the unit which is less than 1 hectare in area;

(b) it would consist of, or include, the erection, extension or alteration of a dwelling;

(c) it would involve the provision of a building, structure or works not designed for agricultural purposes;

(d) the ground area which would be covered by—

    (i) any works or structure (other than a fence) for accommodating livestock or any plant or machinery arising from engineering operations; or

    (ii) any building erected or extended or altered by virtue of Class A,

would exceed 465 square metres, calculated as described in paragraph D.2 below;

(e) the height of any part of any building, structure or works within 3 kilometres of the perimeter of an aerodrome would exceed 3 metres;

(f) the height of any part of any building, structure or works not within 3 kilometres of the perimeter of an aerodrome would exceed 12 metres;

(g) any part of the development would be within 25 metres of a metalled part of a trunk road or classified road;

(h) it would consist of, or include, the erection or construction of, or the carrying out of any works to, a building, structure or an excavation used or to be used for the accommodation of livestock or for the storage of slurry or sewage sludge where the building, structure or excavation is, or would be, within 400 metres of the curtilage of a protected building; or

(i) it would involve excavations or engineering operations on or over article 1(6) land which are connected with fish farming.

Conditions

A.2(1)—Development is permitted by Class A subject to the following conditions—

(a) where development is carried out within 400 metres of the curtilage of a protected building, any building, structure, excavation or works resulting from the development shall not be used for the accommodation of livestock except in the circumstances described in paragraph D.3 below or for the storage of slurry or sewage sludge;

(b) where the development involves—

(i) the extraction of any mineral from the land (including removal from any disused railway embankment); or

(ii) the removal of any mineral from a mineral-working deposit,

the mineral shall not be moved off the unit;

(c) waste materials shall not be brought on to the land from elsewhere for deposit except for use in works described in Class A (a) or in the provision of a hard surface and any materials so brought shall be incorporated forthwith into the building or works in question.

(2) Subject to paragraph (3), development consisting of—

(a) the erection, extension or alteration of a building;

(b) the formation or alteration of a private way;

(c) the carrying out of excavations or the deposit of waste material (where the relevant area, as defined in paragraph D.4 below, exceeds 0.5 hectare); or

(d) the placing or assembly of a tank in any waters,

is permitted by Class A subject to the following conditions—

(i) the developer shall, before beginning the development, apply to the local planning authority for a determination as to whether the prior approval of the authority will be required to the siting, design and external appearance of the building, the siting and means of construction of the private way, the siting of the excavation or deposit or the siting and appearance of the tank, as the case may be;

(ii) the application shall be accompanied by a written description of the proposed development and of the materials to be used and a plan indicating the site together with any fee required to be paid;

(iii) the development shall not be begun before the occurrence of one of the following—

(a) the receipt by the applicant from the local planning authority of a written notice of their determination that such prior approval is not required;

(b) where the local planning authority give the applicant notice within 28 days following the date of receiving his application of their determination that such prior approval is required, the giving of such approval; or

(c) the expiry of 28 days following the date on which the application was received by the local planning authority without the local planning authority making any determination as to whether such approval is required or notifying the applicant of their determination;

(iv)

(a) where the local planning authority give the applicant notice that such prior approval is required the applicant shall display a site notice by site display on or near the land on which the proposed development is to be carried out, leaving the notice in position for not less than 21 days in the period of 28 days from the date on which the local planning authority gave the notice to the applicant;

(b) where the site notice is, without any fault or intention of the applicant, removed, obscured or defaced before the period of 21 days referred to in sub-paragraph (aa) has elapsed, he shall be treated as having complied with the requirements of that sub-paragraph if he has taken reasonable steps for protection of the notice and, if need be, its replacement;

(v) the development shall, except to the extent that the local planning authority otherwise agree in writing, be carried out—

(a) where prior approval is required, in accordance with the details approved;

(b) where prior approval is not required, in accordance with the details submitted with the application; and

(vi) the development shall be carried out—

(a) where approval has been given by the local planning authority, within a period of five years from the date on which approval was given;

(b) in any other case, within a period of five years from the date on which the local planning authority were given the information referred to in sub-paragraph (d)(ii).

(3) The conditions in paragraph (2) do not apply to the extension or alteration of a building if the building is not on article 1(6) land except in the case of a significant extension or a significant alteration.

(4) Development consisting of the significant extension or the significant alteration of a building may only be carried out once by virtue of Class A (a).

Class B Development on units of less than 5 hectares

Permitted development

B.—The carrying out on agricultural land comprised in an agricultural unit of not less than 0.4 but less than 5 hectares in area of development consisting of—

(a) the extension or alteration of an agricultural building;

(b) the installation of additional or replacement plant or machinery;

(c) the provision, rearrangement or replacement of a sewer, main, pipe, cable or other apparatus;

(d) the provision, rearrangement or replacement of a private way;

(e) the provision of a hard surface;

(f) the deposit of waste; or

(g) the carrying out of any of the following operations in connection with fish farming, namely, repairing ponds and raceways; the installation of grading machinery, aeration equipment or flow meters and any associated channel; the dredging of ponds; and the replacement of tanks and nets,

where the development is reasonably necessary for the purposes of agriculture within the unit.

Development not permitted

B.1—Development is not permitted by Class B if—

(a) the development would be carried out on a separate parcel of land forming part of the unit which is less than 0.4 hectare in area;

(b) the external appearance of the premises would be materially affected;

(c) any part of the development would be within 25 metres of a metalled part of a trunk road or classified road;

(d) it would consist of, or involve, the carrying out of any works to a building or structure used or to be used for the accommodation of livestock or the storage of slurry or sewage sludge where the building or structure is within 400 metres of the curtilage of a protected building; or

(e) it would relate to fish farming and would involve the placing or assembly of a tank on land or in any waters or the construction of a pond in which fish may be kept or an increase (otherwise than by the removal of silt) in the size of any tank or pond in which fish may be kept.

B.2—Development is not permitted by Class B (a) if—

(a) the height of any building would be increased;

(b) the cubic content of the original building would be increased by more than 10%;

(c) any part of any new building would be more than 30 metres from the original building;

(d) the development would involve the extension, alteration or provision of a dwelling;

(e) any part of the development would be carried out within 5 metres of any boundary of the unit; or

(f) the ground area of any building extended by virtue of Class B (a) would exceed 465 square metres.

B.3—Development is not permitted by Class B (b) if—

(a) the height of any additional plant or machinery within 3 kilometres of the perimeter of an aerodrome would exceed 3 metres;

(b) the height of any additional plant or machinery not within 3 kilometres of the perimeter of an aerodrome would exceed 12 metres;

(c) the height of any replacement plant or machinery would exceed that of the plant or machinery being replaced; or

(d) the area to be covered by the development would exceed 465 square metres calculated as described in paragraph D.2 below.

B.4—Development is not permitted by Class B (e) if the area to be covered by the development would exceed 465 square metres calculated as described in paragraph D.2 below.

Conditions

B.5—Development permitted by Class B and carried out within 400 metres of the curtilage of a protected building is subject to the condition that any building which is extended or altered, or any works resulting from the development, shall not be used for the accommodation of livestock except in the circumstances described in paragraph D.3 below or for the storage of slurry or sewage sludge.

B.6—Development consisting of the extension or alteration of a building situated on article 1(6)   land or the provision, rearrangement or replacement of a private way on such land is permitted subject to—

(a) the condition that the developer shall, before beginning the development, apply to the local planning authority for a determination as to whether the prior approval of the authority will be required to the siting, design and external appearance of the building as extended or altered or the siting and means of construction of the private way; and

(b) the conditions set out in paragraphs A.2(2)(ii) to (vi) above.

B.7—Development is permitted by Class B (f) subject to the following conditions—

(a) that waste materials are not brought on to the land from elsewhere for deposit unless they are for use in works described in Class B (a),(d) or (e) and are incorporated forthwith into the building or works in question; and

(b) that the height of the surface of the land will not be materially increased by the deposit.

Class C Mineral working for agricultural purposes

Permitted development

C.—**The winning and working on land held or occupied with land used for the purposes of agriculture of any minerals reasonably necessary for agricultural purposes within the agricultural unit of which it forms part.**

Development not permitted

C.1—Development is not permitted by Class C if any excavation would be made within 25 metres of a metalled part of a trunk road or classified road.

Condition

C.2—Development is permitted by Class C subject to the condition that no mineral extracted during the course of the operation shall be moved to any place outside the land from which it was extracted, except to land which is held or occupied with that land and is used for the purposes of agriculture.

Interpretation of Part 6

D.1—For the purposes of Part 6—

'agricultural land' means land which, before development permitted by this Part is carried out, is land in use for agriculture and which is so used for the purposes of a trade or business, and excludes any dwellinghouse or garden;

'agricultural unit' means agricultural land which is occupied as a unit for the purposes of agriculture, including—

(a) any dwelling or other building on that land occupied for the purpose of farming the land by the person who occupies the unit, or

(b) any dwelling on that land occupied by a farmworker;

'building' does not include anything resulting from engineering operations;

'fish farming' means the breeding, rearing or keeping of fish or shellfish (which includes any kind of crustacean and mollusc);

'livestock' includes fish or shellfish which are farmed;

'protected building' means any permanent building which is normally occupied by people or would be so occupied, if it were in use for purposes for which it is apt; but does not include—

(i) a building within the agricultural unit; or

(ii) a dwelling or other building on another agricultural unit which is used for or in connection with agriculture;

'significant extension' and 'significant alteration' mean any extension or alteration of the building where the cubic content of the original building would be exceeded by more than 10% or the height of the building as extended or altered would exceed the height of the original building;

'slurry' means animal faeces and urine (whether or not water has been added for handling); and

'tank' includes any cage and any other structure for use in fish farming.

D.2—For the purposes of Part 6—

(a) an area calculated as described in this paragraph comprises the ground area which would be covered by the proposed development, together with the ground area of any building (other than a dwelling), or any structure, works, plant, machinery, ponds or tanks within the same unit which are being provided or have been provided within the preceding two years and any part of which would be within 90 metres of the proposed development;

(b) 400 metres is to be measured along the ground.

D.3—The circumstances referred to in paragraphs A.2(1)(a) and B.5 are—

(a) that no other suitable building or structure, 400 metres or more from the curtilage of a protected building, is available to accommodate the livestock; and

(b)

    (i) that the need to accommodate the livestock arises from—

        (a) quarantine requirements; or

        (b) an emergency due to another building or structure in which the livestock could otherwise be accommodated being unavailable because it has been damaged or destroyed by fire, flood or storm; or

    (ii) in the case of animals normally kept out of doors, they require temporary accommodation in a building or other structure—

(a) because they are sick or giving birth or newly born; or

(b) to provide shelter against extreme weather conditions.

D.4—For the purposes of paragraph A.2(2)(c), the relevant area is the area of the proposed excavation or the area on which it is proposed to deposit waste together with the aggregate of the areas of all other excavations within the unit which have not been filled and of all other parts of the unit on or under which waste has been deposited and has not been removed.

D.5—In paragraph A.2(2)(iv), 'site notice' means a notice containing—

(a) the name of the applicant,

(b) the address or location of the proposed development,

(c) a description of the proposed development and of the materials to be used,

(d) a statement that the prior approval of the authority will be required to the siting, design and external appearance of the building, the siting and means of construction of the private way, the siting of the excavation or deposit or the siting and appearance of the tank, as the case may be,

(e) the name and address of the local planning authority, and which is signed and dated by or on behalf of the applicant.

D.6—For the purposes of Class B—

(a) the erection of any additional building within the curtilage of another building is to be treated as the extension of that building and the additional building is not to be treated as an original building;

(b) where two or more original buildings are within the same curtilage and are used for the same undertaking they are to be treated as a single original building in making any measurement in connection with the extension or alteration of either of them.

D.7—In Class C, 'the purposes of agriculture' includes fertilising land used for the purposes of agriculture and the maintenance, improvement or alteration of any buildings, structures or works occupied or used for such purposes on land so used.

PART 7
FORESTRY BUILDINGS AND OPERATIONS

Class A

Permitted development

A.—The carrying out on land used for the purposes of forestry, including afforestation, of development reasonably necessary for those purposes consisting of—

(a) works for the erection, extension or alteration of a building;

(b) the formation, alteration or maintenance of private ways;

(c) operations on that land, or on land held or occupied with that land, to obtain the materials required for the formation, alteration or maintenance of such ways;

(d) other operations (not including engineering or mining operations).

Development not permitted

A.1—Development is not permitted by Class A if—

(a) it would consist of or include the provision or alteration of a dwelling;

(b) the height of any building or works within 3 kilometres of the perimeter of an aerodrome would exceed 3 metres in height; or

(c) any part of the development would be within 25 metres of the metalled portion of a trunk road or classified road.

A.2(1)—Subject to paragraph (3), development consisting of the erection of a building or the extension or alteration of a building or the formation or alteration of a private way is permitted by Class A subject to the following conditions—

(a) the developer shall, before beginning the development, apply to the local planning authority for a determination as to whether the prior approval of the authority will be required to the siting, design and external appearance of the building or, as the case may be, the siting and means of construction of the private way;

(b) the application shall be accompanied by a written description of the proposed development, the materials to be used and a plan indicating the site together with any fee required to be paid;

(c) the development shall not be begun before the occurrence of one of the following—

(i) the receipt by the applicant from the local planning authority of a written notice of their determination that such prior approval is not required;

(ii) where the local planning authority give the applicant notice within 28 days following the date of receiving his application of their determination that such prior approval is required, the giving of such approval;

(iii) the expiry of 28 days following the date on which the application was received by the local planning authority without the local planning authority making any determination as to whether such approval is required or notifying the applicant of their determination;

(d)

(i) where the local planning authority give the applicant notice that such prior approval is required the applicant shall display a site notice by site display on or near the land on which the proposed development is to be carried out, leaving the notice in position for not less than 21 days in the period of 28 days from the date on which the local planning authority gave the notice to the applicant;

(ii) where the site notice is, without any fault or intention of the applicant, removed, obscured or defaced before the period of 21 days referred to in sub-paragraph (i) has elapsed, he shall be treated as having complied with the requirements of that sub-paragraph if he has taken reasonable steps for protection of the notice and, if need be, its replacement;

(e) the development shall, except to the extent that the local planning authority otherwise agree in writing, be carried out—

(i) where prior approval is required, in accordance with the details approved;

(ii) where prior approval is not required, in accordance with the details submitted with the application;

(f) the development shall be carried out—

(i) where approval has been given by the local planning authority, within a period of five years from the date on which approval was given,

(ii) in any other case, within a period of five years from the date on which the local planning authority were given the information referred to in sub-paragraph (b).

(2) In the case of development consisting of the significant extension or the significant alteration of the building such development may be carried out only once.

(3) Paragraph (1) does not preclude the extension or alteration of a building if the building is not on article 1(6) land except in the case of a significant extension or a significant alteration.

Interpretation of Class A

A.3—For the purposes of Class A—

'significant extension' and 'significant alteration' mean any extension or alteration of the building where the cubic content of the original building would be exceeded by more than 10% or the height of the building as extended or altered would exceed the height of the original building; and

'site notice' means a notice containing—

(a) the name of the applicant,

(b) the address or location of the proposed development,

(c) a description of the proposed development and of the materials to be used,

(d) a statement that the prior approval of the authority will be required to the siting, design and external appearance of the building or, as the case may be, the siting and means of construction of the private way,

(e) the name and address of the local planning authority,

and which is signed and dated by or on behalf of the applicant.

PART 15
DEVELOPMENT BY THE NATIONAL RIVERS AUTHORITY

Class A

Permitted development

A.—Development by the National Rivers Authority, for the purposes of their functions, consisting of—

(a) development not above ground level required in connection with conserving, redistributing or augmenting water resources,

(b) development in, on or under any watercourse or land drainage works and required in connection with the improvement, maintenance or repair of that watercourse or those works,

(c) the provision of a building, plant, machinery or apparatus in, on, over or under land for the purpose of survey or investigation,

(d) the maintenance, improvement or repair of works for measuring the flow in any watercourse or channel,

(e) any works authorised by or required in connection with an order made under section 73 of the Water Resources Act 1991 (power to make ordinary and emergency drought orders),

(f) any other development in, on, over or under their operational land, other than the provision of a building but including the extension or alteration of a building.

Development not permitted

A.1—Development is not permitted by Class A if—

(a) in the case of any Class A (a) development, it would include the construction of a reservoir,

(b) in the case of any Class A (f) development, it would consist of or include the extension or alteration of a building so that—

(i) its design or external appearance would be materially affected,

(ii) the height of the original building would be exceeded, or the cubic content of the original building would be exceeded by more than 25%, or

(iii) the floor space of the original building would be exceeded by more than 1,000 square metres,

or

(c) in the case of any Class A (f) development, it would consist of the installation or erection of any plant or machinery exceeding 15 metres in height or the height of anything it replaces, whichever is the greater.

Condition

A.2—Development is permitted by Class A (c) subject to the condition that, on completion of the survey or investigation, or at the expiration of six months from the commencement of the development concerned, whichever is the sooner, all such operations shall cease and all such buildings, plant, machinery and apparatus shall be removed and the land restored as soon as reasonably practicable to its former condition (or to any other condition which may be agreed with the local planning authority).

PART 16
DEVELOPMENT BY OR ON BEHALF
OF SEWERAGE UNDERTAKERS

Class A

Permitted development

A.—Development by or on behalf of a sewerage undertaker consisting of—

(a) development not above ground level required in connection with the provision, improvement, maintenance or repair of a sewer, outfall pipe, sludge main or associated apparatus;

(b) the provision of a building, plant, machinery or apparatus in, on, over or under land for the purpose of survey or investigation;

(c) the maintenance, improvement or repair of works for measuring the flow in any watercourse or channel;

(d) any works authorised by or required in connection with an order made under section 73 of the Water Resources Act 1991 (power to make ordinary and emergency drought orders);

(e) any other development in, on, over or under their operational land, other than the provision of a building but including the extension or alteration of a building.

Development not permitted

A.1—Development is not permitted by Class A (e) if—

(a) it would consist of or include the extension or alteration of a building so that—

(i) its design or external appearance would be materially affected;

(ii) the height of the original building would be exceeded, or the cubic content of the original building would be exceeded, by more than 25%; or

(iii) the floor space of the original building would be exceeded by more than 1,000 square metres;

or

(b) it would consist of the installation or erection of any plant or machinery exceeding 15 metres in height or the height of anything it replaces, whichever is the greater.

Condition

A.2—Development is permitted by Class A (b) subject to the condition that, on completion of the survey or investigation, or at the expiration of 6 months from the commencement of the development concerned, whichever is the sooner, all such operations shall cease and all such buildings, plant, machinery and apparatus shall be removed and the land restored as soon as reasonably practicable to its former condition (or to any other condition which may be agreed with the local planning authority).

Interpretation of Class A

A.3—For the purposes of Class A—

'associated apparatus', in relation to any sewer, main or pipe, means pumps, machinery or apparatus associated with the relevant sewer, main or pipe;

'sludge main' means a pipe or system of pipes (together with any pumps or other machinery or apparatus associated with it) for the conveyance of the residue of water or sewage treated in a water or sewage treatment works as the case may be, including final effluent or the products of the dewatering or incineration of such residue, or partly for any of those purposes and partly for the conveyance of trade effluent or its residue.

PART 20
COAL MINING DEVELOPMENT BY THE COAL AUTHORITY AND LICENSED OPERATORS

Class A

Permitted development

A.—Development by a licensee of the Coal Authority, in a mine started before 1st July 1948, consisting of—

(a) the winning and working underground of coal or coal-related minerals in a designated seam area; or

(b) the carrying out of development underground which is required in order to gain access to and work coal or coal-related minerals in a designated seam area.

Conditions

A.1—Development is permitted by Class A subject to the following conditions—

(a) subject to sub-paragraph (b)—

(i) except in a case where there is an approved restoration scheme or mining operations have permanently ceased, the developer shall, before 31st December 1995 or before any later date which the mineral planning authority may agree in writing, apply to the mineral planning authority for approval of a restoration scheme;

(ii) where there is an approved restoration scheme, reinstatement, restoration and aftercare shall be carried out in accordance with that scheme;

(iii)if an approved restoration scheme does not specify the periods within which reinstatement, restoration or aftercare should be carried out, it shall be subject to conditions that-

(a) reinstatement or restoration, if any, shall be carried out before the end of the period of 24 months from either the date when the mining operations have permanently ceased or the date when any application for approval of a restoration scheme under sub-paragraph (a)(i) has been finally determined, whichever is later, and

(b) aftercare, if any, in respect of any part of a site, shall be carried out throughout the period of five years from either the date when any reinstatement or restoration in respect of that part is completed or the date when any application for approval of a restoration scheme under sub-paragraph (a)(i) has been finally determined, whichever is later;

(iv)where there is no approved restoration scheme—

(a) all buildings, plant, machinery, structures and erections used at any time for or in connection with any previous coal-mining operations at that mine shall be removed from any land which is an authorised site unless the mineral planning authority have otherwise agreed in writing, and

(b) that land shall, so far as practicable, be restored to its condition before any previous coal-mining operations at that mine took place or to such condition as may have been agreed in writing between the mineral planning authority and the developer,

before the end of the period specified in sub-paragraph (v);

(v) the period referred to in sub-paragraph (iv) is—

(a) the period of 24 months from the date when the mining operations have permanently ceased or, if an application for approval of a restoration scheme has been made under sub-paragraph (a)(i) before that date, 24 months from the date when that application has been finally determined, whichever is later, or

(b) any longer period which the mineral planning authority have agreed in writing;

(vi) for the purposes of sub-paragraph (a), an application for approval of a restoration scheme has been finally determined when the following conditions have been met—

(a) any proceedings on the application, including any proceeding on or in consequence of an application under section 288 of the Act (proceedings for questioning the validity of certain orders, decisions and directions), have been determined, and

(b) any time for appealing under section 78(right to appeal against planning decisions and failure to take such decisions), or applying or further applying under section 288, of the Act (where there is a right to do so) has expired;

(b) sub-paragraph (a) shall not apply to land in respect of which there is an extant planning permission which—

(i) has been granted on an application under Part III of the Act, and

(ii) has been implemented.

Interpretation of Class A

A.2—For the purposes of Class A—

'a licensee of the Coal Authority' means any person who is for the time being authorised by a licence under Part II of the Coal Industry Act 1994 to carry on coal-mining operations to which section 25 of that Act (coal-mining operations to be licensed) applies;

'approved restoration scheme' means a restoration scheme which is approved when an application made under paragraph A.1(a)(i) is finally determined, as approved (with or without conditions), or as subsequently varied with the written approval of the mineral planning authority (with or without conditions);

'coal-related minerals' means minerals other than coal which are, or may be, won and worked by coal-mining operations;

'designated seam area' means land identified, in accordance with paragraph (a) of the definition of 'seam plan', in a seam plan which was deposited with the mineral planning authority before 30th September 1993;

'previous coal-mining operations' has the same meaning as in section 54(3) of the Coal Industry Act 1994(obligations to restore land affected by coal-mining operations) and references in Class A to the use of anything in connection with any such operations shall include references to its use for or in connection with activities carried on in association with, or for purposes connected with, the carrying on of those operations;

'restoration scheme' means a scheme which makes provision for the reinstatement, restoration or aftercare (or a combination of these) of any land which is an authorised site and has been used at any time for or in connection with any previous coal-mining operations at that mine; and

'seam plan' means a plan or plans on a scale of not less than 1 to 25,000 showing—

(a) land comprising the maximum extent of the coal seam or seams that could have been worked from shafts or drifts existing at a mine at 13th November 1992, without further development on an authorised site other than development permitted by Class B of Part 20 of Schedule 2 to the Town and Country Planning General Development Order 1988, as originally enacted;

(b) any active access used in connection with the land referred to in paragraph (a) of this definition;

(c) the National Grid lines and reference numbers shown on Ordnance Survey maps;

(d) a typical stratigraphic column showing the approximate depths of the coal seam referred to in paragraph (a) of this definition.

Class B

Permitted development

B.—Development by a licensee of the British Coal Corporation, in a mine started before 1st July 1948, consisting of—

(a) the winning and working underground of coal or coal-related minerals in a designated seam area; or

(b) the carrying out of development underground which is required in order to gain access to and work coal or coal-related minerals in a designated seam area.

Interpretation of Class B

B.1—For the purposes of Class B—

'designated seam area' has the same meaning as in paragraph A.2 above;

'coal-related minerals' means minerals other than coal which can only be economically worked in association with the working of coal or which can only be economically brought to the surface by the use of a mine of coal; and authorised by virtue of section 25(3) of the Coal Industry Act 1994 (coal-mining operations to be licensed) to carry on coal-mining operations to which section 25 of that Act applies.

Class C

Permitted development

C.—Any development required for the purposes of a mine which is carried out on an authorised site at that mine by a licensed operator, in connection with coal-mining operations.

Development not permitted

C.1—Development is not permitted by Class C if—

(a) the external appearance of the mine would be materially affected;

(b) any building, plant or machinery, structure or erection or any deposit of minerals or waste—

    (i) would exceed a height of 15 metres above ground level, or

    (ii) where a building, plant or machinery would be rearranged, replaced or repaired, the resulting development would exceed a height of 15 metres above ground level or the height of what was rearranged, replaced or repaired, whichever is the greater;

(c) any building erected (other than a replacement building) would have a floor space exceeding 1,000 square metres;

(d) the cubic content of any replaced, extended or altered building would exceed by more than 25% the cubic content of the building replaced, extended or altered or the floor space would exceed by more than 1,000 square metres, the floor space of that building;

(e) it would be for the purpose of creating a new surface access to underground workings or of improving an existing access (which is not an active access) to underground workings; or

(f) it would be carried out on land to which the description in paragraph F.2(1)(b) applies, and a plan of that land had not been deposited with the mineral planning authority before 5th June 1989.

Conditions

C.2—Development is permitted by Class C subject to the condition that before the end of the period of 24 months from the date when the mining operations have permanently ceased, or any longer period which the mineral planning authority agree in writing—

(a) all buildings, plant, machinery, structures and erections and deposits of minerals or waste permitted by Class C shall be removed from the land unless the mineral planning authority have otherwise agreed in writing; and

(b) the land shall, so far as is practicable, be restored to its condition before the development took place or to such condition as may have been agreed in writing between the mineral planning authority and the developer.

Class D

Permitted development

D.—Any development required for the purposes of a mine which is carried out on an authorised site at that mine by a licensed operator in connection with coal-mining operations and with the prior approval of the mineral planning authority.

Development not permitted

D.1—Development is not permitted by Class D if—

(a) it would be for the purpose of creating a new surface access or improving an existing access (which is not an active access) to underground workings; or

(b) it would be carried out on land to which the description in paragraph F.2(1)(b) applies, and a plan of that land had not been deposited with the mineral planning authority before 5th June 1989.

Condition

D.2—Development is permitted by Class D subject to the condition that before the end of the period of 24 months from the date when the mining operations have permanently ceased, or any longer period which the mineral planning authority agree in writing—

(a) all buildings, plant, machinery, structures and erections and deposits of minerals or waste permitted by Class D shall be removed from the land, unless the mineral planning authority have otherwise agreed in writing; and

(b) the land shall, so far as is practicable, be restored to its condition before the development took place or to such condition as may have been agreed in writing between the mineral planning authority and the developer.

Interpretation of Class D

D.3—The prior approval referred to in Class D shall not be refused or granted subject to conditions unless the authority are satisfied that it is expedient to do so because—

(a) the proposed development would injure the amenity of the neighbourhood and modifications could reasonably be made or conditions reasonably imposed in order to avoid or reduce that injury, or

(b) the proposed development ought to be, and could reasonably be, sited elsewhere.

Class E

Permitted development

E.—The carrying out by the Coal Authority or a licensed operator, with the prior approval of the mineral planning authority, of development required for the maintenance or safety of a mine or a disused mine or for the purposes of ensuring the safety of the surface of the land at or adjacent to a mine or a disused mine.

Prior approvals

E.1(1)—The prior approval of the mineral planning authority to development permitted by Class E is not required if—

(a) the external appearance of the mine or disused mine at or adjacent to which the development is to be carried out would not be materially affected;

(b) no building, plant or machinery, structure or erection—

  (i) would exceed a height of 15 metres above ground level, or

  (ii) where any building, plant, machinery, structure or erection is rearranged, replaced or repaired, would exceed a height of 15 metres above ground level or the height of what was rearranged, replaced or repaired, whichever is the greater,

and

(c) the development consists of the extension, alteration or replacement of an existing building, within the limits set out in paragraph (3).

(2) The approval referred to in Class E shall not be refused or granted subject to conditions unless the authority are satisfied that it is expedient to do so because—

(a) the proposed development would injure the amenity of the neighbourhood and modifications could reasonably be made or conditions reasonably imposed in order to avoid or reduce that injury, or

(b) the proposed development ought to be, and could reasonably be, sited elsewhere.

(3) The limits referred to in paragraph E.1(1)(c) are—

(a) that the cubic content of the building as extended, altered or replaced does not exceed that of the existing building by more than 25%, and

(b) that the floor space of the building as extended, altered or replaced does not exceed that of the existing building by more than 1,000 square metres.

Interpretation of Part 20

F.1—For the purposes of Part 20

'active access' means a surface access to underground workings which is in normal and regular use for the transportation of coal, materials, spoil or men;

'coal-mining operations' has the same meaning as in section 65 of the Coal Industry Act 1994 (interpretation) and references to any development or use in connection with coal-mining operations shall include references to development or use for or in connection with activities carried on in association with, or for purposes connected with, the carrying on of those operations;

'licensed operator' has the same meaning as in section 65 of the Coal Industry Act 1994;

'normal and regular use' means use other than intermittent visits to inspect and maintain the fabric of the mine or any plant or machinery; and

'prior approval of the mineral planning authority' means prior written approval of that authority of detailed proposals for the siting, design and external appearance of the proposed building, plant or machinery, structure or erection as erected, installed, extended or altered.

F.2(1)—Subject to sub-paragraph (2), land is an authorised site for the purposes of Part 20 if—

(a) it is identified in a grant of planning permission or any instrument by virtue of which planning permission is deemed to be granted as land which may be used for development described in this Part; or

(b) in any other case, it is land immediately adjoining an active access which, on 5th December 1988, was in use for the purposes of that mine in connection with coal-mining operations.

(2) For the purposes of sub-paragraph (1), land is not to be regarded as in use in connection with coal-mining operations if—

(a) it is used for the permanent deposit of waste derived from the winning and working of minerals; or

(b) there is on, over or under it a railway, conveyor, aerial ropeway, roadway, overhead power line or pipe-line which is not itself surrounded by other land used for those purposes.

PART 21
WASTE TIPPING AT A MINE

Class A

Permitted development

A.—The deposit, on premises used as a mine or on ancillary mining land already used for the purpose, of waste derived from the winning and working of minerals at that mine or from minerals brought to the surface at that mine, or from the treatment or the preparation for sale, consumption or utilization of minerals from the mine.

Development not permitted

A.1—Development is not permitted by Class A if—

(a) in the case of waste deposited in an excavation, waste would be deposited at a height above the level of the land adjoining the excavation, unless that is provided for in a waste management scheme or a relevant scheme;

(b) in any other case, the superficial area or height of the deposit (measured as at 21st October 1988) would be increased by more than 10%, unless such an increase is provided for in a waste management scheme or in a relevant scheme.

Conditions

A.2—Development is permitted by Class A subject to the following conditions—

(a) except in a case where a relevant scheme or a waste management scheme has already been approved by the mineral planning authority, the developer shall, if the mineral planning authority so require, within three months or such longer period as the authority may specify, submit a waste management scheme for that authority's approval;

(b) where a waste management scheme or a relevant scheme has been approved, the depositing of waste and all other activities in relation to that deposit shall be carried out in accordance with the scheme as approved.

Interpretation of Class A

A.3—For the purposes of Class A—

'ancillary mining land' means land adjacent to and occupied together with a mine at which the winning and working of minerals is carried out in pursuance of planning permission granted or deemed to be granted under Part III of the Act (control over development); and

'waste management scheme' means a scheme required by the mineral planning authority to be submitted for their approval in accordance with the condition in paragraph A.2(a) which makes provision for:

(a) the manner in which the depositing of waste (other than waste deposited on a site for use for filling any mineral excavation in the mine or on ancillary mining land in order to comply with the terms of any planning permission granted on an application or deemed to be granted under Part III of the Act) is to be carried out after the date of the approval of that scheme;

(b) where appropriate, the stripping and storage of the subsoil and topsoil;

(c) the restoration and aftercare of the site.

Class B

Permitted development

B.—The deposit on land comprised in a site used for the deposit of waste materials or refuse on 1st July 1948 of waste resulting from coal-mining operations.

Development not permitted

B.1—Development is not permitted by Class B unless it is in accordance with a relevant scheme approved by the mineral planning authority before 5th December 1988.

Interpretation of Class B

B.2—For the purposes of Class B

'coal-mining operations' has the same meaning as in section 65 of the Coal Industry Act 1994 (interpretation).

Interpretation of Part 21

C.—For the purposes of Part 21

'relevant scheme' means a scheme, other than a waste management scheme, requiring approval by the mineral planning authority in accordance with a condition or limitation on any planning permission granted or deemed to be granted under Part III of the Act (control over development), for making provision for the manner in which the deposit of waste is to be carried out and for the carrying out of other activities in relation to that deposit.

ASSESSMENT OF SBS

The checklist below will help to determine whether an office is a sick building. To determine if the building is sick, each question in each section should be recorded. This should be undertaken for the building as a whole and, depending on the circumstances, for each office in the building.

The number of 'yes' and 'no' answers are counted up and the number put in the subtotal box. When the grand total in the summary sheet shows a high proportion of 'no answers', an alternative building may be the preferred course of action.

However, the cost should also be borne in mind here, because even a lot of 'no' answers could mean that it is still worthwhile undertaking necessary remedial actions or changing the design.

Ventilation

YES   NO

1 Has the building been designed to Chartered Institution of Building Service Engineers (CIBSE) or American Society of Heating, Refrigeration and Air Conditioning (ASHRAE) recommended air change rates?

2 Are these rates achieved in practice?

3 Is the percentage of fresh outside air used in the system above 10%?

4 Are the air intake vents sited away from sources of contamination?

5 Is the prevailing wind direction likely to disperse potential sources of pollution?

6 Are the specified air filters for the plant used?

7 Are the filters fitted correctly?

8 Are there any openable windows to allow staff to ventilate space as required?

9 Have all air diffusers been connected to the ducting plant?

10 Are there any diffusers blocked by furniture?

11 Is there at least one inlet and one extract vent in each room?

12 Do air diffusers give correct air circulation?

13 Have spaces been tested for correct air change rates and dead spots?

14 Are exhaust luminaries used?

15 In the event of a plant breakdown, is there an alternative source of fresh air provision?

16 Do no cold draughts exist?

Subtotal

Humidity

                                                 YES   NO

1 Is the relative humidity level maintained at between 40% and 60%?

2 Is a steam humidification system used?

3 Is it purged at least once per day?

4 Is the humidification system free from organic growth?

5 Is the humidification system fully serviceable?

6 Is there no carry over of water spray past the humidifier station?

7 Is a biocide or any chemical treatment used in the system?

8 Is a weekly inspection of the system carried out?

9 Are dehumidification coils correctly operated?

10 Is there an air break on the condesate drain?

11 Are there no static electricity problems in the space?

Subtotal

Heating

		YES	NO
1	Is the space temperature greater than 22°C in the heating season?		
2	Is the space temperature greater than 23°C in the summer?		
3	Are the temperature variations less than 3°C across the working space?		
4	Is the building zoned?		
5	Are there any elements in the space that will affect radiation asymmetry?		
6	Does the heating or air conditioning system have a terminal reheat facility?		
7	Do all the thermostats in the space function correctly?		
8	Have the occupants individual control over the heating/cooling at their workstation?		
9	Is the building a traditional heavyweight shell?		
10	Is the predominant orientation of windows other than south facing?		

Subtotal

Lighting

		YES	NO
1	Is low frequency tubular fluorescent lighting avoided?		
2	Does the system operate on high frequency?		
3	Is an uplighter system used?		
4	Are specific luminaires used to alleviate screen glare on VDUs?		
5	Is task lighting available?		
6	Are CIBSE lighting levels achieved?		
7	Is glare avoided in the space?		
8	Are window shades available?		

9   Is solar reflective glass avoided?

10 Are natural daylighting levels achieved?

11 Are special shading provisions made on south facing elevations?

12 Are there any problems of light contrast in the space?

Subtotal

Contaminants

	YES	NO

1   There has been no refurbishment in the last year?

2   New furniture has not been installed in the last year?

3   Has the use of volatile organic compounds been avoided?

4   Are photocopiers or printers housed in sealed rooms with their own extractor systems?

5   Does the photocopier or printer exhaust system vent directly to atmosphere?

6   Has the building been 'baked'?

7   Is the building constructed on uncontaminated land?

8   Has the existence of ureaformaldehyde insulation been investigated?

9   Has the existence of asbestos been investigated?

Subtotal

Maintenance

	YES	NO

1   Are air filters maintained as per plant manufacturer's specification?

2   Are the manufacturer's plant maintenance schedules adhered to?

3   Is there a planned maintenance system in operation?

4   Are air flow rates at diffusers/vents as per design and commissioning specifications?

5   Are regular inspections of plant above suspended ceilings or below modular floors carried out?

6   Is the heating system regularly descaled and flushed?

7   Are ceilings and walls regularly decorated?

8   Are all condensate drains regularly checked and flushed?

9   Is the lighting system regularly maintained?

Subtotal

Cleaning

YES   NO

1   Is the building fabric regularly cleaned, including exterior windows?

2   Are internal surfaces, including carpets, floors and furniture, regularly cleaned?

3   Does regular damp dusting take place on all hard surfaces?

4   Are cleaning fluids and chemicals used correctly to the manufacturer's specification?

5   Is the cleaning plant used as per manufacturer's specification?

6   Are air vents/diffusers regularly cleaned?

7   Are luminaires regularly cleaned?

8   Are air filters cleaned as per manufacturer's specification?

9   Are ventilation ducts inspected and cleaned as necessary?

10 Are heating/cooling coils regularly cleaned?

11 Are the insides of filing cabinets regularly vacuumed?

12 Are soft furnishings occasionally cool shampooed or steam cleaned?

Subtotal

Furnishing and colour scheme

YES   NO

1   Are plants and small trees located in the office space?

2   Are furnishings, carpets and wall finishes colour co-ordinated?

3   Has office furniture been ergonomically designed?

4   Have staff been consulted on furnishings?

5   Have furniture diffusers been considered?

6   Have furnishings been assessed for fibre loss?

7   Is there a high proportion of open shelving?

8   Has specialist furniture for VDUs and computerware been considered?

Subtotal

Use of Building

YES   NO

1   Is the building occupied by a private organisation?

2   Is the work principally of a managerial or technical nature?

3   Is the building used as per the architect's design brief?

4   Is the office layout cellular?

5   Is the original occupancy level of the building achieved?

6   Has additional electrical equipment in use in the space been taken into account with regard to the plant cooling load?

7   Is dust and pollution from building alterations avoided?

8   Does partitioning take into account the heating and ventilation system?

Subtotal

Building management

		YES	NO

1   Is a computerised building management system in place?

2   Is a remote system avoided?

3   Is temperature and humidity checked by maintenance personnel?

4   Do staff have a complaints procedure if they feel the working environment is unsatisfactory?

Subtotal

Noise

		YES	NO

1   Are CIBSE noise reduction levels achieved in all spaces?

2   Is the building designed with regard to acoustic problems?

3   Are plant rooms constructed to achieve correct noise reduction levels?

4   Are silencers fitted correctly to supply and extractor ducts?

5   Is noisy machinery isolated?

6   Are crosstalk attenuators fitted?

7   There are no sources of vibration within the plant rooms?

Subtotal

Summary sheet

	YES	NO
Ventilation		
Humidity		
Heating		
Lighting		
Contaminants		
Furnishings and colour scheme		
Maintenance		
Cleaning		
Use of building		
Building management		
Noise		

Grand total

BIBLIOGRAPHY

Ahmed, K, 'Minister plans GM rethink' (2000) *The Observer*, 21 May, p 5

Ailing, J, 'Serving many voices: progressing calls for an International Environmental Organisation' (1997) 9(2) JEL 243

Alder, J, 'Environmental impact assessment – the inadequacies of English law' (1993) 5(2) JEL 203

Alridge, J, 'Polluters named and shamed' (1999) *The Observer*, 30 May, p 7

Arnold, C, 'Planning gain – how are State liabilities passed back to landowners?' (1999) JPEL October 869

Athanasiou, T, *Slow Reckoning – the Ecology of a Divided Planet*, 1998, London: Vintage

Bailey, P, 'The creation and enforcement of environmental agreements' (1999) 8(2) EELR June 170

Baldwin, R, Leach SJ, Doggart, J and Attenborough M, *BREEAM 1/90: An Environmental Assessment for New Office Designs*, 1990, Garston: BRE

Baldwin, R, Yates, A, Howard, N and Rao, S, *BREEAM 98 for Offices*, 1998, BRE

Bar and Kraemer, R, 'European environmental policy after Amsterdam' (1998) 10(2) JEL 315

Barnett, A, 'Can buildings make people ill?' (1995) EG supplement: Office Trends 70

Barnett, H, *Constitutional and Administrative Law*, 3rd edn, 2000, London: Cavendish Publishing

Bell, S and McGilvray, D, *Environmental Law*, 5th edn, 2000, London: Blackstone

Birnie, P and Boyle, S, *International Law and the Environment*, 2nd edn, 2000, Oxford: OUP

Birnie, P, *Basic Documents on International Law and the Environment*, 1995, Oxford: Clarendon

Birtles, AA, 'Right to know – the Environmental Information Regulations' (1993) JPL 615

Boch, C, 'The enforcement of the Environmental Assessment Directive into the national courts: a breach in the dyke' (1997) 9(1) JEL 119

Bookchin, M, *The Ecology of Freedom – the Emergence and Dissolution of Hierarchy*, 1991, Montreal/New York: Black Rose

Bosselmann, K and Richardson, B (eds), *Environmental Justice and Market Mechanisms*, 1999, London: Kluwer

Bowman, M, 'International treaties and the protection of birds: Part II' (1999) 11(2) JEL 281

Boyle, A and Anderson, M, *Human Rights Approaches to Environmental Protection*, 1998, Oxford: Clarendon

Boyle, A and Freestone, D (eds), *International Law and Sustainable Development – Past Achievements and Future Challenges*, Oxford: OUP

Boyle, A, 'Saving the world: implementation and enforcement of international environmental law through international institutions' (1991) 3 JEL 229

Boyle, A, 'Saving the world: implementation and enforcement of international environmental law through international institutions' (1991) 3 JEL 229

Boyle, S, 'Making progress towards a fossil free energy future' (1999) 29(2) *The Ecologist* 132

Bradley, A and Ewing, K, *Constitutional and Administrative Law*, 1997, London: Longman

Brearley, C, 'Integrated transport policy: the implications for planning' (1999) JPEL January 408

Brearley, C, 'Integrated transport policy: the implications for planning' [1999] JPL May 408

British Standards Institute (1988 and 1998), Draft for Development DD175 – Code of Practice for the Identification of Potentially Contaminated Land, London: BSI

Brooman, S and Legge, D, *Law of Animals*, 1997, London: Cavendish Publishing

Brown, P, 'Battling to the last ditch' (1998) *The Guardian*, 2 July, p 19

Brown, P, 'Climate change warning signals at red' (2000a) *The Guardian*, 12 May, p 10

Brown, P, 'From nuclear dream to rubbish tip' (1999b) *The Guardian*, 23 August, p 6

Brown, P, 'Sellafield safety only just tolerable' (2000b) *The Guardian*, 19 February, p 4

Brown, P, 'The unloved industry that will not go away' (1999a) *The Guardian*, 30 January, p 12

Brown, P, 'West's pollution blamed for world disasters' (2000c) *The Guardian*, 15 May, p 7

Brown-Weiss, E, *Environmental Changes and International Environmental Law* 1992, Tokyo: United Nations UP

Building Use Studies, Sick Office – Off Sick, *Building* (1988) vol 253, no 7538(11) March 11, pp 66–67

Bunyard, P, 'Fiddling while the climate burns' (2000) 30(2) *The Ecologist* 19

Bunyard, P, 'How ozone depletion increases global warming' (1999) 29(2) *The Ecologist* 85

Cairney, T and H998, London: Eobson, DM, *Contaminated Land – Problems and Solutions*, 2nd edn, E & FN Spon

Caliiess, C, 'Towards a European environmental constitutional law' [1997] 6(3) EELR April 113

Cameron, J, Demaret, P and Geradin, D, *Trade and the Environment – Volumes 1 and 2*, 1997, London: Cameron May

Campbell, D, *International Environmental Law and Regulation – Volumes 1 and 2*, 1997, Chichester: Wiley

Canter, LW, *Environmental Impact Assessment*, 2nd edn, 1996, Oxford: Irwin/McGraw Hill

Carnworth, C, Werkman, S and Roderick, P, 'Environmental litigation – a way through the maze?' (1999) 11(1) JEL 3

Carnworth, R, 'The planning lawyer and the environment' (1991) 3(1) JEL 57

Carson, R, *Silent Spring*, 1962, London: Penguin

Chadwick, A, Glasson, J and Therival, R, *Introduction to Environmental Impact Assessment*, 1994, London: UCL

Cheyne, I and Purdue, M, 'Fitting definition to purpose: the search for a satisfactory definition of waste' (1995) JEL 149

Clapp, B, *An Environmental History of Britain Since the Industrial Revolution*, 1994, London: Longman

Clapp, BW, *An Environmental History of Britain Since the Industrial Revolution*, 1994, London: Longman

Clark, J, and Harrington, K, *The Role of EIA in the Planning Process*, London: Mansell

Clark, S, 'The rights of wild things' (1979) 22 Inquiry 171

Cole, M, 'Examining the environmental case against free trade' (1999) 33(5) J World Trade 183

Cooper, A, 'An obstacle to wind power development' (1998) 22 JPEL March 432

Craig, P, *Administrative Law,* 4th edn, 1999, London: Sweet & Maxwell

Crouch, D and Ward, C, *The Allotment: its Landscape and Culture*, 1997, Nottingham: Five Leaves

Crowhurst, D and Manchester, SJ, *The Measurement of Methane and Other Gases from the Ground*, 1993, London: CIRIA Report 131

Cuell, M, 'Building related sickness' (1993) 15(3) Building Services 21

De Geus, M, *Ecological Utopias Envisioning the Sustainable Society*, 1999, Utrecht: International

De Klem, C and Shine, C, *Biological Diversity Conservation and the Law – Legal Means for Conserving Species and Ecosystems*, 1993, IUCN Environmental Protection and Law Paper no 29

De La Fayette, P, 'International law and the problem of nuclear safety' (1993) 5(1) JEL 31

De Sadeleer, N and Sambon, J, 'The concept of hazardous waste in European Community law' (1997) 6(1) EELR January 9

Department of the Environment, *Preparation of Environmental Statements for Planning Projects that Require Environmental Assessment – A Good Practice Guide*, 1995, London: HMSO

Department of Transport, *Design Manual for Roads and Bridges, Vol 11*, 1994, London: HMSO

Dobson, A (ed), *The Green Reader*, 1991, London: Andre Deutsch

Dobson, A, *Fairness and Futurity: Essays on the Environment*, 1999, Oxford: OUP

Dobson, A, *Green Political Thought*, 1990, London: Unwin Hyman

Dobson, A, *Justice and the Environment: Concepts of Environmental Sustainability and Theories of Distributive Justice*, 1998, Oxford: OUP

Doherty, M, 'The status of the principles of EC environmental law *Gianni Bettati v Safety High Tech* (1999) 11(2) JEL 354

Dollittle, I, 'After implementation, enforcement? The next challenge for European environmental law' (1999) 11(3) Env Law Mgmt 101

Ekersley, R, *Environmentalism and Political Theory – Towards an Ecocentric Approach*, 1992, London: UCL

Environmental Assessment, Special Publication 96, London, Construction Industry Research and Information Association

Erickson, SJ and King, BJ, *Fundamentals of Environmental Management*, 1999, New York: Wiley

Fairleg, S, 'Defining rural sustainability' (1999) Town and Country Planning March 82

Flood, M, *Solar Prospects – the Potential for Renewable Energy*, 1983, London: Friends of the Earth/Wilwood House

Fortlage, CA, *Environmental Assessment – A Practical Guide*, Aldershot: Gower

Foster, M and Masib, C, 'The Landfill Regulations – how will the UK meet the challenge?' (2000) 9(1) EELR 21

French, R, 'Final Report for Compulsory Purchase: an appropriate power for the 21st century?' (1998) JPEL November 1076

Frost, R and Frackish, A, *Directory of Environmental Impact Statements 1988–94*, (1996) Oxford: Oxford Brookes School of Planning

Fry, M, 'Eco vandalism at sites of special scientific interest' (1993) 5(1) JEL 109

Fry, M, *A Manual of Conservation Law*, 1995, Oxford: Clarendon

Fullalove, S, *Millennium Beaches*, 1999, London: Thomas Telford

Garner, J and Jones, B, *Countryside Law,* 3rd edn, 1997, London: Shaw

Garner, JF, *The Law of Sewers and Drains*, 8th edn, 1995, London: Shaw

Garner, R, 'Wildlife conservation and the moral status of animals' (1995) 3 Environmental Politics, Pt 1, p 114

Garner, R, *Environmental Politics*, 1996, London: Prentice Hall

Gerard, N, 'Access to the European Court of Justice: a lost opportunity? *Stichting Greenpeace Council (Greenpeace International) and Others v Commission*' (1998) 10(2) JEL 331

Gillespie, A, *International Environmental Law, Policy and Ethics,* 1997, Oxford: Clarendon

Gillies, D, 'How far should you go? The obligation to classify SPAs: Case C 3/96 *Commission of the EC v Kingdom of the Netherlands*' [1999] 1 ELR 125

Gillies, D, *Guide to EC Environmental Law*, 1999, London: Earthscan

Gillmore, M, Rock, D, Illotson, T and Ohara, J, 'Reforming judicial review: addressing the planning problem' (1999) JPEL Jan 2000 14

Goldman, L, 'How sick is your building?' (1996) EG 129

Goldman, M (ed), *Privatising Nature: Political Struggles for the Global Commons*, 1998, London: Pluto

Graham, C, 'A fair deal for consumers? The Government's Green Paper on utility regulation' (1998) 9(4) Utilities L Rev 149

Grant, M, *Environmental Court Research Project*, 2000, London: DETR

Greenwood, B, *Planning Law Guidance*, 2nd edn, 1999, London: Butterworths

Gregory, M, *Conservation Law in the Countryside*, 1994, Croydon: Tolley

Gunningham, N and Grobosky, D, S*mart Regulation Designing Environmental Policy*, 1998, Oxford: OUP

Gunningham, N, *Pollution, Social Interest and the Law*, 1974, London: Martin Robinson

Guruswany, J, 'Energy and environmental security – the need for action' (1991) 3(2) JEL 209

Haigh, N and Usher, J, *General Principles of EC law and EC Institutions and Legislation*, 1998, London: Longman

Haigh, N and Usher, J, *General Principles of EC Law and EC Institutions and Legislation*, 1998, London: Longman

Hall, C, *Running Water*, 1989, London: Robertson McCarta

Harris, M and Herbert, S, *Contaminated Land, Investigation, Assessment and Remediation*, 1994, London: Thomas Telford

Harrison, J, 'Environmental mediation: the ethical and constitutional dimension' (1997) 9(1) JEL 79

Harrop, S, 'The dynamics of wild animal welfare law' (1997) 9(2) JEL 287

Hart, D, 'The impact of the European Convention on Human Rights on planning and environmental law ' (2000) JPL 117

Harte, J, 'Nature conservation – the rule of law in European Community environmental protection: *R v SOSE ex p RSPB*' (1997) 9(1) JEL 139

Harte, J, 'The extent of legal protection enjoyed by sites of special scientific interest in England and Wales' (1991) 3(2) JEL 293

Harvey, G, *The Killing of the Countryside*, 1998, London: Vintage

Hawke, N and Kovaleva, N, *Agri-Environmental Law and Policy*, 1998, London: Cavendish Publishing

Health and Safety Executive, 'Sick building syndrome in perspective' (1995) 201(23) Architects J 41

Hencke, D, 'Britain steps out of line on incinerators' (2000a) *The Guardian*, 19 May, p 24

Hencke, D, 'Minister enters fray over future of "toxic" Tyneside waste plant (2000c) The Guardian, 13 May, p 11

Hencke, D, 'Tide of polluted landfill "beyond control"' (2000b) *The Guardian*, April 6, p 7

Hildyard, N, 'Down in the dumps', in Goldsmith, E and Hildyard, N, *Green Britain or Industrial Waste Land*, 1986, Cambridge: Polity, p 215

Hill, C, *Liberty Against the Law – some 19th Century Controversies*, 1996, London: Penguin

Hilson, C and Cram, I, 'Judicial review and environmental law – is there a coherent view of standing?' (1997) 6(3) EELR 148

Holder, J (ed), *The Impact of EC Environmental Law in the UK*, 1997, Chichester: Wiley

Holder, J, 'Law and landscape: the legal construction and protection of hedgerows' (1999) 62 MLR 100

Holdsworth, B and Sealey, A, *Healthy Buildings*, 1992, London: Longman

Holliday, J, 'Why not a rural renaissance?' (1999) Town and Country Planning April 128

Hough, P, *The Global Politics of Pesticides: Forging Consensus form Conflicting Interests*, 1998, London: Earthscan

Howarth, W, 'Accommodation without resolution? Emission controls and environmental quality objectives in the proposed EC Water framework Directive' (1999) 1(16) ELR 26

Howarth, W, Water *Pollution Law*, 1998, London: Shaw

Hughes, D, 'Status of self-sufficiency and the proximity principles with regard to the disposal and recovery of waste in the European Community: *Chemical Afvalstoffen Dusseldorp BV and Others v Minister van Volkshuisvesting, Ruimtelijke Ordening en Milieubeheer*' (1999) 11(1) JEL 121

Hughes, D, *Environmental Law*, 3rd edn, 1996, London: Butterworths

Hunter, R, Hendrick, F and Muylle, K, 'Environmental enforcement in Europe' (1998) 7(2) EELR February 47

Hurrel, M and Kinsbury, W, *International Politics and the Environment – Action, Interests and Institutions*, 1992, Oxford: OUP

Hutter, B, *A Reader in Environmental Law*, Oxford: Clarendon

Hutter, B, *The Reasonable Arm of the Law*, 1988, Oxford: Clarendon

Institute of Environmental Assessment, *Digest of Environmental Statements*, 1998, London: Sweet & Maxwell

Institute of Environmental Assessment, *Guidelines for Baseline Ecological Assessment*, 1994, East Kirby

Jacobs, M, *The Green Economy*, 1991, London: Pluto

Jewell, T and Steele, J, *Law in Environmental Decision Making – National, European and International Perspectives*, 1998, Oxford: OUP

Jewell, T, 'Coal mining and colliery spoil disposal' (1999) ELMg 11(1 and 2) Jan–April

Jones, C, Wood, C and Dipper, B, 'Environmental assessment in the UK planning process' (1998) 69 Town Planning Rev 39

Jones, P, 'Health and comfort in offices' (1995) 201(23) Architects Journal 33

Jowell, J and Millichap, D, 'The enforcement of planning law' (1986) JPL 482

Kameri-Mbote, A and Cullet, P, 'Agro-biodiversity and international law – a conceptual framework' (1999) 11(2) JEL 257

Kinnersley, D, *Troubled Water*, 1988, London: Shipman

Kirkwood, J, in Ryder, R and Singer, P, *Animal Welfare and the Environment*, 1992, Melksham: RSPCA, p 139

Kramer, L, 'Public interest litigation in environmental matters before European courts' (1996) 8(1) JEL 1

Kramer, L, *EC Environmental Law*, 1999, London: Sweet & Maxwell

Kronick, C, 'Nuclear power and climate change' (1999) 29(2) *The Ecologist* 135

Kummer, K, *International Management of Hazardous Wastes*, 1999, Oxford: OUP

Kunzlik, P, 'Access to the Commission's documents in environmental cases – confidentiality and public confidence: *World Wide fund for Nature v The Commission of the European Communities*' (1997) 9(2) JEL 321

Kunzlik, P, 'The enforcement of EU environmental law: Art 69, the Ombudsman and the Parliament' (1997) 6(2) EELR February 46

Lamb, R, *Promising the Earth*, 1996, London: Foe Routledge

Lange, B, 'National environmental regulation? A case study of waste management in England and Germany' (1999) 11(1) JEL 59

Last, K, 'Environmental assessment and the designation of special protection areas and special areas of conservation: the Cairngorm Funicular Railway' [1999] 1 ELR 133

Last, K, 'Habitat protection: has the Wildlife and Countryside Act 1981 made a difference?' (1999) 11(1) JEL 15

Layard, A, 'The 1994 Directive on the Incineration of Hazardous Waste Substitute Fuels and Trans – scientific choices' (1997) 6(1) EELR January 16

Lea, A, 'Batneec, BPEO and the variation of IPC consents – a review of recent high court decisions' (1998) JPEL October 913

Leach, BA and Goodger, HK, *Building on Derelict Land*, 1991, CIRIA

Lean, G, 'Where did all the fresh air go?' (1995) *The Independent on Sunday*, 5 March, p 5

Lefevré, J, 'The new Directive on air quality and assessment and management' (1997) 6.4 EELR July 10

Legge, D and Jackson, R, 'Drought – the implications for water metering' (1998) 142(21) SJ 490

Legge, D and Jackson, R, 'Lead contamination – the implications for drinking water quality 142(34) (1998) SJ 490

Legge, D and Jackson, R, 'Water privatisation – ownership disputes and liability' (1998) 142(14) SJ 330

Legge, D, 'Analysis: Ofwat review of utility regulation – submission by the Director General of Water Services' (1998) 8(5) W Law 169

Legge, D, 'Case note: *R v Director General of Water Services ex p Oldham MBC* (1998) 9(3) Utilities L Rev 123

Legge, D, 'From a Victorian to a modern water industry?' (1999) 2 Utilities J 36

Legge, D, 'The future of water regulation' (1999) 10(6) Utilities L Rev 250

Legge, D, 'The periodic review 1999' (1999) 10(3) W Law 113

Legge, D, 'The periodic review – a review of the law' (1994) 5(2) Utilities L Rev 85.

Legge, D, 'The price of water?' (1994) 5(2) Utilities L Rev 50

Legge, D, 'The sustainability of the water industry in a regulated environment' (2000) 12(1) JEL 19

Legge, D, 'Water, water everywhere, nor any drop to drink?'(1998) 9(4) Utilities L Rev 147

Leinster, P, Raw, G, Thomson, N, Leaman, A and Whitehead, C, *A Modular Longitudinal Approach to the Investigation of Sick Building Syndrome*, 1990, Garston: Building Research Establishment

Long, A and Mereu, C, 'Integrated pollution prevention and control: the implementation of Directive 96/61/EEC' (1999) 8(3) EELR, June 180

Long, A, 'The Single Market and the environment: the European dilemma, the example of the Packaging Directive' (1997) 6(1) EELR 214

Lovelock, J, *Gaia: a New Look at Life on Earth*, 1995, Oxford: OUP

Lovelock, J, *The Ages of Gaia – a Biography of Our Living Earth*, 2nd edn, 1995, Oxford: OUP

Lowe, P, Cox, D et al, *The Politics of Farming Forestry and Conservation*, 1989, Aldershot: Gower

Lowe, P, et al, *Countryside Conflicts*, 1986, Aldershot: Gower

Maclaren, N, 'Nuisance law and the Industrial Revolution – some lessons from social history' (1983) 3OJLS 155

Macrory, R, 'The enforcement of Community environmental law – some critical issues' (1992) 29(2) CMLR 347

Marshall, R and Smith, C, 'Planning for nature conservation: the role and performance of English district local authorities in the 1990s' (1999) JEP Mgmt vol 42 (5) 691

Martell, L, *Ecology and Society*, 1994, Oxford: Blackwell

Mc Auslan, P, *Land Law and Planning*, 1975, London: Weidenfield and Nicholson

McAuslan, P, 'The role of courts and other judicial type bodies in environmental management' (1991) 3(2) J Env Law 195

McClaren, N, 'Nuisance law and the Industrial Revolution – some lessons from social history' (1983) 3 OJLS 155

McCormick, J, *The Global Environmental Movement*, 2nd edn, 1995, Chichester: Wiley

McEldowney, J and McEldowney, S, *Environment and the Law – An Introduction for Environmental Scientists and Lawyers* 1996, London: Addison Wesley

McHarry, J, 'Indoor air and noise pollutants' (1994) 200(23) Architects J 42

McIntyre, O and Mosedale, T, 'The precautionary principle as a norm of customary international law' (1997) 9(2) JEL 221

McManus, F, *Environmental Health Law*, 1994, London: Blackstone

Mehta, A and Hawkins, K, 'Integrated pollution control and its impact: perspectives for industry' (1998) 10(1) JEL 61

Millar, C, 'Economics v pragmatism – the control of radioactive wastes' (1990) 2(1) JEL 65

Miller, C, 'Regulation of UK industrial air pollution in the 1990s – continuity and change: *Her Majesty's Inspectorate of Pollution v Coalite Products*' (1997) 9(1) JEL 303

Miller, C, 'The European Convention on Human Rights: another weapon in the environmentalists' armoury – *Guerra and Others v Italy*' (1999) 11(1) JEL 157

Miller, C, *Environmental Rights – Critical Perspectives*, 1998, London: Routledge

Molhave, L, *The Sick Buildings: A Sub-population Among the Problem Buildings*, 1994, London: Institute for Water

Moore, V, *A Practical Approach to Planning Law*, 7th edn, 2000, London: Blackstone

Morris, A and Dennis, P, 'Survey findings of libraries in Great Britain' (1995) 16(3) Library Management, pp 42–47

Morris, P and Therival, R, *Methods of Environmental Assessment*, 1996, London: UCL

Nicholson, M, *The Environmental Revolution*, 1968, London: Hutchinson

Nollkaemper, F, 'Habitat protection in European Community law: evolving conceptions of a balance of interests' (1997) 9(2) JEL 271

Norton, B, *Towards Unity Amongst Environmentalists*, 1991, Oxford: OUP

Nutley, W, 'Saving planning permission proposed amendments to appeal procedures' (2000) JPEL February 113

Ong, D, The 'Convention on International Trade in Endangered Species (CITES 1973): implications of recent developments in international and EC environmental law' (1998) 10(2) JEL 291

Ooi, PL, *Sick Building Syndrome: an Emerging Stress Related Disorder*, 1997, Singapore: Institute of Environmental Epidemiology

Osborn, D, 'Some reflections on UK environment policy 1970–95' (1997) 9(1) JEL 3

Paret, I and De Prez, P, *Public Expectation and Environmental Enforcement: Distortion or Democracy*, (1999) 11(6) Env Law Mgmt, Nov–Dec, pp 224–28.

Park, P, 'An evaluation of the landfill tax two years on' (2000) JPEL January 3

Parker, J, 'The toxic zone' (1993) 15(3) Building Services 24

Parpworth, N, 'Causing water pollution and the acts of third parties' (1998) JPEL August 752

Parpworth, N, 'The draft EC Landfill Directive' (1999) JPEL January 4

Pearce, D, *Measuring Sustainable Development: Blueprint 3*, 1993, London: Earthscan

Pearce, D, *The New Environmental Policy*, 1990, London: Earthscan

Penn, C, *Noise Control: the Law and its Enforcement*, 2nd edn, 1995, London: Shaw

Pocklington, D, 'UK perspectives on the definition of waste in EU legislation' (1999) 8(2) EELR March 72

Poli, S, 'Shaping the EC regime on liability for environmental damage: progress or disillusionment?' (1999) 8(11) EELR November 299

Potter, IN, *Building Services Research and Information Association*, 1988, Technical Note 4/88, London

Privett, KD, Matthews, SC and Hodges, RA, *Barriers, Liners and Cover Systems for Containment and Control of Land Contamination*, 1996, CIRIA

Pugh, C and Day, M, *Toxic Torts*, 1995, London: Cameron May/UKELA

Purdue, M, 'A harpoon for Greenpeace – judicial review of the regulation of radioactive substances' (1994) 6(2) JEL 297

Purdue, M, 'IPC and EPA 1990 – a coming of age in environmental law' (1991) 54 MLR 534

Purdue, M, 'The distinction between using secondary raw materials and the recovery of waste: criminal proceedings against Euro Tombesi and others' (1998) 10(1) JEL 116

Purdue, M, 'The impact of s 54A' (1994) JPEL March 399

Purdue, M, 'The implications of the constitutional functions of regional water authorities' (1979) JPL 119

Purdue, M, 'The merits of statutory nuisance as a means of cleaning up beaches: *R v Carrick DC ex p Shelley*' (1997) 9(1) JEL 103

Purdue, M, 'The relation between development control and specialist pollution control: which is the tail and which is the dog?' (1999) JPEL January 585

Rackham, O, *The History of the Countryside – The Classic History of Britain's Landscape, Flora and Fauna*, 1997, London: Phoenix Giant

Ragner Gerholm, T, 'The Atomic Age is not over yet' (1998) New Scientist Special Supplement, Power to Save the Planet, 25 September pp xxii–xxiii.

Raw, G, and Goldman, L, SBS: A Suitable Case for Treatment, (1996) *Building Research Establishment*, 109/1/3, September 1996

Raw, G *et al*, *Questionnaire design for SBS Part 2: The Effect of Symptom List and Frequency Scale*, 1994, Building Research Establishment, August 1995

Raw, GJ, *SBS: A Review of The Evidence on Causes and Solutions*, 1992, HSE Contract Research Report No 42

Reaka-Kudla, M, Wilson, D and Wilson, E, *Biodiveristy II: Understanding and Protecting our Biological Resources*, 1996, Washington: Joseph Henry

Reid, C, 'Environmental regulation through EC instruments: the example of forestry' (1996) 8 ELM 59

Reid, C, 'Nature conservation orders' (1992) 4(2) JEL 241

Reid, C, Lloyd, M, Illsley, B and Lyrch, B, 'Effective public access to planning information' (1998) JPEL November 1028

Reid, C, *Nature Conservation Law,* 1994, London: Sweet & Maxwell

Richardson, L *et al, Policing Pollution – a Study of Regulation and Enforcement,* 1982, Oxford: Clarendon

Rideout, G, 'Itching to go home' (1995) 260(7897) Building Services (Supplement)

Robertson, AS, 'Sick building syndrome: is there a way forward?' (1991) 9(2) Property Management 157

Robertson, G, 'Indoor air quality – the property manager's role in tenant health (1989) 8(1) Property Management 17

Rodgers, C, 'Environmental management of common land: towards a new legal framework?' (1999) 11(2) JEL 231

Rodgers, C, *Agricultural Law,* 2nd edn, 1998, London: Butterworths

Rodgers, C, *Nature Conservation and Countryside Law,* 1996, Cardiff: Wales UP

Roger, C, 'UWWTD, implications and issues' 1998, 9(1) W Law, Jan–Feb 24

Rooley, R, 'Sick building syndrome – the real facts – what is known, what can be done' (1995) 13(3) MCB Structural Survey 5

Rostron, J, *SBS: Concepts, Issues and Practice,* 1997, London: E & FN Spon

Routledge, R, 'Statutory control of land use on environmental grounds in England 1485–1945' (1981) 3(1) J Legal History 77

Rowan-Robinson, J and Ross, A, 'The enforcement of environmental regulation in Britain' (1994) JPL 200

Rowan-Robinson, J, Ross, A and Walton, W, 'Public access to environmental information: a means to what end?' (1996) 8(1) JEL 19

Rowe, DM, 'Sick building syndrome: the mystery and the reality' (1994) 37(3) Architectural Science Rev 137

Rowe, M, 'Loophole lets builders ravage village greens' (2000) *The Independent on Sunday,* 21 May, p 14

Rowell, A, *Green Backlash: Global Subversion of the Environment Movement,* 1996, London: Routledge

Royal Commission on Environmental Pollution, 12th Report, *Best Practicable Environmental Option,* 1988, London: HMSO

Rugman, A and Soloway, J, *Environmental Regulation and Corporate Strategy,* 1999, Oxford: Clarendon

Rutherford, M, 'Protecting world heritage sites' (1993) 6(2) JEL 369

Ryan, C, 'Unforeseeable but not unusual: the validity of the *Empress* test: *Empress Car Company (Abertillery) Ltd v National Rivers Authority*' (1998) 10(2) JEL 347

Salman, S and Boisson de Chazournes, P (eds), *International Water Courses – Enhancing Co-operation and Managing Conflict*, 1998, World Bank Technical Paper 414, Washington

Sands, P, *Principles of International Environmental Law*, 1995, Manchester: Manchester UP

Scarse, T, 'The judicial review of LPA decisions: taking stock' (1999) JPL August 679

Schumacher, E, *Small is Beautiful*, 1974, London: Sphere

Scott, J, *EC Environmental Law*, 1998, Harlow: Longman

Scrase, T, 'Listed building consent – shifting grounds on fixtures and fittings' (2000) JPEL March 235

Sculthorpe, H, *Freedom to Roam*, 1993, London: Freedom

Seinfeld, JH, *Atmospheric Chemistry and Physics of Air Pollution*, 1996, New York: Wiley

Shapley, C, 'Decision making and the role of the Planning Inspectorate' (1999) JPEL January 403

Sharman, F, 'River improvement in early 17th century' (1982) 3(3) J Legal History 222

Sheate, W, *Making an Impact: A Guide to EIA Law and Policy*, 1994, London: Cameron May

Shelbourne, C, 'Enforcing listed building consent' (1998) JPEL November 1035

Shepley, C, 'Mediation in planning' (1999) 1(1) ELR 2

Shoard, M, *A Right to Roam*, 1999, Oxford: OUP

Shoard, M, *The Theft of the Countryside*, 1989, London: Maurice Temple Smith

Shoard, M, *This Land is Our Land – the Struggle for Britain's Countryside*, 1997, London: Gaia

Shoard, M, *This Land is Our Land*, 1987, London: Collins

Snape, J, 'Tax law aspects of adopting and operating green transport plans' (1999) 1(2) ELR 95

Soil and Air Hygiene, Indoor Air 1987, vol 2, *Proceedings of the 4th International Conference on Indoor Quality and Climate*, West Berlin, 17–21 August 1987, pp 469–73

Somsen, S, 'EC water directives' (1990) 1 W Law 93

Spencer, M, 'The arithmetic of climate protection' (1999) 29(2) *The Ecologist* 41

Spurgeon, A, Non-specific Exposure in the Workplace, 1997, Birmingham: University of Birmingham Institute of Occupational Health

Stanley, N, 'The *Empress* decision and causing water pollution: a new approach to s 85(1) of the Water Resources Act 1991, Strict Liability' (1999) W Law 10(1) Jan–Feb

Stanners, D and Bordeau, P (eds), *Europe's Environment (The Dubris Assessment)*, 1995, Copenhagan: European Environment Agency

Stroup, R and Meiners, R, *Cutting Green Tape: Pollutants, Environmental Regulations and the Law*, 1999, London: Transaction

Sunkin, M (ed), *Sourcebook on Environmental Law*, 1998, London: Cavendish Publishing

Swanson, T, *Global Action for Biodiversity*, 1997, London: Earthscan/IUCN

Sykes, S, 'Environmental insurance solutions as a means of facilitating transactions involving contaminated and environmentally suspect land' (1999) 1(1) ELR 27

Telling, A, and Duxbury, R, *Planning Law and Procedure*, 11th edn, 1999, Butterworths, London

Tennyson, R, 'Building for health' (1991) 9(7) Facilities 118

Therival, R, *Strategic Environmental Assessment*, 1995, Manchester University EIA Centre

Thomas, K, *Man and the Natural World – Changing Attitudes in England 1500–1800*, 1983, London: Penguin

Thornton, J and Tromans, S, 'Human rights and environmental wrongs – incorporating the European Convention on Human Rights: some thoughts on the consequences for UK environmental law' (1999) 11(1) JEL 35

Tong, D, '"Sick buildings": what are they and what is their cause?' (1991) 9(7) Facilities 9

Torres, H, 'Trade and the environment – interaction in the WTO – how can a new round contribute?' (1999) 33(5) J World Trade 153

Trimbos, T, 'Outdoor advertisements: proposals for reform' (1999) JPEL November 978

Tromans, S and Fitgerald, J, *The Law of Nuclear Installations and Radioactive Substances*, 1997, London: Sweet & Maxwell

Tromans, S, 'High talk and low cunning: putting environmental principles into legal practice' (1995) JPEL 779

Tromans, S, 'Is Franz Kafka alive and well and working for the Environment Agency? Transfrontier waste shipments and proportionality: *R v Environment Agency ex p Dockrange Ltd and Mayer Parry Ltd*' (1998) 10(1) JEL 146

Tromans, S, 'Nuclear liabilities and environmental damage' (1999) 1(1) ELR 59

Tromans, S, *Planning Law Practice and Precedents,* looseleaf, London: Sweet & Maxwell

Trudgill, ST (ed), *Water Quality Processes and Policy*, 1999, London, Wiley

Twigg-Fleshner, C, 'The Freedom of Information White Paper – your right to know' (1998) 9(4) Utilities L Rev 157

Tyler, M and Brown, A, 'Sick building syndrome: who is responsible?' (1991) 9(7) Facilities 6

Tyler, M, 'Legal ramifications of sick building syndrome (1991) 9(4) Property Management 317

Tyme, J, *Motorways vs Democracy,* 1978, London: Macmillan

UK Environmental Foresight Project, *Road Transport and the Environment, Vol 2,* 1994, London: Centre for the Exploitation of Science and Technology

Usher, J, *General Principles of EC Law and EC Institutions and Legislation,* 1998, London: Longman

Van Calster, G, 'Amsterdam, the Inter-governmental Conference and greening the EU Treaty' (1998) 7(4) EELR January 12

Vidal, J, 'Trashing the crops' (1998) *The Guardian,* 31 July, p 16

Vogel, D, *National Styles of Regulation,* 1986, Ithaca: Cornell UP

Walker, B, 'Allergic reactions to buildings' (1991) 13(1) Building Services (CIBSE) 39

Walson, J (ed), *Planning and EIA in Practice,* London: Longman

Wathern, P *et al*, *Environmental Impact Assessment – Theory and Practice,* 1988, London: Unwin Hyman

Weale, A, *The New Politicos of Pollution,* 1992, Manchester: Manchester UP

Wells, T, *Environmental Policy – a Global Perspective for the 21st Century,* 1996, New Jersey: Prentice Hall

Weston, J, *Planning and Environmental Impact in Practice,* 1997, London: Longman

White, P, 'Sick building syndrome awareness' (1993) 43(12) *Chartered Surveyors Weekly,* pp 11–12

White, R, 'Land use, law and the Environment' (1991) 18 J L&S 32 (special edition: law, policy and the environment)

Whorton, MD, 'Investigation and work up of tight building syndrome' (1987) 21(2) J Occupational Medicine 29

Wignall, G, Nuisances, 1998, London: Sweet & Maxwell

Williams, R, 'Damage caused by water from abandoned mines: is there greater potential for liability than first apparent?' (1999) EL Mt 11 (4 and 5) 161

Wils, W, 'The Birds Directive 15 years later – a survey of the case law and a comparison with the Habitats Directive' (Feb 1994) JEL 219

Wilson, E, The Diversity of Life, 1992, London: Penguin

Wilson, S and Hedge, H, The Office Environment Survey: a Study of Building Sickness, 1987, London: Building Use Studies

Wilson, W, Making Environmental Laws Work: an Anglo-American Comparison, 1999, Oxford: Hart

Winter, P, 'Perspectives for environmental law – entering the fourth phase' (1989) 1(1) JEL 38

Winterton, M, 'Mineral extraction: a matter of interpretation' (1999) JPEL September 783

Wolf, S and White, AH, Principles of Environmental Law, 1997, London: Cavendish Publishing

Wood, C, EIA – a Comparative Review, 1995, Harlow: Longman

Wood, M, 'Local plans and UDP: is there a better way?' (1996) JPL 808

Woolf, S, 'Are the judiciary environmentally myopic?' (1992) 4(1) JEL 1

World Health Organisation, Indoor Air Pollutants: Exposure and Health Effects, 1983, Copenhagen: WHO/EURO Reports

Wyatt, D, 'Litigating Community environmental law – thoughts on the direct effect doctrine' (1998) 10(1) JEL 9

Wysham, D, 'The World Bank: funding climate chaos' (1999) 29(2) The Ecologist 108

Ynors, C, Listed Buildings, Conservation Areas and Monuments, 3rd edn, 1999, London: Sweet & Maxwell

Young, H, 'Reflections on s 54A Agreement and plan led decision making' (1995) JPL 121

INTERNET SOURCES

DETR	www.detr.gov.uk
Open government – links to institutions, law and policy on the environment	www.open.gov.uk
International Institute for Sustainable Development	www.iisd.ca
European Union's official server – an invaluable gateway into the EC	www.europa.eu.int
European Environmental Agency	www.eea.eu.int
Friends of the Earth	www.foe.org.uk
Greenpeace	www.greenpeace.org.uk
Surfers against Sewage	www.sas.org.uk
Marine Conservation Society	www.mcs.mcmail.com
National Trust	www.nationaltrust.org.uk
Open Spaces Society	www.oss.org.uk
Council for the Protection of Rural England	www.cpre.org.uk
Planning Aid	www.rtpi.org.uk/planaid
Environmental Law Foundation	www.greenchannel.com/elf
UKELA	www.greenchannel.com/ukela
RSPB	www.rspb.org.uk
RSPCA	www.rspca.org.uk
Whale and Dolphin Conservation Society	www.wdcs.org.uk
Ramblers	www.ramblers.org.uk
Soil Association	www.soilassociation.org.uk
National Farmers Union	www.nfu.org.uk
Countryside Alliance	www.countryside-alliance.org.uk
Earth First!	www.earthfirstjournal.org
RCEP – has details of all the Commission's reports	www.rcep.org.uk
ENDS Reports	www.ends.co.uk

Environment Agency Press Releases	www.environment-agency.gov.uk/modules/homepages/MOD44/articlelist-english.html
Environment Agency	www.environment-agency.gov.uk
EUROPEN	www.europen.be
INCPEN	www.incpen.org
Waste Watch	www.wastewatch.org.uk
BRE	www. BRE.co.uk/waste

INDEX